NEW YORK

Tales of the Empire State

Compiled by
Frank Oppel

CASTLE

Contents

Summer Homes on the Hudson (1899)

SUMMER HOMES ON THE HUDSON RIVER.

BY JOHN W. HARRINGTON.

THE PICTURESQUE RIVERSIDE REGION INTO WHICH WEALTH HAS CALLED THE BUILDER AND THE LANDSCAPE GARDENER—THE PLEASURES AND THE COST OF MAINTAINING A WELL EQUIPPED COUNTRY HOUSE.

THE American metropolis has been pictured as a dreary place, where even the rich live in caves cut into the faces of the cañons named streets and lighted by glazed apertures called windows. But New York's pillars of Hercules, happily, do not stand on the banks of the Harlem. The boundaries of the city are really set far beyond Poughkeepsie, so many of the modern Knickerbockers have country seats on the heights on either side of the Hudson River. A trip along the stream which the Dutch navigator discovered is like a journey through a garden of the gods.

When you have driven through this region, you will not wonder when you return to the city to see miles of green hollands closed down over the windows of Fifth Avenue and the adjacent residential quarter. The Hudson helps to keep youth and vitality in the veins of old New York. The Knickerbockers of the present day hasten away earlier every year from their stone palaces without even a pocket handkerchief of a lawn in front, to the regions of verdant fields, cool streams, and waving forests.

Beautiful country seats stretch in almost an unbroken line from Yonkers to Hyde Park, and beyond. The little railroad stations, the names of which appear on the time table, are really so many porters' lodges. Dobbs Ferry, Irvington, Tarrytown, and the rest, are in summer time points of assembly for the carriages surreys, traps, and dog carts which are driven from the heights every morning and evening. The trains are filled at this season of the year, and they will be until the late fall, with Gothamites and their guests, who are hurrying away from the

THE ANCESTRAL HOME OF GENERAL SCHUYLER HAMILTON, ON A BYWAY NEAR THE ARDSLEY LINKS.

From a photograph by W. C. Harris.

ROCKWOOD HALL, NEAR TARRYTOWN, THE COUNTRY HOME UPON WHICH MR. WILLIAM ROCKEFELLER IS SAID TO HAVE SPENT THREE MILLION DOLLARS.

From a photograph by W. C. Harris.

City of Awful Din to the Land of Delectable Summer. Every Saturday afternoon there goes up from Manhattan Island a throng of commuters so happy that they even forget to play whist. Their minds are intent, as are their eyes, upon the beautiful Hudson along which they are being rapidly carried.

The gospel of out of doors is preached more and more every year. Let the student of social economics talk as he will about the deplorable fact that the young men of the farms are hurrying towards the congested cities; the love for the life under the greenwood tree is growing stronger here in New York. The Knickerbockers go away in the early spring, and often linger in the country until the trees take on the autumnal tints of red and yellow. The city men are spending more of their time in the open air. The love for country life is growing, and New York is becoming more of

MR. HENRY VILLARD'S HANDSOME AND COMFORTABLE SUMMER RESIDENCE NEAR DOBBS FERRY.

a workshop, and the surrounding country is gaining favor as a place of residence.

The banks of the historic Hudson claim the New Yorker first of all. Many of the estates along the stream are ancestral. The old Knickerbockers loved this land which the captain of the Half Moon saw and pronounced very good. The patroons had country homes along the Hudson centuries ago, and the settlements still ring with the names of Livingston, De Peyster,

inal sons of the glebe have been driven steadily back from the banks of the Hudson. The farm house has given place to the modern castle, and the dingy barn to the breeding stable of the gentleman farmer.

It is in midsummer that the New Yorker who affects the Hudson thinks only of his place on the river. He hurries to the earliest possible train in the afternoon, and gladly plunges through

THE SUMMER HOME OF THE LATE DAVID DOWS, AT IRVINGTON ON HUDSON.

From a photograph by W. C. Harris.

and Roosevelt. There was a period when the seashore and the Sound held a greater charm for New Yorkers, but of recent years the popularity of the Hudson River country has been steadily growing.

Estates which were falling into decay have been purchased by citizens of Manhattan. The landscape gardener, under the supervision of the new owner, has brought out the old lines anew, and has laid out roads and graded the lawns on other levels. With the assistance of city architects, additions have been placed upon country houses, and the electrician, the plumber, and a host of other artisans have made the old dwellings homes of luxury. Acres of farming land have been transferred to city owners, and the orig-

the roaring, soot filled tunnel. The thoughts of a drive along smooth roads, of a game of golf, of a walk over the springy turf, make him feel at peace with all mankind. The city, with its dust and smoke and the ever present rattle and bang of street cars and trucks, is all forgotten. The New Yorker hastening up the Hudson sees only the little station of rough hewn stone where "she" has come to greet him and to drive him home behind a team of bays.

He who has a country seat along the Hudson may wield the putter on his own golf links, drive on his own roads, hunt in his own preserves, and go aboard his yacht from his own pier. His table is supplied from the richness of his own

A GLIMPSE OF THE HUDSON, AND OF THE CLIFFS OF THE PALISADES
BEYOND, FROM THE ESTATE OF JOHN D. FLOWER,
NEAR DOBBS FERRY.

From a photograph by W. C. Harris.

neighborhood are alike as far as first impressions are concerned. A row of dingy little stores faces the railroad station like a line of grim and ugly sentinels at the gates of an Aladdin's garden. A drive of a few minutes brings us to the realm of waving woods, of sunlit fields, and of winding, shaded roadways.

Here at Dobbs Ferry is the squarely built house of J. J. McComb, a city mansion in a rural setting. The houses up this way are of every variety of architecture, and many of the dwellings still reflect in their style the ideals of the city. The house of Mr. McComb is surrounded by lawns and flower beds in brilliant colors.

On the heights a mile beyond is the residence of Amzi L. Barber, a perfect example of the architecture named after good Queen Anne. Yonder is the solid gray stone dwelling where Robert G. Ingersoll spends his summers. Where two square columns stand like Termes at the entrance of a grove of Daphne is the beginning of the estate of Henry Villard. The road is marked by tall posts of wrought iron supporting incandescent globes by which the way to the house is illuminated at night. The home of Mr. Villard is a long, rambling structure with projecting wings. It suggests comfort and happy ease. A few hundred yards away, on a bend in the river, stands a rustic summerhouse which commands a view of the Hudson for miles. Here the owner could sit all day, if he would, and watch the ever changing surface of the river which flows in splendor between wooded headlands and the gray Palisades.

Further down is the home of John D. Flower, a brother of the late Roswell P. Flower. It was from a summerhouse on the Flower estate that the photographer was enabled to get a view of the river and the Palisades, partly obscured by the overhanging foliage.

land. He is surrounded by a small army of retainers, to whom his every wish is law. Except for the drawbridge and the dungeon keep, his house is as much of a castle as any pile of stone erected by feudal barons on the crags above the river Rhine.

It is not until Yonkers is reached that the beauty of the Hudson River country is revealed. On the heights near this suburb stands old Greystone, celebrated as the home of Samuel J. Tilden. At Riverdale you may get a glimpse of the picturesque gateway which marks the entrance of the estate of Giovanni P. Morosini, who, in his country residence, has gathered what is probably the largest collection of arms and armor in the United States.

Leaving the train at Dobbs Ferry we find ourselves in the very heart of the region which New Yorkers have taken for their own. All the towns in this

THE COUNTRY RESIDENCE OF MR. JOHN D. ARCHBOLD, NEAR TARRYTOWN—"A HOUSE OF LONG PIAZZAS AND COOLING SHADE."

From a photograph by W. C. Harris.

The road leads towards Ardsley. A turn to the left brings us to the grounds of General Sam Thomas, where a square, comfortable house looks forth from a high plateau. Another byway descends to the old home of General Schuyler Hamilton, and then we emerge at the Ardsley Casino, surrounded by golf links and encircled by smooth roads.

And here is Irvington, a favorite resort of New Yorkers for these many generations. There is the house where David Dows lived for many years, and yonder the handsome residence of Charles L. Tiffany. Men famous in the history of this country have made their home in this neighborhood. The house of Cyrus Field is still occupied. There stands the old home of the Mairs family. Beyond Barney Park Dr. Warner has built a modern castle of red stone.

We are in old Broadway, the old post road overarched by giant trees. Traps and smart road carts roll along where once was heard the rumble of stages and the shrill blast of the postilion's horn. We halt before Sunnyside, world famous as the home of the genial soul who gave the name of Knickerbocker to the men whose descendants have come up from the city to possess this land. We have passed the home of Edwin Gould and of other New Yorkers whose names are well known in the history of finance and commerce. Now we are approaching Tarrytown, the place linked in the minds of all American school boys with the capture and the untimely death of the young British officer whose body lies in Westminster Abbey.

THE SOLID GRAY STONE DWELLING IN WHICH COLONEL ROBERT G. INGERSOLL SPENDS HIS SUMMERS, NEAR DOBBS FERRY.

Lyndhurst, the house of Miss Helen Gould, stands between Tarrytown and Irvington. It is a gray stone building resembling a Scottish castle. It is surrounded by stately linden trees, from which it derives its name. Miss Gould purchased the place from the Gould heirs several years ago, and has since made it her home practically all the year. Lyndhurst was designed by the late Jay

are raised. In the Spanish-American war many invalid soldiers were brought to the Tarrytown hospital at the expense of Miss Gould. Every morning a wagon from Lyndhurst was driven to the hospital with a load of butter, eggs, milk, and fruits from the farm. Woody Crest, a summer home for children conducted under the supervision of Miss Gould, stands near Lyndhurst's gates. The waifs

COLONEL JOHN JACOB ASTOR'S HUDSON RIVER RESIDENCE, FERNCLIFF, NEAR RHINEBECK.

From a photograph by Burger, Poughkeepsie.

Gould to be the most magnificent country seat in the United States.

A drive through this estate is like a journey through the forest of Arden. On either side of the road are beds of brilliantly hued flowers gathered from every clime. The greenhouses of Lyndhurst are widely celebrated. There are seven of them, all connected by a large central dome. Each house is devoted to the culture of a particular class of plants. The dome is filled with palms; another house is given over to the raising of orchids, and another has beneath its glass roof nearly every known variety of ferns. Next to the river is the garden proper, consisting of stretches of green lawn diversified by winding walks, flower beds, groups of trees, and flowering shrubs. Divided by the highway, is the farm part of the estate, where fruits and vegetables

from the city may wander over this lovely estate at will.

Miss Gould makes her house the headquarters of her varied philanthropic labors. She and her secretary are busy several hours a day in arranging the affairs of the numerous charities in which she is interested. Lyndhurst is the home of a modern Lady Bountiful.

"Majestically plain and substantially good" some one has described Rockwood Hall, the Tarrytown home of William Rockefeller. It is situated north of Tarrytown in the midst of a tract of one thousand acres of fertile land. The splendid house stands on the site of the mansion of General Aspinwall, which was torn down to build lodges for the keepers. Rockwood Hall is constructed of stone taken from the Hastings quarries, not far away. It is as solid as a fortress, and

THE DURKEE HOUSE, NEAR POUGHKEEPSIE—"OVERLOOKING THE RIVER AND ENCOMPASSED BY VENERABLE TREES."

yet its squareness of outline is relieved here and there by softer lines and by its sloping roof of red tiles. The building and the land cost Mr. Rockefeller two million dollars, and the furnishings are said to represent an expenditure of a million more. Much of the estate is a forest preserve, teeming with game. Here are squirrels and wood pigeons by the thousand. Hidden among the trees is a lake two acres in extent, stocked with trout. Down on the river bank is a handsome boat house.

John D. Rockefeller has a villa at Po-

MR. A. C. FIELDS' RESIDENCE, ON CLINTON AVENUE, DOBBS FERRY—A TYPICAL MODERN COTTAGE OF THE HUDSON RIVER REGION.

From a photograph by W. C. Harris.

cantico Hills, two miles distant, and his Hudson River estate is almost as extensive as that of his brother. The house its white pillars gleaming against a background of forest. The soul of an artist would take delight at the sight of the

SUNNYSIDE, WASHINGTON IRVING'S OLD HOUSE AT IRVINGTON—"WORLD FAMOUS AS THE HOME OF THE GENIAL SOUL WHO GAVE THE NAME OF KNICKERBOCKER TO THE MEN WHOSE DESCENDANTS HAVE COME UP FROM THE CITY TO POSSESS THIS LAND."

stands on a steep hill, and on the ridge above is a tall observation tower from which may be seen miles of forests and farms. Not far from Tarrytown is the home of John D. Archbold, a house of long piazzas and cooling shade.

Going five miles further north we reach

Pompeiian gardens within a short distance of the dwelling. Here stand groups of classic columns around which are arranged beds of flowers in dazzling colors.

Brayton Ives, the banker, has recently purchased the old Moore mansion, a mile from Sing Sing, and is remodeling it. The

THE HANDSOME, OLD FASHIONED COUNTRY RESIDENCE OF MR. EDWIN GOULD, AT IRVINGTON.

the country home of Mrs. Elliott F. Shepard, near Scarborough. The house, a mansion in the Colonial style, stands on level ground, on the crest of a hill, with

property was once the home of Dr. Clement Moore, author of "The Night Before Christmas." The Moore family were a race of amateur horticulturists and

THE RESIDENCE OF MR. J. J. McCOMB, ONE OF THE MOST CONSPICUOUS PLACES AT DOBBS FERRY—"A CITY MANSION IN A RURAL SETTING."

From a photograph by W. C. Harris.

botanists, and on the estate are plants and trees from every clime under the sun.

Perched on the hills about Garrisons, New York, are summer homes reached by winding roads, the construction of which was a herculean task. Across the river, near Newburgh and West Point, are scores of handsome villas. John Burroughs, the naturalist of the Hudson, has a handsome residence on the river and a den in the woods near West Park. Returning to the east side of the river, we are in a land of flocks and herds. The New Yorker be-

IN THE GROUNDS OF THE VILLARD PLACE, NEAR DOBBS FERRY—"A RUSTIC SUMMER HOUSE WHICH COMMANDS A VIEW OF THE HUDSON FOR MILES."

A RUSTIC GATE AT THE ENTRANCE TO MR. CHARLES L. TIFFANY'S GROUNDS, AT IRVINGTON.

From a photograph by W. C. Harris.

Rhinecliff, fifteen miles from Poughkeepsie and two miles back from the Hudson River. Here are one thousand acres of pasture, forest, and closely sheared lawn. At one time Mr. Morton devoted much attention to the raising of cattle. The greenhouses and the gardens of Ellerslie are among the show places of the neighborhood. Mr. Morton and his family are extremely fond of country life, and it is to Ellerslie that they go each year to spend the spring and summer.

When John Jacob Astor came back from the war a colonel, he went as soon as possible to his country home, Ferncliff, near Rhinebeck. Here his faithful retainers came forth to greet him and caused the dells to ring with the music of their own brass band. Ferncliff was purchased more than forty five years ago by William Astor, the father of the present owner. It consisted originally of fifteen small farms. The estate now extends a mile and a half along the Hudson and as far back into the country. It comprises about fifteen hundred acres.

comes a real farmer up Dutchess County way. The banks of the river are the boundaries of fertile estates assembled about imposing country mansions.

Fair Ellerslie, the home of former Governor Levi P. Morton, is situated at

The entrance to the grounds is guarded by a porter's lodge of gray granite. A driveway twenty feet wide and overarched

DRIVEWAY AND GATE POSTS IN THE GROUNDS OF THE VILLARD PLACE, NEAR DOBBS FERRY.

From a photograph by W. C. Harris.

by elms leads to the house. Set in niches in the foliage and shrubbery along this avenue are classic statues which stand out vividly from the living green. In front of the house is a great flower bed.

The comfortable country home of the Astors stands on a plateau, and from its windows may be obtained a view of Rondout Creek and of the distant Shawangunk Mountains. The dwelling is built in the

vators of rare flowers, and as patrons of everything which pertains to turf, field, and farm. In the summer time and in the autumn there are fairs and flower shows at which the New Yorkers are recognized as judges and as experts. Who does not remember the glories of the old Dinsmore estate, the owner of which was known as a horticulturist? His name lives in the Dinsmore rose, and

THE ENTRANCE TO THE GROUNDS OF DR. WARNER'S RESIDENCE, ONE OF THE FINEST PLACES AT IRVINGTON.

From a photograph by W. C. Harris.

Italian style. The entrance is a great vestibule sixty feet in length. The hallway is decorated with Persian rugs and hangings, with deer heads and other spoils of the chase, and with oil paintings of famous race horses which Mr. Astor has owned. You could easily imagine yourself in the home of a fox hunting English country gentleman.

Dutchess County and all the region around Poughkeepsie is preëminently the place of country seats. On every road leading from the placid Hudson may be seen the high stone posts which mark the entrance to lordly estates. Here many New Yorkers live practically all the year round. It is a land where they become enthusiasts as breeders of cattle, as culti-

every man in the county who is interested in horses and cattle of fancy breeds will talk of "The Locusts," the country place of the Dinsmores.

Ogden Mills has built in this neighborhood a splendid house fashioned on classic lines. Its white and shining front can be seen for many miles. It is one of the most beautiful country houses on the continent. Then there are the substantial homes of the Durkees and the Merritts, fine old country homes overlooking the river and encompassed by venerable trees.

Frederick W. Vanderbilt has acquired a country seat at Hyde Park. An army of workmen has for several years been remodeling the old estate, laying out roads and regrading the lawns. The house, which stands on a double terrace, has been practically rebuilt under the supervision of a well known firm of archi-

To conduct such an estate, the services of farm hands, gardeners, laborers, teamsters, stablemen, coachmen, and grooms are required. Many of the New Yorkers

BROADWAY, THE HISTORIC HIGHWAY THAT RUNS NORTHWARD FROM NEW YORK THROUGH YONKERS, IRVINGTON, AND TARRYTOWN, PASSING MANY FINE COUNTRY RESIDENCES.

tects. The estate consists of about six hundred acres of fertile land, a large part of which is in the original forest.

Most of the properties along the Hudson are divided into a "park side" and a "farm side." The division is generally made by a country road. A superintendent is employed who is responsible for the care of the entire establishment. The number of men employed on the average country place varies with the season and the amount of work to be done. It may be anywhere from ten to two hundred.

who have purchased country places that have been neglected for years find it necessary to build roads, establish grades, cut down dead trees, and completely change the face of the landscape.

The care of the ten or fifteen acres of lawn which form a part of most estates requires the constant attention of five or six men. On one place as many as thirty three men have been seen groping on their hands and knees upon the grass, laboriously pulling out small weeds by the roots and replacing them with a few

THE CONSERVATORIES AT LYNDHURST, FAMOUS FOR THEIR WONDERFUL DISPLAY OF RARE FLOWERS.

THE COUNTRY HOME OF MR. OGDEN MILLS, NEAR POUGHKEEPSIE—"ITS WHITE AND SHINING FRONT
CAN BE SEEN FOR MANY MILES."

From a photograph by Burger, Poughkeepsie.

grass seeds taken from a little bag which they carried. These lawns must be carefully mowed every day or so, and along the edges of the driveways the grass must be neatly cut with shears. To keep the verdure fresh and green the use of the hose and the automatic sprinkler is constantly required.

The construction of the driveways represents thousands of dollars. One of the first things which the New York owner does is to build a road that will not wash out. He digs down to the depth of about four feet and places a layer of stone in the trench. Upon this are placed glazed drains on either side and a smaller porous drain in the middle. Then loads of cobble stones are dumped upon the drains, and the whole is thickly covered with broken stone, which is thorough-

ly rolled. Such a road as this costs from three dollars and fifty cents to five dollars a yard. By the time a few miles of these costly pathways have been built, the New Yorker finds that it takes money to maintain a Hudson River estate.

Next to the superintendent, the most important man on a country place is the

LYNDHURST, THE "GRAY STONE BUILDING RESEMBLING A SCOTTISH CASTLE,"
BUILT BY THE LATE JAY GOULD, AND NOW THE RESIDENCE OF
MISS HELEN GOULD.

head gardener. He directs the operations of the men in the greenhouses, lays out the flower beds, and is responsible for

information replied by saying, "How high is a tree? How many persons can you put on a yacht?" The cost depends

ELLERSLIE, THE COUNTRY HOME OF EX VICE PRESIDENT LEVI P. MORTON, NEAR RHINECLIFF—"HERE ARE ONE THOUSAND ACRES OF PASTURE, FOREST, AND CLOSELY SHEARED LAWN."

the care of the lawns. Every morning at six o'clock the superintendent calls the roll and sends the various employees to their posts of duty. It requires as much bookkeeping and management to conduct one of these country seats along the Hudson as it does to direct the affairs of a business house.

It is a very natural question, "What is the cost of conducting such a place?" That is an inquiry which it is difficult to answer. One man to whom I applied for

entirely upon the tastes of the owner. On one estate not far up the Hudson about thirty laborers are employed, whose monthly wages are thirty five dollars each. A competent superintendent may be obtained for a thousand dollars a year, and the salary of a first class gardener is six hundred dollars. You must add to this the wages of the stable force, usually ten men in all, and the household servants, who number half a score. Here are fifty or sixty retainers whose

ARDSLEY TOWERS, THE COUNTRY HOUSE OF THE LATE CYRUS W. FIELD, AT IRVINGTON, NOW OCCUPIED BY MR. BELTZHOOVER.

wages amount to nearly twelve thousand dollars annually. A country place, taking into consideration its extent and the tastes of its owner, may cost anywhere from ten thousand dollars to fifty thou-

honored by the electors of Rhinebeck. And like the lordly estates that are the pride of rural England, the country places of the Knickerbockers are usually opened to the public, provided the public

THE RESIDENCE OF AMZI L. BARBER, NEAR DOBBS FERRY—"A PERFECT EXAMPLE OF THE ARCHITECTURE NAMED AFTER GOOD QUEEN ANNE." ITS WINDOWS COMMAND A VIEW OVER A WIDE STRETCH OF PICTURESQUE COUNTRY.

sand dollars a year. We read much of the poultry, the eggs, and the milk which come to the market from the "farm sides" of some of these estates along the Hudson. In spite of these sales, the gentleman farmer generally finds that his agricultural operations are on the wrong side of the ledger. Next to maintaining a first class steam yacht the most expensive pursuit is conducting a country seat.

Most of the New Yorkers who live along the Hudson in the summer take an interest in the affairs of the community in which they dwell. They attend the churches, contribute to the fairs, and some of them even hold offices. Colonel John Jacob Astor has several times been

comes in carriages. The pedestrian and the bicyclist, as a rule, are not especially welcome visitors.

The principal amusements of the Knickerbocker at his Hudson home are golf, yachting, and driving. He takes delight in being in the open air and in drinking in the prospect of the waving forests and the ever changing river. Often he comes up from the city on his own yacht, and reaches a club station or his own pier in the twilight. He finds pleasure in driving the white rubber ball, and in raising a thirst for oatmeal water, and perhaps for Scotch whisky, as he tramps over the links. Whatever he does, this Hudson River country makes him a happier and a freer man.

Montauk Point, Long Island (1871)

HARPER'S
NEW MONTHLY MAGAZINE.

No. CCLVI.—SEPTEMBER, 1871.—Vol. XLIII.

MONTAUK POINT, LONG ISLAND.

THE MONTAUK LIGHT.

MONTAUK POINT—the eastern extremity of Long Island—is a region comparatively unknown, except to a few sportsmen, attracted thither by its very wildness, and to such tourists as find especial charms in its seclusion, and in the bold and picturesque scenery of its defiant promontory, upon which the wild Atlantic incessantly beats, and sometimes with tremendous violence. We had been informed that these tourists had a "hard road to travel," leading, after all, only to a "wild, desolate country, infested by mosquitoes and snakes."

Nevertheless I was glad to escape from the monotony of every-day routine, and, with two congenial friends, venture forth upon this tour, which, whatever might be the difficulties attending it, was certainly unhackneyed. No sedulous Murray or Fetridge had preceded us. Even *Harper's Magazine*—that universal cyclo-

"THE RIVER SWARMING WITH CRAFT."

pedia of travel, discovery, and adventure, which had explored the most secret recesses of Africa, the arctic mysteries, the isles of the Pacific, and the wilderness beyond the "high Rockies" —had, by a sort of telescopic instinct, overlooked this brave little headland right under its nose. Neither pen nor pencil had taken off the edge of the novelty and romance of our *terra incognita*.

We chose a beautiful October afternoon of last autumn for the commencement of our excursion. We took the boat for Sag Harbor. The last bell expressed our glad adieus to the dusty metropolis, the gang-plank was taken aboard, and our pretty little steamer—the *Eastern City*—was soon out in the stream, heading eastward. Rounding Corlaer's Hook, we passed the Brooklyn Navy-yard on our right, with its ship-houses and spacious workshops; the quaint hull of the old line-of-battle ship *Vermont*, standing out in marked contrast with the more graceful models of our modern ships of war and Ericsson's "cheese-box" monitors. What manifestations of life and incessant activity throng the river, which is swarming with craft of every description—stately three-masted schooners, sloops, fishing-smacks, and ferry-boats, and, darting hither and thither, the lively little tugs, always in haste, and seemingly out of breath! Here we are passing the old Novelty Works on our left, now almost silent and lifeless, where, years ago, the machinery of the pioneer ocean steamers—the *Washington*, *Hermann*, and the Collins ships—was manufac-

tured. In those days both shores of this East River were lined with ship-yards in full operation. We pass Blackwell's and Randall's islands—devoted to the noble charities of New York city—and through Hell Gate, soon, we hope, to be deprived of its ancient terrors, as the government engineers are silently boring their way into and under the solid rock, expecting by one blast to destroy this perilous reef. With Ravenswood and Astoria on our right, we thread our way by and around the lovely wooded points out into Flushing Bay. Then past Riker's Island and beautiful Whitestone, with its charming bay—the place of rendezvous of the New York Yacht Fleet—and directly we are abreast of Fort Schuyler, frowning with heavy guns from its battlements. Past the fort, out into Long Island Sound. On the left, and westward, lies City Island, famed for its oysters.

All this time we have been passing through a fleet of eastward-bound vessels, that, sped by a fair tide and favorable wind, reaches to the dim horizon. Looking backward to the setting sun, what a flood of beauty fills our view, vividly bringing to our mind those radiant verses of Samuel Longfellow:

"The golden sea its mirror spreads
    Beneath the golden skies,
And but a narrow strip between
    Of land and shadow lies.

"The cloud-like rocks, the rock-like clouds,
    Dissolved in glory float,
And, midway of the radiant flood,
    Hangs silently the boat.

"THE GOLDEN SEA."

"The sea is but another sky,
　The sky a sea as well,
And which is earth, and which the heavens,
　The eye can scarcely tell.

"So when for us life's evening hour
　Soft-fading shall descend,
May glory, born of earth and heaven,
　The earth and heavens blend.

"Flooded with peace the spirit float,
　With silent rapture glow,
Till where earth ends and heaven begins
　The soul shall scarcely know."

The sun has gone, and as the twilight deepens, the full, silver-faced moon rises above the picturesquely wooded " Sands Point;" and the star in the light-house grows in brilliancy as the darkness increases. We are loath to leave the deck, but supper is ready, and our appetites, sharpened by the fresh air, persuade us to go below.

One hour later the pageant of the evening has dissolved, and now the moon looks down, throwing her silvery light in gentle ripples to our feet. The air is full of mystic softness. Our artist friend talks of the Mediterranean, of

Capri—its rocks and grottoes—of Venice, of Turner, the great interpreter, of life in Rome; and art, with all its inspiring memories, crowds upon us. The bachelor of our party chants in a minor key,

"Ask me no more: the moon may draw the sea;
　The cloud may stoop from heaven and take the
　　shape,
　With fold to fold, of mountain and of cape;
But, oh, too fond, when have I answered thee?
　　　　　　　　Ask me no more."

Our cigars are ashes. "Good-night! Good-night!"

The next morning, on waking, we found the boat fast at her dock in Sag Harbor, and the stage waiting. We concluded to go on at once and breakfast at East Hampton, and were soon rolling out of the old town, which years ago enjoyed a prosperous business, owning and sending to sea forty vessels engaged in whaling, and one hundred and thirty in the cod-fishing and coasting trade. Our road left the town in a southeastward direction, and proved much better than we had anticipated, winding through

SANDS POINT.

"THROUGH A BEAUTIFUL LANE."

J. HOWARD PAYNE.

a young growth of dwarf oak and pine, and with only one house for five miles of the way. As we approached East Hampton the woods gave place to clearings and cultivated fields. Presently, at a turn in the road, we caught a glimpse of the old church spire above the roofs and foliage; and passing through a beautiful lane, that reminded us of some of Birket Foster's bits of English landscape, we entered the main street, which is twice the width of Broadway, carpeted with emerald-green turf, with wagon ruts running through the centre. Weather-beaten houses stood close to the foot-paths, embowered in foliage; and here and there we saw large flocks of geese stretching in undulating lines across the road. Passing the first church, shingle-covered, rotten and crumbling with the wear of one hundred and fifty-three years, its bent and rusty vane creaking in the wind, just across the street stands "Clinton Academy," once holding high rank among the educational institutions of the State; and here, in close proximity, is the birth-place of J. Howard Payne, author of "Home, Sweet Home." In the distance we catch a view of the great arms of a windmill moving slowly,

"Its delicate white vans
　　against the sky,
So soft and soundless,
　　simply beautiful."

Our driver put us down in front of the hospitable house of Mr. ——, one and a half hours from Sag Harbor; and here, while breakfast is being prepared, let us take a backward glance at East Hampton, and ascertain what manner of men settled this quaint, drowsy old village, gray and moss-covered with age, and telling of pre-Revolutionary times.

We learn that at the time the great struggle between king and Commons was beginning in England—during the time of John Hampden and Milton—a band of Puritan neighbors, most-

WINDMILL ON THE ROAD TO AMAGANSETT.

OLD CHURCH AT EAST HAMPTON.

ly farmers, left their comfortable homes in Maidstone, Kent, on the river Medway, thirty miles from London. They first landed at Salem, Massachusetts, and a short time afterward found their way to the easterly end of Long Island, and founded the town of East Hampton in the year 1649, purchasing the lands from the Indians as far east as Montauk for the sum of £30 4s. 8d. sterling. It was then an unbroken wilderness, and the Indians were numerous on every side. On the east, at "Montaukett," the royal Wyandanck swayed the sceptre; on the north, at Shelter Island, his brother, Poggotacut, ruled the tribe of "Manhassetts;" and a third brother ruled over the "Shinecocks." And here, in the dark and gloomy forest, in silence unbroken save by the Indian war-whoop, the cry of the wild beasts, or the solemn roar of the ocean, they made their earthly home, and laid the foundations of a government insuring to all the people the largest civil and religious liberty.

"Amidst the storm they sang;
    And the stars heard and the sea;
And the sounding aisles of the dim woods rang
    To the anthem of the free.

"The ocean eagle soared
    From his nest by the white wave's foam,
And the rocking pines of the forest roared:
    This was their welcome home."

One hundred and twenty-five years later the sons of this good old stock voted, June 17, 1774, to "co-operate with our brethren in this colony to defend our liberties." During the Revolutionary war the town suffered many heavy blows; but through the long seven years of hardship and struggle it is not known that any Tory ever made his home on its sacred soil. "The intelligence and morals of her people and the genius of her sons have been among the brightest ornaments of the Empire State."

The "old church" represented in the vignette was built in 1717. The bell and clock are over a century and a quarter old. Its first pastor received for his support "forty-five pounds annually, lands rate free, grain to be first ground at the mill every Monday, and one-fourth of the whales stranded on the beach." On the death of Dr. Buel, the third pastor, in the year 1799, Rev. Lyman Beecher was settled over the church. Referring to Dr. Beecher's

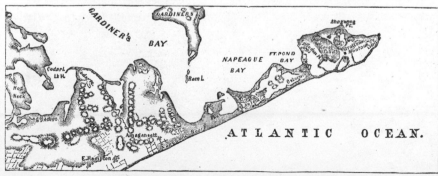

MAP OF THE LONG ISLAND COAST FROM SAG HARBOR TO MONTAUK POINT.

KITCHEN FIRE-PLACE IN THE PAYNE HOMESTEAD.

autobiography, we do not find that he makes any positive statement as to the addition made to his income through the misfortunes of "stranded whales;" but we do learn, however, that "as late as about 1700 it is said that a woman named Abigail Baker, in riding from East Hampton to Bridgehampton, saw thirteen whales along the shore between the two places." Dr. Beecher married immediately after his settlement, and the following narrative, communicated to his children, shows the difficulties which he and his wife encountered in setting up housekeeping. "There was not a store in town, and all our purchases were made in New York by a small schooner that ran once a week. We had no carpets; there was not a carpet from end to end of the town. All had sanded floors, some of them worn through. Your mother introduced the first carpet. Uncle Lot gave me some money, and I had an itch to spend it. Went to a vendue, and bought a bale of cotton. She spun it, and had it woven; then she laid it down, sized it, and painted it in oils, with a border all around it, and bunches of roses and other flowers over the centre. She sent to New York for her colors, and ground and mixed them herself. The carpet was nailed down on the garret floor, and she used to go up there and paint. She took some common wooden chairs and painted them, and cut out figures of gilt paper, and glued them on and varnished them. They were really quite pretty."

H. B. STOWE. "That carpet is one of the first things I remember, with its pretty border."

CHARLES. "It lasted till my day, and covered the east room in our Litchfield home."

H. B. STOWE. "Well, father, what did East Hampton folks say to that?"

"Oh, they thought it fine. Old Deacon Tallmadge came to see me. He stopped at the parlor door, and seemed afraid to come in. 'Walk in, deacon, walk in,' said I. 'Why, I can't,' said he, ''thout steppin' on't.' Then, after surveying it a while in admiration, 'D'ye think you can have all that, *and heaven too?*'"

In writing of the town the author of "Home,

BOAT IN SAND-DRIFT.

WRECK OF THE "CATHARINE."

Sweet Home" says : " It is twenty minutes' walk from the ocean. A beautiful oasis, so surrounded by sands and barrenness that the inhabitants are confined to farms barely sufficient to enable them, with patient industry and rigid economy, to draw thence the means of sustaining their families......The traditions of the place are few, but mysterious. I first sought them in the town records; but vast, indeed, was my perplexity on only encountering notices of various inexplicable hieroglyphics granted to the Zephaniahs and Ichabods and Jeremiahs, through many generations, for the respective 'ear-marks' of each. Eventually, however, it was relieved. I found out that these mystical 'ear-marks' were merely registers of the stamps on the ears of the cattle under which the towns-people entered them for a portion of the pasturage at Montauk, to which each freeholder had a right."

After breakfast we directed our steps toward the birth-place of Payne—a modest, unpretending house, nestling under the shadow of the Academy building, where his father, we were told, was once a tutor. How many touching associations crowd upon us as we remember the many weary hearts whose thought and aspiration have found expression through the singer who first saw the light in this out-of-the-way nook, and whose fate it was to die away from home and kindred in a foreign land !

" Hearts there are on the sounding shore
   (Something whispers soft to me),
   Restless and roaming for evermore,
   Like this weary weed of the sea ;
   Bear they yet on each beating breast
   The eternal type of the wondrous whole,
   Growth unfolding amidst unrest,
   Grace informing with silent soul."

But I must not loiter, contenting myself with the thought that I have said sufficient to show that there is at least one spot, not far from the metropolis of the New World, that has not felt the improvement of the age, and that it is just the place to dream away leisure hours. We were busy all day sketching the many picturesque objects, and retired to rest delighted with our day in East Hampton.

Early the next morning we start toward the rising sun, reaching the village of Amagansett about eight o'clock. Here we strike Napeague Beach, and halt to sketch a fish-cart and a boat, partly covered by the sand, and a little further on the wreck of the ship *Catharine*, the surf breaking in bursts of spray, and creaming in and over her barnacled timbers. Eastward

" The sunlight glitters keen and bright,
      Where, miles away,
   Lies stretching to my dazzled sight
   A luminous belt, a misty light,
      And wastes of sandy gray."

Mile after mile we walked by the sea; the beach was a pure clean sweep, free from seaweed, pebbles, or stones. Tiny sandpipers were running along in front of us, following the curves of the incoming and receding waves. Fragments of wrecks were frequent. Toward noon we stopped to rest, and found some beach plums, which proved to be sweet and palatable.

| Nick. | Slope. | L. | Hole. | Slit. | Hollow. | U. | Halfpenny. |

EAR-MARKS.

FRAGMENTS OF WRECKS ON THE BEACH.

After resting a while we continued our way, the walking growing more difficult, as the tide is higher here, and the beach begins to be broken. Stones and shells seemed to be frequent as we approached nearer the end of the Point. The weather was perfectly delicious, the sky without a cloud, the sea a soft blue, growing green as it breaks on the shore, fresh and pure from the broad Atlantic. For hours we had been passing over the "dreaded" Napeague Beach, which we had been told was impassable.

Gradually the land began to rise out of the broken, sandy dunes, and to grow into irregular bluffs. Here we began to look out for the first house, and about two o'clock caught sight of it from the bluff, close to the shore, and were soon refreshing ourselves in the comfortable parlor with some home-made blackberry wine, and cool water from the well. We obtained from Mr. Lawrence a sketch of some of the "ear-marks" now in use in marking cattle. During the past season fifteen hundred head of these, one hundred horses, and seven hundred

sheep had been pastured on the downs east of this house, at a charge per head for common stock of $2 50, and of $5 for the field or fattening pasture. There are three keepers, living about four miles apart, whose duty it is to shift the cattle from point to point, as the water or pasture may require. They are furnished with a comfortable house, and as much land as they may require for farming purposes, with the privilege of keeping a certain number of cattle, sheep, etc., with every opportunity to raise chickens, geese, ducks, and turkeys.

Life-saving stations are scattered about four miles apart along the coast, containing boats ready to launch at a moment's notice; but we were told by old wreckers that, owing to their great weight, it is impossible to launch them through the heavy surf, and that practically they are of no use.

After dinner we continued our walk, following the coast till sundown; then on over the downs, through the deepening twilight into the gloaming, the music of the everlasting and monotonous roar of the sea sounding in our ears,

OSBORNE'S.

THE SHIPWRECK AT NIGHT.

until we reached Mr. Osborne's, near the beach, after dark. Soon we were comfortably seated in his cozy parlor, chatting with the family like old friends. An examination of the "register" revealed a very different record from the books of this kind usually found in hotels. Here we have a description of a successful day's sport— ducks, wild-geese, snipe. On another page regrets at leaving such home-like quarters. Here, again, a series of comic sketches by our friend Dr. C——. Then we have a tale of wreck and disaster: how a ship was driven ashore one wild night, a few years ago; how brave men gathered to the rescue; how the crew, one after another, dropped into the sea, some of them being saved

from the jaws of the angry waves; of a mother washed ashore, dead, clasping a babe in her arms; the wild figures of the wreckers on that dark, stormy night of horrors, lit up by a great fire of drift-wood, made up a picture not easily effaced from our minds; the morning dawned at last, but the ship had disappeared—she had been beaten to pieces, and the shore was strewn. for miles with broken timbers of the wreck. Another record, in a neat female hand, reads thus, "Good-by, dear old Montauk, till another winter."

But it is growing late. Our hostess asks if we will sleep on feathers or straw. Sleepy voices echo, "Straw! straw! straw!" Three

"DESOLATE GRAVES."

snowy beds. We drew lots for the choice, and were soon fast asleep.

Early next morning we visited some lonely graves. One of the sleepers had reached the age of ninety-nine years. The sea,

"It keeps eternal whisperings round desolate graves."

Close to the house is Fort Pond, well known to sportsmen, who are now beginning to arrive. Ducks are already quite plenty. We were shown a beautiful wood-duck that had been shot the night before. Breakfast over, we push for the water's edge. There are evidences every where of fearful storms,

"Where surge after surge would leap enorm,
 Cliffs of emerald topped with snow,
 That lifted and lifted, and then let go
 A great white avalanche of thunder,"

tearing and goring gaps and seams into the coast, which is at this spot quite low. Here a sea-wall has been piled up, and the sand gathering about it forms a slight barrier to the encroachments of the ocean. Looking east along the wide beach, what a sight greets our view! Extending full half a mile, the débris of wrecked ships, a chaos of splintered fragments, bleached and broken—a tremendous illustration of what Walt Whitman calls

"The spasm of the sky and the shatter of the sea."

Here we stop to sketch part of a broken mast, then the charred remains of what seems to have been a schooner. Partially buried, and protruding from the sand like skeleton fingers, were great iron bolts, rusted and bent. After heavy gales it is found that the character of the beach often changes. Wrecks that have long been buried and forgotten are exhumed, and again the fierce winds and heavy seas cover them from sight. Further on we pass heaps of coal ; parts of the vertebræ of a whale, bleached perfectly white ; a bit of rail, or broken spar and tackle-block—what memories of disappointed hopes, unwritten tragedies, lying here in this grave-yard of the sea ! Still further on the bluffs begin to rise to a height varying from twenty to fifty feet, in bright sunlight against the dark blue of the sky. Their color is a fresh yellow ochre, broken with gray and purple.

Toward noon we clambered to the heights through a ravine, and were glad to discover "Stratton's"—the third house—about a mile away, and perhaps half a mile inland on the high ground, looking in the distance like a huge granite boulder, harmonizing and blending with the dun color of the hills. Here we saw large numbers of cattle feeding on the slopes that surround Great Pond ; and further east, for the first time, we sighted the light. While dinner was being prepared our pencils were busy, and we enriched our sketch-books with the picturesque barn-yard filled with corn, and the hay and grain stacks, attesting the richness of the lands for agricultural purposes. For dinner we had a pair of black ducks, which, a little later in the season, visit this locality with other game in great numbers.

Then again we were by the edge of the sea. The shore is here cumbered with large stones

CATTLE ON THE SLOPES.

"THE SHATTER OF THE SEA."

and boulders of considerable size. Looking west were the rolling downs stretching into the purple distance against the evening sky —a picture of profound and solemn beauty never to be forgotten.

> "We walked beside the sea,
> After a day which perished silently
> Of its own glory....
>
> "For though we never spoke
> Of the gray water and the shaded rock,
> Dark wave and stone, unconsciously, were fused
> Into the plaintive speaking that we used
> Of absent friends and memories unforsook;
> And, had we seen each other's face, we had
> Seen, haply, each was sad."

We reached Montauk Light, and the end of our second day's tramp, a little after dark. Later in the evening we accompanied the keeper (Mr. Ripley) on a tour of inspection. Going through a passage-way we found ourselves in the oil-room, neatly paved with colored tiles, the oil being stored in large tanks on one side of the room. The ascent is, by one hundred and thirty-seven steps, winding around the central shaft, and the walls are of enormous thickness; the tower, erected in 1796, was some years since strengthened by building a solid brick lining inside of the original structure. Immediately below the lamp is the keeper's room and the apparatus which keeps the revolving "flash" in operation. Here through the long weary watches of the night, one hundred and eighty feet above the sea, exposed to the full force of the wild Atlantic storms, these faithful sentinels keep vigil. On their fidelity and constant watchfulness depends the safety of the many thousand vessels that annually traverse this highway of the sea.

AGRICULTURAL PROSPERITY.

"Steadfast, serene, immovable, the same
　Year after year, through all the silent night,
Burns on for evermore that quenchless flame,
　Shines on that inextinguishable light!"

A few steps higher and we are in the lantern, containing a "Fresnel" flash light of the first order, made by Henry Lepante. It is a miracle of ingenuity in the scientific concentration of the lenses. We step inside the lenses as the "flash" slowly revolves, and the next moment are inclosed in light which is visible thirty-six miles seaward. The flash throws a flood of brilliant light around the entire circle, disappearing and re-appearing every two minutes.

Mr. Ripley explains to us that the lamp has two reservoirs—an upper and a lower; the former being five feet above and directly over the lower one. They are connected by two pipes. The lower reservoir contains a pump, by which the oil is forced through one of the pipes into the upper reservoir. The feed-pipe connected with the lamp has a chamber which contains a small float, by which the flow of oil is regulated, allowing 120 drops per minute. The oil that is not consumed passes down into a receiver under the lamp, to which a small tube is attached, conveying it through a wire-cloth strainer into the lower reservoir, to be again pumped up. During the long winter nights the lamp will consume two and one-half gallons of refined lard-oil, and the oil will flow four hours without pumping. The upper reservoir will contain nine gallons. The flash is propelled by clock-work, which, when wound up, will run three hours. The lenses are twelve feet in height and six feet in diameter. The lamp is placed inside of the lenses, having four wicks, the largest being three and a half inches in diameter. During the day the lenses are covered with linen curtains, to prevent the rays of the sun from striking the lamp and unsoldering the brass-work. The height of the lantern is nine feet, the frame of solid iron. No wood of any kind is used in the tower.

Much trouble is experienced in keeping the oil from congealing during the cold winter nights, owing to the want of stoves in the oil-room. Attention to this matter by the Light-house Board would add much to the comfort of the keepers and the efficiency of the light. There is a curious history connected with the light. It was presented by the French government to the United States, and lay a long time in the Custom-house in New York; was then sold to pay the duties, and finally, after much dickering, was purchased back again by "Uncle Sam."

Stepping out on the balcony that surrounds the tower, the glorious panorama of the moon-lit sea lay all about us, and at that moment two ships were crossing the glinting light of the moon. The raw, chilly night air soon drove

SCRUB-GROWTH.

KING AND QUEEN OF THE MONTAUKS.

us below to the comfortable fireside of the keeper's family, where we sat listening to stories of storms from the southeast, during which the whole weight of the Atlantic is thrown directly upon Montauk Head. The light-house is built of granite, and, founded on a rock, stands on the bluff sixty feet above the beach. The sea is silently eating its way toward the tower, and this will soon compel a removal to the higher ground west.

Early the next morning we were sketching the sunrise, but the fishermen were up before us, trolling for blue-fish. We had arranged to have a team sent to take us off, and by eight o'clock we started homeward, the road leading over and around the knolls, at times following the beaten path, at others over the unbroken sod. To the left we caught a glimpse of the sea and the curved column of smoke on the distant horizon. Then we descended down into a deep dell, by the dry bed of a former pool, now covered with the dead leaves of the pond-lily. Rising again, to the north of us lies Gardiner's Island and the distant Connecticut shore, and still further eastward, in the faint blue distance, Rhode Island, and off due east from the Point, Block Island. The sky and water are an intense blue, while the sand spits and points on the northerly side look like golden beaches in the morning light. Now and then we pass clumps of scrub-growth clad in russet and gold.

Our driver pointed out a few scattered houses, forming the village of the once powerful Montauk Indians, who have now dwindled to about a dozen persons. In 1660 their ancestors conveyed to certain parties of the plantation of East Hampton "all the neck of land called Montauk, with all and every part and parcel thereof from sea to sea, from the utmost end of the land eastward to the sea-side, unto the other end of the said land westward, adjoining to the bounds of East Hampton,......with meadow, wood, stone, creeks, ponds, and whatsoever doth or may grow upon or issue from the same, with all the profits and commodities, by sea or land, unto the aforesaid inhabitants of East Hampton, their heirs and assigns, forever. ......And in token thereof have digged up a

piece of the said lands, and delivered as our act and deed."

The mark of Wianambone, O
The mark of Sachem Squa, X
The mark of Zoquabone, Q
The mark of Shobanow, —
The mark of Massaquit, ⋈
The mark of Yombo, ∞

A further bond, made by Wyandanah and Sassakatako, sachems of Montauket, 1687, with the consent of the Montauket Indians, conveyed to the trustees of the freeholders of yᵉ town of East Hampton "all the tract of land at Montauket, from sea to sea." And the trustees, for themselves and the freeholders, engaged that the Indians "have leave to plant what corn soever they have occasion for to plant from time to time, where they see cause, themselves and their heirs forever, upon the land as purchased of them by us." The two hundred descendants of the original purchasers are waiting for the time when the tribe will be extinct, and there shall be no lien upon the land. The Indians are said to be idle and worthless, except their king and queen, who are industrious, quiet citizens. The king, David Pharaoh, was that day attending court at Riverhead; therefore we concluded it would not pay to visit them.

The wood begins to grow more dense on the north side, and we are gradually leaving the glorious downs, dotted here and there with herds and flocks. The air is pure and bracing, the autumn tints of surpassing beauty, and all things conspire to make a perfect day. We give way to the exhilaration we feel, and freely express our delight. Over hill and vale, through lovely copses of piperidge, alder, and oak—flaunting tints of crimson, gold, and purple, with long gray moss pendent from the older trees—we shortly strike the edge of the dreary "Napeague Beach" region. Barberry, stunted cedar and pine, and masses of "deerfeed" vary the monotony of this sandy desert, rendered uninhabitable during the summer season by the myriads of mosquitoes. Along the north shore there are deep bays, the resort of fishermen. Vast quantities of moss-bunkers are caught and worked into oil. Napeague, from ocean to sound, must remain the waste it is; but the land east, for about eight miles in length by a width of a mile or more, will, some day not far distant, become a place of summer resort for the dwellers on the main-land. It has an average elevation of fifty feet above the sea. Swept from all points by the breeze from the water, can its equal be found? It had been the fortune of some of our party to visit the coasts of Italy, to wander over the downs on the Isle of Wight, to ramble on the heathery hills of Scotland, and to visit Newport, Nahant, Cape Ann, and Long Branch; but the two days' tramp along the beach, and the ride over the downs of Montauk on that memorable October day, stand in strong relief above all other similar experiences. We reached home in the evening *via* the Long Island Railroad, having been absent a little over four days.

The New Croton Aqueduct (1889)

THE NEW CROTON AQUEDUCT.

RDINARILY, a dwelling-house, measuring say 33 by 35 feet, and standing where the rainfall is not less than 45 inches in a year, will collect on an average about 90 gallons of water per day; that is, supposing that all the water that falls in the area of the building is saved, that none is allowed to evaporate, and that the cistern is big enough to hold the excess of water that falls in the wet winter months. Practically, such a roof will not give on an average ninety gallons a day, and in a dry year will yield very much less. Such a dwelling-house may be supposed to contain a family of five people, and at even ninety gallons a day this would be only eighteen gallons apiece. A tenement house five stories high and of the usual New York area has about the same roof surface. In such a tenement five families, or twenty-five people, would find homes, and if the theoretical ninety gallons were divided among them, they would have only a trifle over three and a half gallons each.

When in the rapid growth of New York City the population reached three hundred thousand it became necessary to obtain more water than could be supplied by the wells or roof tops. A small supply had been obtained near by, but it was not enough, and it became very evident that the needed water must be brought from some distant water-shed far beyond any injury from the smoke, dust, and refuse of a great city. There were some who looked to the Housatonic Valley in Connecticut. Others thought the pure, deep lakes among the mountains of New Jersey would be nearer and more abundant. Next to these was the valley of the Croton River, about thirty miles north of the city. The Croton was within the State of New York, and its many branches, winding among wooded hills and meadow-dotted valleys, covered over 360 square miles of thinly settled country. It was for these reasons the most available water-shed in easy reach, and was selected as the big roof from which to fill the municipal water-barrel.

The original Croton aqueduct was begun in 1837 and finished in 1842. It is a brick conduit built on or near the surface, and extends from the dam at Croton Lake (which is artificial) along the Hudson River to High Bridge, crossing the deep valley of the Harlem on that beautiful structure—a true aqueduct that suggests the grand aqueducts of Rome. The capacity of the aqueduct is from ninety-five to ninety-eight million gallons of water every twenty-four hours. For the New York of the 'forties this was an abundant supply, and a curious result seems to have followed the use of such a vast quantity of water by such a comparatively small population. Three hundred gallons in a day for each person—no one could use so much water. Why take thought of its use? The people of New York never did, and they became, so far as water was concerned, a wasteful people, and they have never been cured of the habit. Prayers, entreaties, threats, fears of a water famine, have made no impression.

Within the life of one generation the average daily supply of ninety-seven million gallons has come to be insufficient. The people on the lower floors continued to go on in the same cheerful wastefulness, with no thought of their neighbors or of the morrow, until all up-stairs New York was reduced to very short commons. Then thousands of small pumping engines were put into the tenements and many roofs carried a water-tank. With the ever-growing population the share of water for each individual has rapidly decreased. The public fountains have been shut off and the use of private hose has been restricted. In 1884 the Bronx River aqueduct was built, and for a while it served to help the upper part of the city. To-day, even with this extra supply, there are only 115,000,000 gallons daily to be divided among 1,500,000 people. Even this apparently liberal supply implies plenty of rain. If the season be dry and the rainfall scant there will be serious trouble at once.

When in the early 'eighties it was proposed to bring more water into the city it seemed best to go once more to the Croton.

Speaking roughly, the Croton River and its branches cover about 360 square miles of hilly country in Dutchess, Putnam, and Westchester counties, New York, and also a narrow strip of the western edge of Connecticut. The main river flows in a southwesterly direction into the Hudson, the lower part following a narrow and winding valley among high hills, the upper portion spreading out into three main channels called the East, West, and Middle branches. It is naturally a country of brooks and ponds, and is musical in spring with the sound of many waters. If the entire surface on which the falling rain seeks an outlet above the present Croton Dam is measured, hills, fields, and lakes, we have 338.82 square miles of available water-shed. Of course all the territory below the Croton Dam is virtually useless as a water-shed. The rain indeed falls, but it flows away and is lost in the salty waters of the Hudson. There are therefore two water-sheds, one the present water-shed above the dam, and the larger district (including the former) below the dam, and which might be used were a second dam built lower down the river. This larger water-shed would give a surface of over 360 square miles. As this lower dam is not yet built, it may be best first to consider the smaller water-sheds now available above the present dam.

The Croton Valley is distinctively a dairy country. The underlying rock is a micaceous gneiss of remarkably uniform character. This rock is greatly broken up on the surface and appears in steep, irregular hills scattered about in great confusion. Glacial action in the past is plainly marked, and the surface is covered with a thin, gravelly soil, or is bare and stony. Woods formerly completely covered the entire country; but the early settlers cleared off the forests, and to-day there is a second growth of woods covering the steeper and rougher hills. The cleared lands are almost exclusively pasturage and hay-fields, and only a portion of the soil is available for crops. In the southern and eastern parts of the water-shed the few towns are scattered along the main stream of the Croton, for the sake of the water power. Towards the north and west the population is more scattered, and the hills rise to wild and deeply wooded mountains. In point of fact the water-shed is a part of the Highlands of the Hudson, the center being directly opposite West Point, and the mountains are, as it were, foothills of the great Appalachian backbone of the Atlantic seaboard. These stony hills and sloping pastures, these woods and fields, make the great roof on which the rains and snows deposit their pure waters that New York be not athirst. So far as nature is concerned, it is as good and sweet a place to collect water as may be found in the world. If there be any injury to the water, it must come from known and preventable artificial sources. The gneiss rock is practically watertight, and all the water that falls is saved, less the amount that is lost by evaporation. The soil that covers the surface is a filter to restrain any natural impurities that may contaminate the rain or snow. The grass, trees, and vegetation serve as a sponge to hold the water after every rain and let it escape slowly and evenly into the streams. The only possible contamination that can come to the water collected on such a surface must come from the habitations of men and animals. Twenty-five years ago the population of the Croton Valley was very small, and the actual contamination of the water was so small that it was hardly worthy of notice. The ordinary waste of a farm, manure, etc., spread upon grass or plowed land, can do no harm, because the pure, sweet soil and the air are disinfectants and purifiers.

Within the last few years a third railroad has been built across the Croton water-shed, the towns have rapidly increased in size, a large number of summer hotels and boarding-houses have been built, and manufactories have multiplied. From all these may come contaminations. The population of this valley are plain folks, quite as selfish, quite as indifferent to sanitary laws, and quite as firm in their belief in their right to do as seems to them fit, as the rest of us. The Croton gives them water power, its bed is a good place to deposit refuse. Why, they doubtless say, why not use it for water power and a sewer? From the piazza of a farmhouse it is difficult to sympathize with a tenement house. A number of committees and commissions have from time to time inspected the Croton water-shed with the view of ascertaining the possible and probable injury to the water that may arise from the neglect or carelessness of the people living there. The last investigation was made by the State Board of Health in 1887, and from their report and from other sources it is evident that the danger from contamination is rapidly increasing. In the opinion of experts the danger is not yet serious. The point is that it grows, and grows rapidly. So evident is this danger that laws have been passed to police the entire district. It therefore depends wholly upon the officers appointed to conserve the water-shed whether we drink in the future pure water or impure water. Had the citizens of New York any real faith in the persons whose duty it is to care for the cleanliness of our big drinking-cup they might rest in peace. Unfortunately so long as they permit certain " private clubs " to decide who shall hold public office that faith must be at least a trifle unstable.

The annual rainfall in the Croton River, as recorded at Boyd's Corner from 1870 to 1886, ranged from 38.52 inches in 1880 to 55.20 inches in 1882. These were the dryest and the most rainy years, and were exceptional, the average being 45.97 inches. This, in a water-shed of about 360 square miles, is ample for a much larger city than New York for a generation to come. There is, of course, a large percentage of loss by evaporation from the surface of the reservoirs and from the ground, yet there should be gathered here sufficient water, provided it is all properly managed, for several generations to come, and enough to form the larger source of supply for a century or longer. There is water enough and to spare. The question is how to economize it, a problem some of the ablest hydraulic engineers in the world have done much to solve.

The rainfall is never evenly distributed through a year, or even through a series of years, and while the average rainfall may be sufficient, the actual supply will be so irregular as to be wasteful and even dangerous. The engineers who have at different times been in charge of the public works of New York have recognized for a long time that the entire rainfall must be conserved. The restraining influence of the woods and ponds must be extended by artificial means. The abundant rains of winter must be saved for use in the dry season of midsummer. Two plans have been proposed. One is to construct, at intervals along the upper waters of the Croton, a large number of artificial ponds or reservoirs, by erecting dams across the streams and impounding the water. Another plan is to erect one large and several smaller dams on the lower parts of the main streams, and thus to collect and store virtually all the water falling into the entire basin. The first of the plans, that of having a series of small storage reservoirs, has already been carried out in a limited way, and is now being extended. The second plan is still under advisement, and will, no doubt, ultimately be carried out, thus combining the two plans. The peculiar character of the country in the Croton basin makes it comparatively easy to construct artificial storage reservoirs, and two have already been built. The first of these, at Boyd's Corner, is on the upper waters of West Branch in the northwest corner of the basin, among the wildest and highest mountains of the district. The second is on the Middle Branch of the Croton near the center of the watershed, between the villages of Carmel and Brewster's. Croton Lake is too shallow to be regarded as a storage reservoir, for its chief duty is to lift the water of the main stream to a level with the mouth of the old aqueduct.

The plan on which this system of reservoirs is operated is very simple. In wet weather the water in the two reservoirs flows away through the "spillways" or waste weirs beside the dams, and runs down the river into Croton Lake. Here a portion of the water is drawn

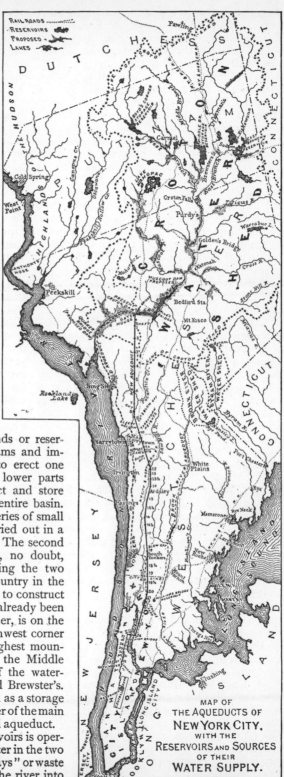

MAP OF
THE AQUEDUCTS OF
NEW YORK CITY.
WITH THE
RESERVOIRS AND SOURCES
OF THEIR
WATER SUPPLY.
SCALE OF MILES

off into the aqueduct, and the remainder flows over the dam and is lost in the Hudson. In dry weather the surplus water escaping through the spillways beside the dams grows less and less, and finally stops, leaving the reservoirs full of stored water. The river immediately below each dam ceases to flow, and would dwindle to a mere thread of water did not new supplies come in from the hills on each side. The drain on Croton Lake through the aqueduct soon absorbs the entire flow, and the water ceases to run to waste over the dam. The engineer in charge then asks the gate-keeper at Boyd's Corner to open the gates and permit the stored water to run down the river into the lake. In the same way he draws upon the Middle Branch reservoir, and in this manner the supply is kept up through the dry weeks of summer. Besides these two artificial reservoirs, there are a number of natural and partly improved ponds, Lake Mahopac being the largest. These ponds can also be drawn upon for extra supplies in case of necessity.

Boyd's Corner reservoir contains 2,727,-000,000 gallons of water, and Middle Branch 4,004,000,000 gallons, and this represents our reserve capital put away, so to speak, in bank against a dry day. So long as the old aqueduct drew less than one hundred million gallons a day these two reservoirs were sufficient insurance against a drought. When more water was required and a new and very much larger aqueduct was proposed the entire question assumed another aspect. As early as 1858 it was recognized that the storage capacity of the basin must be largely increased, and surveys were made for some new and very large reservoirs. While all of these reservoirs were not built, and more recent surveys have shown that some of the sites selected were not available, it may be observed that the necessity for such storage lakes has become imperative, and three reservoirs are now in process of construction. A passing study of this work may serve to show how a great storage reservoir is made and used.

Taking the town road from the village of Brewster's on the New York and Harlem Railroad, we drive down a long hill into the valley of the East Branch until the works of the Borden Milk Condensing Company are reached. Here the road follows the little river under a bridge of the New York and New England Railroad and again climbs over the hills till the little village of Sodom is reached. There the stream turns to the south through a narrow rocky gorge and then winds off to the east between high, wooded hills. At this point is being erected a magnificent masonry dam closing the portal between the hills and designed to create an irregular lake where now are farms, meadows, and deep woods. The

new reservoir will eventually consist of two distinct bodies of water formed by four dams. The first of these dams is of solid rubble masonry faced with dressed granite. To the east of this dam, on the crest of the hill and at right angles with the stone dam, will be a long, low dam of earth and having a heart or core of masonry. North of the dam, on the other side of the rocky hill, are two more earth dams, designed to impound the waters of a little pool called Lake Kishowana and a small brook that flows out of it. Under the hills is to be a tunnel connecting the two reservoirs. The building of the three earth dams is comparatively simple. The work on the stone dam is quite complicated. The first steps were to bore into the hills on each side of the stream and in the bed of the river with diamond drills to ascertain the character of the bed-rock. The borings having shown that the rock is comparatively uniform in character, the river was diverted by means of a temporary crib-work dam, and then a deep trench was blasted out of the bed of the river and out of the steep sides of the hills to form a safe support for the dam. In this trench the foundations of the dam are laid. In the center, near the bottom, large iron pipes with gates are built into the foundations, the pipes being eventually the escape or outlet for the water, and while the dam is being built they serve as a waste weir or outlet for the river. The dam is 500 feet long, 53 feet wide at the base, 12 feet wide at the top, and 78 feet high. The earth dam is 700 feet long, and there will be a roadway on the top of each dam with a turning-place at the end. When finished it will be a magnificent drive, with the broad lake on one side, the deep, rocky valley on the other, with its white fountains below and the wide spillway at the end of the dam, where the surplus water will pour in an enormous waterfall down the rocky face of the cliff. The present hill, where stands the white church, will be like an isthmus between the two reservoirs, the tunnel to connect the two being directly under the crest of the hill. The accompanying pictures give one an excellent idea of the character of the country above the dam, and show the work in operation just as the walls of the great stone dam began to rise above the massive foundations sunk in the hills. The first two illustrations show the deep trench cut in the hills as a foundation for the dam, and the cable hoist used in handling stone. The third picture gives an idea of the character of the country to be eventually submerged.

It is a curious commentary on the demands of modern civilization to observe the effect of building this dam. The million people in the city need a reserve of drinking water, and twenty-one families must move out of their

EXCAVATION FOR SODOM DAM.

shed is not yet by any means exhausted, and as fast as needed more of these storage reservoirs will be provided at different places. One will probably be placed near Purdy's, on the little Titicus River. An excellent site for the dam has already been found where the stream passes through a narrow, rocky gorge. A dam will here flow a very large tract of fine farming country to the east and give another sweet, clean drinking-cup for the city. Still others are under consideration near Carmel, and above Croton Lake on Muscoot River.

In addition to this plan of storing the surplus water in a number of reservoirs at the upper part of the Croton basin is the proposal to erect, far down on the main stream of the Croton, one very large dam, which with the others will impound virtually all the rainfall of the Croton basin and save thousands of millions of gallons that are now lost. This proposed dam is to be placed within one or two miles of Quaker Bridge. If built it is to be the largest dam in the world, and will impound more than thirty thousand million gallons of water. The lake will be on an average 3000 feet wide and 72,000 feet long, with an average depth of over 30 feet. The dam will add

quiet rural homes and see their hearths sink deep under water. The entire area to be taken for the reservoir is 1471 acres. Twenty-one dwellings, three saw and grist mills, a sash and blind factory, and a carriage factory must be torn down and removed. A mile and a quarter of railroad track must be relaid, and six miles of country roads must be abandoned. A road twenty-three miles long will extend around the two lakes, and a border or "safety margin" three hundred feet wide will be cleared all around the edge to prevent any contamination of the water. This safety border will include a carriage road, and all the rest will be laid down to grass. As the dam rises, the water will spread wider and wider over fields, farms, and roads. Every tree will be cut down and carried away. Every building will be carted off, and the cellars burned out and filled with clean soil to prevent any possibility of injury to the water. Fortunately there is no cemetery within the limits of the land taken for the reservoir. Had there been one it would have been completely removed before the water should cover the ground. Fifty-eight persons and corporations, holding one hundred and eleven parcels of land, will be dispossessed in order to clear the land for the two lakes and the dams, roads, and safety borders.

This East Branch reservoir will give the city two good-sized additional storage reservoirs, and while they will add considerably to the present supply, they will not meet the wants of the city in a year of drought. The Croton water-

CABLE AND BUCKET AT SODOM DAM.

115 square miles to the now available watershed, and save about all the water now lost on this great surface. Very much has been written both for and against this great dam, but the consensus of opinion appears to be in favor of its erection. That it can be built is beyond discussion. It can also be built with entire safety, both in a sanitary sense as a storage place for water, and in a mechanical sense as a structure absolutely safe against overthrow by floods. The key to the safety of any dam is found in the spillway. Given a good

be, for a generation at least, any danger of a water famine, even should two dry years like 1880 follow each other.

When it was first proposed to build a new aqueduct to bring down more water from the Croton water-shed it was suggested that the new and larger dam should be built at once and that the aqueduct should start at the great dam. It was also suggested that the aqueduct should start just above the old dam at Croton Lake. The points in favor of this last plan were these: The water could be let into the aque-

A FUTURE LAKE AND ISLANDS AT BREWSTER'S.

design, good materials, and good work, a dam may be as secure as any structure that can be built. Its life therefore depends on the provision for relieving extra pressure. The water behind the dam rises as the rainfall increases. Before it can reach the top and flow over it finds an outlet in the spillway and runs harmlessly away. It is believed that American engineers are in the front rank of their profession, and modern science places in their hands the exact data of rainfall, water pressure, and strength of materials. It becomes, therefore, only common sense dealing with large figures; and this dam, great as it may seem on paper, is within the ability of our engineers, and its construction and maintenance are within "the limits of safety." The smaller reservoirs will not be useless when the large dam is built, and all these proposed small dams should be built as well as the greater work. It will take five years to build the big dam. Each of the smaller dams can be built in two or three years, and New York cannot go on another year without more water. True wisdom suggests both plans, the smaller reservoirs on the head waters, the larger lake below. Both systems can be used together and be controlled from one point, and then there will not

duct as soon as completed and without waiting for the new dam. If it were afterwards decided to build the great dam and submerge the present dam, the water could be just as well taken there as at the dam itself. If the dam were built a part of the old aqueduct would be submerged, and it could be used as a supply pipe for conveying the water back from the new dam to the new aqueduct. The old aqueduct could also be connected with the new reservoir at or near the new dam, tapping the river several miles below the present inlet. This plan, therefore, seemed the best, and the new aqueduct was laid out along a line beginning at a point just below Croton Dam.

The Croton Valley at the foot of Croton Lake is very narrow and the stream is walled in by steep, rocky hills. This very fact led to the erection of the present dam at this place. The old aqueduct is on the south bank and follows the line of the country road close under the steep cliffs that line the shore. The new aqueduct would require a gate-house, and, as there was no room on the bank without interfering with the old aqueduct, it was decided to blast out an excavation directly in the side of the hill. This excavation, like an enormous scar on the side of the hill, made the first important

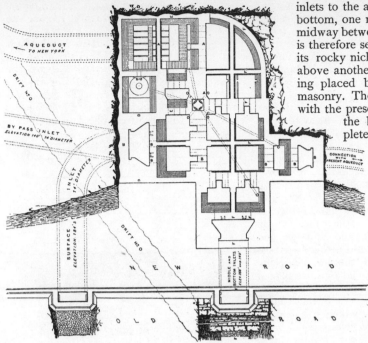

GENERAL PLAN OF THE NEW GATE-HOUSE.

inlets to the aqueduct — one near the bottom, one near the surface, and one midway between. The new gate-house is therefore set high up on the bank in its rocky niche with three inlets one above another, the building itself being placed behind a massive wall of masonry. The middle inlet is on a level with the present road on the bank, and the bottom inlet, when completed, will pass directly under the old aqueduct, and will be many feet under the present surface of the lake. All this is, of course, provisional and for the future. For immediate use there is a fourth, temporary, inlet, called the "by-pass inlet," that takes the water from the lake a few hundred feet above the dam. This inlet is the only one that can be used at present, and we must take the water, as we do now, from a point near the surface of the old Croton Lake. Another point with respect to the future had also to be considered. The old aqueduct passes in front of the new gate-house, and by connecting it with the gate-house the water for the old aqueduct could be controlled from the new gate-house and the old gate-house could be given up.

The new gate-house must be regarded as a masterly piece of engineering, both in design and in construction. It is a nearly square structure, built of granite and brick and divided into a number of compartments or vaults. The aqueduct being below the level of the river, it will be impossible to permit the water to rush directly into it under pressure. The aqueduct is here a "flowing conduit." That is, the water does not fill it, but occupies only about four-fifths of the tunnel and flows easily along like an underground river. The water enters the gate-house through the by-pass under pressure, and to relieve this pressure and permit the water to escape into the aqueduct with only its natural pressure or weight it is passed through a series of reducing chambers until its force is spent and it is ready to start easily and slowly on its long, dark journey to the sea. This grand gate-house gives us the key to the whole great engineering work before us.

Walking over the iron floor of the immense room within we may before long peer down into the deep black caves where the great waters are to flow. Here the engineer may guide a whole

step in the great work of moving the rainfall of the Croton basin into New York. The aqueduct itself begins just opposite the iron bridge, seventy feet below the ground and below the bed of Croton River.

The most simple way to connect an aqueduct with its reservoir, or source of supply, is to place the end of the aqueduct below the level of the water and to put a gate in the conduit to control the inflow of water. This was the plan followed in the old aqueduct. The latest science leads to grave doubts whether this is the best way. Water stored in a reservoir is in different temperatures and in different conditions at different depths. It may be warm near the surface and cool below. It may contain minute forms of life near the surface and be barren below. The engineer should therefore be able to draw the water from different points according to the season and according to the temperature and condition of the water. It is evidently better to let the cold bottom water flow into the city in summer than the tepid surface water. A gate-house is necessary in any event, and in planning the gate-house for the new aqueduct provision was made for the future control over the selection of the water to be sent to New York.

Very soon the great dam must be built. When it is built the water will rise forty feet above the present dam, and the lake opposite the new gate-house will be deep enough to give three

river under the hills, selecting, mixing, and controlling from day to day the water sweeping with ceaseless roar through the caverns below. Looking down into one of the great vaults of the gate-house the portal of the aqueduct can be seen. It is like the entrance of a cave under the hills. It seems hardly possible that this black archway, so deep under ground, is the direct road to New York, and that the water will easily flow away into the blackness on its long journey to the Central Park reservoir.

When it was proposed to build a second aqueduct two plans were suggested. One was to parallel the present aqueduct with a second one placed on or near the surface. Two serious objections were found to this route. If the aqueduct were placed so near the Hudson it would interfere with the old aqueduct and could be easily shelled and destroyed by hostile ships that might force their way into the Hudson, or even be destroyed by guns placed on the New Jersey shore, and the city would be without water and at the mercy of the enemy. Some such route must be taken if a surface aqueduct be built; and even were it safe from attack from the river the very fact of the aqueduct being on the surface would always be a menace, as it could be easily destroyed by a mob. Common sense and military prudence plainly pointed to a tunnel placed deep under ground out of reach and easily guarded at the few points where it might come to the surface. Besides this, land owners are content to accept a very small fee for right of way if the tunnel is a hundred feet under their houses and the inconvenience of surface operations is avoided.

These considerations led to the construction of the new aqueduct in the form of a continuous tunnel extending from Croton Dam to High Bridge. The path of the aqueduct is a perfectly straight line from the gate-house to a point just

FRONT ELEVATION OF BLOW-OFF.

west of Tarrytown Heights and north of Sleepy Hollow. It then turns slightly to the east, passes under the hills, and enters the valley of the Saw-mill River. It then passes, with an occasional slight turn to right or left, directly to the great siphon where the water is to pass under the Harlem River. Reaching Manhattan Island near 180th street, it follows Tenth Avenue to the new gate-house at 135th street, where the aqueduct will end and the pipe lines begin. The pipe lines will then convey the water to Central Park reservoir and to other points for distribution through the upper part of the island. For the entire distance from Croton Lake to 135th street the aqueduct is built of solid brickwork and masonry, reënforced in places with wood and iron, and all, except at three points covering a few thousand feet, is sunk to an average depth of 170 feet and underground. The aqueduct itself is divided into two portions, each part being of different size and shape. The larger part, extending from the lake to a point near the city line, is a horseshoe section and is a flowing conduit; that is, the tunnel is filled to about four-fifths of its capacity. The other portion, extending from the city line to 135th street, is smaller and of

BUILDING THE FOUNDATION OF A GATE-HOUSE AT SOUTH YONKERS.

a circular section, and here the water fills the entire tunnel and is under pressure.

In planning an aqueduct two things have to be considered. There must be arrangements made for the steady filling or supply of the aqueduct and for the safe conveyance of the water without contamination and without loss. There must also be provision for shutting off the supply and emptying the aqueduct in order to clean or repair it. We have seen how the new aqueduct is to be supplied from Croton Lake, and its ability to carry the water without harm or loss can be studied as we travel along its route. The fact that the aqueduct is deep underground insures the safety and purity of the water. The next problem was more serious, and involved a long and thorough preliminary study of the country through which the aqueduct passes. A pipe placed deep underground and full of water is difficult of access if at any time it becomes necessary to clean or repair it. If it be of a uniformly descending grade it is possible to empty it by shutting off the supply of water. The water will gradually run out, and the tunnel can then be entered from either end. In the case of the new aqueduct this would hardly be practicable, because of its great length. There must be numerous places where it can be entered, and a number of outlets or "blow-offs" where the water can be drawn off from the whole or a part of the tunnel. There must also be waste weirs for the escape of surplus water, and for maintaining the flowing water at a uniform height in the aqueduct. The actual problem in the case of the new aqueduct was even more difficult, because it was necessary to make at two points sunken loops or inverted siphons. The first of these was made to avoid a swamp, by diving under it, and the second and deeper siphon is under the Harlem River. In emptying the aqueduct the water would lodge in these low places and provision must be made for lifting it out. At other points advantage was taken of the contour of the country, and outlets or "blow-offs" were placed in low valleys, where the water could be allowed to flow away into neighboring streams.

A study of the gate-house and blow-off at South Yonkers will give a general idea of the plan on which these outlets are arranged. Here the aqueduct appears at the south side of a hill and is then built for a short distance in an open cut. As the land falls the aqueduct comes to the surface and is built on the ground and covered with an embankment. At this point a small brook is diverted from its old bed and passes, through stone culverts, directly under a massive granite gate-house. The gate-house consists of a large chamber on the line of the aqueduct and of the superstructure or building (one room) overhead where the gates are controlled. This chamber is built of massive blocks of granite and is divided into two parts by a cross wall or partition parallel with the aqueduct. In this partition are eight openings, four being placed at the bottom on a level with the floor of the chamber, and four placed about ten feet above the first. All of these openings lead directly into the culvert below. The four lower openings can be closed by gates controlled by shafting from the room above. When the aqueduct is in use the water fills the chamber up to the lips of the upper openings or waste weirs.

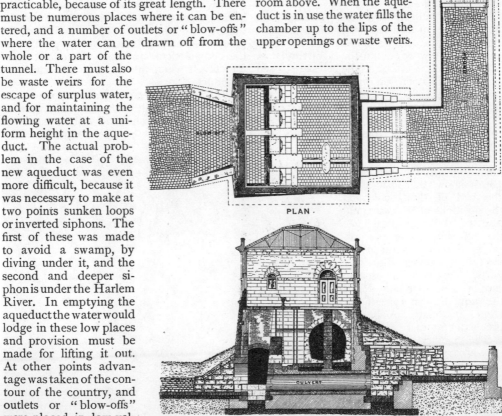

PLAN.

BLOW-OFF AND WASTE WEIR AT SOUTH YONKERS.

BLOW-OFF AT SOUTH YONKERS, LOOKING NORTH.

had been laid, also the floor of the chamber, the gates, and the lower part of the central column. A portion of the aqueduct is seen to the north just as it emerges from the hill.

The accompanying pictures from photographs in the gate-house reveal the massive character of the stone-work, and also give an impression of the comparative size and shape of the aqueduct at this point. One of these pictures gives a view from the chamber looking north into the aqueduct. Another is from a photograph taken within the aqueduct and looking south across the chamber into the south portal of the aqueduct, and showing the massive walls of the gate-house and the dividing column in the center of the chamber. The picture on the opposite page shows the partition with the gate openings below and the waste weir above. At the left the arch shown in the other picture appears at the lower part of the gate, daylight showing under the crown of the arch. The elevation of the gate-house, on page 212, shows its position on the embankment, and also the openings of the culvert where the brook passes under the aqueduct.

These waste weirs are provided with channels or grooves cut in the stone-work, and by sliding planks into these grooves and thus forming a wooden dam, the height of the water in the aqueduct can be maintained at any point desired.

If at any time it is required to empty the aqueduct or to shut the water off below this point, the gates can be opened and the entire contents will sweep out into the culvert and then into the brook. As soon as the gates are closed the water will again flow on through the chamber towards the city. In the same way the water may be turned aside at Ardsley or at Pocantico, or be shut off at the lake and allowed to escape at any of these points until the aqueduct is empty.

The plan and section and elevation on the preceding pages show the position of the bed of the brook and the positions of the gates, and also of the two portals of the aqueduct. Near one portal is seen a column dividing the chamber into two parts. This is to be used to support a wooden dam across the aqueduct in case it becomes necessary to shut off the water at this point.

The picture showing the gate-house while being constructed will also assist to a correct understanding of the work. The construction had reached a point where the "invert" or floor of the aqueduct on each side of the gate-house

When it had been decided that a new aqueduct should be built in the form of an underground tunnel, careful and elaborate surveys were made of the country to the south of

LOOKING SOUTH ACROSS GATE-HOUSE AT SOUTH YONKERS.

Croton Lake to determine the best route. The hills and valleys were searched for the best positions from which to reach the line of the proposed tunnel by means of shafts sunk in the ground. Diamond drills were employed to test the character of the rock in order to find out if it would be sufficiently strong to sustain the roof of the tunnel while the excavations were being made. The cores brought up by the drills showed the bed-rock to be of a generally uniform quality of gneiss with a few belts of limestones, over the entire thirty miles between the lake and a point near 135th street on the west side of the city. Careful studies of all the data collected in the field showed that a tunnel could probably be excavated directly through the rock at an average depth of 170 feet below the surface. The surveys showed that after passing under the high hills to the south of the lake the valley of the little Saw-mill River offered a route to the Harlem that would not require very deep shafts to reach the line of the tunnel. This route would also give two or three points where the tunnel would come to the surface and give opportunities for the building of gatehouses, blow-offs, and waste weirs. From these studies the final plans were made and the drawings and specifications drawn up for the entire work.

The plans showed that the line of the tunnel could be reached by thirty-two shafts and four open cuts. To gain time, the number of shafts was afterwards increased to thirty-five. For convenience the work was divided into five divisions and these again divided into fifteen sections. The first four sections extended from the lake southward to a point near East Tarrytown and included the open cuts at Pocantico, a distance of about thirteen miles. These sections included the deepest shafts and made the longest portion of the tunnel entirely underground. Sections 5 to 9 inclusive carried the tunnel to the city line and under lower hills, the tunnel twice coming to the surface. Sections 10 and 11 included all the route to the Harlem River, and here the tunnel dropped down deeper under the ground, because if continued on that grade it would have approached too near the surface. Section 12 included the great siphon under Harlem River, and Sections 13 and 14 carried the work to the gate-house at 135th street, where the aqueduct ends and

the pipe lines begin. The grade established for the aqueduct was about nine inches' fall in the mile for the flowing portion extending from the lake to a point about a mile south of the city line. The drainage for this portion, in case of repairs, escapes at Pocantico, Ardsley, and South Yonkers. Where the aqueduct changes from a horseshoe section to a circle the tunnel dips deeper into the earth, as already mentioned, and the drainage is into the inverted siphon at the Harlem River, where the water can be pumped out through a blow-off and discharged into the Harlem. South of the river the tunnel gradually rises and the drainage flows north and escapes into the Harlem.

It was estimated that the most economical distance at which a heading could be driven

BLOW-OFF AND WASTE WEIR.

from the bottom of a shaft would be about half a mile, and the next step was to define the positions of the shafts. The selection of the sites was guided in part by this distance of one mile (half a mile each way), in part by the valleys, and in part by convenience in disposing of the "spoil," or waste rock. The bottom of a valley would give the shortest shaft, but leave no room for dump-heaps, and thus all the shafts, while in valleys, were really on the sides of the hills above the bottom or lowest part of the depression to give room for the gigantic heaps of broken stone (spoil) that would gather about the mouths of the shafts. These considerations finally resulted in the selection of thirty-five shafts to be excavated directly into the earth. For convenience the shafts were numbered from 0 to 32, and it is curious to observe the variety of places in which they were started. "Number 0" is a straight drift into the hills from the edge of Croton River below the dam, and the

HEAD-HOUSE OF SHAFT ON TENTH AVENUE.

dump-heaps form a gigantic embankment along the south side of the river. Shafts from Nos. 1 to 17 are either in woods or on farms, some of them being deep in the hills far from any town or village. Shafts 24 and 25 are directly on the banks of the Harlem. Shafts 27 to 30 are placed in the middle of Tenth Avenue, between the tracks of the cable road, and some of them in a thickly built-up neighborhood. The accompanying illustration gives a good idea of the way some of the shafts are placed in the center of Tenth Avenue. The deepest shaft at the great siphon at Harlem River is 419 feet, the deepest among the hills near the lake is 370 feet, and the shortest shaft is only 32 feet.

The actual work of sinking the shafts began about the middle of January, 1884, twenty-four shafts being very soon under way. The first shaft to be excavated to the depth of the top of the tunnel was shaft No. 11A, thirty-one feet deep. Other short shafts were soon after completed and the work of excavating the tunnel was begun. The deepest shaft in the hills, No. 3 (370 feet), was completed in thirty-four weeks from the start, there being five weeks when for various reasons little or no progress was made. The short shafts along Tenth Avenue were not begun until February, 1886, and were completed in from ten to twenty-two weeks. The maximum progress in any one week was forty-two feet in the drift No. 0, and the maximum progress in the vertical shafts was twenty-one feet.

The actual work of driving the tunnel began in shaft No. 11A, in March, 1885, the progress

for the first week being forty feet to the north and twenty-four feet to the south. By the 1st of April work was under way in four more shafts, and by May 9 work was in progress in ten shafts. By the 1st of July nineteen shafts had reached the level of the tunnel, and in thirteen of these the tunnel was advanced in one or both directions. The first piece of excavation to be completed was near Shaft 14. It was only fifty-five feet long, and extended to the open cut at Ardsley. The next piece of excavation to be finished extended from Shaft 9 north to Pocantico cut, a distance of 1727 feet. In September, 1886, four more of the drifts either met under ground or had reached an open cut, and in October three more connections had been made, and the tunnel had begun to assume something of its grand proportions. Up to January 1, 1887, a period of ninety-six weeks from the start, the maximum progress in the heading from the shafts or portals (open cuts) had been 84 feet in one week, and the highest average weekly progress in any one heading had been 45 feet. The highest average weekly rate of approach between the headings (south from the shaft, north from the next) was 70 feet, and in many places it ranged from 50 to 60 feet. This was for the time when work was actually going on.

Up to January 1, 1887, the tunnel and open cuts had been excavated for a total distance of twenty-two miles, leaving at that time only eight miles, which were completed in the spring of 1889. The excavation was soon large enough to admit the masons, and work in the tunnel lining began. Parts of the tunnel did not need any interior support, but it was thought best to reënforce it with a brick lining called the "tunnel lining," this brick-work being in turn firmly braced at the sides and roof against the walls of the excavation. The work of making the tunnel lining began in Shaft 9, September 28, 1885. During 1886 the work was under way in one or both directions from a number of shafts, and on the 1st of January, 1887, the side walls of the finished tunnel had advanced 32,382 linear feet, and the "invert," or floor, had been laid for 7722 feet, while the arch, or roof, had been completed for 16,713 feet. The entire brick-work of the tunnel is now completed, and makes a continuous tunnel 29.63 miles long. The total number of bricks exceed 163,000,000, or sufficient to construct thirty-three buildings like the "Tribune" building in New York City.

In this enormous labor at one time ten thousand men were employed, with hundreds of mules and horses and a great number of steam engines, and their labors underground were lighted by scores of electric lights. The mere handling of this vast amount of material involved important questions of transportation. The line of the aqueduct is several miles back from the line of the Hudson, and touches tidewater only at the Harlem River near High Bridge. The only railroad convenient to the line is the New York City and Northern, a short, single-track route reaching from the elevated railroad on Eighth Avenue at 155th street to the Croton River basin. Fortunately it has docks on the Harlem, and could load cars with brick and cement from barges and canal boats sent up from the East River. Whenever convenient, materials were sent by this route. For the portions within the city materials were sent by team from points on the Hudson. The enormous mass of broken rock (spoil) taken out in making the excavations involved the purchase of land on which it could be dumped. The material itself is practically valueless, except for filling on town roads or railroads. It has been tried for road surfacing, but is wholly useless, as it soon grinds up to fine powder.

However carefully the plans for such a great engineering work as this are drawn, there must be an element of uncertainty in the actual work. It is impossible to foresee what difficulties may be met deep under the hills. For instance, in sinking Shaft 24, on the east bank of the Harlem, water was encountered in great quantities, so that the work had to be performed under the greatest difficulties. Costly pumping engines were erected and put in operation. After-

wards, when for certain reasons a second shaft had to be sunk still lower, a new position was selected for this shaft not twenty feet away, and this second shaft was as dry as a bone. The diamond drill might have gone a few inches to one side and not have told the exact truth about the rock.

The first serious difficulty was met at a place called Gould's Swamp, in Section 5. The soil proved to be a wet muck overlaying sand with boulders — in fact, a swamp. The only way to avoid this soft spot was to go round it or to pass, deep in the bed-rock, under it. This was finally done, and two shafts were sunk, Nos. 11A and 11B, on the hillsides on each side of the swamp, and these were connected by a short tunnel, thus forming a bend or inverted siphon.

Another serious difficulty was met at shaft No. 30, near 149th street. Soft, crumbling rock was found that threatened to cause dangerous leakage of water, and it became necessary to line the interior of the tunnel with plates of cast iron. These plates were bolted together to

REËNFORCING THE TUNNEL.

form a circular pipe the size of the aqueduct at this point (13 feet 3 inches), and outside of this iron pipe the brick-work was laid as in the other portions of the aqueduct. The illustration on the preceding page shows this work of reënforcing the aqueduct. This iron-lined portion of the aqueduct extends for about 230 feet in the south heading and is about 400 feet south of the shaft.

The most serious difficulty met in the entire work was encountered in crossing the Harlem. Two shafts on each bank of the river, Nos. 24 and 25, had been sunk to what seemed to be a proper depth, and headings had been driven east and west across the river where a fissure was met near the west bank of the river, and it was decided to sink the shaft deeper. Shaft No. 25 was continued to a depth of 419 feet; headings were then started, and in due time they met and were lined with brick. The work was not alone one of the greatest difficulty, but it may also be regarded as of the first importance from an engineering point of view. Shaft 25 is one of the largest in this country; it is

THE SITE OF THE GREAT SIPHON.

double, one portion being used for the water and the other for the bucket that is used in lifting the water out of the siphon in case of inspection and repairs. The arrangements for emptying the aqueduct at this point are specially interesting, because not only is the part under the river very deep, but only at this place could a blow-off be arranged for draining that part of the aqueduct south of this point. Here are being built a gate-house, pumping station, and blow-off, and they will form perhaps the most interesting spot, from an engineering point of view, in the entire work. The aqueduct is here under pressure, and the water rising in the shaft after its passage deep under the river must again rise on its passage to the gate-house at 135th street. The top of the shaft must therefore be closed at a point under the surface where it joins the aqueduct that extends along Tenth Avenue, and it must also have gates to permit the escape of all the water in the aqueduct to the south, a distance of two miles. Shaft 26, a few hundred feet from Shaft 25, is arranged with an overflow and blow-off, and it virtually acts as a safety-valve for all that portion of the aqueduct to the south. The overflow here regulates the height of the water in the gate-house at 135th street, two miles south. A short pipe line connects Shaft 26 with the blow-off at the foot of the bluff at

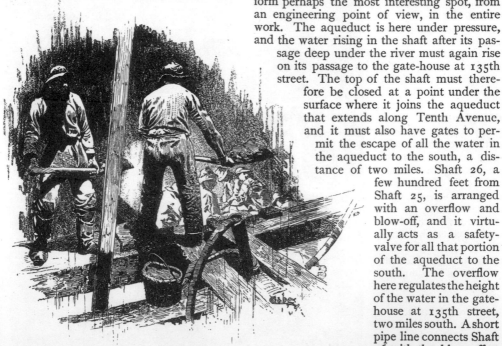

IN SHAFT 25.

Shaft 25. Shaft 24 has also a blow-off for the water to the north as far as South Yonkers.

There are, therefore, three grand hydraulic works concentrated within a few hundred feet and in the midst of what promises to be a populous part of the city. Moreover, these works, though partly unseen, are placed between two other great works that testify to the skill of American engineers. To the south is High Bridge, justly famous as a lofty and beautiful stone structure, and to the north is the Washington Bridge. This new bridge is formed of two immense steel arches, the largest single arched spans in the world. The picture on the opposite page gives an idea of the character of the Harlem Valley at this point. The picture gives a view across the river, and shows the head-house and other works at Shaft 24. At the left is seen a portion of the new bridge, and below, on the river banks, are the two landing stages where the brick, cement, and other materials used in the aqueduct were landed. It also gives a view of the inclined railway for bringing brick and stone up from the river to Shaft 25.

In addition to the larger and unexpected difficulties met in building the aqueduct more trouble was looked for in the way of soft, broken, and weak spots in the rock. These were overcome by means of timbering, as in a mine. However, the amount of timbering required was not excessive, only about 39,000 feet of the aqueduct tunnel being supported by timbers outside the brick lining. This timber-work was put in before the bricks were laid, and in some cases was left in position when the lining was put in. Completely inclosed from the air, it will last for a long time; and even if it decays no harm can follow, as the tunnel lining is backed up by masonry and is amply strong enough to carry the weight of the rock.

The difficulties at all points along the aqueduct have now been overcome and the great engineering work is virtually complete. The

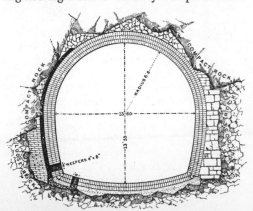

THE HORSESHOE SECTION FOR FLOWING WATER.

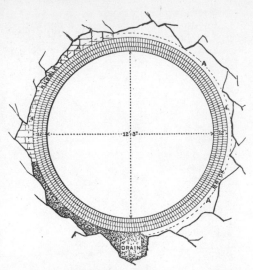

THE CIRCULAR SECTION FOR WATER UNDER PRESSURE.

upper part from the lake to a point near the city line is of a horseshoe section, the interior dimensions being 13.60 feet wide at the top of the side walls and 13.55 feet high in the center. The accompanying section shows the shape of the tunnel lining. The lining consists of three and sometimes four cornices of brick laid in cement. The actual excavation, as shown in the diagrams, is larger than the tunnel lining, and the space between the lining and the sides of the excavation is represented as filled with masonry or with additional brick-work. This exterior work was essential in order to brace the arched lining against the weight of the rock overhead. Without this masonry at the sides and top of the lining the pressure of the rock might crush or distort the brick-work and destroy or seriously obstruct the aqueduct.

The tunnel south of the city line descends deeper underground and is circular in section and smaller in diameter, and will connect with an additional storage reservoir to be built at Jerome Park. The section above gives a good idea of this part of the excavation and of the round tunnel lining. It also shows the masonry backing used to reënforce and protect the lining and assist in carrying the weight of the rock above. The diameter of the circular part of the aqueduct is twelve feet three inches, except under the Harlem River, where it is reduced to ten feet six inches.

Not long ago the writer walked for a mile or more through both the arched and circular portions. Entering by an unfinished portal, left open on account of repairs, the first impression was rather depressing. The ladder was wet with clay, and the sunlight fell upon the curved walls and a wide and rapid brook flowing between

CAVE OVER CROWN OF ARCH.

them. A rubber hat, rubber coat, and long rubber boots were awkward but comfortable. There was a cool wind blowing from the two black-arched caves, and it was but a moment's change from bright sunshine to intense darkness, relieved only by the lantern in the hand. The floor had a gentle slope towards the center and for about a foot on each side was comparatively dry. The sense of walking half in a brook and half on its slippery bank was peculiar at first, but in a little while the trick of walking on the edge of the water close to the side wall had been learned.

The spot of sunlight behind us faded away to only a yellow star that at last went out. The intense darkness was blacker by contrast with the black walls that here and there in the light of the lamps sparkled with drops of moisture. Occasionally a white mark gleamed with strange distinctness on the walls, showing where the engineers or inspectors had measured the work or left traces for future measurements or inspections. The silence, the cool air gently moving through the tunnel, the narrow circle of light about the lantern, appealed strongly to the imagination. Every splashing footfall echoed strangely, and there seemed at times to be a deep murmur in the air. We paused and listened, but heard nothing save the faint ripple of the water. Then might come

a distant sound, or rather reverberation, like the ghost of a thunder peal. Standing in the water in the center of the tunnel and looking either way there was only deep blackness, and it was difficult to decide from which direction came the faint rolling sound. A word spoken seemed to start tremendous echoes, and a note sung loudly floated away and came back again in a long-drawn-out sigh. Several words spoken quickly were repeated distinctly out of the black void beyond the little circle of light. Again we heard the far-away booming, and the engineer said that men were at work perhaps a mile away. We might meet them yet.

The lines of bricks stretch on and on in uniform, unbroken precision. The sloping floor never changes its exact angle, the walls are ever exactly in line, and high above the head is the arched roof. It is the perfection of mechanical work stretching ever onward through darkness. We pass a gate-house and cross its magnificent stone floor, and listen to the roar of the escaping water, and watch the curious effects of light shining upward through the gates and bringing out the massive blocks of granite into startling relief. Again the great arch welcomes to darkness.

Ahead there appears a faint, white cloud, or nebulous spot of light. In a moment we are close to it, and find it some workman's tools covered with white canvas. It is only a hundred feet distant, and yet seems immensely removed. All sense of distance is lost in such deep darkness. Looking up, a circular opening is seen where daylight streams faintly down a shaft, lighting an iron ladder. This is one of the finished shafts, and the light shining on the white canvas spread over the tools at the bottom gave that peculiar nebulous appearance in the gloom. Nearly all the shafts are completely closed, and only a few are left like this—permanently open. The ladder ends in a little house that serves as a protection from the weather and from improper visitors to the tunnel.

As we walk on there are sounds in the air, echoes from yet unseen workmen. Soon through the murky air are seen star-like spots of light. There is a flash from an electric light and we meet piles of brick, stone, and cement. There are voices and a sound of tools and we come to a wooden staging, or "false work," and climb a short ladder and stand close to the roof among a group of workmen. There is a square hole cut in the arched ceiling, and with much scrambling we crawl through and sit down directly on the top of the tunnel lining. The space between the lining and the rock is

not high enough to enable one to stand upright, yet high enough for a comfortable seat on the top of the work. The cave-like place extends for some distance in both directions. The candles light up the wet, ragged rocks overhead, some heavy timbers in the distance, and the clean red bricks of the arch.

This space over the tunnel lining is only one of a great number that have been found at different points along the aqueduct. They appear sometimes at the top, sometimes at the sides, sometimes extend completely over the tunnel lining from side to side. In the specifications for the work all these spaces are marked as filled up solid with rubble masonry. The masonry is necessary to the strength of the aqueduct, and it was to be supplied in all cases for the whole length of the tunnel. It was not so supplied in this and in many other places. Moreover, the specifications call for three, and in some cases five, courses of solid brick laid in cement. The upper course in this cave is not laid in cement at all. The bricks on the top of the arch are as clean as on the day they were made. No cement was used, and the bricks were merely laid loosely in place and left there. The hole cut in the arch was made by the engineers to test the work, which was found wanting.

CAVE AT SIDE OF ARCH. (FROM A PHOTOGRAPH.)

That this statement may not seem exaggerated, two pictures are presented on the preceding pages from photographs taken in two of these caves. In the first the hole cut in the arch is shown with one course of brick properly laid, two courses badly laid, and two courses simply left out. More bad work can also be seen in the other picture. The rock above is the roof of the excavation, and all the empty space represented in the picture was paid for by the citizens of New York at the rate of about five dollars a cubic yard. In some of these caves cross-walls were built to deceive the engineer and lead him to think all the space had been built in solid. In one of the pictures such a cross-wall is shown with a hole knocked in it to show that another cave existed beyond. It is now known that these defects occur in the larger part of the aqueduct, and that over one million dollars were at one time paid out for work that was never performed, and that was certified to have been performed by those appointed to watch the work.

Happily the faults of which these pictures are such unimpeachable witnesses have been repaired, at the expense of the contractors, but they resulted in a complete change in the administration of the work, and the whole business is now but a bad memory. We can only hopefully look forward to the day when "practical politics" shall no longer rule our great public works. The time is fast coming when the selfish greed of political " halls " and the personal necessities of aspirants for public office can no longer thrive on the robbery of the people. Some day the American people will insist that neither governors nor mayors shall appoint public servants at the behest of political managers.

The aqueduct itself ends at the gate-house at 135th street and Tenth Avenue. The water rises through a shaft into the great vaults of the gate-house and then flows through eight lines of huge iron pipes into the city. Four of the lines of pipes lead directly to the reservoirs at Central Park, and four of them branch off at different points to supply the upper and central parts of the city. The laying of these pipes was of itself a great piece of work. The gate-house is a few hundred feet east of Tenth Avenue, and the pipe lines all start from the bottom of the gate-house deep underground. The surface slopes rapidly to the south, and advantage was taken of some partly unoccupied land to lay out a new street extending in a southeast direction from the gate-house to 125th street. This new street, now called Convent Avenue, made a bed for the eight lines of pipes. A trench was cut out the entire width of the street, and in it the pipes were laid. At one or two places the pipes came to the surface, and here the street was raised to cover them. The illustrations on other pages give an idea of the size of these great pipe lines and of the manner in which they were laid. At 124th street gates were put in the pipe lines, and

WORKING ON THE PIPE LINE.

PIPE LINE ON CONVENT AVENUE, FROM GATE-HOUSE.

blow-offs were arranged in connection with the sewers. At 125th street the pipe lines begin to branch off, one line turning east along that street. The other lines go on towards the south along the east side of Morningside Park. Other lines diverge at different points, and the four lines for Central Park pass down Eighth Avenue until they enter and cross the park to the old reservoir.

Compared with other tunnels, the new aqueduct is easily at the head of all works of a like character in the world. The cities of Chicago and Cleveland are each supplied with water through tunnels extending out into a lake. The first Chicago tunnel is 5 feet in diameter and 10,567 feet long. The second tunnel is 7 feet in diameter and 31,490 feet long. The Cleveland tunnel is only 5 feet in diameter and 6661 feet long. All of these tunnels were laid in comparatively soft materials. The Baltimore water supply includes a rock tunnel, twelve feet in diameter and seven miles long, and is lined with brick-work for about two miles. The old Roman aqueducts were several of them longer than the Croton Aqueduct, but they were all very small, and were merely masonry conduits a few feet in diameter. The Liverpool water supply is conveyed by an aqueduct about twice as long as the Croton Aqueduct, but it is mainly a surface aqueduct, there being only a little tunnel-work. A portion of the aqueduct is merely a pipe line. The supply is from a reservoir formed like that at Croton or at Sodom, by building a dam across a narrow gorge in a valley among the mountains in Wales. The dam is larger than

that at Sodom, being 136 feet high, while that at Sodom is only 78 feet. Compared with the proposed dam it will be small, as the new dam is to be over two hundred feet high, and will be the highest dam in the world. The aqueduct tunnel, when compared with railroad tunnels, is a little smaller in diameter than the three most famous tunnels, but is very much longer. The Hoosac Tunnel is only 24,000 feet long, the Mont Cenis is 8 miles long, and the St. Gothard 9½ miles long, while the new Croton Aqueduct, as we have seen, is nearly 30 miles long.

In conclusion it may be observed that with the new aqueduct completed New York City can draw 318,000,000 gallons of water from Croton Lake. Combined with the old aqueducts it can have on tap, as it were, 415,000,000 gallons every 24 hours. In rainy years like 1888 and 1889 it will be able to use this great supply of water freely.

At the present time we have the Boyd's Corner reservoir, holding 2,700,000,000 gallons, and the Middle Branch reservoir, holding 4,004,000,000 gallons. These, with the 2,000,-000,000 in Croton Lake, give a reserve of 8,704,000,000 gallons. The new reservoir at Sodom, now nearly finished, will add 9,000,-000,000, and the reservoirs on the Titicus and Muscoot rivers and at Carmel, to be finished within three years, will give 22,000,000,000 gallons; so we are sure next year of 17,704,-000,000 gallons, and of 39,704,000,000 two years later. Thus we have to-day a reserve of 17,700,000,000, or enough to last a few months only in a year of drought; but when the large

Albany Fifty Years Ago (1857)

I.—VANDERHEYDEN PALACE

ALBANY FIFTY YEARS AGO.

I AM an Albany Knickerbocker—a Dutchman of purest Belgic blood—and I justly claim to be heard, as the last as well as the most loyal of the fading cocked-hat generation, who mourn over the barbarisms of despotic Fashion and the hot haste of society in these degenerate days, when steam and iron have usurped the power of honest breath and muscle, and the lightning has become the obedient chariot of thought.

Albany, the Beverwyck, the Willemstadt, the Fort Orange of Colonial times—the oldest city in the United States except St. Augustine—has a claim to the reverence not only of every true-hearted Dutchman who loves his pipe, his krout, and his freedom, but of the universal Yankee nation, which has no geographical limit this side of Saturn's rings.

Standing still, as a Dutchman ought, I have become a second Columbus, for I have discovered a New World indeed in the changes wrought around me during the last fifty years. I am a bachelor of eighty, erect as a liberty-pole, and I thank Heaven fervently that I have neither sons nor daughters to mortify me with the absurdities of this absurd hour in our social retrogression, as I call what zealots name progress. My hair is like the snow or the hoar-frost, and no longer needs the aromatic powder of the good old time. So far, good; but when I look at the dear old three-cornered hat upon the peg in my chamber, how I doubly loathe the glistening stove-pipe I am compelled to wear upon my head in winter and in summer, in deference to the god of the tailor and the milliner. And when I contemplate my velvet small-clothes, with the bright silver knee-buckles, or even the Wellington boots and graceful tassels of a later day, how I sigh for the restoration of the elegant breeches and the abolition of the dangling pantaloon!

Well do I remember the great innovation when cocked hats and long bodices were doomed. It was after the French Revolution had given free reign to extravagant fancies in politics, religion, and social life that the mighty overturn in the world of fashion commenced, and the costumes in which our fathers fought and our mothers suffered for freedom, were banished from our best society to give place to the mongrel modes of French fanatics and servile English imitators. The phenomenon appeared even in the staid Dutch city of Albany, where French politics could find no rest for the sole of its foot. I was then a gay young man, and had been accustomed to adore the ladies (as I do yet) in ample skirts, waists showing Hogarth's line of beauty, flowing sleeves, and faultless head-dresses, albeit their hair was sometimes thick with pomade or frizzled into a bush. As suddenly as the bursting of a balloon did the ladies' dresses seem to collapse from the longitudinal display of our own time to the economical dimensions of a white covering for a bean-pole. The bodice disappeared, the cincture went up directly under the arms, and the immense Mademoiselle Parpluies became nobodies, and might sing,

"Shepherds, I have lost my waist,
    Have you seen my body?
Sacrificed to modern taste,
    I'm quite a hoddy-doddy.
Never shall I see it more,
    Till common sense, returning,
My body to my legs restore,
    Then I shall cease from mourning."

Nor were the fair creatures solitary sufferers. Cocked hats, powdered hair, elegant wigs, exquisite queues, and even the breeches of the gentlemen were proscribed, and at last were compelled to succumb toward the close of the century. The hat assumed all sorts of shapes, but the prevailing absurdity was a very small crown and a very wide brim turned up at the sides. I remember turning out of State Street into Market Street one morning in September, walking arm-in-arm with my old friend General Tenbroeck, then mayor of the city, when a young married couple belonging to one of our most aristocratic families, who had lately returned from their wedding tour in Europe, appeared just in front of Myndert Van Schaick's elegant three story mansion, displaying the new fashions to the fullest extent; indeed that couple were the pioneers of the innovation in Albany. The husband's hat was of orthodox dimensions. His coat, with narrow skirts, fitted closely, and so did his pantaloons, while his legs were encased in enormous Hessian boots. His cravat was full and high, and in his bosom was a magnificent linen frill. The lady had "lost her waist," and her dress—something like a petticoat tied round her neck, with her arms put through the pocket-holes—was a rich lilac color. Upon her head was a small hat, not unlike her husband's in form, over which was piled in profusion a great bunch of wheat-ears, the wearing of straw having then become the rage abroad. Well did the epilogue satirize this fashion:

> "What a fine *harvest* this gay season yields!
>   Some female heads appear like *stubble-fields*.
> Who now of threatened famine dare complain,
>   When every female forehead teems with *grain?*
> See how the *wheat-sheaves* nod amid the plumes!
>   Our barns are now transferred to drawing-rooms;
> While husbands who delight in active lives,
>   To fill their *granaries* may *thrash* their wives!"

I remember seeing a fine caricature by Gillray at about that time, representing John Bull in the act of being dressed in the large-appearing but really tight-fitting French coat of the day, by a Paris tailor, who exclaims, "Aha! dere my friend, I fit you to de life!—dere is liberté!—no tight aristocratical sleeve to keep you from do vot you like!—aha!—begar! dere be only vant von leetle national cockade to make look quite *à la mode* de Paris!" John stands in stiff Hessian boots, evidently very uneasy, and exclaims, "Liberty! quoth'a! why zounds, I can't move my arm at all, for all it looks so woundy big! Ah! damn your French *à la mode*, they give a man the same liberty as if he was in the stocks! Give me my old coat again, say I, if it is a little out at the elbows!" And so felt our bride and groom very soon, for the people stared, and the boys giggled, and the dogs barked at them as they passed by. Yet they had planted the infection in the goodly city of my birth; and from the hour of their advent the doom of the cocked hat, at least, was pronounced. Long and faithfully I defended the cherished ornaments of my young manhood, but my queue daily dwindled, my velvet breeches elongated and turned into broadcloth or nankeen, my chapeau rounded and loomed up, and after ten long years of fruitless opposition, and when all my compeers were vanquished by the tyrant, I yielded. Ever since I have followed loyally in the train of the conqueror. *Vive la bagatelle!*

Nor was it upon personal adornment alone that change, iconoclastic change, then commenced its work. There seemed to be a spirit of unrest abroad early in the present century, and a won-

II.—STATE STREET, LOOKING EAST.

derful impulse, for weal or woe, was given to commerce and social life in Albany, which has since swept away almost every vestige of its external appearance and domestic simplicity, so familiar to me in the days of my young manhood. Albany to-day, with its almost sixty thousand inhabitants, and its twenty millions of dollars worth of real and personal property, and Albany of fifty years ago, with its seven thousand people and its fifteen hundred houses, are as unlike as a rural village and a metropolitan city.

All my life I have been fond of the arts of design. Even now, when my eyes are becoming somewhat dim, and my fingers are less supple than they were a score of years ago, I delight in using the pencil in delineating objects of interest, thus impressing their images indelibly upon my own memory, and preserving them for the benefit of posterity. My full portfolios attest this taste and industry; and now, when the storms are abroad, or the hot sun smites, I amuse myself, hour after hour, in my snug little library, within a quiet mansion near the Capitol, in looking over these pictorial records, and recalling, by association, the scenes and incidents, the men and things, of other days. Come, take my arm, dear reader, and go with me to my study, and I will show you some sketches of streets and buildings in Albany as they appeared fifty years ago. This way, if you please. Be careful of your footsteps on these winding stairs. Sit down in this arm-chair with green velvet cushion. Here are slippers and a cricket, and on this quartette-table we will lay the portfolio. Like the exhibitor of a panorama, I will give an explanatory lecture as we proceed. Let us take the drawings up in numeral order.

No. II. (opposite) is a view of State Street in 1805. We are supposed to be standing near the head of the street, in front of St. Peter's Church, and on the site of old Fort Frederick, a strong quadrangular fortification, with a bastion at each corner, which stood upon a high hill there. The altitude of its heavy stone walls was equal to that of the roof of St. Peter's at the present day. It was built when Cornelius Schuyler was mayor of Albany, before the French and Indian war. Its northeastern bastion occupied the site of St. Peter's, a portion of which is seen on the extreme left of the picture. We are looking eastward, down the then rough and irregular, but now smooth and broad street, and see the old Dutch Church at the intersection of Broadway. Beyond the Hudson River are seen the hills of Greenbush, which form a portion of the Van Rensselaer manor.

St. Peter's, known in earlier times as "The English Church," stood in the middle of State Street, opposite Barrack (now Chapel) Street, as represented in the engraving No. II. It was built of stone, and was erected in 1715. The tower was wanting when Peter Kalm, the Swedish naturalist, visited Albany, in 1749. Peter, by the way, had a very poor opinion of the Albanians at that time. He says they

III.—ST. PETER'S CHURCH.

fleeced strangers unmercifully; and he has recorded his opinion that if a Jew, who can generally get along pretty well in the world, should settle among them, "he would be ruined." In *my* good old cocked-hat times they were different, but I will not vouch for them in these degenerate days. I remember the church, with a tower which my father told me was built in 1750. The next year, a fine bell—the same that now calls the worshipers to St. Peter's—was cast in England, and sent over and hung in the tower. The road, since my recollection, passed up the hill on the south side of the church and fort, and in the rear of the latter it passed over Pinkster Hill, on which the State Capitol now stands.

Pinkster Hill! What pleasant memories of my boyhood does that name bring up! That hill was famous as the gathering-place of all the colored people of the city and of the country for miles around, during the Pinkster festival in May. Then they received their freedom for a week. They erected booths, where gingerbread, cider, and apple-toddy were freely dispensed. On the hill they spent the days and evenings in sports, in dancing, and drinking, and love-making, to their heart's content. I remember those gatherings with delight, when old King Charley, a darkey of charcoal blackness, dressed in his gold-laced scarlet coat and yellow breeches, used to amuse all the people with his antics. I was a light boy, and on one occasion Charley took me on his shoulders and leaped a bar more than five feet in height. He was so generously "treated" because of his feat, that he became gloriously drunk an hour afterward, and I led him home just at sunset. When I look into the State Capitol now when the Legislature is in session, and think of Congress Hall filled with lobbying politicians, I sigh for the innocence of Pinkster Hill in the good old days of the Woolly Heads.

A word more about St. Peter's, and we will resume the consideration of No. II. The house seen on the right is that of Philip S. Van Rensselaer, a younger brother of the Patroon, who was mayor of Albany from 1799 to 1814. The same building is seen prominently in No. II., with two birds just above it. Under the chancel of the church, in a leaden coffin, are the remains of young Lord Howe, who was killed near Ticonderoga in 1758. His friend, Captain (afterward General) Philip Schuyler, conveyed his body to Albany and placed it in his family vault. Many years afterward, when it was removed to the church, the coffin was opened, and Lord Howe's hair, which was short at the time of his death, had grown to long and flowing locks, and was very beautiful. Now let us turn again to No. II.

The two houses next to Van Rensselaer's belonged to the brothers Webster, the early printers in Albany; and the frame building next to them was their office, and was familiarly known as "The Webster Corner." They were twin brothers. Charles commenced business in 1782, as a newspaper publisher, and in 1784 he established the *Albany Gazette*. It was afterward called the *Advertiser*, and lived until 1845, a period of almost sixty years. A complete file of it is preserved in the State Library. The brothers commenced the publication of a quarto, in 1788, which they called the *Albany Journal*. They also published books; and from that noted corner cart-loads of Noah Webster's spelling books were scattered over Northern and Western New York by those enterprising men.

Next below Webster's is seen the Livingston House and elm-tree, and the Lydius House, occupying opposite corners, and delineated in detail in No. V. A house with gable in front, just below the Lydius Corner, yet remains, and is occupied by the State Bank. Peirson, a tobacconist, and Doctor Dixtre, a druggist, occupied the next taller building. Almost in front, and at the steepest part of the street, is seen one of the old well-curbs of the city, used before the construction of the water-works which now supply the inhabitants with a pure beverage.

IV.—THE STEVENSON HOUSE.

They are all gone now, and will be entirely forgotten when another generation shall have taken our places. All the old travelers and tourists described the well water of Albany as peculiarly offensive to the taste, it being filled with insects which, on account of their size, might have looked down with contempt upon the infusoria.

The old Dutch Church seen near the foot of the street we will consider presently. The tall house seen over its angle on the left belonged to one of the Kanes, well-known merchants who made a large fortune by dealings with the white people and the Indians of the Mohawk valley. A greater portion of their dwelling and store house in the valley may yet be seen near Canajoharie. An anecdote is related, in connection with the Kanes, which illustrates the proverbial shrewdness of the New Englanders, and the confiding nature of the old stock of Dutchmen in that region. A Yankee peddler was arrested for traveling on Sunday, contrary to law, and was taken before a Dutch justice. The peddler pleaded the urgency of his business. At first the Dutchman was inexorable, but at length, on the payment to him of a small sum of money as a bribe, he agreed to furnish the Yankee with a written permit to travel on. The justice requested the peddler to write the "pass." He wrote a draft on Messrs. J. and A. Kane, for fifty dollars, to be paid in goods, which the unsuspecting Dutchman signed. The draft was presented and duly honored, and the Yankee went on his way rejoicing. A few days afterward the Dutchman was called upon to pay the amount of the draft. The whole thing was a mystery to the Belgic magistrate, and it was a long time before he could comprehend it. All at once light broke in, and the victim exclaimed vehemently, in bad English, "Eh, yah! I understands it now. Tish mine writin', and dat ish de tam Yankee pass!" He paid the money, and resigned his office, feeling that it was safer to deal in corn and butter with his honest neighbors than in law with Yankee travelers.

The house on the right of the church, in range with the most distant lamp-post, belonged to Dr. Marchion, and there the city post-office was kept. The perspective in the drawing in this street view, of this side, is so nearly on a straight line that the forms of the buildings in the lower part of State Street can not well be defined. In the portion of the street opposite the Livingston Elm were two noble but dissimilar buildings: one of them was erected by Harman Wendell in 1716; the other was built by John Stevenson, and completed in 1780. The former was in the ancient Dutch style. The owner was a rich fur-trader, and many a traffic with the Indians were made within its walls. The Stevenson House was then a wonder in architecture, it being in a style quite different from any thing in Albany. It was purely English throughout, and it was known as the "The rich man's house." Both of these buildings were demolished in 1841.

Coming up State Street, on the south side,

V.—NORTH PEARL AND STATE STREETS.

we find the spacious brick mansion of George Merchant, over which five birds are seen. Mr. Merchant was a fine scholar, and for some time occupied the "Vanderheyden Palace," on North Pearl Street, as an academy. There many boys, of Revolutionary times, learned their Greek and Latin under Mr. Merchant's instruction. Among them was my elder brother, who figured quite conspicuously in public affairs at the time when the Federal Constitution was under discussion throughout the country. He made a patriotic speech at the dinner in the great *Federal Bower* (erected on the spot where the State Capitol now stands), on a hot August day, in 1788, at the close of the great procession in honor of the ratification of the Constitution.

The peaks and chimneys beneath the single bird are those of the old Geological Hall, which stood back of Merchant's house, and occupied the site of the present Geological rooms. The building with a projecting ridge for hoisting, was a carpenter's shop; and the last one seen on the right of the picture, was the chair factory of Mr. M'Chesney, a Scotchman, who died a few years ago at an advanced age. He always had his timber sawed in front of his establishment.

No. V. exhibits the corners of North Pearl and State Streets, looking up Pearl. The most conspicuous objects are the ancient building known as the Lydius House (6), with its terraced gable, and the adjoining mansion (7) of William Pitt Beers. The corner house was built expressly for a parsonage, to accommodate the Reverend Gideon Schaets, who arrived in Albany in 1652, and became the pastor of the Reformed Dutch Church. The materials for the building were all imported from Holland— bricks, tiles, iron, and wood-work. They came over with the church bell and pulpit in 1657. When I was quite a lad I visited the house with my mother, who was acquainted with the father of Balthazar Lydius, the last proprietor of the mansion. To my eyes it appeared like a palace, and I thought the pewter plates in a corner cupboard were solid silver, they glittered so. The partitions were made of mahogany, and the exposed beams were ornamented with carvings in high relief, representing the vine and fruit of the grape. To show the relief more perfectly, the beams were painted white. Balthazar was an eccentric old bachelor, and was the terror of all the boys. Strange stories, almost as dreadful as those which cluster around the name of Bluebeard, were told of his fierceness on some occasions; and the urchins, when they saw him in the streets, would give him the whole sidewalk, for he made them think of the ogre growling out his

"Fee, fo, fum,
I smell the blood of an Englishman."

He was a tall, thin Dutchman, with a bullet head, sprinkled with thin white hairs in his latter years. He was fond of his pipe and bottle, and gloried in celibacy until his life was in "the sere and yellow leaf." Then he gave a pint of gin for a squaw, and calling her his wife, he lived with her as such until his death, in 1815. His fine old mansion was demolished in 1832, when it was believed to be the oldest brick building in the United States. The modern Apothecaries' Hall was erected upon its site.

On the opposite side of the street is seen the frame building (1) known as Webster's Corner, already alluded to as their printing-office. The white house (2) next to it was the residence of Philip Livingston, one of the signers of the Declaration of Independence. The elm-tree (yet standing on the corner of Pearl and State streets) was planted by Mr. Livingston about one hundred years ago. It was then merely a twig; and it is said that Mr. Livingston severely rebuked a young sailor, one morning, who was about to cut it down for a switch or a cane. To the minds of us Albanians, in summer, that now noble tree forms a grateful monument to the memory of its planter.

Looking up Pearl Street, we see a large building (3) with two gables in front, which was known as the *Vanderheyden Palace*, a sketch of which is given at the head of this article. It was just below Maiden Lane, on the site now occupied by the Baptist Church. It was erected by Johannes Beekman, one of the old burghers of Albany, in 1725. The bricks and some of the other materials were imported from Holland, and it was one of the finest specimens of Dutch architecture in this country. The Beekman family occupied it until a short time previous to the Revolution, when the proprietor had been dead more than a dozen years, and his daughters were all married. Jacob Vanderheyden purchased it in 1778, but it continued to be used as an academy by Mr. Merchant and others until the great fire in 1797, after which Mr. Vanderheyden, whose dwelling had been consumed,

made this his residence. There he lived in the style of the old Dutch aristocracy, until his death in 1820. His family left it soon afterward, and from that time it was used by a variety of people for miscellaneous purposes until its demolition in 1833. This old mansion figures in Washington Irving's story of Dolph Heyliger, in "Bracebridge Hall," as the residence of Heer Antony Vanderheyden. The iron vane, in the form of a horse at full speed, now occupies the peak of the southern gable of *Sunnyside*, the delightful residence of Mr. Irving on the Hudson River. That gable is almost a fac-simile of the one of Vanderheyden Palace, over which the vane turned for more than a century.

A little beyond the Palace is seen the homestead of the Pruyn family, a stately Dutch house (4), with terraced gable fronting the street. Dr. Samuel Woodruff, an old and eminent physician, owned the next (5) more modern residence, on the corner of Maiden Lane and Pearl Street. Adorned with yellow paint, it made a conspicuous and favorable appearance among the dingy Dutch houses of that quarter —the brick gables of an earlier date.

No. VI. presents a continuation of Pearl Street, from Maiden Lane northward. The Woodruff House (1) is first seen, and the smaller building (2) next to it was Dr. Woodruff's office. At that time dentistry, as a distinct profession, was not practiced in Albany. Physicians usually connected it with their own. I well remember when I went tremblingly up those steps, sat in the Doctor's leather-cushioned chair, and thought my neck was broken

VI.—NORTH PEARL STREET, FROM MAIDEN LANE, NORTHWARD.

VII.—NORTH PEARL STREET.

when the huge turnkey drew an aching molar from my jaw for the first time. Next to the Doctor's office was a stately Dutch building (3) erected by Mr. William Eights, of the city of New York. Being a Whig, Mr. Eights was compelled to leave the city when the British took possession of it, in the autumn of 1776. He erected this mansion soon afterward, and resided there for some time. The frame building adjoining was long occupied by "Bob Thompson," as he was familiarly called, who was quite celebrated as a pastry-cook. He used to serve parties at the houses of the Albany gentry, half a century ago. The next house, with terraced gable (6), was the dwelling of Widow Sturtevant, in the immediate rear of which is seen the present church edifice, over the congregation of which the Rev. Dr. Sprague is pastor. This is much more modern than the other buildings, and is introduced, in outline, to show to the eyes of the present generation their relative position.

The tall yellow building (7) next to Widow Sturtevant's was then occupied by Dr. C. C. Yates; and its quite fanciful companion of the same color was the residence of Brewer, the renowned sexton and bell-ringer of the old Dutch Church, of whom I shall speak presently. The next building (9) was painted a lead color. It was the famous *Uranian Hall*, then the great school of Albany. It was erected by the Society of Mechanics, whose children were educated there. The school was supported partly by the funds of the Society, and for a long time it was the best institution of the kind in the city. On the site of these two last-named buildings (8 and

9) the edifice of the Albany Female Academy now stands. That institution was founded in 1814, under the title of the Union School. The Academy was incorporated in 1821, and its first president was the late Chancellor Kent. The present building was erected in 1834.

No. VII. is a continuation of No. VI., showing a portion of North Pearl Street. This section will appear familiar to some of my Albany friends who were boys fifty years ago, for they will recognize in 15 the little district school-house and its surroundings, where they went to get whipped, and to be seated upon a hard high bench six or seven hours each day. The first house in this sketch (10) was the dwelling of Mr. William M'Clellan, an eminent Scotch physician. In the next (11) broad and spacious house dwelt the very distinguished John B. Romeyn, D.D., of the Presbyterian Church. Doctor Romeyn was quite remarkable for his obesity. An anecdote connected with him is related, which exhibits the often lurking humor of the grave and taciturn Indian. One very hot day in July, during the administration of Governor Jay, the Doctor was present just at the conclusion of a council with Mohawk and Oneida Indians, at Schenectada. The Indians have a custom of adopting white people of eminence into their tribes, and giving them significant names, and the honorary title of chief. At the Doctor's urgent solicitation he was adopted by the Oneidas. The day was excessively sultry, and he sat there perspiring at every pore. When the ceremony was ended, he inquired what was his new name. With great gravity the old Sachem gave it in the Iroquois language, while not a muscle of the face of his dusky companions was moved. The Doctor wished an interpretation, and the Sachem, with equal gravity, replied, "The Great Thaw." The Indians sat unmoved, while the whole white portion of the audience roared with laughter.

Next to Dr. Romeyn's stood a house of more ancient pattern (12), in which resided Nicholas Bleecker, one of the wealthiest merchants of the city. Peter Elmendorf, an eminent lawyer, dwelt in the adjoining house (13); and between that and the little school-house (15) was the play-ground for the boys. Looking over that inclosure, and among the trees, is seen the top of the old family mansion or homestead of the Bleeckers, at the corner of Chapel and Steuben streets. There Harmanus Bleecker, our Minister at the Hague a few years ago, resided at the time of his death. I believe the property has since passed out of the possession of the family. I remember seeing there, during the latter years of the late Mr. Bleecker, a fine portrait, cabinet size, of John Randolph of Roanoke, painted by Ward of Philadelphia. Bleecker and Randolph were warm friends while they were in Congress together in 1811; and, as a token of that friendship, they exchanged portraits with each other.

The last house (16) was the residence of John Andrews, a well-known police-constable, who was the terror of evil-doers in the good old Dutch city fifty years ago. He might always be seen at the polls on election days, with a stout leather cap, similar to those worn by firemen, and an ugly-looking hickory cudgel with two huge knobs on the larger end.

No. VIII. is a continuation of the west side of Pearl Street, from Fox (now Canal) Street to Patroon Street. These buildings possess very little special interest, except the church with its two steeples. They have all long since passed away. They were of wood, all painted red, and gave a very dull appearance to the street. On the left is seen (1) a portion of the Vandeberg mansion. Adjoining it was the shop (2) of John Bantum, a white-and-blacksmith. The smaller building next, was occupied by a little crabbed Irish schoolmaster named Crabbe, who made it a religious duty to whip the whole school at least once a week, so as to be certain that no sinner had been deprived of the necessary chastisement. He generally commenced the duties of the day by imbibing a mug of flip at Jemmy Fleet's, a countryman of his, who kept a few groceries and a great deal of liquor in an adjoining building. Back of these (4) is seen the tool-house of the church; and upon the distant eminence beyond, then known as Arbor Hill, is seen the country seat (5) of General Tenbroeck, of the Revolution, who was mayor of Albany from 1796 to 1799. Arbor Hill is now occupied by Thomas W. Olcott, President of the Mechanics' and Farmers' Bank of Albany. Next to the last of the small buildings in the direction of the church was then occupied by Saughler, a celebrated chocolate manufacturer; and in the last (7) the sexton of the church resided.

The most prominent as well as the most elegant of all the buildings seen in No. VIII. is the edifice of the North Dutch Reformed Church, with two steeples. It was erected in 1798, and Rev. John Bassett, an associate with Dr. Wes-

VIII.—NORTH PEARL STREET.

IX.—MARKET STREET.

terloo in the old State Street Church, became its first pastor. He was succeeded in 1804 by the learned and eloquent John Melancthon Bradford. The heart of many an old Albanian will glow with delight at the mention of his name. He was a man of noble port, tall, commanding, and handsome. His mind was far in advance of his generation, and his eloquence kept all the emotions in constant play. And oh! how many of my old companions will also sigh at the mention of his name, when they think of that brilliant sun, setting amid the storm-clouds of domestic woe. I can not bear to think of it. And there in after years, how Hooper Cummings, another sun, blazed out occasionally in that pulpit, and, like the noble Bradford, went down among the clouds, a warning to the self-confident, who pray not hourly for the shield of God's grace against the Tempter.

Fox Creek formerly flowed across the street (now under it) where the fence is seen, adjoining 7; and so between the trees. Opposite the church is seen a small building, with a door and window, which was then occupied by Bocking, a very celebrated cake-baker. The light from his oven at night was reflected by a window in one of the steeples of the church, and for a long time, the origin of the illumination being unknown, the story was current that the church was haunted. The superstitious were afraid to pass it in the night, and some would not go to the bakery after dark. The two little figures in this picture represent a fashionable couple in Albany in 1805. The lady has not yet "found her waist," and the gentleman has his round-head hat, his narrow-skirted coat, and huge white-topped boots, then just beginning to be worn by the ton.

Here we will leave Pearl Street, where not a house of all that we have seen now remains; and we will go down to Broadway (formerly Market Street), where as great changes have since taken place. Our first view in No. IX. is that portion of Old Market Street, east side, from State Street to Maiden Lane. The public market, which gave the name to the street, is seen in its centre; and at the extreme right is the old Dutch Church in the middle of State Street. Beginning on the left, we have a view of the residence (1) of Paul Hochstrasser, a wealthy German merchant in Albany fifty years ago. The next (2), on the corner of Maiden Lane, was the house and store of General Peter Gansevoort, one of the most active of the Revolutionary officers in the Northern Department. The larger house (3) adjoining it was occupied below by Hill, a glover and leather-breeches maker. In the upper part, Fairman, the eminent engraver, started business; and there Murray, a Scotch peddler, first met him, and afterward became his business partner. The more stately brick mansion (4) was the residence of the Rev. Mr. Bassett while pastor of the North Dutch Church; and next to that, and partly concealed by the market (5), was the store of Barent and John B. Bleecker, eminent merchants at that time. The terraced gable of Ford's carpet-store is seen next beyond it; and then, looming above all, is the grand mansion of David Fonda (7), a merchant who kept dry-goods, groceries, and liquors for sale, next door to General Tenbroeck, some twenty years earlier. At this time he was a retired merchant, and owned one of the nine fine private carriages then in Albany. That mansion is now the City Hotel.

Passing the market, we see an auctioneer's store; and rising above it (9) is seen a large brick building, the store and dwelling of the brothers Kane (John and Archibald) already mentioned. Back of these is seen the roof of the building now the Exchange. Archibald Kane had his hand very badly shattered by the discharge of a gun at Canajoharie, where it was amputated by Dr. Jonathan Eights. I remember seeing him frequently in his store after the accident with his arm in a "sling" made of stuff resembling mohair. Next to Kane's we see Dr. Marchion's apothecary store, where, as we have already noticed, the city post-office was kept; and more prominent than all others is the old Dutch Church edifice (11), which we will consider presently.

The Market-house was built in 1791, at an expense of £222 sterling. It was removed several years ago, when the street was named Broadway. That market was a great gathering-place for the inhabitants of the neighborhood, at the period in question, on warm afternoons, when the butchers had departed. They would take their chairs there, and smoke and gossip for hours. With many the privilege of leisure to enable them to enjoy such a luxury was highly prized; and it became a saying expressive of independence, "If I had a thousand pounds I could afford to sit in the market, and would not call the Patroon *uncle*." How many political schemes have been concocted and discussed under the broad roof of that old market-house! How many plans which controlled the destinies of the Empire State may have been matured in these daily social councils!

We will now, in No. X., stand in Court Street, south of State Street, and look northward up Market Street. Here we have a near view of the old Dutch Church, and a distant one of the Market; and some of the houses we shall describe in Nos. XI. and XII. On the extreme left (1) is the stove and iron store of John Stafford; and next to it (2) is the store of Stafford and Spencer, coppersmiths. The adjoining building was the store of John J. P. Douw, a hardware merchant; and the one on the corner (4), with gable in front, is now known as Douw's Building. It was occupied fifty years ago by James and Walter Clarke, hardware merchants. On the left is the "English hat store," kept by an Englishman named Daniels. That was the great emporium of the modern abominations. There I purchased, on a Christmas-eve, my first stiff round hat, and then I hung up my cocked hat forever.

The smaller building near, painted yellow, was the store of Richard Deane and Son, Scotch merchants; and the large peaked gable (9) was the store of the rather eccentric Henry Lansing, who kept teas and dry-goods. I remember him well half a century ago—an old, thin, tall Dutchman, with a three-cornered hat and remarkable queue. He would seldom allow his

X.—COURT AND MARKET STREETS.

XI.—MARKET STREET, NOW BROADWAY.

customers to enter his store. He would take to the door whatever was asked for, and sell it there. It was a strange whim, and had its origin in his doubts of the honesty of most people. Adjoining his brick store was a frame building erected over a brook, and occupied by Thomas R. Gould, a hardware merchant, with whom my esteemed townsman, the earnest advocate of Temperance, Edward C. Delavan, was a clerk for a while. But the most interesting object in this picture is the old Dutch Church. We are looking at its south front, in which was its entrance. This edifice, built of stone, was erected in 1715, over a smaller one built in 1656, at the intersection of Yonkers and Handelaer's streets, now State Street and Broadway. The old church within was occupied until the walls and roof of the new one were completed, and so there was an interruption in the stated public worship for only three Sabbaths. The pulpit and bell were sent over from Holland; and in the window near the northeast corner of the edifice were the arms of the Van Rensselaer family, wrought in stained glass. The portion of the window containing the arms is now in possession of General Stephen Van Rensselaer, the proprietor of the old manor house at the northern termination of Broadway. The history of this church during a century and a half is exceedingly interesting, but I have not time to give it. I may only give a general description of the edifice itself. It was a curious one inside. There was a low gallery; and the huge stove employed in heating the building was placed upon a platform so high that the sexton went upon it from the gallery to kindle fires. Perhaps in those days heat descended, instead of ascending, as in these degenerate times. The pulpit was octagonal in form, made of oak, and in front was a bracket on which the minister placed his hourglass when he commenced preaching. The pulpit with the bracket may yet be seen in the North Dutch Church. The bell-rope hung down in the centre of the church, and to that cord hung many a tale of trouble for Mynheer Brower, the bell-ringer, who lived in North Pearl Street.

Every night at eight o'clock he went to the church, pursuant to his duty, to ring the "suppawn bell." This was the signal for all to eat their "suppawn" or hasty-pudding, and prepare for bed. It was equivalent to the English curfew bell. On these occasions the wicked boys would teaze the old bell-ringer. They would stealthily slip into the church while he was there, unlock the side door, hide in some dark corner, and when the old man was fairly seated at home, and had his pipe lighted, they would ring the bell furiously. Down he would go; the boys would slip out at the side door before his arrival, and the old man after some time would return thoughtfully, musing upon the probability of invisible hands pulling at his bell-rope. He thought, perhaps, those

——"People—ah, the people,
They that dwell up in the steeple
    All alone;
And who, tolling, tolling, tolling,
    In that muffled monotone,
Feel a glory in so rolling,
    On the human heart, a stone;
They are neither man nor woman—
They are neither brute nor human—
    They are ghouls!"

The dead were buried under the old church; and only four or five years ago some of the coffins were exhumed by workmen when excavating for water-pipes. That venerable building was demolished in 1805-6, and the stones were used in the construction of the new one, with two steeples, in North Pearl Street.

Nos. XI. and XII. present the appearance of Market Street (now Broadway) in 1805, and will give the people of Albany to-day an opportunity for perceiving the great changes that have been wrought within fifty years. It has been almost total. First, on the extreme left (1), we have a corner of the old Dutch Church; then (2) a low, yellow building, known as Robinson's corner, where the loftier edifice of the Albany Museum now stands. Next (3) was the fine brick dwelling-house and store of my kinsmen, Myndert and John Van Schaick, then eminent merchants, and the former since a long resident of New York city. In the two-story white frame building (4) Davis Waters sold groceries; and in the adjacent brick building (5) lived David Newland, a Scotch settler. Elbert Willet lived in the next brick building; and in the taller one adjoining it was the Albany Bank, incorporated in 1792. This was the first banking institution in Albany. Its nearest neighbor was the spacious brick dwelling-house of John Maley, one of the merchant princes of Albany. It has survived the battles of change, and is now known as the Mansion House Hotel. Abraham Ten Eyck's bookstore was next to Maley's, and the smaller house, with a huge chimney, belonged to Douw B. Slingerland, a merchant. His neighbor (11) was Barent G. Staats, also a merchant.

In the small building on the corner of Maiden Lane, and next to the last one in the sketch, lived Teunis Van Vechten, a wealthy burgher, whose son Teunis (then a student at law), I well remember, was secretary of a meeting of young men who were preparing for the bar, convened on account of the death of Alexander Hamilton, in July, 1804. Nowhere did the death of Hamilton make a more profound impression than in Albany, and nowhere was the hatred toward Burr, his destroyer, more intense.

The last house (13) seen in the sketch we are considering was built of brick imported from Holland, and at the period under consideration it was occupied as a toy-shop and dwelling by Mrs. Douglas, on the right, and on the left, by John and Abraham Brinkerhoff as a hardware store. We will now pass to the consideration of the last extended street view.

No. XII. The first complete building seen on the left of the sketch was of wood, painted red, and there, fifty years ago, Peter Annelly sold looking-glasses. I can not now recall the names of the occupants of the next two (15 and 16), one of which was painted red, the other blue. The tall building (17) next to the blue store was the residence of Barent Bleecker, another of the merchant princes of Albany. It was painted yellow, and appeared very gay by the side of its neighbor (18), a dull-red house, built, in the antique Dutch style, of Holland brick, and then occupied by Major John H. Wendell, a Revolutionary officer. Adjoining it was the office of Stephen Lush, an eminent lawyer, whose daughter was the wife of the Rev. Dr. Bradford, already mentioned. Looming above all was the grand house (19) of my excellent friend Dr. Samuel Stringer, who was one of the most eminent men of the day, and who adhered to the cocked hat as long as there was a shred left by the destructive hand of fashion. I remember seeing the foundation of his house laid about the year 1804, I think. Then, for the first time, white marble was used in Albany as sills and caps for windows, and attracted great attention. The house was demolished in 1856 to make way for stores. Next to it was Dr. Stringer's office, separated by an alley from the large brick house (20) of Andrew Brower. Dudley Walsh occupied the old Dutch house, of Holland brick, next to Brower's; and on the corner of Steuben Street is seen the old brick house of Sanders Lansing, a celebrated cake-baker of that day. He particularly excelled in making "Dead Cakes," as they were called, for funerals. These were thick discs, about four inches in diameter, and similar in ingredients to our New-Year cake. They were distributed among the attendants at funerals after their return from the grave, when a glass of spiced wine was also handed to each. The "Dead Cakes" were often kept for years—sometimes through two generations—as mementoes of the departed, like the wreaths of *immortelle* in France. Very recently I saw one of these cakes at the house of an old friend in Westerloo Street, which bore the monogram of Sanders Lansing. It appeared like an old acquaintance, for they were common in my youth and young manhood.

Opposite the cake-baker's is seen the fine old brick residence of Chancellor Lansing, who was mayor of Albany from 1786 to 1790. With this we close our examination of views in Market Street (Broadway) in the olden time; then,

XII.—MARKET STREET, NOW BROADWAY.

as now, one of the principal business streets of the city.

XIII.—WIDOW VISSCHER'S.

Here are two smaller views. The first is the fine old dwelling-house upon the side-hill, on the northeast corner of Pearl and Columbia streets, then the residence of the buxom Widow Visscher. It was specially distinguished as the lodging-place for the Indians when they came to Albany for the purpose of trading their furs, too often for rum and worthless ornaments. There many stirring scenes transpired, when the Indians held their powwows, and became uproarious under the influence of strong drink. At such times the widow would use her broomstick freely. It was a potent sceptre in her hands in restoring order, for the most stalwart Indian who had once felt its power looked upon it with awe. That house has survived the general sweep of so-called improvement. It is now owned by Eben Pemberton, and is occupied as a grocery and provision store.

The second small sketch is a view of the northern entrance to the city of Albany, as it appeared in 1805. On the left is seen a part of the Van Rensselaer manor-house inclosure. On the opposite side is seen an old store-house, which was used by the Patroon as an office wherein the business of his vast estate was transacted. That old building has been demolished, and a pretty modern one erected upon its site, where the agent of General Stephen Van Rensselaer, the son and successor of the last Patroon, now lives. The old trees remain, standing in all their wonted vigor and beauty.

And here we will close the portfolio. I have enjoyed these reminiscences of the Past most heartily, and I trust you have not spent the hour unpleasantly nor unprofitably. A little while and I shall be like those old buildings—prone among the buried things of the Past; and yet a little while, and you, too, will be a forgotten item on the day-book of the living. But it is better to laugh than to weep, and so I will close my sermon here at the end of the text. Here is a glass of fine old Rhenish, imported by my friend Barent Bleecker. We may never meet again on the earth; so with the sparkling goblets in our hands, I will say, God bless you! Adieu!

XIV.—NORTHERN ENTRANCE TO ALBANY.

Sunnyside, The Home of Washington Irving (1856)

HARPER'S
NEW MONTHLY MAGAZINE.

No. LXXIX.—DECEMBER, 1856.—Vol. XIV.

EAST FRONT

SUNNYSIDE

THE HOME OF

WASHINGTON IRVING.

THE GATE

THE quaint historian, Diedrich Knickerbocker, says it was traditionary in his family, that when the worthy Master Hendrick Hudson first laid eyes upon the marvelous beauties of the great waters which now bear his honored name, astonishment and admiration wrung from his taciturn lips the remarkable exclamation, "See there!" That the susceptible navigator really did give expression to his unwonted emotions in these supreme terms, or at least "in words to that

UP THE HUDSON, FROM ABOVE SUNNYSIDE.

effect," there is very little doubt; inasmuch as the echo thereof has never ceased to be heard among the hills, through all the two and a half centuries since gone by. Indeed, it has rung, and is ringing, more audibly and more eloquently every passing day; for enchanting as was the vision which dazzled the eyes of the drowsy skipper of the *Half-Moon*, when the prow of that adventurous craft was first turned toward the waters of the unknown river, yet from that hour to this, still has the wonder grown. The mountains yet stand in their ancient dignity and grandeur, the valleys and glades wear their old sweet smile, and the floods roll on in the same "simple, quiet, majestic, epic flow;" while about all there has gathered many an added grace.

Time has embellished the scene, until the silent river and the desert shore are now alike musical with the ceaseless hum of busy, happy life; and the rose blooms and breathes every where in the once trackless forests. Poetry and romance have bewitched it with the enchantment of song and story, and history with thrilling memories of great and gallant deeds; while at this day there is rapidly growing around it a newer and yet sweeter charm, in its close association with the actual life, the daily joys and sorrows of many of those gifted ones whose genius and works have endeared their names to our imaginations and hearts.

It is amidst these charmed scenes that our venerable ex-President Van Buren has exchanged the uneasy chair of state for the snug fireside seat in his peaceful retreat of Linden-

wold. It was in a beautiful home, directly overlooking the Hudson, and commanding the grand panorama of the Catskills, that the lamented painter Cole lived, and labored, and died; and where these noble hills first bless the sight in the ascent of the river, are the broad lawns and slopes of Placentia, where that veteran pioneer in our literature, Paulding, is passing a kindly and genial age in elegant seclusion among kindred and friends. Not far below him is the pleasant abode of Morse, who has snatched the lightning to bear his name and fame through the world. Lossing, the amiable historian, is near by. Yet below, among the Highlands, a whole flock of singing birds have built their dainty nests. Here, in the village of Newburgh, lived the landscape gardener, Downing, to whose genius the river owes so much of its horticultural and architectural adornment. A little distance southward is his own favorite creation, the picturesque villa at Cedar Lawn, the residence of Headley. Poor Downing, who was an ardent lover of the Hudson, was gazing upon its moonlit charms with even more than his wonted delight, as he sat on the piazza here, on the very eve of the fatal day which gave him so early a grave beneath its waters. Between Cedar Lawn and Newburgh there is a charming retreat—once the home of the painter Durand—and in the immediate vicinage of the village, on the other side, Mr. H. K. Brown, the sculptor, is now setting up his household gods. His gifted brother of the chisel, Palmer, lives above at Albany. On his broad and elevated mountain terrace, guarded by the ever-watch-

DOWN THE HUDSON, FROM ABOVE SUNNYSIDE.

ful Storm-king, and peering down, down upon crag and cascade, Willis holds intimate and loving companionship with Nature at Idlewild; while on the opposite shore, in the heart of the Highland group, is beautiful Undercliff, the abode of his friend Morris. The quiet studio of Weir stands upon the grand esplanade of West Point, and within the same evening shadow of the crumbling walls of old Fort Putnam is the island home of the fair sisters of the "Wide, Wide World." Hereabout, too, lives the polished scholar Gulian C. Verplanck. Yet further below, and looking far down upon the broad waters of the Tappan Sea, is Cedar-Hill Cottage, the savory *cusine* whence come the dainty viands of the *Knickerbocker* "Table;" while yet nearer to the city, Mr. and Mrs. Sparrowgrass live and recount the pleasant incidents of their simple lives.

Lower yet, at Manhattanville, within the limits of the great city, but as yet unprofaned by its touch, is the revered resting-place of that devoted friend of the feathered world, Audubon.

Last, and perhaps the dearest to us of all these household names which come so gratefully to our remembrance, doubling the charms of the scene as we journey up the fair river, is that of Irving, who, of all our authors, here fittingly finds a home amidst the altars upon which he has devoutly offered up the love and worship of a long life, and upon which he has reverently placed many of the sweetest fruits of his genius.

The Hudson, he says, has ever been to him a river of delight; and here, after many wanderings, he has "set up his rest," thanking God that he was born upon its banks, and brought up in

POCANTICO POINT, FROM IRVINGTON.

THE PALISADES, FROM IRVINGTON.

that companionship with its glorious scenes, from which has come so much of what is best and most pleasant in his nature. It is, he says, in a manner his first and last love, and after all his seeming infidelities he has returned to it with a heart-felt preference over all the other rivers of the world.

Through a varied life passed in many climes, he has ever treasured the fondest and most enthusiastic remembrance of the scenes which brightened his dawning life, and which now shed a mellow radiance upon its decline; and eloquent expressions of this noble attachment are to be found every where throughout his works, though written afar off, now in one land, now in another.

Mr. Irving has laid his hearth-stone upon the site of his boyhood's haunts, and amidst the early inspirations of his muse; on the very spot, indeed, which long, long ago he said he should covet, if he ever wished "for a retreat, whither he might steal from the world and its distractions, and dream quietly away the remainder of a troubled life." Happily he has not reached his sighed-for haven, wrecked upon the rocks of trouble and disappointment; for, later, we find him writing thence in a spirit of glad content: "Though retired from the world, I am not disgusted with it."

Sunnyside, the apposite and familiar name of Mr. Irving's charming cottage, lies hidden among the jealous trees, some twenty-two or three miles up the Hudson, on the eastern shore of that first and greatest of its famous expan-

sions, the Tappan Bay. It is a region scarcely less beautiful, though not so striking in its character as the more renowned Highlands. In historic story it is equally rich, and far more so in romantic association.

In an hour's ride, and at almost any hour, the railway will convey you from New York to the station at Irvington, a little walk below the Sunnyside Cottage; or to Tarrytown, the distance of an agreeable ride above. To see the setting of this sparkling little jewel of a home properly, though, you should make your approach by water, which is at all times, in the river travel, the most enjoyable way. One gets but a very inadequate glimpse of the beauties of the Hudson by the railroad route; indeed, it seems to us that in process of time the popular estimate of the landscape must grow to be very false and unjust; every body imagining that in their railway glance they have learned all about the subject, when really they remain in most profound ignorance. Even the voyage of the steamer fails to give one a fair idea of the scene. This is to be obtained only by long and loving study, afloat and ashore, in the neighboring valleys, and on the near and distant hill-tops. Every new visit which we make to the Hudson assures us that we have it yet to see.

It is a glorious sight which greets our eyes, as, leaving the noisy city wharf, we push our way through the crowding sails out into the broad waters, and onward toward the vailed meeting of the distant shores. On one side stretches the seemingly interminable Island

City, and on the other lie the suburban villages and villas of New Jersey, now crowning rocky heights, and now nestling by the river's narrow marge, until we reach those grand columnal walls, the famous Palisades, happily contrasted, in all the journey of twenty miles to the Tappan Bay, by the village and cottage-dotted slopes of the opposite shore. The Palisade rocks form the speciality of the landscape in this part of the Hudson; and so, still, in all the views looking south from the vicinage of Mr. Irving's dwelling. They are admirably seen from the shore at Irvington, and again, over a richly cultivated intervale, from the hill terraces above. Both situations give equally attractive glimpses of the river, overlooking that topographical will-o'-the-wisp Point-no-Point, the villages of Irvington and Tarrytown, and the mystic precincts of Sleepy Hollow. Three miles away across the wide bay are the busy little towns of Nyack and Piermont, with their background of bold hills, led by the brave Tower Rock. Piermont is the river terminus of the great Erie Railway, and it was in the sanguine expectation of advantage as a lighter to the freights of this road that the opposite village of Irvington, once Dearman, was laid out. It came to pass, however, that the Erie highway found an outlet elsewhere, and Irvington remains to this day but little more than it was at first—a capital beginning. The neighboring village of Tarrytown has drawn off all its springs of local business, insomuch that it possesses only one small store, and not even an apology for a hotel.

Tarrytown, in the reckoning of this fast age, is an ancient burgh, mossed and lichened with old traditions and historic reminiscences. Mr. Irving tells us, in his "Legend of Sleepy Hollow," not, he says, to vouch for the truth, but to be precise and authentic, "that there is a story that in the olden time its name was given to it by the good housewives of the adjacent country from the inveterate propensity of their husbands to linger about the village tavern on market days."

Tarrytown, and all the country round, was a region of stirring incident and interest in the days of the Revolution. Then it was scarcely less bustling, both river and shore, than now, when it has become the environs of a metropolis and the crowded highway of commerce. It lay between the territory of the enemy, who occupied the city and island of New York, and the patriot forces encamped under the Highlands at Peekskill, and was the ill-fated Africa into which both parties carried the war, under the marauding banners of the chivalric Skinners and Cow Boys, claiming to serve respectively under *carte blanche* American and British commissions; and with such zeal, says Mr. Irving, with his characteristic pleasantry, "as often to make blunders, and to confound the property of friend and foe, neither of them, in the heat and hurry of a foray, having time to ascertain the politics of a horse or cow which they were driving off into captivity; or when wringing the neck of a rooster, to trouble themselves whether he crowed for Congress or King George."

Here, in the quiet bay, lay the armed ships of the foe, stealthily watching for an opportunity to slip through the guarded pass of the Highlands, and thus gaining possession of the river, to open a communication with their forces in Canada. With what anxious hearts must not Washington and his brave men, from their threatened position above, have watched the moves of this deadly game—so nearly lost through Arnold's treacherous play. It was in this immediate vicinity, the very spot now marked by a monument in the heart of Tarrytown, that the possession of the river was secured to the patriots by the timely arrest of André. This region was the theatre also of the closing scene of the sad drama thus opened. Here, just across the river at old Tappantown, hidden from view by the intercepting hills of Piermont, the unfortunate soldier was tried and executed. The house from which he was led to the gallows is still in good condition, and is now a wayside inn, under the name of the "Old Stone House of '76." We visited it last summer on the occasion of a ball given in commemoration

POINT-NO-POINT, FROM IRVINGTON.

ACROSS.

DOWN. UP.

RIVER VISTAS, FROM THE LAWN.

of the "capture." Of the troubles and trials of the people of this portion of the river when the enemy's ships anchored in their bays, and of other revolutionary incidents of the vicinage, Mr. Irving gives us detailed and graphic accounts in the second volume of his "Life of Washington."

In "Wolfert's Roost" our author narrates an ancient legend of the Tappan Sea, so pleasant in itself, and so marked with the quiet humor with which he tells such a story, that we are tempted to repeat it. "Even the Tappan Sea," he says, "in front (of Sunnyside), was said to be haunted. Often in the still twilight of a summer evening, when the sea would be as glass, and the opposite hills would throw their purple shadows half across it, a low sound would be heard as of a steady vigorous pull of oars, though not a craft was to be descried. Some might have supposed that a boat was rowed along unseen under the deep shadows of the opposite shores; but the ancient traditionists of the neighborhood knew better. Some said it was one of the whale-boats of the old water-guard, sunk by the British ships during the war, but now permitted to haunt its old cruising grounds; but the prevalent opinion connected it with the awful fate of Rambout Van Dam, of

graceless memory. He was a roystering Dutch-man of Spiting Devil, who, in times long past, had navigated his boat alone one Saturday the whole length of the Tappan Sea, to attend a quilting frolic at Kakiat, on the western shore. Here he had danced and drunk until midnight, when he entered his boat to return home. He was warned that he was on the verge of Sunday morning; but he pulled off nevertheless, swearing he would not land until he reached Spiting Devil if it took him a month of Sundays. He was never seen afterwards; but may be heard plying his oars, as above mentioned, being the Flying Dutchman of the Tappan Sea, doomed to ply between Kakiat and Spiting Devil until the day of judgment."

With this peep at the surroundings, let us now look for the cottage itself; for it must, like its occupant, be looked for, lying, as it does, like "modest violet in hedge-row hid," and venturing to peep out from its timid seclusion only, as Mr. Irving himself describes it, "with half-shut eyes." When once congratulated upon the absolutism of his jealously-vailed domain, "Yes," said he, in his pleasant way, and straining his eyes to take in the whole wide compass, to wit, the little tree-encircled farm, "yes, I'm monarch of *all* I survey!"

The most imposing view (though, as we have intimated, it is not the cue of Sunnyside to be imposing) is that of the east side, seen in our initial picture, and approached by a shady lane, through the simple but characteristic gateway beneath. This is the only carriage access. The nearest way to reach it from the station at Irvington is on the railroad track, up to the foot of the lawn upon which the cottage stands. Among our pictures is a view of this approach, also of the little glimpse of the south end or porch, which it once afforded and still would, if a few obscuring boughs were to be trimmed away. We have preserved, too, a sketch of the rustic stile and path which leads from the railroad up the bank, and opens upon that part of the lawn where we picked up our picture of the north and west side of the cottage, and the group of vistas up, down, and across the river.

It is a sweet scene of rural simplicity and comfort which is disclosed to us by either approach ; as the open sunlit lawn, so affectionately embraced by its protecting trees and shrubbery, which, though permitting little peeps here and there from within, deny all vagrant observation from without. One can scarcely believe himself as thickly surrounded as he really is here by crowding cottage and castle, so entire is the repose and seclusion of the spot. Years ago, when Mr. Irving first took up his abode at Sunnyside, he was all alone by himself, yet now every inch of the adjacent country is gardened, and lawned, and villaed, to the extreme of modern taste and wealth ; yet all so charmingly under the rose, that you always stumble upon the evidences unexpectedly, as you dreamingly pursue the thicket-covered and brook-voiced wood-paths. It is like the discovering of birds'-nests amidst forest leaves. Seen from the opposite shore of the river, the whole hillside is glittering with sun-tipped roof and tower, but like the Seven Cities of the Enchanted Island, it all vanishes as you approach.

The cottage, with its crow-stepped gables and weathercocks overrun with honey-suckle and eglantine, with the rose-vine and the clinging ivy, is a wonderfully unique little edifice, totally unlike any thing else in our land, but always calling up our remembrances or our fancies of merrie rural England, with a hint here and there at its old Dutch leaven ; in the quaint weathercocks, for instance, one of which actually veered, in good old days gone by, over the great Vander Heyden Palace in Albany, and another on the top of the Stadt House of New Amsterdam. A lady would be apt to call the Sunnyside cottage

NORTH AND WEST SIDE OF THE COTTAGE.

RAILWAY APPROACH TO SUNNYSIDE.

"the dearest, cosiest, cunningest, snuggest little nest in the world." Mr. Irving describes it as "a little old-fashioned stone mansion, all made up of gable-ends, and as full of angles and corners as an old cocked hat." "It is said, in fact," he continues, "to have been modeled after the cocked hat of Peter the Headstrong, as the Escurial was modeled after the gridiron of the blessed St. Lawrence."

A gentleman passing up the river before the trees had so entirely obliterated Sunnyside, was told by an intelligent cicerone that Mr. Irving had brought the pagodaish-looking tower, on the north end, from the ruins of the Alhambra. It is cruel, of course, to destroy poetic beliefs, but, to be conscientiously exact, we must, though it pains us, confess that there is reason to think it was conceived and executed by a Tarrytown carpenter, all unknown to fame.

As painters are given to using their wives for models, when available, so perhaps Sunnyside was made to "sit" for our author's pleasant picture of a home on the Hudson, in his story of "Mountjoy:" a home "full of nooks and crooks and chambers of all sorts and sizes; buried among willows, and elms, and cherry-trees, and surrounded with roses and hollyhocks; with honey-suckle and sweet-briar clambering about every window; a brood of hereditary pigeons sunning themselves upon the roof, with the nests of hereditary swallows and martins about the eaves and chimneys, and hereditary bees humming among the flowers." As in this romantic homestead, so in the dreamy atmosphere of Sunnyside, one might very easily invest all the scene, as did the imaginative Mountjoy, with an ideal character and sentiment; very

naturally transform the humming-birds and the bees into tiny beings from fairy land, and see their dainty homes in the flower-cups, and long for Robin Goodfellow's power of transformation to be able to compress his form into utter littleness; to ride the bold dragon-fly, swing on the tall, bearded grass, follow the ant into his subterranean abode, or dive into the cavernous depths of the honey-suckle.

Before the intrusion of the railroad, which has profaned so much of the river shore, the quiet beach, with its little cove, into which a rural lane debouched, was one of the sweetest features of Sunnyside. This part of the domain is beautified by a sparkling spring, draped, like all the region round, as we shall see by-and-by, in the fairy web of romantic fable. " Geoffrey Crayon" tells us, in his patient researches into the early history of the neighborhood, that this storied spring was, according to some authorities, invested with rejuvenating powers by one of its aboriginal owners, who was a mighty chieftain and a most cunning medicine-man; while the old Dutch tradition says that it was smuggled over from Holland in a churn by Femmetie Van Blarcom, wife of Goosen Garret Van Blarcom. "She took it up," says the worthy Geoffrey, "by night, unknown to her husband, from beside their farm-house near Rotterdam; being sure she should find no water equal to it in the new country—and she was right!" You may at this day descend the gentle slope of the green lawn, step over the moss-grown wall, and pushing aside the protecting tendrils, yet imbibe the provident widow's Rotterdam nectar; but very likely, with a startling whew and whiz, there will rush past you engine and car, shaking the hills around, and mortally terrifying all your growing fancies. The road passes so near to the cottage, though entirely hidden from view, as to drown the voices within. It must for a while have been a sore annoyance to the quiet-loving Prospero of Sunnyside. Happily he is a philosopher—and a good-humored one—as well as a dreaming romancer, and so has made the best of it, accepting the convenience of the thing as compensation for the poetry it has driven away. It serves him as the always needed moral of the skeleton at the feast, and calls him healthfully back to mortal mundane fact, when lawless fancy bears him too far away. In the best-tempered view of the matter, however, Poetry and Steam can not be made to harmo-nize. They will always give each other the cold shoulder.

The acres of Sunnyside, all told, are not many; and yet so varied is their surface, so richly wooded and flowered, and so full of elfish wind-ing paths and grassy lanes, exploring hillsides and chasing merry brooks, that their numbers seem to be countless; a pleasant deception greatly aided by that agreeable community of feeling between Mr. Irving and his neighbors, which has so banished all dividing walls and fences, that while you think you are roaming over the grounds of one, you suddenly bring up among the flower-beds of another. Especially is this the case in respect to the beautiful seat of Mr. Moses H. Grinnell, nearest to Sunnyside on one hand, and the residence of Dr. M°Vic-kar on the other.

The woodland of Sunnyside is very happily varied, offering every variety of sylvan growth, beech, birch, willow, oak, locust, maple, elm, linden, pine, hemlock, and cedar; while on the the lawns are evergreen and flowering shrubs; and, trailing over the vagrant walls and fences, honey-suckle, rose, trumpet-flowers, and ivy. The latter plant, which is very abundant, is of the famous stock of Melrose Abbey. The gar-den, which is in keeping with its surroundings, is watched by a favorite retainer, for whom Mr.

Irving has built a snug cottage, fronting the lawn in face of his own mansion. This little edifice is especially interesting, from its having been designed by Mr. Irving himself; his only venture, he once told us, as an architect. It brings to mind that only published example of his skill as a painter, the outline picture of the broad Stratford sexton in the "Sketch-Book," so boldly signed "Geoffrey Crayon, *del*." He may have other conceptions in his portfolio, for he is an earnest lover of the pencil, which once disputed with the pen for the preference as the interpreter of his fancies. He came, indeed, long ago, very near being able to repeat the famous boast, "*Sono anch' pittore!*" This was during his first visit to Europe, when he fell in with Allston, as both were entering the earliest years of manhood. As they rambled together among the art-treasures of the Old World, the thought, he says, suddenly presented itself, "Why might not he remain there and turn paint-er?" He mentioned it to his friend, who caught at it with eagerness, and offered him all the assist-ance in his power, with enthusiastic predictions of success. "I promised myself," he says, "a world of enjoyment in the society of Allston, and other artists with whom he had made me acquainted, and pictured forth a scheme of life all tinted with the rainbow hues of youthful promise. My lot, however, was differently cast. Doubts and fears gradually cooled over my pros-pects; the rainbow tints faded away; I began to apprehend a sterile reality, so I gave up the transient but delightful prospect of remaining at Rome with Allston and turning painter." We can not regret this early disappointment when we think of the happy results of his devotion to the more successful rival art.

We have referred to the welcome presence at Sunnyside of the picturesque English-like lane. Among our pencil memoranda the reader will find two illustrations of this attractive feature, looking toward and from the little cove where lies the widow Femmetie's wizard spring. We have preserved, also, some passages in the merry

THE COTTAGE FROM THE RAILROAD.

PATH FROM THE RAILWAY.

THE RIVER, FROM THE LANE.

brooklet which trips so gayly through the woods to meet the river at their rendezvous by the cove. They will be easily found, with other scenes of the same type. Our picture of the wood-path stile, though not a literal portrait, is a fair example of one of the most charming features of the landscape.

Separated from the lawn around the cottage by the belt of trees in which stands the gardener's dwelling, is another open area occupied by a pretty lakelet "expansion" of the brook—an echo of the great bay beyond. The painter gives unity, and harmony, and force to his picture by distributing throughout the work its leading sentiment or story and its prevailing color; so, in the artistic composition of Sunnyside, its chief feature, the great "Mediterranean" of the river, as Mr. Irving calls the Tappan Bay, with its fleet of white sails thick as the passing clouds, is repeated by the little "Mediterranean" of the brooklet and its fleet of snowy ducks.

Before we relieve the reader's impatience to join the happy circle in-doors, let us glance briefly at the past history of the Sunnyside cottage. In his own serio-comico description of his home, Mr. Irving speaks of it as being "one of the oldest edifices, for its size, in the whole country;" and as, "though of small dimensions,

yet, like many small people of mighty spirit, valuing itself greatly upon its antiquity." Pleasant are his fanciful pictures of the spot, in the old fabulous age of Indian rule, when "the unsophisticated inhabitants lived by hunting and fishing, occasionally recreating themselves with a little tomahawking and scalping." And diverting, too, is his story of the second epoch in its history, in the good Dutch days of Peter Stuyvesant, when it fell into the hands of that hardheaded hero's privy counselor, Wolfert Acker, who inscribed upon its walls his favorite motto of "Lust in Rust" (pleasure in quiet), and thus gave it the name of "Wolfert's Rust," afterward corrupted into Roost "by the uneducated who did not understand Dutch; probably from its quaint cock-loft look, and from its having a weather-cock perched on every gable." The next lustrum in its life was in the days of the Revolution, when it became the homestead of the great family of the Van Tassels, by whose name it was known down to the time when Mr. Irving came into the possession, and baptized it "Sunnyside." The valiant Van Tassel, Mr. Irving tells us, was "a flagitious rebel" in the war-time, and his Roost was a pestiferous den of the rampant marauders of the region. Indeed, so greatly annoyed were the enemy by the machinations therein concocted, that they made it a special mark of their vengeance, and thumped it into a more fearful effigy of a cocked hat than ever.

It was at the Roost that Diedrich Knickerbocker, according to Mr. Irving's grave story, found the invaluable state papers rescued by the thoughtful and patriotic Wolfert from the archives of the conquered city of New Amsterdam, upon which his marvelous History of the Dutch Dynasty was built; and here he pursued his erudite researches in the very room which is now our author's sanctum.

Katrina, the mischievous heroine of the Legend of Sleepy Hollow, and the idol of the rival swains Ichabod Crane and Brom Bones, was of the gallant family of the Van Tassels, and the Roost is supposed to be the very house where was given that famous quilting frolic, in returning from which the ill-fated Ichabod was so relentlessly pursued by the rollicking Brom Bones, under the awful guise of the Headless Horseman. Here, in the little garden, grew, no doubt, the veritable pumpkin which so materially assisted in this tragic scene! The present aspect of the old church toward which Ichabod flew for sanctuary on the night of that fearful ride, is seen in one of our pictures.

The Roost wore its old Dutch aspect (of which there is a faithful drawing extant) when Mr. Irving purchased the domain. The alterations which he has since made were begun in 1835, and completed in the autumn of the following year, at which time he took possession.

The air of graceful simplicity and cozy comfort which so strongly marks the exterior of the Sunnyside cottage, is felt quite as vividly within doors. It is cut up into just such odd, snug little apartments and boudoirs as the rambling, low-walled, peak-roofed, and gable-ended outside promises. The state entrance is by the porch at the south end; the household exit is from the drawing-room, across the piazza, to the lawn on the east or river front. It is on this side of the cottage that the family chat or read the news of the great world, away, on summer days and nights. On the north side of the

THE PORCH.

drawing-room there is a delightful little recess, forming a boudoir some six or eight feet square, the whole front of which is occupied by a window looking across the lawn, and through the up-river vista chronicled in our portfolio. It is, in summer, neatly matted and furnished with little stands of books, and flowers, and statuettes, and the low-toned walls are hung with drawings and sketches by Leslie, Stuart Newton, and others—mementoes of Mr. Irving's sojournings and friendships in England—with some of Darley's admirable etchings from Rip Van Winkle and the Legend of Sleepy Hollow. It is a little nook which you would set down at once as under special female guardianship. Perhaps it is the veritable chamber haunted by the sleepless ghost of the young lady who, the tradition says, "died somewhere in the Roost of love and green apples."

The graceful simplicity which marks the appointments of this Lilliputian sanctum is seen through all the furniture and adornments of the mansion. The spirit throughout is that of refinement without affectation, elegance without display, comfort without waste.

This winsome and delicate frame is in delightful keeping with the picture of social and domestic life within it; for, though a bachelor, Mr. Irving has not, as, in his sweet story of "The Wife," he tells us a single man is too apt to do, "run to waste and self-neglect; to fancy himself lonely and abandoned, and his heart to fall to ruin, like some deserted mansion, for want of an inhabitant." On the contrary, he has, happily,

THE SOUTH END OF THE COTTAGE.

VIEW IN THE LANE, EASTWARD.

of thought, which always reminds us of certain peculiarities in his movement and bearing, and of an expression coming from his habit of inclining his head always a little to one side. There is about the cottage, as about himself, an air of reserve, without coldness, which, while cordially inviting approach, creates instinctively and willingly a respectful deference. The sweet, sunny sentiment of his home is ever seen in his genial smile, and his kindly and benevolent nature in its aspect of cheerfulness and benignity; while its odd twists, and turns, and unexpected vagaries speak of the quaint and whimsical, yet refined and delicate humors of his character.

Of Mr. Irving's fragrant penchant for dream-land, to which we owe his exquisite fairy tales of poetic superstition, romance, and chivalry, there is an early and amusingly extravagant hint of recognition in Disraeli's story of "Vivian Grey," where "Geoffrey Crayon" is rallied upon a mood so obliviously *distrait* as to be utterly unconscious of being transferred by his waggish friends from one party of pleasure to the revels of another. His humor, cheerful, gently enjoyable, and lasting, rather than bold, uproarious, and transient, giving the especial charm to another class of his imaginings, runs through all his every-day conversation and gossip. He was once alluding to the passing away of his years and youthful strength, when, pointing to the twin elms framing the up-river lawn scene, which, years ago, he had planted with his own hand, "Those trees," said he to us, with a quaint smile, "I once carried on my shoulder; but I could not do it now!"

We recognized the genial, "golden-hearted" "Geoffrey Crayon" of our old stolen midnight readings, when, talking of his trees, he remarked that he once entertained the black-walnut and the butternut, but as they were whining misanthropes, who cowardly shed their autumn leaves and put on long wintry faces while all their companions were lifeful and merry, he had turned them out. "I banished them," said he, "as incorrigible *croakers*."

made himself "monarch of a little world of love" in the "domestic endearments of the kindred he has gathered under his roof, and the reverent affection of the friends who share his generous hospitality."

In the society of his nieces, who have long been to him as daughters, and of their father, his elder and only surviving brother; in the companionship of tried friends, and in the genial pleasures of his literary occupations, all sweetened by the grateful reminiscences of a long and eminently useful life, his little home, let us hope, is to his own heart within as true a "Sunnyside" as it is to the world without.

We have yet to instance beauties and harmonies in our charming picture. It has grown up out of our author's own heart, and both in unity and in detail it is a striking reflex of his character, and even, fanciful as the parallel may seem to be, of his physique and manner. In its very modest yet well-balanced proportions we see his figure of healthful manliness, though scarcely reaching to the middle stature. There is, too, about the odd little mansion, an air of quiet, true dignity, mingled with a feeling of sly mischievousness; unconscious, yet observant; dreaming, yet wide-awake; silent, yet full

Of the goodness and loving-kindness of his heart we once heard a gentle anecdote, which we hope it will not be improper to repeat. Speaking of the growing deafness of his favorite brother, who has long been a member of his family circle at Sunnyside, "Alas!" said he, "he can not now hear half I say to him; but, thank God, we can yet *see* each other!"

In his professional and private life Mr. Irving has ever been much swayed by a constitutional waywardness of character, now indolent and dreaming, now impulsive and active. "I have wandered," he says, in his character of "Geoffrey Crayon," "through different countries, and witnessed many of the shifting scenes of life. I can not say that I have studied them with the eye of a philosopher, but rather with the sauntering gaze with which humble lovers of the picturesque stroll from the window of one print shop to another; caught sometimes by the delineations of beauty, sometimes by the distortions of caricature, and sometimes by the loveliness of landscape." In his preface to the last revised edition of the "Sketch-Book" there are some confessions of this humor in a correspondence, referring to the publication of that work, between himself and his friend Sir Walter Scott. He is in London, long years ago, asking Scott's counsel, which he intimates is especially desirable to him, since reverses of fortune have made the successful employment of his pen all-important.

THE GARDENER'S COTTAGE.

Scott, in reply, and acting upon his hint at necessities, generously proposes to him the office, in his gift, of editor of a new weekly periodical then about to be established in Edinburgh, with emoluments to the amount of five hundred pounds sterling per annum, and the prospect of further advantages. Mr. Irving, in declining this tempting gift, says: "I feel myself peculiarly unfitted for the situation offered to me, not merely by my political opinions, but by the very constitution and habits of my mind. My whole course of life has been desultory, and I am unfitted for any periodically recurring task, or any stipulated labor of body or mind. I have no command of my talents, such as they are, and have to watch the varyings of my mind as I would those of a weather-cock. Practice and training may bring me more into rule; but at present I am as useless for regular service as one of my own country Indians or a Don Cossack. I must, therefore, keep on pretty much as I have begun—writing when I can, not when I would. I shall occasionally shift my residence, and write whatever is suggested by objects before me, or whatever rises in my imagination; and hope to write better and more copiously by-and-by. I am playing the egotist; but I know no better way of answering your proposal than by showing what a very

OVERLOOKING SUNNYSIDE.

GLEN ON THE BROOK.

good-for-nothing kind of being I am. Should Mr. Constable feel inclined to make a bargain for the wares I have on hand, he will encourage me to further enterprise; and it will be something like trading with a gipsy for the fruits of his prowlings, who may at one time have nothing but a wooden bowl to offer, and at another time a silver tankard." This vagrancy of mind he seems to have conquered, at least for brave intervals, in later years; otherwise we should not now possess the fruits of those sustained and laborious efforts, his classic "Columbus," and his "Columbus and his Companions," and his latest, though we trust not his last work, the "Life of Washington." Still he is the same retiring lover of quiet and seclusion as of yore, shrinking from popular remark, and cherishing an especial distaste for all or any active participation in public affairs. Though it is said that once, and for a moment, he was moved by friendship to attend a political meeting across the bay from Sunnyside, to take the stump, and hurrah for "Tippecanoe and Tyler too!"

Mr. Irving is now in his seventy-fourth year, having been born on the 3d of April, 1783, in the city of New York, in a house which but lately stood on what is now the corner of William and Fulton streets. His father, who was a native of Scotland, and his mother, an English lady, had settled in America some twenty years before his birth. He is the youngest of five sons, who were all addicted to literary pursuits, excepting the one who now lives, with his daughters, under his brother's roof at Sunnyside.

William Irving, the eldest of the brothers, was a writer in the famous Salmagundi papers, to which he contributed most of the poetical pieces, the letters and verses "from the Mill of Pindar Cockloft." He was a member of Congress from 1813 to 1819, and died in 1821. "He was," say the Messrs. Duyckinck, in their admirable "Cyclopædia of American Literature," "a merchant at New York, with the character of a man of wit and refinement, who had added to a naturally genial temperament the extensive resources of observation, and a fresh experience of the world, gathered in his border life."

Peter Irving, the second brother, studied and graduated in medicine, but never practiced. He established and edited the *Morning Chronicle* newspaper; wrote a stirring tale of piratical adventure called "Giovanni Sfogarro," and assisted his brother in the conception of the comic "Knickerbocker History." He died in 1838.

Ebenezer Irving was once a merchant, but has long since retired from the cares of business, and is now one of the family at Sunnyside. His son, Theodore Irving, the author of "The Conquest of Florida," was formerly Professor of History and Belles Lettres in Geneva College, and afterward at the New York Free Academy. He is now an Episcopal clergyman in Western New York.

John T. Irving, the fourth brother, practiced the profession of the law so successfully that he rose to the bench, and presided over the Court of Common Pleas in New York for seventeen years. He died in 1838. His son, John Treat Irving, is well known as the "Quod" correspondent of the *Knickerbocker Magazine*, in the columns of which were first published his successful novels, "The Attorney," and "Harry Harson, or the Benevolent Bachelor." He has written also a series of spirited "Indian Sketches"—reminiscences of an expedition to the Pawnee tribes.

The intimation which this glance at the literary tastes of his brothers gives us of the atmosphere in which Mr. Irving's boyhood was passed will readily explain the early manifestation of his love of books; and the classic character of the volumes which then happily fell into his hands, reveals the secret of that pure, simple, old-fashioned art which, from his earliest efforts, has ever marked his style. His literary *début* was made in 1804, in a series of essays upon the manners, amusements, and fashions of the town and the time, under the signature of "Jonathan Oldstyle." They were contributed to his brother's paper, the *Morning Chronicle*, and were afterward issued, though without his approval, in pamphlet form.

His career had thus scarcely begun when his health failed, and, apprehensive of a pulmonary complaint, he thought it necessary to remove to the south of Europe. During two years' rambles amidst the natural beauties and the attractive associations of many lands—France, Italy, Sicily, Switzerland, Flanders, and Holland—he formed that attachment to the Old World which at another time led him from home through the long lapse of seventeen years, and again for an interval of four years. In these residences abroad he amassed the valuable material from which has grown so much of his literary labor — the Pictures and Tales of English Rural Life, in the "Sketch-Book" and "Bracebridge Hall;" the Memories of Abbotsford and of Newstead Abbey, in the "Crayon Miscellany;" the "Tales of a Traveler;" and the volumes relating to Columbus and to his Companions, to Granada and the Alhambra. Through these works are scattered, however, many of his choicest American themes; proving that, though far from, he was not unmindful of his native home.

Before going abroad he began the study of the law, which he resumed on his return to New York in 1806. He was the same year admitted to the bar, but with no sequence, as he never practiced the profession. We soon again find him in the literary ranks, contributing, with his brother William Irving, and his friend James K. Paulding, to the "Salmagundi," a semi-monthly journal of "whimwhams and opinions," humorous and satirical. In this work, which was continued during one year, the follies and fancies of the day were attacked with such amusing and effective skill that it was eagerly looked for at the time,

THE BROOK, FROM THE LANE.

THE "LITTLE MEDITERRANEAN."

and is referred to with interest now. It was the most popular and successful American production of the day, and in its rich and racy humor gave clear promise of the genius afterward developed by its authors.

Mr. Irving's next appearance was two years later, in 1809, with that most unique and surprising volume in our literature, Diedrich Knickerbocker's "History of New York, from the Beginning of the World to the End of the Dutch Dynasty;" which at once elevated the author to the first rank among native writers. It opens with such profound Dogberry gravity that no wonder the unsophisticated reader, not forewarned, took it seriously at its word until its irresistible drollery grew too rampant to be longer masked. A story is told of a solemn judge who smuggled a copy of the work into court, and actually collapsed over it while upon the bench. In his preface to the revised edition of the work, the author explains all the circumstances under which it was written; how it was his first intention simply to parody a pretentious Guide-Book to the City, and "to burlesque the pedantic lore displayed in certain American works; how, as his material extended, he found that he should have enough to do, if he confined himself, as he did, to the period of the Dutch ascendency only; and how, in his droll pictures of our phlegmatic fathers, he was only in fun, and meant no offense to the general." When he found, he says, "how few of his fellow-citizens were aware that New York had ever been called New Amsterdam, or had ever heard of the names of its early Dutch governors, or cared a straw about their ancient Dutch progenitors," the matter broke upon him "as the poetic age of the city; poetic from its very obscurity; and open, like the early and obscure days of ancient Rome, to all the embellishments of heroic fiction." And so well has he availed himself of the "doubt and fable" of his theme, that he has created pictures and scenes which will forever remain pleasurably associated with all the local recollections of the Gothamites. So happily did he hit the popular fancy, that "Diedrich Knickerbocker" has almost become the tutelary saint of his native city; the people, generally, are Knickerbockers; they eat Knickerbocker ices and Knickerbocker oysters, travel in Knickerbocker coaches and Knickerbocker steamboats, read Knickerbocker magazines, pray in Knickerbocker halls, and, by-and-by, will, no doubt, go to Knickerbocker graves, in hope of a Knickerbocker heaven. The "good-humor and good fellowship" which the History inspires is made to sweeten many healthful pills of needed satire and sage instruction; for there are, and always will be, the world over, many dreaming Oloffes, and doubting Walters, and testy Williams, and headstrong Peters.

The Knickerbocker completed, we find the current of our author's literary life subsiding for a while, with here and there only a sparkling bubble; among them a Biographical Sketch of Campbell, written at the solicitation of the poet's brother—who was then residing in New York—to help the sale of an American edition of "O'Connor's Child," just received from Lon-

STILE IN THE WOODS.

don. This paper led afterward to a pleasant acquaintance between the American and the English author.

In this interval of repose Mr. Irving entered into commercial life, as a silent partner of two of his brothers; but the second war with Great Britain soon following, he became infected with the popular enthusiasm, and assumed the editorship of the *Analectic Magazine*, in Philadelphia, for which he wrote a series of succinct and elegant biographies of the American Naval Captains. His patriotic feelings not finding sufficient vent through the quiet channel of the pen, he seized the sword, and donned the epaulet, in the character of aid-de-camp and military secretary to Governor Tompkins, of New York, and, for a while, was honorably known as "Colonel Irving."

Among the commercial disasters caused by the war, was the destruction of the house of "Irving and Brothers," which suddenly cast our author—who had gone to England on the business of his firm when peace was restored—once more upon his literary resources. He now prepared to bring out his "Sketch-Book," for which he had gathered already so much material in his experience and observation of English life and manners. Some portions of the work had been already published in America, and the apprehension of a piratical edition in London, where they had attracted very favorable notice, accelerated his measures for their issue by himself, and for his own advantage. It was this occasion that produced the passages of correspondence with Scott to which we have previously referred. Not finding such a publisher as he desired, he determined to print at his own cost and risk; but afterward, through the mediation of Sir Walter, Mr. Murray was induced to take hold of it; which he did with so much success that he gave the author two hundred pounds in addition to a like sum which he had already paid for the copyright. This charming budget of tales—the most read, perhaps, of all Mr. Irving's works—gives us every example of those excellences of theme, thought, treatment, and style which have made his fame. It touches all chords of feeling, from the most *riant* humor to the tenderest pathos. It is not to be wondered at that it instantly made its way both at home and abroad, containing, as it does, among its gems, those masterly expressions of gentle emotion, the "Wife" and the "Broken Heart," and the immortal legends of "Rip Van Winkle and "Sleepy Hollow." His peaceful little valley, made forever famous as the scene of the last-mentioned fancy, is one of the most attractive features of the landscape about the author's home. Apart from its romantic associations, it is a most interesting spot; one in which the visitor might easily dream dreams for himself, if they were not already served to his hand. In our explorations of its quiet lawns and glens we were surprised to note the

THE HUDSON, FROM SLEEPY HOLLOW.

"PHILIPSENS' CASTLE."

literalness with which Mr. Irving had sketched its features. In the close portraiture we could scarce persuade ourself that the lank Ichabod and his mischievous urchins, the malicious Brom Bones and the blooming Katrina, were only phantasies of the brain; for there, before our very eyes, lay the brook and the bridge over which old Gunpowder bore his terrified master on that eventful night when he was so relentlessly pursued by the ghostly Hessian; and yonder, on the hill, stood the old church toward which he fled for sanctuary. There, too, was the homestead, or "castle," of the once mighty family of the Philipsens, its ancient walls and chimneys reflected in the bright waters of the Pocantico; and hidden away in one of the most secluded haunts of the same lovely stream, far up in the mysterious valley, we heard the clank of the wheel of "Carl's Mill."

Besides the descriptions of the Hollow which are given in the legend, we find in the opening chapter of "Wolfert's Roost" much poetic history. There, Mr. Irving tells us how the region won its somnolent name from a charm laid by a rival chieftain upon its ancient people—a charm so potent, that they sleep among the rocks and recesses to this day, with their bows and arrows beside them. "Often," he says, "in secluded parts of the valley, where the stream is overhung by dark woods and rocks, the plowman, on some calm and sunny day, as he shouts to his oxen, is surprised at hearing faint shouts from the hillsides in reply; being, it is said, the spell-bound warriors, who half start from their rocky couches, and grasp their weapons, but sink to sleep again." "Carl's Mill" figures in our author's fancies as the haunted house, occupied by an old, goblinish-looking negro, from whom, he says, Diedrich Knickerbocker gleaned, as he chatted with him on the broken mill-stone, many valuable facts, and among them "the surprising though true story of Ichabod Crane" itself. The old church of Sleepy Hollow was once a pure specimen of the good, solid Dutch architecture, but of late years its harmony had been destroyed by the incongruous addition

of a Greek portico. In speaking of this ancient relic, in the droll chapters from which we have already quoted, Mr. Irving says that it was once graced by two weather-cocks, "one perched over the belfry and the other over the chancel. As usual with ecclesiastical weather-cocks, each pointed a different way, and there was a perpetual contradiction between them on all points of windy doctrine; emblematic, alas! of the Christian propensity to schism and controversy." "The drowsy influence, too, of Sleepy Hollow," he adds, "was apt to breathe into the sacred edifice; and now and then an elder might be seen with his handkerchief over his face to keep off the flies, and apparently listening to the dominie, but really sunk into a summer slumber, lulled by the sultry notes of the locusts from the neighboring trees."

But lest we too catch "the witching" influence of the air, which Mr. Irving assures us still affects all who enter the wizard valley, we will hasten to make our way out, and resume the record of our author's literary achievements, which our long digression has so irrelevantly interrupted.

Mr. Irving's next volumes, written in Paris, were those of "Bracebridge Hall." This work is a continuation of the "Sketch-Book," especially of those portions dealing with English rustic life, manners, and pastimes, of which it presents pictures never rivaled by England's own best painters. Our pleasant Christmas introduction to the hearty old Squire and his factotum, Master Simon, in the pages of the "Sketch-Book," made us glad to improve their genial acquaintance and that of their worthy neighbors, General Harbottle and Master Ready Money Jack Tibbetts, under the frank and hospitable roof of Bracebridge Hall.

We next find Mr. Irving wandering along the Rhine, and among the German capitals; wintering in Dresden in 1822, and back again the following year to Paris. In 1824 he published the "Tales of a Traveler," which provoked some fault-finding by the English critics, who had become tired of calling Aristides the Just. These envious shafts, however, proved very harmless, for the public verdict declared the author's original and rare genius, well sustained in the strange stories of the Nervous Gentleman, in graphic pictures of literary life found in the Experiences of Buckthorne and his Friends, in the romantic episodes in Italian life, and in the novel character of American tradition and adventure. Moore, who during the preparation of this work was with the author in Paris, says, in his Diary, that the publisher, Murray, purchased it at the price of fifteen hundred pounds, and would have given, if it had been asked, two thousand pounds. The poet also expresses his surprise at the rapidity with which it was written—one hundred and thirty printed pages having been made in the brief space of ten days. This must have been during one of Mr. Irving's happiest moods; for, as a general thing, we believe that literary composition is a slow and careful process with him. His is the laborious, though unseen art, which conceals art.

By this time Mr. Irving's reputation had spread far and wide, and his works, which had become in universal demand, were translated into all the languages of the Continent. In 1826, two years after the appearance of the "Tales of a Traveler," he went to Spain, and took up his residence at Madrid. Here, availing himself of the important series of documents then recently collected by Navarrete, he prepared his elegant and classic "History of the Life and Voyages of Columbus," and afterward of the "Discoveries and Voyages of Columbus's Companions." The first of these works gained for him the compliment from George the Fourth of one of two fifty-guinea gold medals which that king had offered for eminence in historical composition. So well suited to the turn of his mind was the dramatic and adventurous spirit of the age and land of Columbus, that his task was one of love; and without prejudice to philosophy and fact, his narratives have all the charms of a tale which is told.

So completely, indeed, was his imagination taken with the romance of his theme, that he was led to give further expression of his interest in a "Chronicle of the Conquest of Granada," and an exploration of the poetic marvels of the Alhambra. Following Columbus, as he did, step by step, in his close attendance upon the Spanish monarchs, in court and camp, through all the changing scenes of the Moorish war, up to the final catastrophe before the walls of the Moslem capital, he had, like him, become almost an eye-witness of the scenes he was called upon to narrate. Thus, in the "Chronicle," while truthfully detailing historical events, he has yet draped all in the airy garb of romance; and from the "Alhambra," that fountain of poesy, where he was less fettered by the sober shackles of Fact, and his fancy had freer play, he has drawn wells of winsome story even *plus Arabe qu'en Arabie*. In this Spanish Sketch-Book, as it has been called, we read the tales of dauntless chivalry, bold emprise, generous valor, and devoted love, as though we were, like the poetic Moslems of old, listening to the

DISTANT VIEW OF THE OLD CHURCH IN SLEEPY HOLLOW.

NEAR VIEW OF THE OLD CHURCH IN SLEEPY HOLLOW.

mingled speech of mystic bard and falling fountain.

In 1829 Mr. Irving was awakened from his dreams in the ruined halls of the Alhambra, where he had passed three happy months, by a call to the post of Secretary of Legation to the American embassy in London. This unsolicited office he filled until the Minister, Mr. M'Lane, returned home, when he was left for a while as *Chargé d'Affaires*. In his diplomatic character he officiated at the coronation of William the Fourth, and he received from that monarch and the royal family, as well as from various distinguished personages of the court, many marks of high esteem.

At this time, too, the English University at Oxford conferred upon him, in compliment to his genius, the honorary degree of LL.D. This distinction he received in person, and amidst the cordial acclamations of the students and graduates, and of a brilliant and learned assemblage.

In 1832 he returned home from his second residence in Europe, which had lasted seventeen years. The fame which he had acquired in this long interval won him the heartiest reception from his countrymen. The public enthu-

siasm was indeed so great, that, had it so pleased him, his tour through his native land, which soon followed, might have been one continued and most sincere ovation. From this display, however, he naturally shrunk, declining all invitations save one to a public dinner in his own city of New York.

From the journeys in the United States which Mr. Irving made soon after his return home, and especially from his rambles over the prairies and wildernesses of the Far West, have grown his "Tour on the Prairies," embodied in the revised and uniform edition of his works recently published by Putnam; in the "Crayon Miscellany," his "Adventures of Captain Bonneville," and the "Astoria" narrative. In these works, all marked by the author's habitual elegance and grace of style, we have striking pictures of the wild trapper-life and adventure of our Rocky Mountain and Pacific regions.

In 1837 and 1840 Mr. Irving contributed, at intervals, to the columns of the *Knickerbocker Magazine*. Among these papers are, "The Early Experiences of Ralph Ringwood," and "Mountjoy; a Passage in the Life of a Castlebuilder," which, with other stray waifs from the

English annuals and elsewhere, have been recently collected and published, under the title of "Wolfert's Roost." In the little sketch of "The Creole Village," in this volume, he claims to have first used the now common phrase, "the almighty dollar;" and as the expression, he says, "has been questioned by some as savoring of irreverence, he owes it to his orthodoxy to declare that no irreverence was intended even to the dollar itself, which he is aware is daily becoming more and more an object of worship."

Among his latest published works is his loving life of his favorite author, Goldsmith, to whose genius his own has been so often and so appositely compared, and his history of "Mahomet and his Successors," another wave from the flood of his Moslem researches.

In February, 1842, he made his third and last visit to Europe, where he passed four years in the honorable position of American Minister at the court of Madrid. Since his return he has lived at the homestead made so attractive in his works as "Wolfert's Roost," and now so gracefully known to us as Sunnyside.

Here he is at present, industriously employed upon his "Life of Washington." The publication of this noble work was commenced during the past year (1855). Three volumes have been already issued, in which the charmed reader is led, with never-flagging interest, through the varied and eventful scenes of the Revolution. The fourth and last volume, which it is understood will be devoted to the Presidential life of his hero, will, no doubt, be very soon completed.

There is a pleasant and authentic anecdote about the presentation of our author, when a child in arms, to Washington. "May it please your Excellency," said his nurse, following the General into a Broadway shop, "here's a bairn that was named after ye!" Whereupon he placed his hand kindly on the boy's head, and prayed God to bless him; thus perhaps exorcising the malign influence popularly supposed to accompany the inheritance of a great name. As Washington was the political, so is his namesake the literary Father of his country.

The scope of our paper has permitted a brief allusion only to the characteristics of Mr. Irving's genius—to the freshness and fullness of his invention—to the individuality of his conceptions—to his rich poetic fancy—to his catholic sympathies, reaching the heart in all its moods, from hearty mirth to pensive sentiment—to the simplicity, good sense, honesty, and manliness of his thought—all heightened by the marvelous ease and grace of his "mellow, flowing, softly tinted style;" and to that ever-present charm of personality, which, as he himself says of Goldsmith, "seems to bespeak his moral as well as his intellectual qualities, and makes us love the man, at the same time that we admire the author."

Thus have we peeped into the pleasant face of Sunnyside, and conned the magic by which it has bewitched the public heart. Long after its modest walls shall have crumbled away will the charm cling to its memory, for its associations with one who, building always upon the true foundations of life—Truth and Beauty—has reared to himself a perpetual and fragrant altar in the pantheon of the world's literature.

"CARL'S MILL," IN SLEEPY HOLLOW.

The City of Buffalo
(1885)

THE CITY OF BUFFALO.

LOOKING across Niagara River from the crumbling ruins of Fort Erie, whose most frequent visitors to-day are the cows of the neighboring farmers browsing peacefully on the grass-grown ramparts, whence seventy years ago General Peter B. Porter made his brilliant sortie, one sees the granite tower of the City Hall of Buffalo rising commandingly above the surrounding miles of warehouses and factory chimneys, hooded in an atmosphere of smoke and steam.

Northward, past the high bluff crowned by the ruins of Fort Porter and the stone copings of "The Front," flows the Niagara with a constantly accelerating velocity. Parallel with it, "packed with long lines of freighted boats towed by slow-paced horses," is the Erie Canal, "the author and sure conservator of the fortunes of Buffalo."

South and westward Lake Erie spreads out in endless billows; and at the east, forming a noble background to the city, rise the Chautauqua hills and the highlands of Evans and Wales.

In the neighborhood of the old Canadian fortress all is stagnation. Peaceful country roads lead off through green lanes, and in the half-decayed frame mansions, surrounded by tall Lombardy poplars, and supported from foundation to cornice by Corinthian columns, is a reminder of that departed grandeur which made Fort Erie in by-gone days what her neighbor over the river is to-day—a centre of gay life.

To understand the past, present, or future of Buffalo as a port of entry, the results of her characteristic industries, and the pluck of her early settlers—and no city in the United States more directly owes her present prosperity to the energy of a few far-seeing pioneers—one must approach her from the harbor side.

In the foreground stands the most imposing row of bread-distributers on the lakes, the mammoth grain elevators of Buffalo Creek, nearly forty of them, making an elephantine procession a mile long, with a combined storage capacity of 9,250,000 bushels, and a transfer capacity of 3,102,000 bushels, or, in other words, the power of receiving from lake vessels and transferring to canal-boats and cars daily 3,000,000 bushels of wheat, a rate unequalled at any other port in this country. It is not uncommon to see a large lake vessel unloading and two canal-boats and two trains of freight-cars loading at the same time.

The site of the Bennett elevator, at the junction of the creek and the Evans ship-canal, is historic as marking the scene of an experiment only less interesting than the first voyage of Robert Fulton's steamboat, for it was here, in 1842, that a Buffalonian, Joseph Dart, built the first steam storage transfer elevator, on the well-known elevator and conveyer principle of Oliver Evans, in the face of the jeers of his townsmen, who predicted that he would find to his cost that "Irishmen's backs were, after all, the cheapest elevators."

The capacity of Joseph Dart's elevator was but 55,000 bushels, with a power of raising 1000 bushels an hour. To-day such an elevator as that of the connecting terminal railroad, having a capacity of 1,000,000 bushels, can elevate 19,000 bushels an hour. Watching the legs of the two towers of this huge elevator drop upon a mass of wheat in the hold of a lake vessel moored at its wharf, the machinery start, and the twelve-quart buckets dip down into the grain and rush with light-ning speed up into the roof of the building, where they deposit their load in the bins, it is not difficult to believe that a cargo which by the old method of "Irishmen's backs" would have required a month to discharge can now be stowed away in five hours.

Buffalo Creek is interesting not only for its connection with an invention which, by facilitating the movement of bread-stuffs, has a vital concern for all mankind, but as the stream—"a ford then only waist deep"—from across whose entrance some sixty years ago a few citizens, determined that Buffalo should be the western terminus of the Erie Canal, dug away the sand bar which choked its channel. Buffalo Creek Harbor was begun, carried on, and completed principally by three private individuals, who mortgaged the whole of their estate in its behalf. The river is now protected north and south by two breakwaters, but the capacious harbor thus obtained is insufficient for the growing commerce of the city, and the United States government is making an outside harbor by the construction of a breakwater designed to be four thousand feet long, fronting the entrance of the river about a half-mile from the shore. With the completion of this breakwater facilities will exist for the building of new wharves aggregating an additional five miles, making the available water-front about nineteen miles. In other words, the commerce of Buffalo Creek is destined one day to rival the gigantic traffic of the river Mersey, when the harbor of this queen city of the lakes will vie with that of Liverpool in her endless docks and warehouses.

Mr. Henry James banishes one of his characters from the Eternal City to "Buffalo" as to the wild West, forgetting or unaware that the name of this lake city is not without Old World precedent. Bosporus means ox-passage, and Oxford a ford for oxen. That the city derives its name from the river is certain, but whether the river was so called because the buffalo had at one time grazed in the shade of the basswood-trees along its margins, now lined with elevators, floaters, lumber-yards, coal pockets, chutes, and trestles, or from a mistake in the Indian title, has not been satisfactorily determined. The name of the city first appears in a treaty made at Fort Stanwix—now Rome—between the United States and the Iroquois Confederacy.

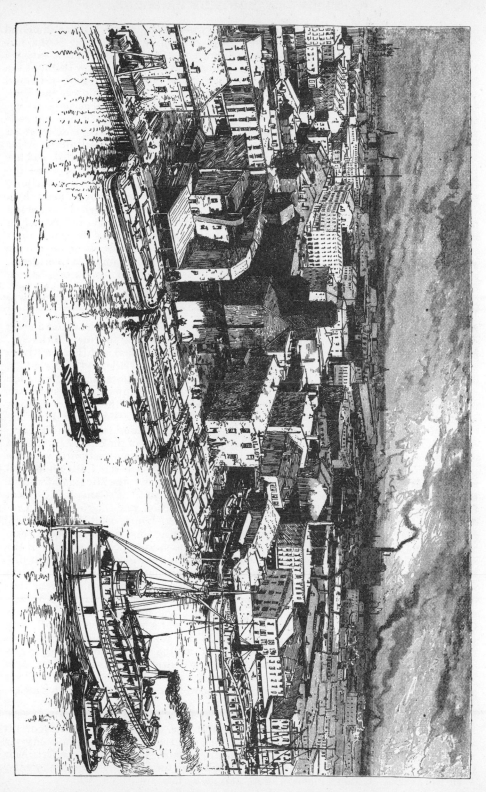

THE CITY OF BUFFALO.

All through the summer the harbor is full of life—tugs dart hither and yon, lake vessels, big and little, receive their cargoes, huge steamers and propellers take on passengers or freight for the upper lakes, while numerous pleasure-yachts, named for sea-nymphs and dryads, steam toward the International Bridge, which opens in the centre with massive swing, and permits them to pass through on their way "down the river." Finally, and most important, stretching in all directions, are the iron rails over which the commerce of the Great West reaches the Eastern sea-board.

To win the heart of this queen city to-day you must court her in the rôle of a railway king. You must come as the projector of a new trunk line, prepared to lay your millions at her feet in return for a site from which to throw another iron girdle around the city, and with thousands more to invest for a commanding lot on Delaware Avenue, "The Circle," or fronting one of the many park approaches, whereupon to erect a palace of Medina sandstone, or a cypress-shingled villa rivalling those of Newport or the famous Jerusalem Road.

Never was the imperial position of Buffalo appreciated as now, when all signs point to the realization of the prophecy that she is destined to sit "like a commercial Constantinople stretching along the Bosporus of the broad Niagara, and holding the keys of the Dardanelles that shall open and shut the gates of trade for the regions east and west." A study of the globe will show why, from the founder of the city in 1797 down to the latest railway manager of 1885, eager to obtain an approach to the International Bridge, already inadequate to the demands of traffic and mooting the revival of the old scheme of tunnelling under the Niagara, every sagacious person has predicted a great commercial future for the Queen City of the Empire State. With the completion of the Northern Pacific Railroad the whole world will pay her tribute. Not only will the products of the immense wheat fields of the Red River, the coal, oil, and iron of Pennsylvania, the lumber of Michigan and the Southern States, the ores of Lake Superior, and the live stock of the great western prairies pass through her gates, but the commerce of Asia with the Atlantic States, with England, and the Continent.

In the year of Buffalo's incorporation,

1832, when there were but one hundred miles of rail in the United States, was granted the first permit to put a railroad through Erie County. Now, without the repetition of a rod, over nine thousand miles of travel are possible on the lines centring at Buffalo alone, as the starting-point or terminus of twenty different railway lines. No city, save one, owes so much to railroads as does Buffalo. Her terminal facilities are unequalled, and her transfer yards at East Buffalo are the largest in the world, with the outlying country encompassed for miles about by a net-work of tracks, approaching closer and closer as they near the city, and extending around the harbor-side to pour their freight of coal, salt, and petroleum into the lake vessels in return for a cargo of grain, flour, lumber, iron, and copper ore. Commercial Buffalo is like a portly and self-satisfied spider, supreme in the centre of her web.

The business man has his choice among six different routes to New York city. The New York Central and Hudson River; the New York, Lake Erie, and Western; the New York, West Shore, and Buffalo; the Delaware, Lackawanna, and Western; the Lehigh Valley; and the Buffalo division of the Buffalo, New York, and Philadelphia—all lead east amid the beautiful scenery of the interior of the State. Stretching away in an opposite direction toward the western prairies are the Lake Shore and Michigan Southern, the Michigan Central, the Grand Trunk of Canada, the Great Western division, and the New York, Chicago, and St. Louis, or "Nickel Plate." The remaining nine roads are local lines. Among the most important of these is the Buffalo Creek Railway, a belt freight line four miles in length, extending down on either side of the ship canal. Every railroad entering the city has a connection with this, and by the terms of the city's grant its rates are uniform to all, thus placing the railroads on equal terms.

Within the city limits railroad corporations own 2746 acres, or more than four square miles of territory. There are 436 miles of standard gauge track—more miles of rails than are contained in any other city on the globe. Within the corporate boundaries of his own town the Buffalonian could enjoy a railroad journey equal to a trip to New York over the Lackawanna, with twenty-six miles to spare.

AMONG THE ELEVATORS.

From photograph by George Barker, Niagara Falls.

THE COAL DOCKS.

What gives unusual interest to the marvellous railroad improvements in Buffalo since 1880, from which year dates the "new era" of prosperity, is the fact that to this construction all the newer scientific principles have been applied. The railroad kings of America have discovered that the traffic capacity of railroad lines is limited mainly by the extent of their terminal facilities, and with this conviction have been developing the terminal facilities of Buffalo most assiduously. The Lehigh Valley Railroad affords a notable illustration of a successful application of the modern theory, for although it has not a line of its own to Buffalo, but sends its coal-laden cars hither from Waverly over the Erie, the company has nevertheless expended millions in the acquisition of unsurpassed terminal facilities in the southern part of the city for the purpose of transshipping its coal, and sending it up Lake Erie and over other roads. Indeed, the opinion has been expressed that the improvements making on the Tifft Farm property—a tract of 425 acres, belonging to this road, at a cost of $4,000,000, will prove of greater value to Buffalo than any public work since the opening of the Erie Canal. These improvements consist chiefly in the turning of the city ship-canal into the farm, and so cutting it backward

and forward at right angles in huge parallelograms as to endow the city with eight additional miles of docks—an amount of water-frontage equal to all she had before—and giving the railway corporations a total of fourteen miles of water-front available for the transfer of freight from lake to rail. The most discreditable fact about the railroad growth is that, notwithstanding the exceeding generosity of the city in the matter of land grants, not one of the roads centring at Buffalo has paid her the compliment of erecting a fine railway station. Those of many New England country towns are far superior.

In no direction has the sudden broadening of Buffalo's business interests been more remarkable than in coal, both for home consumption and distribution. A few years ago the coal traffic was confined to the car-loads necessary for local use. As the city developed into a manufacturing centre the cry went up, "Give us cheap coal." This caused the opening of direct railroad communication between the Pennsylvania mines and the wholesale dealers. The Buffalo, New York, and Philadelphia, in addition to its railroad property, controls extensive coal mines and lands in Pennsylvania, from which it feeds Buffalo with a constantly increasing coal, oil, lumber, bark, and grain commerce.

A few years ago vessels started up the lakes carrying coal as ballast, in order to bring return cargoes of grain. To-day, the freights of the two shipments are day ranks as the third coal depot of America, also as the most important distributing point for anthracite coal, nearly all of which goes through the city. The bi-

ALONG THE WHARVES.

about the same. Coal as an up freightage is fully as important as the down cargo of grain. Nearly two million dollars of property is engaged, it is estimated, in carrying the product of the coal fields from this port, exclusive of rolling stock.

In the amount of tonnage, Buffalo to-tuminous coal trade shows a progressive growth which, if prognosticated a few years ago, would have been deemed incredible. In the year 1874 the receipts were 327,467 tons; in 1884, 1,921,354 tons. Bituminous coal is largely used by the manufacturers of the city, and is one of the

LIGHT-HOUSE AT ENTRANCE OF HARBOR.

standing local grievances, on account of the soot it showers over the town. The enormous growth of the anthracite coal trade is shown by the fact that in 1874 the receipts were 472,262 tons; in 1884, 2,451,410 tons.

Thus, were Buffalo not a railway centre, she would be known as a coal depot. Take away both these interests, and she would be reputed one of the leading live-stock markets of the country. Without even this, her grape-sugar factories would endow her still with a world-wide name. Remove the grape-sugar works to the neighborhood of the Western corn fields, and she would yet be famed on both sides of the Atlantic Ocean for the greatest engineering feat of modern times—the cantilever bridge of the Michigan Central Railroad which spans the gorge of the Niagara, built in 1883 at the Central Bridge Works, now the Union Bridge Company, of Buffalo. Aside from these larger and wider-known establishments, there are over two thousand manufactories, numbering among the more important, car-wheels, stoves, and engines, boots and shoes, oil refineries, malt-houses, breweries and distilleries, flouring mills, chemical works, ship-yards, agricultural implements, and minor industries without number. The mail of one large establishment last year was greater in amount than the entire receipts of the post-office in 1872.

In Buffalo, which practically controls this industry, originated the manufacture of grape-sugar. One alone of the three glucose factories of Buffalo, the American, consumes 10,000 bushels of corn every twenty-four hours, requiring as feed for a single day the average annual product of 434 acres of corn fields, or more than half the entire annual product of all the New England States, more than one-sixth of the entire product of New York, and more than 0.0022 of the total crop of the United States.

daily newspapers in judicious editorial management are unexcelled. The Buffalo *Daily Courier*, which is a descendant of the *Star*, the first daily paper in Buffalo, has had a long line of able editors, among whom was the late William A. Seaver, afterward associated with *Harper's* Drawer.

As she is to-day a highway for the commerce of the nineteenth century, so was Buffalo and Erie County at an earlier period a well-trodden pathway across which passed a motley train of pilgrims and warriors—French hunters and trappers striding to the Northwest, Cardinal Richelieu's Jesuit missionaries holding up the cross, and the Indians of the Long House to put out the camp fires of the Kahquahs and Eries. Since first her soil was

JOSEPH ELLICOTT.

An enormous capital is invested by the *Courier*, *Express*, and *Commercial Advertiser* in the printing, lithographing, and engraving business. Buffalo claims also that, in proportion to population, her

seen by white men the habitations of three distinct races have in turn occupied it; and it is less than sixty years since the second of these, the Seneca Indians, the successors of the Kahquahs, were hunting deer on the present site of the State Insane Asylum, whose symmetrical red-tiled towers, designed by Richardson, loom up imposingly at the head of Richmond Avenue.

Following North Street, one of the fashionable neighborhoods of Buffalo, which intersects Richmond Avenue at the Circle, down Porter Avenue, nearly at right angles to it—a route almost identical with the "Guide Board Road" of the period when the Indians and their English allies crossed from Canada to Black Rock to burn Buffalo—we come out upon the Front, another now favorite residence neighborhood. Here the Buffalonian gets his one "marine" view, and here, too, he has a perpetual reminder of the original owners of the soil. More than two centuries have elapsed since the smoke wreaths of the Kahquahs' lodges rose on both sides of the gorge which witnesses the nuptials of the fairest of the Great Lakes with the most powerful of rivers. They named the stream that divided their ancient domain the Onniagahra, or Niagara.

In the summer of 1687, says the local historian, the Baron la Hontan ascended the rapids of the Niagara River in his light birchen canoe to Lake Erie. His military eye taking in the commanding situation at once, he recommended the site to the French government for a fort, and marked it Fort Supposé on the map that illustrated his travels. The fort was intended as a check against the neighboring Iroquois and Seneca Indians. This, the earliest historical notice of the site of Buffalo, was more than a hundred years prior to the Holland land purchase and the laying out of the city.

"In her many diagonal streets, all radiating from a common centre, Buffalo, as I have heard, bears an intentional resemblance to Washington. But where is the Capitol?" queried one of the newer settlers lately.

It is not to the credit of Buffalo that she has as yet perpetuated by neither statue nor memorial, save in the name of a single street, his fame who not only first predicted her commercial destiny, but what is almost unparalleled in the history of cities, selected her exact site and laid out in the then wilderness at the foot of Lake Erie a city on a scale commensurate with his inspired belief in her destiny. As agent for the Holland Land Com-

SOLDIERS' AND SAILORS' MONUMENT.

A REMINDER OF HOLLAND.

pany, Joseph Ellicott, in the year 1804, completed the survey of the broad streets, diagonal avenues, and public squares, some of which are to-day included in her extensive park system, and all of which form adequate approaches to the newer suburbs of the Buffalo of 1885. To her singularly open and attractive topography it is to be regretted that she does not add that next-to-godly attribute, cleanliness.

Joseph Ellicott was the brother of Andrew Ellicott, then Surveyor-General of the United States. Fresh from assisting his kinsman to lay out the city of Washington preparatory to its becoming the seat of government, he followed the same general plan in surveying the streets of "New Amsterdam," as he proposed to call it, out of respect to his Dutch employers, the members of the so-called Holland Land Company. The chief business thoroughfare now bears the commonplace name of Main Street—one which, to all save the ears of towns-people accustomed to it, wonderfully becomes its still semi-countrified air and the non-imposing character of many of its buildings; for everywhere in her business sections old and new Buffalo jostle each other picturesquely. Had Joseph Ellicott been allowed to complete his design in the nomenclature and laying out of the main

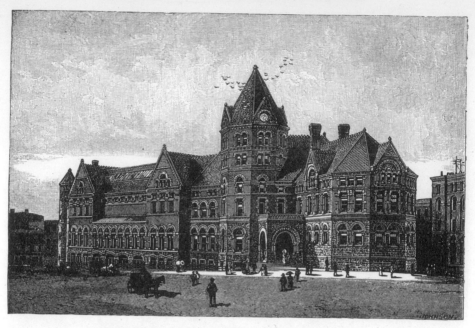

NEW LIBRARY BUILDING OF THE YOUNG MEN'S ASSOCIATION.

thoroughfare of trade, Main Street would have been Willink Avenue below "the Churches," and Van Staphorst above, for what was designed to be the site of the Capitol of New Amsterdam forms now the three blocks in Main Street bounded to the north and south by Eagle and Swan streets.   Here Mr. Ellicott proposed to erect his palace, with broad vistas opening to view in all directions.   The eye of the prince of New Amsterdam could have gazed at pleasure up Van Staphorst Avenue to the rising ground at the north, down Willink Avenue to the harbor, and out Vollenhoven Avenue (Erie Street) to the lake and Canada, along Stadnitski Avenue (Church Street) to the State reservation, and up Shimmelpennick Avenue (Niagara Street) past the elegant residences circling around Niagara Square, which was to be the centre of his city, straight to the setting sun.   The westerly limit of this manor, extending beyond the present west side of Main Street, suggested the title of "Ellicott's bow-window" to the towns-folk.   So practical a man as President Fillmore expressed just regret that the democratic spirit of that time, jealous of so baronial an establishment, cut the beautiful semicircle by running Main Street through instead of around it,

dividing the tract of about one hundred acres by North and South Division streets, since Mr. Ellicott would have left a splendid building for the display of the fine arts and a beautiful park in the midst of the city.   It is a curious circumstance that the site was again selected by the visionary and famous Rathbun for his proposed magnificent Chamber of Commerce.   Rathbun's dream, unlike Ellicott's, was destined to be fulfilled in part in 1884, when the commerce of the lakes and canal joined hands with the manufacturing and mercantile interests to erect, further down-town, the Merchants' Exchange.   The Buffalo Board of Trade, which sunk its identity in the Merchants' Exchange, was a corporation with a noble record.   To its unceasing energy and patriotism is due the promotion of many enterprises affecting deeply the commercial interests of the city and nation.

While no one would dare to advance a claim for Buffalo in the months of March and April, she has a thousand charms as a summer home.   With a turn of the faucet one may drink of or plunge in the cool waters of the upper lakes.   The fruit and vegetables on the breakfast table come fresh and crisp each morning from the market-gardens about the city.   The fish

IN THE CRÈCHE.

were caught before daylight from the depths of Niagara, and the beefsteak selected from the herds waiting transportation at the East Buffalo stock-yards, where larger moneyed transactions on a cash basis take place daily than in any other quarter of the city. The roses and the lilies which brighten the morning meal were plucked in the door-yard. If the resident be a man of some leisure and fond of horseflesh, he takes an early morning turn behind his flyer around the Driving Park, one of the best and fastest tracks in the country, and famous in trotting annals as the scene of Dexter's and Goldsmith Maid's best time. The yearly meet on these grounds the first week in August brings a crowd of horsemen and racers to the city. The Driving Park Association own an elegant club-house, in the old colonial style, from the verandas of which there is a fine view over the city to the lake and the river.

The old resident who has somewhat thrown off the cares of active business visits his office summer mornings to read his letters and give directions to his clerks, then steps aboard his steam-yacht with a party of friends. After a good haul of black bass on the river, he drops anchor at Falconwood to join his neighbors and their wives, or perhaps members of his own family, whom the club boat has brought down earlier in the day, at a six-o'clock dinner. The yachts are headed up-stream just at the twilight hour, when

the outlines of the Canada shore, across which tall poplar-trees throw their long shadows, are fading into indistinctness, and make their dock at the famous Fort Erie Ferry, where coaches are waiting to take the summer idlers home by way of the park boulevards.

This sketch of summer life would be incomplete without the suggestion that Lake Erie's zephyrs have so tempered the heated midsummer atmosphere that a blanket tends to promote the luxurious slumbers which follow the evening hours spent in the piazza with one's neighbors. The popularity of this form of pleasuring was voiced by the Buffalonian who said, "When I build, I shall build a veranda, with possibly a house attached."

Buffalo now ranks among the gayest and most hospitable cities in America. Her commercial growth has been traced. It would be no less interesting to note how this has reacted on private habits. Since her earliest years she has been a community of great friendliness and hospitality, of comparative simplicity in social forms, and of a singularly democratic spirit. While she is no exception to the rule that so soon as the business quarter of a town takes on the character of a metropolis, there is a tendency toward increasing decorum and stateliness in social life.

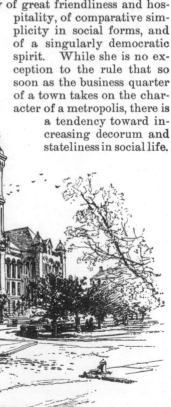

THE CITY HALL.

agreeableness and intelligence, not size of purse, are, as before she became a Mecca for capitalists, the standard of her representative families. Among the innumerable pleasant home centres of Buffalo

frontier. To Mr. Marshall's efforts was due largely the organization of the Buffalo Historical Society, which has done diligent and honorable service in collecting and preserving the records of early days.

LANDING AT FALCONWOOD.

is that of the Hon. James O. Putnam, lately United States Minister to Belgium. In his high public record, no less than in his liberal culture and exceptional social qualities, Mr. Putnam's fellow-townsmen take great pride.

Buffalo has much reason to honor the literary attainments of the late Orsamus H. Marshall, the historian of the Niagara

While several private individuals have reached what Mr. Howells terms "the picture-buying stage" of development, as a city Buffalo gives no encouragement to the fine arts. Founded in 1862, the Fine Arts Academy presents a curious example of arrested development, and of the stagnation usual to art enterprises in commercial centres. The most beautiful work

ON THE CANAL.

that adorns its gallery, "The Dead Pearl-Diver," by Paul Akers (owned by his heirs), was immortalized by Hawthorne in *The Marble Faun.*

The Academy owns over two hundred paintings, among them Phillipoteaux's brilliant panoramic picture of the French revolution of '48, an immense canvas, destined to be historic, containing over a hundred figures, remarkable for fine drawing. The interest of the Jewett Fund insures the purchase of a good picture every year or two, and many have been contributed by representative American artists. Mr. L. G. Sellstedt, the able superintendent, for years has given of his time unstintingly and hopefully for the future growth of art in Buffalo.

The Buffalo Club and the City Club are the largest as well as the representative men's clubs. The Buffalo Club, whose first president was Millard Fillmore, is the older and more exclusive organization, and is to that city what the Somerset Club

DELAWARE AVENUE.

is to Boston. It also upholds the city's reputation for hospitality to distinguished men, dividing the honor in this regard with Falconwood. Ordinarily it is considered the whist centre of the town.

The City Club, for some years the only business men's exchange, numbers over three hundred members, and is an outgrowth of the newer commercial interests. It is the down-town lunching centre. While womankind is discussing the characters of the latest magazine serial, or her newest possessions in pottery and porcelain, over candle-lighted luncheon tables up-town, coal, lumber, oil, grain, and the latest railroad grant, as well as Blackstone and Chitty, furnish the divers topics of the City Club.

Buffalo is remarkable for the number of her fine amateur pianistes, and for the many musical organizations which she sustains—a development due in part to the predominance of the Teutonic element. A year ago the Philharmonic Society, a string orchestra, was started, with a subscription of $14,000. The oldest German musical organization, and one of the oldest in the country, is the Liedertafel.

In 1886, the semi-centennial year of the Young Men's Association, its new library building, designed by Cyrus L. W. Eidlitz, and intended as a home not only for the Young Men's Association Library, but for the Grosvenor (a free reference library), the Historical Society, and the Fine Arts Academy, will be finished, at a cost of nearly $300,000. As the custodian of the chief public library, and promoter of many liberal projects, the Young Men's Association has for nearly half a century been foremost in furthering the literary culture of Buffalo. In its long line of presidents are numbered the most honored names of the city. The new library building is directly in the rear of Lafayette Square. Already crowned by the Soldiers' and Sailors' Monument, with the noble façade and towers of the Young Men's Association in the background, its graceful Norman arches adorned with busts of men eminent in *belles-lettres*, art, science, and music, this square in the heart of the city will do equal honor to Buffalo and to the distinguished name it bears.

Considering that Buffalo ranks as the third city of the State, with over two hundred thousand inhabitants, and talks of numbering half a million when she rounds the century, she has little as yet to be proud of in public buildings. In the imposing Venetian-looking square occupied by the City and County Hall, and in the fair proportions of a few of the newer structures, there is, however, much hope for the future, architecturally speaking.

Old Franklin Square, the first village burying-ground, now occupied by the City and County Hall, is a historic site. In its woods Colonel Cyrenius Chapin reluctantly surrendered the village to the British and their Indian allies December 30, 1813, on condition that they would respect the rights of private property—a condition which they failed to fulfill; for there is no darker chapter in the war of 1812 on this frontier than the burning of the village of Buffalo. To-day the site is interesting to the nation as the scene where its President began his public career. The City Hall extends longitudinally north and south in the form of a double Roman cross, with its main façade in Franklin Street. Opposite its Delaware Avenue front, and connected with it by an under-ground passage, is the jail—a massive limestone structure. The City Hall is surrounded by a terraced lawn bordered by granite copings, and broken here and there by brilliant floral parterres. Clark's Island, Maine, furnished the clear gray granite which in a rough form composes the first story, and in finished blocks completes the two upper stories. From the observatory in the tower, the four corners of which are surmounted by colossal statues of Justice, Mechanic Arts, Agriculture, and Commerce, one of the finest views of the city is obtainable.

Inside the building, which cost less than a million and a half, and was built "without a steal," all the municipal and county business is transacted. To its granite hitching-post the farmer from Willink, Eden, or Wales, dismounting from his rickety straw-stuffed wagon, ties old rawbones, and helping his wife down off her high perch, joins the crowd of lawyers, judges, jurymen, city and county officials, that pours in and out of the building all day long in an unceasing stream. The Surrogate's Court, whither perhaps the old couple wend their way, was the scene of the trial of the famous Fillmore will case, wherein the descendants of the historic American families Jay and Clinton were engaged as opposing counsel.

The Mayor's office now has a peculiar fascination for ambitious country boys, who approach reverentially the portals of the spacious presence-chamber wherein only three years ago President Cleveland transacted his official duties, furnishing the office with a pattern which tax-payers of whatever political affinities demand shall be copied by his successors.

Although in church architecture Buffalo is behind the times, St. Paul's Protestant Episcopal Church, a perfect specimen of Early English Gothic, is the noteworthy exception, being the most beautiful church edifice in Western New York. St. Joseph's Roman Catholic Cathedral contains the celebrated Hook organ from the Centennial Exposition, as well as the finest set of chimes in the country, from the Paris Exposition of 1867, where they took the first prize.

About the site of St. Paul's, the mother parish of Buffalo, and but a stone's-throw from the city buildings, there lingers one of the strangest and most picturesque traditions of Western New York. What could be more romantic or more incongruous than to lay in the chancel of a Protestant Episcopal Church the corner-stone of a Hebrew city within whose precincts it was intended to gather together all the lost tribes of Israel?

The year 1825 is most memorable in the early history of Buffalo. Then occurred the hanging of the three Thayers for the murder of John Love, much celebrated in song and story; then also the reception of General Lafayette at the Eagle Tavern. That year pedagogue Millard Fillmore, who boarded around among the families of his pupils, began to be considered a rising young man; some of the wiseacres thought he might come to be a justice of the peace; others, more sanguine, did not think the Assembly Chamber at Albany beyond the reach of his ambition.

On the 26th of October, 1825, was celebrated the opening of the Erie Canal. About a month before, when the community, eagerly anticipating a connection with tide-water, was excited with visions of prospective greatness, and ready for any display, there arrived from New York Major Manuel Mordecai Noah, high sheriff of the county of New York, consul at Tunis, and self-styled Judge of Israel. He came with glittering robes and insignia of office, to establish the city of Ararat on Grand Island, then covered with a dense forest. Although a loyal and devoted son of Abraham, Major Noah had not succeeded in arousing enthusiasm in his scheme among those of his own faith. As a shrewd man of the world, an able lawyer, a successful politician, and the editor of the principal organ of the Tammany party in New York, and withal sanguine that the city would prove a mine of wealth to its founders, he had no difficulty in persuading some of his Gentile friends, among whom was the father of the late Gerritt Smith, to buy nearly the whole of Grand Island, then just surveyed and offered for sale by the United States government.

On this lonely but extensive island, between the forks of the Niagara, and lying midway between Lake Erie and the Falls of Niagara, he determined to build a city of Oriental splendor. Already, before his arrival on the scene, a flag-staff bearing the "grand standard of Israel" had been erected on the chosen site, and a stone having an inscription in Hebrew and in English

THE STATE INSANE ASYLUM.

THE MARKET.

had been prepared to dedicate with imposing ceremonies. This stone, always known in local history as "Mordecai's corner-stone," was intended rather as a memento of the founding of the magnificent city of the Jews than as the support of any particular building. In those days the luxurious steam-yachts of wealthy citizens, which now plough the rapid current of the Niagara, existed not in the imagination of the veriest dreamer; even row-boats were wanting with which to convey the crowd eager to behold the spectacle presented by the birth of an Oriental city in the depths of the forest. The brilliant and audacious Noah conceived the idea of having the ceremony celebrated with due pomp within the walls of St. Paul's Church, twelve miles from the site of his city. To this end were invoked the willing services of all the dignitaries of the town, the military and the Masons, Major Noah the central figure appearing as the "Judge of Israel" in black, wearing judicial robes of crimson silk, trimmed with ermine, and a richly embossed golden medal suspended from his neck.

The bright September day opened with the booming of cannons. The grand procession embraced the best that the town could offer. Halting at the church door, the troops opened each way, and the pageant entered; while the band played the grand march from *Judas Maccabeus*, the corner-stone of Ararat, the city of refuge for the people who rejected Christ, was laid on the communion table of a Protestant Episcopal church, and dedicated by Hebrew ritual. The Masonic rites were performed with the typical corn, wine, and oil, the choir sang "Old Hundred," and the rector, in full canonicals, pronounced a Christian benediction.

Mordecai Noah never saw the site of Ararat, and the Hebrew race disregarded his grandiloquent proclamation and the tax levied for its building; but its corner-stone, after many curious migrations, occupies a conspicuous place in the rooms of the Buffalo Historical Society, where relic-hunters are frequently seen copying its inscription.

The old church in which these ceremonies took place has yielded to the present beautiful stone edifice of Early English Gothic architecture crowned by a graceful spire. This, with the "Old First" (Presbyterian), gives the neighborhood the name of "The Churches." They stand opposite the square originally intended for Joseph Ellicott's Capitol.

Unique as is the story associated with Grand Island's past, in its private clubs of to-day, Falconwood, Oakfield, and Beaver Island, which crown its western bluff with beautiful villas facing the Canada shore, their lawns sloping trim-shaven to the river, Buffalonians and their hosts of mid-summer guests find still greater fascination. Contiguous to Falconwood, cradled by the Niagara, in itself, says N. P. Willis, "the best cradle nature could possibly form for the family of a luxurious exclusive," the "father of the greenback," the Hon. Elbridge Gerry Spaulding, spends his summers. Connected with his country-seat, "River Lawn," is a large stock-farm, famous for its thorough-bred cattle.

Adjacent to this is the farm of the Hon. Lewis F. Allen, the venerable historian of Grand Island, uncle by marriage of President Cleveland, and the pioneer stock-raiser of this region. To a few Buffalo capitalists Erie County owes largely the rapid advance of its important stock interests. Within the city limits, and adjoining the park, is a stock-farm having a herd of short-horned cattle which in numbers and pedigree are not excelled in this country or in England, where its owner employs special agents. But the already famous stock-farms of Erie County are far too numerous for even cursory mention.

Covering territory of about thirty-nine miles, an area greater than is occupied by any municipality in the United States except Philadelphia, the freeholders of Buffalo far outnumber those of any other city. So great a proportion of the laboring class of the population owning their homes gives an air of unusual thrift to the foreign quarter—a vast, closely built tract lying east of Main Street. When, on the occasion of a brief stay in Buffalo, Herbert Spencer was by his own request driven through the thickly settled wards of "Germantown," he remarked particularly upon the hundreds of one and two story cottages which line these streets, and are almost universally in good condition as to paint and window-blinds, and with every inch of the little plot of surrounding land cultivated with vegetables or flowers.

To the early influence of one man, the late Stephen Van Rensselaer Watson, a citizen whose far-seeing genius for practical affairs gave Buffalo her present comprehensive system of street railroads, is due much of the independent comfort now enjoyed by the foreign element of her population. Coming to the city in 1844, he invested largely in uncleared land on the east side. This he divided, and sold out in lots on long payments, principally to Germans, whom he aided not only with money, but with sagacious advice.

It is a significant fact that the first civilized man to settle on the present site of Buffalo was a German. Of few Northern cities can it be affirmed, as of this, that the Teutonic element constitutes nearly one-half the entire population. The Germans of Buffalo have their own press, literary and musical associations, churches, theatres, and, it is unnecessary to add, beer gardens, while in public spirit they have in one notable instance shown themselves

DINING IN THE CRÈCHE.

ahead of the Americans. Not only are German names frequent on the business signs of the American quarter, but the Germans have their own long business street running diagonally out through "Germantown," and the German population has been represented frequently in city, county, and State offices.

Artists in search of models and authors making character studies will find few fields richer in local color than the German quarter of Buffalo and her two large markets. These markets are distinctive, and help to make living cheap. Each market occupies a block, and at the stalls everything, from crockery, yarn, buttons, and shining tins, to the finest cuts of beef, poultry, fish, and green truck of all kinds, is exposed for sale. In midsummer they are the market-places of flowers. Pretty young girls in fresh muslins tie their pony-carts outside, and come tripping in among the stalls to cull out bunches of mignonette, sweet-peas, and pansies, jostling against baby wagons, match venders, long-aproned butchers, white-capped Vienna roll men, and German fraus with a generous bulk of waist and shoulders.

Ever since the days when Christy's Minstrels, which originated in Buffalo, merrily sang,

"Oh, Buffalo girls, are you coming out to-night,
  Are you coming out to-night,
  To dance by the light of the moon?"

the belles of the city have been renowned in two continents. While the ever-increasing social obligations of a gay city life require them to be out at night more than ever, the strict regard for etiquette which now prevails in the rarefied atmosphere of Buffalo society decrees that they shall be accompanied by their chaperons. Of a city that is neither Eastern nor Western, it is natural that the best type of Buffalo womanhood should blend in her personality the salient characteristics of the women of each section of the country; in other words, she has the individuality which is inevitable from her environment. To the mental alertness of the New-Englander she superadds the fearless originality of the belle of the prairie, but without her aggressiveness or tendency to crudeness.

A vital concern for poor and suffering humanity is not characteristic of Buffalo women only, but there are few cities the philanthropic institutions of which are

managed so generally by women, and who in their very positive relations toward the charities of Buffalo are, as has been remarked, "the salt of the city."

In 1832 an ambitious young merchant, Benjamin Fitch, settled in Buffalo, where he made a fortune. His subsequent benefactions to the city, amounting in all to about $300,000, entitle him to a name among the great philanthropists of America. Just fifty years after his coming the corner-stone of the Fitch Institute was laid, at which ceremony Mayor Cleveland spoke eloquently of Mr. Fitch's generosity. The old man answered, in simple phrase, "I have done but my duty."

Under the French and Gothic roof of the Fitch Institute, on the corner of Swan and Michigan streets, erected at a cost of over $60,000, there are many and divers philanthropic interests, and its illuminated clock tower is a beacon-light for the working people who pass up and down the crowded thoroughfare. Both the Fitch Institute and the Crèche are managed by the Charity Organization Society, the oldest of the associated charity systems of this country. Buffalo adopted the London method of organized charities in 1877. The Charity Organization Society, officered by the younger professional and business men chiefly, has been indirectly the source of inspiration for many of the newer movements by which Buffalo has striven to cast off her slough of conservatism.

Think of having to take care of twenty thousand babies! This is what the Fitch Crèche has done since 1879. This great public cradle is the most interesting charity in Buffalo, because the most unique. Founded on the model of the London Day Nursery to care for little children whose mothers earn their support as char-women, it has so far outstripped its progenitor as to be called the model crèche of the world.

Delaware Avenue, which "takes its rise in a jail and ends in a tomb," as a wag, sneering at its aristocratic pretensions, said, is shaded its full length of three miles with double rows of elms and maples, which arch overhead. Its beautiful houses and villas standing alone, amid broad lawns, and embowered in vines, give the long avenue the elegantly rural aspect of a suburban rather than a city street. In summer, masses of shade trees, and foliage wreathing itself over side walls and porticoes, serve to soften or conceal the architectural incongruities of some of the older

LAKE IN THE PARK.

and too elaborate houses. Its reputation as one of the finest of residence streets is likely to grow, rather than diminish, with the city. For when completed on the plan of the original survey, Buffalo Street at Niagara Falls Village and Delaware Avenue will be one long highway, and the most beautiful avenue in America. Then the City Hall of Buffalo and the proposed International Park at Niagara Falls will be connected by the same boulevard. The aspiring Buffalonian goes farther, and predicts that there will be one day a river boulevard from Buffalo to Youngstown, from Lake Erie to Lake Ontario.

Perhaps it is to offset a pardonable conceit over this nearness to the greatest of nature's wonders that Buffalo's immediate suburbs are so strictly commonplace. The city sprawls out in a north and easterly direction over an area as flat as the proverbial pancake. He who tries to drive out into the country is held fast in a net-work of railway tracks. To beautify the city within its limits by creating a continuous circle of driveways was a necessity which gave birth, in 1869, to the park system, comprising over eight hundred acres of pleasure-grounds connected by boulevards, which together afford a drive of over ten miles.

Watching the gay and interminable procession of coaches, landaus, dog-carts, and English phaetons, with their liveried grooms, passing over the asphalt or macadamized park roads in midsummer, one has to rub one's eyes to believe that the first family carriage ever seen in Erie County, owned and driven by Samuel Pratt, rolled into Buffalo only eighty years ago. There are three large parks, the Park proper, about three miles north of the City Hall, the Parade, which is in the precincts of "Germantown," and the Front, on the banks of the Niagara. On the broad and undulating Park meadow the polo club play many of their best games, and horseback parties make this their favorite rallying point. Beneath this smooth-clipped turf, guarded by two monarchs of the forest, lie, unknowing and unknown, three hundred soldier dead, regulars of the United States army, the victims of typhoid fever in the winter of 1812. Haunted in midsummer, not by shades of these departed patriots, but by thousands of picnic parties, many of which come from the lower and more crowded parts of the city to get a breath of pure country air, the Park not alone conduces to beautify, but subserves a nobler end as a health-giving outlet and a provider of refreshing recreation at little cost.

Adjacent, sloping down to " Gala Water," freighted with gondolas, canoes, and row-boats, is the white encampment of Forest Lawn, wrapped in a silence broken only by the light tread of the squirrel or chipmunk running boldly up the side of one of the ancient oaks that abound in the well-wooded cemetery.

Among the distinguished dead who rest in Forest Lawn is the late General Albert J. Myer, whose widow is the daughter of Ebenezer Walden, the first lawyer in Erie County, and its first judge. The family mausoleum, overlooking the Park lake, is close by the Pratt Monument, also commemorative of a family prominent among the earliest settlers of Buffalo.

On that panel of the square of granite over the grave of Samuel Wilkeson which faces the harbor is chiselled:

"Urbem condidit. He built the city by building its harbor."

To tell how Buffalo and Black Rock were arrayed against each other as hostile camps in battle, each striving to be the terminus of the Erie Canal, is but to repeat an oft-rehearsed story. Buffalo, through the agency of a few resolute men, with Samuel Wilkeson at their head—who waded Buffalo Creek, and labored with the diggers on the sand bar—having succeeded in scooping out a harbor, argued with success the case against Black Rock.

In her new-found allegiance to the railway king, Buffalo does not forget her foster-mother. As a free highway the Erie Canal holds the balance of power. It regulates the transportation rates by rail, and preserves the supremacy of the great State of New York as the chief thoroughfare of commerce—a supremacy which the railways could not maintain unaided. The statistics of the past year show that the canal did as well as its rivals by rail or water, and has by no means, as has been intimated, survived its usefulness.

In the name of the rivulet which flows through Forest Lawn, Scajaquada Creek, is a reminder of the aboriginal owners of these lawns and woodlands. Another will soon be there, for under the auspices of the Historical Society is now rising a monument whose apex will be surmounted by a bronze statue of Red Jacket. This monument marks the resting-place of the recently re-interred bones of Sa-go-ye-wa-tha, the Rienzi of the Iroquois, and other distinguished chiefs of the Six Nations.

All through the earlier history of Buffalo the aboriginal lion, Red Jacket, stalks a picturesque figure. Realizing that it was the precursor of the extinction of his nation, Red Jacket was jealous of the encroachments of the white people. Naturally, therefore, although always courteous, he felt unfriendly toward Mr. Ellicott. One day the two met in the Tonawanda Swamp, and sat down together on a log. After a few moments of silence, which Mr. Ellicott knew too much of Indian custom to interrupt, Red Jacket exclaimed, "Move along, Joe." The request was complied with. After a few moments it was repeated. Red Jacket gave the peremptory order several times, until by degrees Mr. Ellicott had moved to the extreme verge of the log. Again came the mandate, "Joe, move along." "But there is no room left," was the answer. "That," cried Red Jacket, "is the way the white man treats us. He first says move along a little, then a little more. When we have moved as far as we can, he shoves us out of the world."

The Tonawanda Swamp, wherein this dialogue was held some seventy years ago, is now covered with the lumber-yards of Buffalo capitalists, for Tonawanda, the great lumber port of the Western lake territory, and Buffalo, are one lumber market to-day, with identical interests. The descendants of Red Jacket, former owners of the soil, are relegated to the Cattaraugus and Alleghany reservations, or have been "shoved" as far west on their way toward the end of the log as the distant reservations of Kansas.

Buffalo has become one of the cosmopolitan cities of the country. Germans, French, English, Italians, Swedes, Poles, Japs, Turks, and Arabs jostle each other in the crowded thoroughfares, and buy and sell in the markets. She has had her saengerfests, her great musical festivals, innumerable conventions, political, scientific, and literary, and has given the United States two Presidents and two cabinet officers.

Saratoga Springs (1876)

BROADWAY, FROM CONGRESS PARK, SARATOGA.

THE first white man who (so far as is known) visited Saratoga Springs was Sir William Johnson, Bart. Sir William, under a commission of major-general from George II., defeated the French army under Baron Dieskau at the battle of Lake George, on the 8th of September, 1755. In this action he received a wound from which he never recovered, and was frequently subject to serious illness. It was during one of these attacks that the Mohawks revealed to their "beloved brother," War - ra - ghi - ya - ghy (Johnson), the medicinal properties of the "High Rock Spring." Nor, perhaps, could there have been a stronger proof of the affection in which he was held by the Indians than this act of giving to him the benefits of that which they had always sacredly guarded as a precious gift to themselves from the Great Spirit. Accompanied by his Indian guides, the baronet, on the 22d of August, 1767, being too feeble to walk, was placed on a litter and borne on the shoulders of his faithful Mohawks through the woods to the spring. Here he remained in a rude bark lodge for four days, by which time he was so much benefited as to be able to return to Johnstown, part of the way on foot.

The popularity of Saratoga Springs as a watering-place may be said to date from this visit. "My dear Schuyler," writes the baronet to his intimate friend General Philip Schuyler, "I have just returned from a

129

visit to a most amazing spring, which almost effected my cure; and I have sent for Dr. Stringer, of New York, to come up and analyze it." Hence it was that the fact of so distinguished a personage as Sir William having been partially restored by the water soon became noised through the country, inducing others to make the trial. In 1770 a Dr. Constable, who resided at Schenectady, examined the water at Saratoga and pronounced it highly medicinal. In October, 1777, Major-General Mooers, of Plattsburg, who was stationed after Burgoyne's surrender in the vicinity, visited the spring; and in 1783 Dr. Samuel Tenney, a regimental surgeon in camp at Fish Creek, also paid a visit to the spring, and made some judi-

uated in a marsh. There is no convenience for bathing except an open log-hut, with a large trough, similar to those in use for feeding swine, which receives the water from the spring. Into this you roll from off a bench."

In 1783 General Washington, accompanied by his aids, Alexander Hamilton, George Clinton, and Colonels Humphreys and Fish, visited the High Rock on their return from an inspection of the northern forts, their attention having been directed to it by General Schuyler while guests at the latter's house at Schuylerville. On their return route through the woods, when near the present village of Ballston, they lost their way. Near the bridle-path lived one

SIR WILLIAM JOHNSON'S VISIT IN 1767.

cious remarks on its uses as a medicine. In the summer of the same year General Schuyler cut a road through the forest from Schuylerville to the High Rock, and erected a tent, under which his family spent several weeks, using the water. For many years after its discovery the High Rock continued to be the resort of people from all sections of the country; and when other springs were found in the neighboring village of Ballston, in 1770, the chief drive of the visitors there was through the woods to the "High Rock." The accommodations, however, for a long time were of the most primitive character. "These waters," writes Elkanah Watson, in visiting the High Rock in 1790, "are sit-

"Tom" Conner, who was chopping wood at his cabin door. They inquired the way, and Tom gave the requisite directions. The party accordingly retraced their steps a short distance, but, becoming bewildered, rode back for more explicit directions. Tom had by this time lost his temper, and peevishly cried out to the spokesman of the party, who happened to be Washington, "I tell you, turn back and take the first right-hand path, and then stick to it: any darned fool would know the way." When poor Tom learned whom he had thus addressed, he was greatly chagrined. His neighbors for a long time tormented him on his "reception of General Washington."

The next year, 1784, another distinguished person visited the High Rock, brought there by the advice of Washington, viz., Colonel Otho H. Williams; and in 1790 the mother of the late Hon. Theodore Dwight also visited the spring, coming from Hartford on horseback. On reaching the spring, Mrs. Dwight found but three habitations, and those but poor log-houses on the high bank of a meadow. The log-cabins were full of visitors, and she found it almost impossible to obtain accommodations even for two nights.

Among the visitors to the High Rock in the spring succeeding Mrs. Dwight's visit were a Congressman (John Taylor Gilman) and an aged gentleman, his friend and fellow-traveler. One day, as the former, accompanied by a young son of the woodsman with whom they were stopping, was returning from a hunt along a foot-path leading to the cabin, the aged gentleman meanwhile sitting on the door-step awaiting their coming, the boy, highly elated, ran forward, exclaiming, "Oh, mother, we've found a new spring!" To the question, "Who found it?" the son replied, "The Congress." The aged gentleman then said, laughingly, to Mr. Gilman, who had now come up, "The spring shall always be called the 'Congress.'" Thereupon the entire household "turned out" and went down to see the wonderful discovery. At this peri-

od it was necessary to climb over logs waist high to gain access to the new spring, the water issuing from a fissure in the rock, and being conducted to the glass through a wooden spout fastened into the crevice. The village now rapidly increased; new springs were discovered; a large frame house was built in 1802 by Gideon Putnam on the site of the present Grand Union, having for its sign a quaint representation of the adventure of "Putnam and the Wolf," and thenceforth the "Springs" became the resort of those who were in pursuit of health and pleasure.

The fountains of Saratoga will ever be the resort of wealth, intelligence, and fashion. As a political observatory no place can be more fitly selected. Gentlemen are continually coming from and going to every section of the country; information from all quarters is received daily; and it is the best of all places for politicians to congregate. The great "combination" of opposite parties and opposing interests, by which General Jackson, Mr. Eaton, and Mr. Van Buren were brought into power, and John Quincy Adams turned out, was chiefly formed here; and it was here that the old Clintonians were sold out to "Jackson and Co." Saratoga, too, for a series of years, was the head-quarters of the "Albany Regency," under the leadership of Edwin Croswell and John Cramer—a combination which has

CONGRESS SPRING, SARATOGA, IN 1816.

never been equaled in its influence over the political destinies of New York State, and, through it, upon the nation.

During three-quarters of a century Saratoga has entertained more persons distinguished in letters, human and divine, than any other place of the kind. Time would fail to mention in detail the reception of the "Great Magician," who, in the autumn of 1832, like the hero of a German melodrama, came clothed in a storm; the arrival of Senator Douglas, amidst the thundering of cannon, in the summer of 1860; the great Whig gathering during the Harrison campaign in 1840, and the speech of Daniel Webster on that occasion to an audience of fifteen thousand; the tributes paid to Scott, Madison, Clinton, Clay, Calhoun, Tyler, Fill-

UNITED STATES HOTEL.

more and Seward, and Sir Allan M'Nab; or to descant upon the genial Irving, who for many seasons occupied a cottage at the "United States," or the individual traits of Wayland, Fuller, Murray (Kirwan), Cheever, Kent, and a host of others equally distinguished. All that may be done is to photograph a few characters as they flit across the camera of memory.

In 1825 Joseph Bonaparte, the ex-King of Spain, who with a numerous retinue was stopping at the "United States," was present at a dinner party given in his honor by Mr. Henry Walton. He was accompanied by his sister, Caroline Murat, and his two daughters. Though a king, he looked very much like other mortals. His manners, dress, and equipage were wholly unassuming, quiet, and unpretentious, as was the case with the ladies of his family. The rank was there, and needed no demonstration. In the course of the dinner, Bonaparte suddenly turned deadly pale, and, with the perspiration standing on his forehead, turned imploringly to his host, gasping out, "*Un chat! un chat!*"

"John," said Mr. Walton to his waiter, "take away the cat; it disturbs this gentleman."

"Cat, Sir?" echoed John; "I can see no cat!"

The other members of the family now joined in the search; and at last, sure enough, crouched under the sideboard was discovered a little frightened kit-

FAC-SIMILE OF PUTNAM'S SIGN, STILL IN EXISTENCE.

ten. But it was not until Bonaparte had lain down for some hours that he recovered from the prostration into which the presence of the feline had thrown him.

The dinner was followed in the evening by a brilliant party. Among other literary gentlemen present were Theodore S. Fay, Percival, Paulding, Irving, Verplanck, and Joseph R. Chandler. M'Donald Clarke, the "mad poet," was also among the guests. Clarke did not remain long, nor did he circulate among the company. Most of the time he stood by the door, his pose and style the familiar attitude of the classic Napoleon, with arms folded. His head rested not upon his breast, but his eyes looked up to the ceiling, while on one foot was a jack-boot, and on the other a large clumsy shoe. After he had left, Colonel Stone related to the company the history of the stanza by Clarke that had lately appeared in the Commercial. It seems that Lang, in his New York Gazette, had alluded to "M'Donald Clarke, that fellow with zigzag brains." The insulted poet rushed into the sanctum of the Commercial, blazing with fury.

"Do you see, colonel," said he, "what Johnny Lang says of me? He calls me a fellow with zigzag brains."

"Well, and so you are," said the colonel. "I think it is a very happy description of you."

"Oh! that's very well for you to say," retorted M'Donald. "I'll take a joke from you; but Johnny Lang shall not destroy my well-earned reputation. Zigzag brains, forsooth! Zigzag brains—think of it, colonel! I must have a chance to reply to him in your paper."

"How much space would you want?" inquired the colonel.

"I think I could use him up in a column and a half," said M'Donald.

"A column and a half!" said the colonel. "Stuff! You shall have no such space. I'll give you just four lines; and if

THE "MAD POET."

that will answer, fire away; but not one line more."

The poet, thus driven into a corner, instantly wrote off the following neat epigram:

"I can tell Johnny Lang, in the way of a laugh,
  In reply to his rude and unmannerly scrawl,
That, in my humble sense, it is better by half
  To have brains that are zigzag than no brains at
    all."

"There, colonel," said he, "let Johnny Lang put that in his pipe and smoke it."

In August, 1828, Judge Cowen gave a farewell reception to James Fenimore Cooper, who was to sail in a few days for Europe. From the diary of a gentleman who was

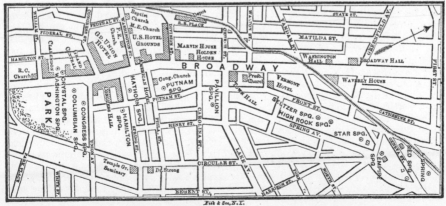

MAP OF SARATOGA, SHOWING LOCATION OF THE PRINCIPAL SPRINGS.

HATHORN SPRING.

present I quote the following reflections brought out by seeing Cooper at this time: "To Mr. Cooper the loss of his property has probably been of more real advantage than the money ten times over would have been. It has called forth the slumbering energies of his mind, and given vigor and richness to his imagination, by the exertion of which he has acquired a proud name among the distinguished writers of his country."

Saratoga has also been the residence of many distinguished lawyers, men who have adorned the bench by their individual and professional worth. Indeed, during one period of its existence the village was the centre of a galaxy of legal minds that cast a halo around whatever came within the circle of its influence. The names of Walworth and Willard, Cowen and Hill, Lester and Barbour, will occur to the reader, while the names of others now living in Saratoga, and also eminent in their profession, show that the mantles of the departed have fallen upon worthy successors.

On the corner of Broadway and Vandam Street yet stands the old homestead of the Walworth family, embosomed in a grove of stately pines. These trees are all that remain of a large wood formerly used as a public ground, and a favorite resort for guests and villagers. Swings hung down between the tall pines, which in fair weather were in almost constant motion. Here the

Indians encamped, sold their bows, canes, and baskets, and shot at pennies to show their skill; and here, too, the militia met for drill, armed with umbrellas and broomsticks, or, in default of those articles, with corn stalks.

Pine Grove was for a long period of years a much-frequented place. Few residences have seen more of the great celebrities of the country, especially of her distinguished jurists and statesmen. It has known Daniel D. Tompkins, De Witt Clinton, Martin Van Buren, Enos T. Throop, Silas Wright, Churchill C. Cambreling, William L. Marcy, Francis Granger, Stephen A. Douglas, Millard Fillmore, James Buchanan, Chancellor Kent, Judge Story, Judge Grier, Washington Irving, James Fenimore Cooper, William L. Stone, Catharine Sedgwick, Mrs. Sigourney, Gerrit Smith, Generals Scott, Wool, and Worth, Gottschalk the pianist, and a host of others—Governors, Senators, and Congressmen, celebrated authors and soldiers, who have chatted in its parlors, dined at its table, and walked about under the shade of its pines. Chancellor Walworth never forgot an acquaintance. Every morning during the summer season he looked carefully over the list of arrivals, and hastened to call on those he knew. The "Grove" has known the portly form of Joseph Bonaparte in tights, and the squat figure of Mar Yohannan, the Nestorian bishop, in multitudinous folds of cloth. Clergymen always found a welcome here, whatever their type of faith or form of worship. Its traditions array such names as Eliphalet Nott, Lyman Beecher, Drs. Sprague and Bethune, Francis Wayland, Archbishops Hughes, M'Closkey, Purcell, Kenrick, and Spalding, Cardinal Bedini, and Bishop Alonzo Potter. Methodist bishops have visited there, and at a very

bers of the bar, who, by going there instead of to Albany, were able to combine a little business with a trip to the Springs. A wood-box being covered with a carpet, an arm-chair was placed upon it, and a long-legged desk before it, and the little office was thus converted into a court-room. Here for many years distinguished counsel came to make, defend, and argue motions in chancery. Hither came Ambrose Spencer, Chief Justice of New York, John C. Spencer, Joshua Spencer, Charles O'Conor, Samuel Stevens, Mark Reynolds, Elisha Williams, Benjamin F. Butler of New York, Daniel Lord, William H. Seward, David Graham, and many other men of equal mark, though of a later generation. Here once William Kent and George

PINE GROVE—THE RESIDENCE OF THE LATE CHANCELLOR WALWORTH.

early date a Catholic bishop from Canada, in quaint knee-breeches and large buckled shoes, whose zeal in the cause of temperance brought him in connection with the chancellor. Thither also came at various times innumerable missionaries from foreign parts, and occasionally a russet-coated elder from the Shaker settlements.

The front-room in the north wing was the chancellor's office for forty-three years. Any one passing the house might see him hard at work throughout the day, and his lamp was burning there still until two, three, and often four o'clock in the morning. In this same office the chancellor held his "motion courts." This was not only a convenience to himself, but generally agreeable to the mem-

Griffin were pitted against Daniel Webster in a case involving the Illinois State bonds, which crowded the room, piazza, and sidewalk with anxious listeners, until, out of consideration for these, the chancellor adjourned to the Universalist church. "This cause does not end here," said Griffin, in a tragic tone of voice; "we shall meet again at Philippi." "Ay," replied Webster, with a grim humor that convulsed the audience, "the learned counsel will meet us again at Philippi; but will they pay us when we get there?"

At "Pine Grove" the celebrated "spike case" dragged its "slow length along" for many years, in which nearly all our great lawyers had a finger. It was a reference

CHANCELLOR WALWORTH.

referee was to ascertain the increased profits of a party of manufacturers so rapping as aforesaid, and the consequent damages to the other party having the exclusive right so to rap as aforesaid. Mrs. Walworth once, in conversation with Governor Seward, said, "I wish you would explain what this everlasting spike suit is about; I don't understand it." "Indeed, madam," he replied, "I should be very much ashamed if you did. I have been engaged in it for several years, and I don't understand it yet."

Chancellor Walworth had certain peculiarities while presiding in court which were well known to the lawyers who frequented the little forum at the Grove. In endeavoring to master the points of a case he had a method of his own, and it was necessary for counsel to conform to it in their arguments. Those who frequented his court soon learned to humor him in this respect, but strangers were often annoyed by his interruptions and contradictions. He required not only the names of the parties and the general nature of the motion, but the peculiar character of each one's interest clearly stated, before he would listen to any argument or to any rhetorical preambles. A noted lawyer of Brooklyn once, after reading his affidavits, was endeavoring to enter upon his argument in support of his motion. But the chancellor was not satisfied. "I think," he said, "that Widow Van Bummel ought to be heard from in this matter." "Indeed, your honor," replied the counsel, "I do not see how the

case, which the chancellor undertook after the abolition of his office. The original suit was brought in the United States Court for the infringement of a right to give a peculiar rap to the head of a spike in the process of formation, and the question before the

INDIAN CAMP, PINE GROVE.

COWEN'S STONE OFFICE.

widow Van Bummel can have any possible interest in the motion." He endeavored to proceed, but was soon interrupted again : " I should like to know what the widow Van Bummel has to say." After a hard contest for liberty to proceed, despairing at last of success, the counsel began tying up his papers, and said, testily, " Well, your honor, I will hunt up this widow Van Bummel, and see if she has any thing to say; and if there is any other old woman in the United States or elsewhere that your honor would like to see, I will bring her into court."

Another old landmark yet standing is the " Stone Office," built by Esek Cowen in 1812, and in which were written *Cowen's Evidence* and the *Notes on Phillipp's Evidence*—works which are, perhaps, more extensively consulted than any other law-books extant. The latter of these represents a labor of eleven years, in the last three of which he was assisted by Nicholas Hill and William L. F. Warren. Here were written those learned opinions which illumined the Reports in the best days of our jurisprudence; and here, also, was written Judge Cowen's famous opinion in the celebrated " M'Leod case," in which were discussed the question of perfect and imperfect war and other great national principles, and which by its learning and ability attracted universal attention.

Judge Cowen was a man of untiring zeal in intellectual labors, with fixed habits of intense application; and while yet young he became a ripe and varied student, earn-

ing the reputation of being one of the most finished scholars as well as one of the most erudite judges of the nation. He devoted never less than fourteen hours a day to study, often protracting his labors far into the night. At such times he never consulted his watch, but used wax candles, starting with fresh ones every evening; when they had burned to the socket it forced him to bring his labors to a close. On one occasion he substituted for them a lamp, as requiring less attention in snuffing. The hours wore on, and the oil being unexhausted, daylight found him still at his labors. He made the trial a second night, but with no better success, and was obliged to return to his candles.

A little distance from the " Stone Office" stood, until within two years, the house in which those talented sisters Lucretia Maria and Margaret Miller Davidson lived and died. It was an old-fashioned wooden building, with gable ends and moss-grown porch, and surrounded by magnificent elms, whose branches, meeting over the roof, had intertwined and clasped hands as though desirous of protecting the occupants within. It was, in fact, the ideal home for a dreamy poetic nature.

The earliest of Lucretia's poems which are preserved were written at the age of nine years; and although a great portion of her compositions were destroyed, two hundred and seventy-eight yet remain. Margaret, sharing her elder sister's precocity, began to write when she was six. At ten she wrote and acted in a drama at New York; and notwithstanding her sister's fate, her intellectual activity was not restrained. So early, ardent, and fatal a pursuit is unparalleled, except in the cases of Chatterton and Kirke White. Catharine Sedgwick and Washington Irving were, when visiting Saratoga, loved and welcome guests of the Davidson family; and on the death of Margaret her poems were published under the auspices of the latter. The remains of both the sisters, together with those of their brother, the lieutenant, also a writer of elegant verse, lie in the cemetery of the village —a cemetery which, without the showiness of Greenwood, or the clustering memories of Mount Auburn, or even the picturesque-

making the toll one-twelfth, was Tom's idea of money; for when on a certain occasion he was asked to pay a bill of one dollar, he indignantly exclaimed, "A dollar I will not give, but I have no objection to pay ten shillings!"

The greatest and most historical occasion, however, in which Tom figured was in 1849, during one of the visits of Madame Jumel to the village. Madame Jumel, whose criminal intimacy with Aaron Burr had brought her into contempt (those were the days when free-love doctrines were estimated at their true value), was then staying at the "United States," and she endeavored by a magnificent equipage to dazzle the understanding, and thus atone for her

LUCRETIA MARIA DAVIDSON.　　　　　MARGARET MILLER DAVIDSON.

ness of Laurel Hill, still attracts by the quiet beauty of its surroundings.

It would be passing strange if Saratoga should not have known during its existence many curious characters. Of these none, perhaps, have excited more notice of a certain kind than a colored man who was known as "Tom Camel." This person was decidedly an original genius. Like Yorick, "a fellow of infinite jest," and withal of great shrewdness in some respects, he yet at times was in his simplicity a perfect specimen of the Southern negro. Like the wisdom of the Canadian miller, who sought to better the condition of his craft by declaring that the miller's toll (one-tenth) was too small, and therefore proposed a law

dismissal from the ranks of Diana. It was therefore determined to administer to her a lesson.

Accordingly, one afternoon, when her carriage, with a numerous retinue of outriders, drew up in front of the "United States" to take her to the lake, lo! just as she drove off, another equipage appeared directly following her. This carriage was driven by a villager in full livery, and behind, in a huge clothes-basket for a seat, sat another villager in footman's dress, while plainly visible within the open carriage, and dressed up in woman's clothes, sat Tom Camel, representing the former mistress of Aaron Burr. It was the custom of Madame Jumel, before going out of the town, to drive slowly through the main village street, that the rustic inhabitants might have a proper sense of their own insignificance; and before the trick was discovered, madame's carriage, followed by her counterfeit in "double," had paraded the entire length of the street, Tom Camel, meanwhile, fanning himself with a large fan, and bowing and courtesying to the crowds, which had now gathered on every side. Madame Jumel by turns threatened and pleaded and offered bribes. But Tom was inexorable; and the two equipages went to the lake and back in the same order.

CLARENDON HOUSE.

Owing to this exhibition, Madame Jumel made this her last visit to the Springs.

A striking feature of American scenery is the great number and beauty of its small fresh-water lakes. One of the most beautiful of these is Lake Saratoga, the best view of which is obtained from the top of Caldwell's Hill, on the eastern bank. There the scene which meets the eye is calm and beautiful rather than sublime. Nothing can surpass the gracefulness of the sweep of the hills which come down to the further shore, or the charm of the prospect which the scene presents of native forest and cultivated fields, in one part stretching up the hill-side, and in others spreading out into rich plains. At a distance of one mile from this stand-point the lake takes a turn to the right, and is merged in the Fishkill, through which

GRAND UNION HOTEL.

it enters the Hudson. The lake can be seen from nearly every point of the compass. From the Catskills on the south, from the Kayaderosseras Mountains on the west, and from the French Mountains at Lake George on the northwest, it is distinctly visible; while from the top of "Potash Kettle," near the Sacandaga River, Lake Saratoga, as well as the vicinity of the Indian Pass in the Adirondacks, may be plainly discerned.

The lake is about five miles in length, with an average width of one mile, it being the broadest opposite the promontory known as Snake Hill. This hill, which has of late years become so familiarly known as the starting-point of the intercollegiate regattas, has formed the frame-work of a Rev-

out of the box to show their docility. Not, perhaps, liking the familiarity of a tipsy keeper, one of them bit him in the hand, and his death ensued on the following day.

In the vicinity of Snake Hill there lived, a year or two since, a half-breed Indian of the St. Regis tribe, by name Pete Francis. To his little cottage it was the custom of epicures to make regular pilgrimages, for no one—so they all agreed—could cook a fish as delicately and serve it as temptingly as Pete. When Pete Francis cooked the Lake Saratoga bass, fresh from the cold translucent depths, whence he had lured them with a skill that none could equal, criticism became dumb, and the appetite enjoyed a feast that lingered long, like

INTERCOLLEGIATE REGATTA ON SARATOGA LAKE—SNAKE HILL IN THE DISTANCE.

olutionary romance from the pen of the late Daniel Shepherd, of Saratoga. The name was given to it by the early settlers in consequence of a formidable den of rattlesnakes that formerly existed half-way up its side. President Dwight, when visiting Saratoga in 1820, was informed that a few years previously there was a man living near Snake Hill who had the singular power and still stranger temerity to catch living rattlesnakes in his naked hands without wounding the snakes or being wounded by them. He used to accumulate them in great numbers for curiosity and sale. But one evening, arriving at the Springs with a pair of these amiable playthings, in a box, and having disregarded the principles of the temperance society, he heedlessly took them

the memory of some pleasant ecstasy. As Charles Lamb said of a canvas-back duck, the eating of one formed an era in a man's existence. Pete, like all great geniuses, was eccentric and peculiar. With strong likes and dislikes, he had a keen appreciation of character, and was a great favorite with his distinguished patrons, among whom he numbered Governors, judges, members of Congress, and hosts of connoisseurs of all degrees of prominence. For the most part, he was a quiet, good-natured soul, strolling about with a subdued aspect, an easy and deliberate gait, in a state of entire freedom from restraint, reflection, and want, and without any impulse strong enough to call forth his latent manhood, save—and with this solitary exception—when he had hooked a five-pound bass at the end of his line. Then, presto! what a change! His muscles would stiffen, his eyes sparkle, his nostrils dilate, and his whole frame fairly quiver with emotion. Pete was started in business some thirty years ago by the late Hon. James M. Cook; and though he was handsomely remunerated for his many years of unrivaled catering, yet, like Daniel Webster, he never

PETE FRANCIS.

knew what it was to be wealthy. No bass ever escaped his clutch when once it was hooked, but dollars somehow slipped through his fingers with marvelous celerity. Upon first coming into this region he was, when quite young, employed by that renowned French caterer and keeper of the old Sans Souci Hotel at Ballston, Andrew Berger, and by him taught to prepare fish in a manner in which, I believe, he has never been excelled.

Lake Saratoga was formerly quite noted for its remarkable fishing; and during the interregnum between the first and second battles of Bemis's Heights, when the British army were in want of food, the Indians were accustomed to supply General Burgoyne's table, with trout of a delicious flavor caught in its waters. Shad and herring also were in the habit, before the mills were erected at the junction of the Fishkill and the Hudson, of running up into the lake. Up to the year 1825 the lake was filled with trout; and even so late as 1832 the late Colonel William L. Stone, writing from the Springs to his paper, the New York *Commercial Advertiser*, states that a few of these fish were yet occasionally taken. But pickerel having been introduced into the lake in 1824, the trout very soon disappeared. The lake also has long been famous for its yellow perch (*Perca flavescens*).

But the glory of Lake Saratoga as a place for fine sport has, I am afraid, departed forever. The cause of this is to be ascribed entirely to the pernicious practice of "spearing," and fishing with "set lines" and nets—a custom not only fraught with tenfold more danger to the finny tribe than legitimate fishing, but one that has continued for many years, notwithstanding all endeavors to put a stop to it.

There is an Indian superstition attached to this lake which probably had its source in its remarkable loneliness and tranquillity. The Mohawks believed that its stillness

HIGH ROCK SPRING.

MYNHEER BARHYDT.

was sacred to the Great Spirit, and that if a human voice uttered a sound upon its waters, the canoe of the offender would instantly sink. A story is told of an Englishwoman, in the early days of the first settlers, who had occasion to cross this lake with a party of Indians, who, before embarking, warned her most impressively of the spell. It was a silent, breathless day, and the canoe shot over the surface of the lake like an arrow. About half a mile from the shore, near the centre of the lake, the woman, wishing to convince the Indians of the erroneousness of their superstition, uttered a loud cry. The countenances of the Indians fell instantly to the deepest gloom. After a minute's pause, however, they redoubled their exertions, and in frowning silence drove the light bark swiftly over the waters. They reached the shore in safety, and drew up the canoe, when the woman rallied the chief on his credulity. "The Great Spirit is merciful," answered the scornful Mohawk; "He knows that a white woman can not hold her tongue!"

Stretching around the village of Saratoga Springs on its eastern side is a wide belt of low marshy land known as the Bear Swamp. In the early settlement of the country this region was remarkable for the number and variety of the wild animals it contained. It undoubtedly furnished a large portion of the game which caused Lake Saratoga to be so well known to the Six Nations as "the place where the game abounds," and

after the country was comparatively settled up it still presented fine opportunities for hunting the larger and smaller varieties of animals.

Lying on the southern edge of Bear Swamp, and partly draining it, are two bodies of water—Lake Lonely and Barhydt's Lake. Lake Lonely was originally called by the early settlers "Owl Pond," on account of the quantity of owls which were wont to gather around its shores and make night dismal by their hootings. On its eastern bank steep declivities rise up from the water's edge, covered with tangled firs and hemlocks, some of which, the growth of centuries, rise above their fellows, till their tops, resembling so many spires, seem lost in the clouds. Standing upon the eastern shore and looking northward, the eye, sweeping beyond the smooth sheet of water, takes in the most southerly spurs of the Adirondack region, darkly wooded to their topmost elevation. In the spring considerable torrents pour down the deep ravines into the lake, forming cascades of some magnitude. One of these glens forms an echo almost as distinct and powerful as the celebrated one in the ruined bastion of the old French fortress at Crown Point.

Barhydt's Lake was formerly—between 1820 and 1835—a great resort, having on its banks a public-house kept by Mynheer Barhydt, a Dutch settler. This tarn is called a "lake" by courtesy. Sunk as deep into the earth as the firs shoot above it, it is surrounded by a wilderness of straight columnar shafts, which "branch out at the top like round tables spread for a banquet in the clouds." As late as 1835 it was filled with trout, though even then the shrewd old Dutchman foresaw the future scarcity of this fish. In the summer of that year Colonel Stone writes to the *Commercial Advertiser*, "At Barhydt's the sportsman is obliged to throw all the trout he may take, back into their native element again, and pay by the hour for the privilege besides."

Jacobus Barhydt was in many respects an original character. With all his astuteness, however, he sometimes overreached himself.

When Joseph Bonaparte was at Saratoga in 1825, he offered Barhydt $20,000 for the place. Astounded at such a sum, Barhydt refused it, remarking that he "did not know whether Bonaparte was a fool or a knave." The old Dutchman could not conceive that the beauty of the place had tempted the offer, and suspected some sinister design. "If it's worth that to you," he said, in closing the conversation, "it's worth that to me." Bonaparte, failing to buy in Saratoga, afterward bought a beautiful place at Bordentown, New Jersey, and thus Saratoga lost a king for a citizen.

In 1839 N. P. Willis visited Barhydt's Lake, and gave the following description of the old Dutchman:

"The old man sat under his Dutch stoop smoking his pipe, and suffered us to tie our ponies to his fence without stirring, and in answer to our inquiries if there was a boat on the lake, simply nodded and pointed to the water's edge. Whether this indifference to strangers is innocence merely, or whether Herr Barhydt does not choose to be considered an innkeeper, no one is enough in his secrets to divine. He will give you a dram or cook you a dinner of trout, and seems not only indifferent whether you like his fish or his liquor, but quite as indifferent whether or what you pay him. In his way Herr Barhydt is kind and courteous.

"We descended to the lake, and after rowing about, we returned to partake of the old Dutchman's hospitality and have a little conversation with him. Among other things, we asked him if he was aware that he had been put into a book. 'I've hearn tell on't,' said he. 'A Mr. Wilkins or Watkins has writ something about me, but I don't know why. *I never did him no harm as I know on.*'"

On a ball night the scene on driving into town from the lake is most wonderful. On emerging from the pine groves that skirt the village on the east, a thousand dazzling lights burst upon the view as they shoot forth their beams from the brilliant halls and countless windows of the splendid establishments of this celebrated wateringplace. A very trifling effort of the imagination would at this moment be necessary to transform these mansions into the fairy castles and palaces of Eastern romance, lighted up in honor of some signal triumph or royal bridal *fête*. On these occasions the ballrooms at the three principal hotels are frequently decorated with arches and festoons of flowers, and the halls are finely illuminated.

The hotels at Saratoga are of world-wide reputation. They afford the means of judging of the manners and forming some estimate of the diversified character of our countrymen from the various parts of the extended Union, and enable us to catch a glimpse of the prevailing follies and fashions of the day.

LAKE LONELY.

Cat-boat Cruising
on Long Island Sound
(1885)

CAT–BOAT CRUISING ON LONG ISLAND SOUND.

THERE are many fine bodies of water throughout the United States; but the writer has failed to find one equal to Long Island Sound for yacht cruising. Contiguous to several large cities, and with innumerable fashionable watering-places dotting its shores, and fine harbors on either hand, affording ready shelter in case of storm, this beautiful sheet of water stretches out as far as the eye can reach; to the south its limits are the sandy beaches of Long Island, while its northern confines are the more rocky shores of New York and Connecticut. All the prominent New York clubs devote from one to two weeks each summer in cruising in a fleet upon its waters, though some have ridiculed them for cruising on what has been termed "that petty sheet of water." According to Webster, a yacht is a pleasure-vessel; and the owners of yachts are supposed to use them for pleasure only, and not for knocking about on the ocean with nothing around them but water and sky, and with plenty of hard work for pastime. Having but a week or two in which to sail in company, a cruising-ground is naturally selected that will afford the greatest amount of pleasure to the majority in that time. It has also been insinuated that fear prevents the American yachtsmen from making more extended cruises; from this we beg to differ, as every fall many of our yachts make cruises to Southern ports, to the Bermudas, and West Indies, while others, during the summer, cruise as far to the northward and eastward as Nova Scotia and Newfoundland, and in a few instances to Labrador; then many of our craft have crossed the ocean. As for the Sound being a "petty sheet of water," the writer has seen it many times when these scoffers would have been only too happy to cut and run for a harbor, even when aboard of one of their pet cutters. To return to the subject of our sketch, my friend Potts and myself decided upon a short cruise in our yacht *Sharpie*, which we had recently purchased. Having served our apprenticeship as members of the racing crews of the yachts *Joe Jefferson*, *Sophia-Emma*, and *A. Varian, Jr.*, of the Manhattan and Harlem Yacht clubs, we considered ourselves quite competent to handle our own yacht. A few months previous we had decided to purchase a boat, and looked about for one that would suit as to speed and price, the latter being a very important item. A yacht known as the *Vidette*, of Port Chester, but now of the New Haven Yacht Club, made her appearance at this time in our neighborhood, and impressed us as being about what we wanted. We soon came to terms and the yacht was ours. She was always spoken of as the *Sharpie*, bearing something of a resemblance to the New Haven sharpie, except that the flat bottom and overhanging stern were omitted. She was a cross between the sharpie and skipjack build. Length, 21 feet 2 inches; beam, 8 feet 6 inches; draught, 14 inches; was an open centerboard boat, cat-rigged, and was built by a party of New Haven coachmakers for their own use. The club boys ridiculed our purchase, and as far as appearances were concerned they were justified, but the way "that old box" sailed around the good-looking ones, later on, caused their owners to look with unfeigned astonishment.

It was in the early part of September, several years ago, that, having extended invitations to our friends "Max" and "Doodles," we met at the Knickerbocker Yacht club-house at Port Morris one pleasant Thursday afternoon. Our ages ranged from seventeen to twenty-one, and we made a very boyish-looking crew. The Knickerbocker Yacht Club was then in its infancy. The club-house is situated at the mouth of the Kills on the New York shore, facing East River, about one mile east of and above the turbulent waters of Hell Gate. Having exchanged our good clothes for boat toggery, we proceeded to get our stores on board, using two long, narrow trunks; one in which to pack blankets and extra clothing, the other for our provisions and dishes. These were run under the deck, forward, giving us a free cockpit to move about in. For protection from dew and rain at night, we rigged up a shelter-tent in the following style: placed an upright at the after end of the centerboard trunk, from which we ran a ridge pole to the forward deck; over this we spread a piece of canvas, which we had rendered waterproof with oil and paint, and laced the edges of it securely to the deck, close to the coaming. No rain or spray ever penetrated this tent. The boom swung clear of it, so that in case of rain it could be used during the day without interfering with the yacht's sailing. We had all knocked about in boats, more or less, and cared nothing for a little hard usage and the absence of home comforts. While making our preparations to start, a large fleet of coasting schooners and sloops came up through Hell Gate on the first of the flood-tide, bound to the eastward. A nice breeze was blowing from the south, and all being ready we cast off from our buoy, and fell in at the rear of the fleet as a sort of "whipper-in." Now we are off, all restraint thrown aside, carelessly dressed, and as happy and light-hearted as a lot of boys can be.

The club-house is quickly left astern; then past the old schooner, anchored over the spot where the British frigate *Huzzar* sank during the Revolution, and where for many years past divers have been sent down to search for the immense treasure that is supposed to be at the bottom of the river,— said treasure being chests containing the money to pay off the British army in America. It was generally believed that a number of American prisoners, who were confined in the vessel, perished with her. Although many tons of mud and sand have been hoisted on deck and screened, being first shovelled in bags by divers, those money-chests have failed to come to light. Old guns and cannons have been brought up, but nothing of any greater value. Many doubt if the gold ever went down with the vessel.

On we go through the narrow channel between North and South Brother Islands; the main ship channel is between North Brother and the Port Morris shore. A government lighthouse is located on North Brother, presided over by the gallant "Mary Ann Kelly," as she is familiarly spoken of by the boatmen on the river. To the eastward of South Brother is Riker's Island, which contains several acres of land, and is much larger than the Brothers. Between Riker's Island and College Point, L.I., there is excellent anchorage, and great fleets of coasting vessels are frequently seen here, waiting for favorable winds and tides. All this time we had been closing up with the fleet, and had passed some of the rear-guard. And now we heard volleys of abuse hurled at model and design of our poor old yacht by the crews of the vessels we were in company with; but we had our

revenge; the way the old *Sharpie* walked through that fleet must have caused some astonishment among her slanderers.

Potts related the following little incident that occurred one afternoon when out with a party of friends:

"I was taking a little spin on the river, bound to the eastward," said he, "when a big market-sloop came along bound west, close-hauled, and careened slightly under the influence of the fine breeze that was blowing. Her captain hailed me, and wanted to know, 'if boats like that 'ere thing wasn't built by the mile, and sawed off in lengths to suit the buyer?' No reply was made, but coming about quickly at his stern, and to leeward, we trimmed the *Sharpie's* mainsail in flat, and, giving her a good 'rap full,' held her right to it. Foot by foot we gained on him; and, all the time working up to windward, we were soon abreast of his chain-plates, and a little farther on shot across his bow. When clear of him we lay to, so that he could pass close to us. We gave him a grand shout, and inquired if he didn't want to buy a mile or two of boats like her. As she went by we just heard his emphatic remark, 'Well, I'll be blanked!'"

After passing College Point, the next place of note is Whitestone, on the Long Island shore, whidh suddenly opens up to view from behind a point; it is very prettily situated, in a cove, and has fine surroundings, the worst of which are, of course, the mosquitoes, of which there is a plentiful supply. Wonderful yarns have been related of the powers of these White-stone mosquitoes, but we will refrain from giving them in print. This is a great yachting rendezvous, and many fine craft are to be met anchored near the steamboat dock during the summer months. Here the vigilant *Herald* ship-news reporter is seen in his little row-boat, pulling from vessel to vessel as they pass by, ascertaining their names and whither bound. On the other shore is Throgg's Neck, at the extreme end of which stands Fort Schuyler, opposite which is another large fort on Willett's Point; these guard the narrow entrance to the East River from the Sound proper, which is entered after passing Throgg's Neck.

On our port bow a large bay runs up to Pelham Bridge, which is a great resort for fishermen. On the starboard is Little Neck Bay, a very pretty harbor, made famous by its clams and oysters. Peeping out from its heavily-wooded shores may be seen an occasional house. Then comes the Stepping Stones Reef, extending out from Great Neck ; at its western end there was formerly a can buoy, but now a very fine lighthouse stands as a warning to all sailors to beware of the dangerous reef.

Inquiry was made as to the manner in which the reef obtained its name. Max proceeded to enlighten us by relating the following, which is a sailor's legend : —

" The devil, who, according to this yarn, must have been a native of Long Island (no reflection intended upon Long Islanders), started from his home to make a raid upon the New York shore. As no ferry-boats were running in that section, the only ferry in existence being that operated by the grim ferryman Charon, on the river Styx, he dropped a stone into the water on which to step, from this he cast another a little farther out, and so on until he reached the deep water of the channel. Not having a United States coast survey chart with him, and never having met the City Island fishermen, to be posted, he was unacquainted with the soundings and depth of water in that locality. When he took his last step from where the lighthouse now stands, down he went into deep water, and was seen no more. Hence the name Stepping Stones."

We are now abreast of Hart's Island Roads, a fine harbor, greatly used by coasting-vessels. On the port is City Island, with its ship-yards from which many of New York's famous yachts have been launched. There is quite a fair-sized village on the island, the homes of the ship-carpenters and joiners employed in the ship-yards, and the hundreds of fishermen who ply their vocation in the neighboring waters. The island is connected to the mainland by a bridge at Pelham Neck. On the starboard are Hart's and David's Islands, on the first of which is Potter's Field, the final resting-place of all New York's unknown and pauper dead ; David's Island is a government military post. Continuing on through a narrow channel between numerous small islands and rocks, one reaches New Rochelle. Our course being in another direction, we passed Hart's Island about dusk, Sands' Point lighthouse, on the Long Island shore, sending out its flashes at regular intervals. A little to the north and east is Execution Rock lighthouse, situated, as its name would imply, on a large rock in the middle of the Sound. Our man of history and legends came in again with the infor-

mation that Execution Rock obtained its name from the fact that two or three river pirates were executed there many years ago. At McClellan's Hotel, on City Island (since destroyed by fire), there was on exhibition a plaster cast of the head of one of the pirates, also the noose with which he was hung. I have seen the cast and noose, but cannot vouch for their genuineness.

Darkness set in as we passed Execution light, so we placed our red and green lights. By this time we had worked our way clear of the whole fleet with which we had started, and ours was now the leading vessel. The wind had grown gradually lighter since sundown. On our stern, the bright rays shone forth from the faithful sentinels on Sands' Point and Execution Rock ; while ahead of us, as our guiding star, shone Captain's Island light. We had so thoroughly enjoyed our delighful sail that supper was entirely forgotten. However, this matter finally received proper consideration, after which it was decided to divide the crew into four-hour watches, and sail all night, in order to make as many miles as possible in our limited time. Running close to the Connecticut shore, out of the usual track of vessels, and entirely alone, brought to us a peculiar sense of independence, and a monarchs-of-all-we-surveyed feeling that was decidedly enjoyable.

The off-watch turned in off Greenwich Harbor, leaving the deck in charge of Max and myself. I was on look-out forward, to report the approach of any vessel that might appear. Max was at the tiller sailing by compass, so he said. He had served a short time on a school-ship in the United States navy, and we considered him 'way up in the art of navigation. We sailed along for some time all right, to every appearance, when we suddenly realized that sounds on shore had become very distinct. The night was quite dark, and objects at a short distance invisible. I could hear the rumble of a railway train quite plainly, and knew that that should not be. Suddenly espying a large mass of rock ahead, I shouted to Max to " luff her," which he did promptly, and cleared it. I suggested that if that was an example of steering by compass I preferred to depend on the lighthouses, and sail from one to the other, as can be done the full length of the Sound, save in foggy weather. We held a council of war, and came to the conclusion that we didn't know exactly where we were ; then our talk brought out the other watch, and a good laugh they had at our expense. It was necessary to do something, so Doodles and Potts took the skiff and went ahead to reconnoiter. Then it was found that Max, instead of keeping the yacht on her true course up the Sound to the east had sailed up to the very head of Stamford Harbor.

How we got in there without striking a rock,—for the place is full of them,—was a mystery to all. With the row-boat ahead keeping a sharp look-out for rocks, and with the light breeze which prevailed, we worked the yacht slowly back into the Sound again without accident. Upon examination it was found that the compass was useless,—it was one Max used *for a watch-charm.*

Daybreak found us off Sheffield Island light, at the entrance to Norwalk Harbor. Ahead of us was a fine three-masted schooner, deeply laden and bound to the eastward with every stitch of canvas set, which gave her a splendid appearance. The sunrise effect was very beautiful, for the luminous rim of the sun came peeping over the Long Island hills, and slowly arose until its whole bright face was beaming upon us. tinging everything around a golden hue.

Having completed our toilets, for we found the easiest mode of performing our ablutions was to take a plunge into the clear waters of the Sound, the oil-stove was brought into service and breakfast prepared. Our fare was plain but wholesome, consisting of bacon, eggs, fried potatoes, coffee, and bread and butter.

The wind freshened in the early morning, and the old *Sharpie* bounded along in gallant style. Skirting the Connecticut shore there was much to admire in the ever-changing scene. Here a little cove with a fleet of fishing-smacks at anchor, there, a glimpse of cattle grazing on the hillsides, or neat little farm-houses with plots of well-tilled land about them, and here and there, seemingly dropped along the entire shore, many fine houses, the summer homes of business men of New York and other cities.

Now we are off Black Rock light; and beyond can be seen the George Hotel, a fine, well-kept house that is popular with yachtsmen. It is located a little to the west of Bridgeport, on a fine snug harbor of easy access. Bridgeport is on our port beam and we soon pass it; Stratford Point follows, and then we come ahead of Charles Island, some distance out into the Sound

from Milford, Conn. A sand bar runs from the island to the mainland, and is bare at low-water, affording a line of temporary communication with the shore. The island is now the property of the American (steam) Yacht Club, on which they have a club-house. Away ahead we see New Haven lighthouse, and in a short time West Haven appears, and almost at the same time East Haven shows to view, while off to the northward is the City of Elms itself.

Doodles and I made a wager (dinners for the crew) as to the time of coming to anchor in New Haven Harbor, my wager being that we would reach there by one o'clock. It was a beautiful day, with a fair sailing breeze, and the *Sharpie* rattled off the miles at such a lively rate that we dropped anchor off the City Dock, at the foot of East street at exactly 1.20 P.M. I had lost by twenty minutes. We put in the remainder of the day with a stroll about town, and in the evening, having found two of the *Sharpie's* old owners, were royally entertained by them.

Saturday morning broke cloudy, and with every appearance of an unpleasant day. All hands were on deck early, disappointment depicted on every face, for we had expected a pleasant day for the homeward run. Breakfast being dispatched, the order was given to hoist sail and weigh anchor. Everything was stowed snugly, and the canvas shelter-tent lashed down securely, as it was evident that we were to have a trying day, and so it proved, though far worse than we anticipated. By seven o'clock we were making our way out of the harbor with a strong breeze from the north-west, Oyster Bay, Long Island, being our objective point. The waters of the Sound presented an ugly appearance; stretching out for twenty-five miles to the Long Island shore, and to the east and west as far as the eye could reach, was a mass of white-caps, the angry billows rolling higher and higher as time went on. The only vessel in sight was the iron sloop-yacht *Vindex*. under close-reefed canvas.

A short distance outside of the harbor we were struck with a very severe squall from the north-west, and the water was lashed into a white foam all about us. Down, down went the old *Sharpie* on her side. Potts shoved the tiller " hard down " with his foot, and threw the weight of his body up to windward. Max jumped for the peak halyards, and let them go by the run, while Doodles and the writer hung out to windward as far as they could. Will she ever come up? Swash rushes the water across the deck, threatening every minute to fill the cockpit, but the shelter-tent does its work nobly, and casts most of it back. Up she comes, slowly, with no other mishap than the shipping of a few pails of water. Sail was quickly dropped, and two reefs tied in; and off we go again on our course. The sea by this time was running very high, and the gusts of wind coming harder and oftener. Too much sail! Now she is working along with only the peak of her sail hoisted to keep her on her course, and even this at times proves to be more than enough. The continued pitching and tossing was too much for Potts and Doodles and they became seasick. Heartless Max, busy as we were, keeping the boat free from water, found time to get out a piece of nice fat pork, and proceeded to explain to the seasick ones what delightful eating it would be for them, with the usual pitiable result. All hands were obliged to take turns at bailing out, and a hard fight it was to keep the water below the flooring. Up went the yacht on the crest of a wave, then down she rushed in the trough of the sea, the crest of the succeeding wave hanging over her stern threatening every minute to engulf her.

All hands were growing tired, and Max threw himself down in the cockpit for a short rest; that sufficed, and he joined the other boys in their misery, a sickly, revengeful smile flitting across Doodles' face, as he observed Max's distress; three out of four on the retired list.

And now a large black sloop-rigged fishing-smack, close reefed, is observed coming towards us, standing out from Bridgeport. Nearer she comes, making straight for us. One minute upon the top of a wave with half her length thrown out of water as she bounds forward, the next disappearing so that nothing is visible but her tall mast. Now she ranges alongside, her crew appearing on deck in their yellow oil-skin suits and sou'westers.

"We'll take you off, but we can't tow your yacht in this seaway," comes the shout from the smack's deck.

"Thank you for your great kindness in running out to us," we reply, "but we won't give up the old boat without a harder fight."

"All right, boys," is the response, "good-luck to you!" and she is off.

As she ran across our bow we read her name, "C. D. Smith, of Bridgeport," and it is even now with feelings of deepest gratitude that I think of the "C. D. Smith" and her gallant crew going miles out of their way on an ugly morning to render assistance to fellow-men believed to be in distress.

Shortly after this incident occurred, our skiff filled with water. We attempted to bail it out, but the seas washed in faster than we could bail, so we gave it up. This dead weight dragging astern proved too much for us to tow with our reduced canvas, so we were compelled to cut the skiff adrift. Not another vessel under sail did we see during the day, all coasters were snugly at anchor in some sheltered cove.

It soon became evident that it would be an impossibility to make Oyster Bay; so, when abreast of Stony Brook, L.I., we squared away for that harbor, scudding along most of the time under bare pole, and at times fairly rushing through the water. Approaching the harbor, on either hand we could see great lines of breakers, with a very narrow and shoal channel through which to enter. To miss the channel meant "good-by" to the *Sharpie*, as a few minutes' pounding in such a surf would soon reduce her to kindling wood.

Knowing the harbor, Max took the tiller and piloted her safely in, and by two o'clock in the afternoon we had tied up to a dock and spread out our wet clothing and bedding to dry.

The next morning (Sunday) was a beautiful day; the wind and sea were both down somewhat, and, after waiting for the first of the ebb, — the tide running so like a mill-race at the entrance that we couldn't stem it, — we got under way again.

Working along the shore through Smithtown Bay, past Huntington Harbor, Eaton's and Lloyd's Neck, Cold Spring Harbor, with Oyster Bay opening from it, reached home safely late in the evening.

Alfred Varian.

The Scooter–
A Winged Tobaggan
of Long Island
(1905)

THE SCOOTER—A WINGED TOBOGGAN
OF LONG ISLAND

J. W. MULLER

PHOTOGRAPHS BY JAMES BURTON

STANDING that January morning on Long Island's southern mainland, whose sedgy surface never freezes so hard that it will not sob under foot, a man might look out over the still inland sea of the Great South Bay and beyond it over the white ocean beach to the sharp, dark curve of the unfluttered ocean, and see spring in the world. Frozen fast from shore to beach, from farthest cove to mumbling inlet, the air that crept over the bay was yet so soft, the sky that hung over it so innocently blue, that it seemed as if the marble sheet must surely disappear before another morning.

Three miles away, in the heart of the serene, stiff plain, lay a black furrow, bent in many curves. In it, with main and foresail drawing gently full, a schooner worked toward open sea to escape the ice-lock that had held her for a week. Careless eyes watched her from the mainland, from miles of sleepy marsh, idly desiring to be on her, close hauled for the unrippled Atlantic in that midwinter, summery gentleness of day. Other eyes watched her too; eyes set in keen, hard-lined brown faces, where the life savers of Fire Island regarded her. They saw what the landsmen could not see; what, indeed, only eyes as sharp as the clear gray eyes of gulls might catch—that the baby blue of the cloudless January heaven had a dull shine of hard steel where the sea dipped. They saw, too, high in air, wide sails careening in a steady flight toward shore. The gulls were coming in, long before noon, not pausing for the feast that the lowered tide had spread on the open beach.

Down in the unseen, sunken sea beyond the horizon, straight east as the parallel of Fire Island's latitude runs, a wind was being born—a cold wind and a great wind. It was drawing in with the young flood, moving with its motion, growing with its growth. When the tide was full, the sea

wrinkled and began to move. On the frost-feathered edges of the ice inside of the inlet, a little surf began to run. A mile of ice whimpered. Faint, vague sighs fluttered over the wide plain. Under the floes, the tide turning to run back to sea, strained its green back. Floe moved against floe, creaked, snapped and receded. Again they met and drifted apart. Once more they struck, grinding, and stayed.

The schooner ran no more in an open lane. Her channel had become an archipelago of ice islets, changing each moment. She tacked, and a field, breaking suddenly adrift, shouldered into her course. She lay on the other tack to pass between two floes, and, before her sheets were taut, the two were one.

The beaches drummed. Beyond them, the red sun shone on a running sea. The wind strove hugely to turn back the lusty tide, and the two battled, with ice floes for weapons. Astern of the caught schooner, the secret tide coaxed a floe that bobbed toyingly. Softly it floated, softly it swung under the vessel's counter, with clear splintering sounds it shivered into bits. And at that purring touch, the wheel twirled crazily with its rudder bitten off.

Down went the starboard anchor. It fell on ice and pressed it under, but a fathom deep the floe held, and buoyed up the half ton iron. Out roared the port chain and found mud. But the ice had the schooner. When the chain veered out, the bottom gave way to the pull, for it was not a schooner alone, but an acre of moving ice that pulled at it.

The straining sails spoke, thundering. But louder than they, spoke the inlet—*one!* TWO! THREE!—the tide backing against the wind and cascading on the bar. Even as torn hands pulled in the stiffened drumheads of canvas by main strength, the vessel struck—once with just a dainty scrape and a velvety glide over soft, soft sands,

The fleet of scooters on the Great South Bay.

yielding kindly; twice, with a weary, squatting wallow; thrice, with a smash that shivered to her mast-heads. Below, there came the trill of little water. flowing musically. Her timbers had started, and the Atlantic Ocean was coming in to see what manner of thing this was.

Now here was such a shipwreck as the winter sea loves, with a scene set cunningly to torment its victims before it took them down; for around the bursting schooner lay too much ice to launch a boat, bu were men to creep out on it, they would be met by encompassing hungry water; cold and deep and black.

The staunchest life boat on all the American coast, from Cape Fear to Montauk, could not win through the wicked mass. Yet, from the white dunes of Fire Island, something was coming to help. Little things they were, detaching themselves speck by speck from the beach where the Life Saving Station sits; so little that the lonely figure of the occupant of each loomed up like that of a man sitting on a child's bobsled.

Pitiful things were these to play at taking the place of the mighty lifeboats; neither as large nor as deep as a ducking skiff, and set with a mast scarcely higher than a man. But they came with the speed of the blast itself. Scarcely seeming to touch the surface they skimmed a smooth stretch, with a clinking ring of metal on hard ice.

In their course lay a long mile of hummocks—two and three feet high, cast in rough confusion. Straight at them went the little things, mounted them, dipped into the hollows, mounted again and leaped headlong from the last ones to hit the ice twenty feet away—and still to tear ahead unchecked for even an instant by the wild work. Now they hit mush ice, over which surely no thing made of man can go, any more than things can go through it, for it is too thin for the one and too solid for the other.

Churn! churn! churn! The mush spouts off the bows, and on they go, unhindered, with ice crystals and water spraying high along each side. Out of the mush they spring more easily than ever gull rose from the water, and with a crunch take the hard ice again and speed on faster, faster. But now they are surely doomed! Ahead of them lies black water, five hundred yards

across, and they are pointing for it straight at twenty miles an hour and not a hundred yards to make before they leap in and are engulfed!

In they go! White water smashes over them. But instantly out of the froth the little sails wimple and skim on, undeviating. They hit the ice bank on the other side plumb and do not stop, but slide up on it as a wet seal slides on his floe. Again they take hummocks, almost leaping from top to top of the rough crests. Again they take hard ice, brittle ice, mush ice, ice five feet thick and ice that is only a glare over treacherous, lurking water; and straight and true, unharmed and undelayed they sail and round under the stern of the broken ship.

Next morning her sticks and splintered timbers make dismal black dots along five miles of ice field, and the surf makes catplay with her wreckage from Fire Island to Tiana Beach; but her crew sits safe and warm in the Life Saving Station, thanks to the Long Island life savers' contribution to nautical engineering, the Great South Bay scooter—sail-boat and ice-boat in one, and the nearest thing to a wild duck that the hand of man has produced.

Men are "scootering" for sport now, all over the Great South Bay from Babylon to Moriches; but the sport is not more than three years old, and the scooter has not changed perceptibly in model or rig from the original form devised by the life savers for practical and, often, grim work. No doubt the next few years will see a great evolution under the hands of the sportsman, for the scooter is surely destined to become a craft of world-wide use. But at present it still is delightfully and amazingly simple — nothing except a flat-bottomed, shallow boat shaped like a ducking skiff, shod with a steel or brass runner on each side of the flat keel, and sailed with mainsail and jib, the latter being used to steer the craft, as, manifestly, it cannot carry a tiller.

Anybody can build a scooter, if he can build anything at all. Some of the best on the Great South Bay to-day were built by house carpenters. One of the prizewinners in last year's races was built by a stone mason. The boat that came in third in the scooter race of last winter was built by a boy of eighteen, who had not seen or

Rounding the Stake—Showing Method of Steering with the Jib.

heard of a scooter before that year. The cost of those in use now ranges from seventy-five to one hundred dollars.

Like the Indian canoe, the Eskimo kayak, the Hawaiian surf-riding boats and the Malay proa, the scooter, fully as unique and original as they, was born of simple necessity.

Those strange salt-water lagoons that extend from New York east along the south shore of Long Island to the sandy Hamptons, present an arctic problem of their own in winter. No boat can cross them, for there is never an unbroken reach of open water. No man can walk them, for there is rarely unbroken ice. No ice yacht can sail them, for there may be a five foot thickness of ice in one stretch and not half an inch in another. The restless tides will not let the bays freeze smooth. Each change of current makes hummocks up-rear that would wreck the ice yacht. Each tide opens wind holes and loosens floes in the channels.

Thus the only mode of winning across the treacherous and deadly surface from mainland to beach, for communication or life saving, was to drag a flat-bottomed boat on a sled, sliding it off at mush ice or open water and poling or rowing till hard ice was gained again, when the killing work of dragging the heavy craft was resumed. Often it required half a day for men to cross the bay. No man could expect to cross without breaking through hidden holes. Each winter took a toll of dead.

To ease the work of dragging the boats, the life savers at last hit on the idea of setting a tiny sail on the craft when the wind was fair. Gradually the sails were enlarged. Then a bright spirit fastened sledge runners directly to the boat instead of mounting it on a sled. And then—all at once one man preparing to cross the bay with a mighty wind behind him, asked himself why he should haul the boat at all. In that moment the scooter was born.

First it carried a wisp of a sail. Men who know the Great South Bay have deep respect for it. They knew what it meant to slip over its ice with a wintry gale blowing fifty miles an hour behind them, and they went carefully. Gradually, as they learned what could be done, the sails grew in size.

To-day the typical scooter is from fourteen to fifteen feet long, with a beam of four to five feet. It is well decked all around,

particularly forward, so that the open space forms a cockpit only five or five and a-half feet long and two feet to two and a-half wide. Around the cockpit runs a powerful combing, built to withstand rough knocks and rising at least three inches above deck. The entire deck has a gentle turtle-back curve, fore and aft and across. This curve of the deck is almost duplicated by the bottom of the scooter, thus making a very slight modification of a flat bottom.

Now come the runners—really the only thing that makes the scooter different from any other boat. They are made of brass or steel. Each has its votaries. The men with brass runners can file them true and sharp whenever they need it, especially before a race, without wasting more than a few minutes. There are conditions where steel runners hold the ice better and again at times the softer brass runners are a decided advantage. On a fourteen-foot boat the runners will be ten feet long, slightly rocker-shaped, one inch wide and from one and a-half to one and three-quarters inches high, being so set and ground as to bevel inwards. They are set about twenty inches apart. It is in the shape, set, and location of the runners that further evolution and perfection of the scooter as a racing machine, probably will come.

The mast, which is set well aft, is from nine to ten feet long. The sails may be rigged in any way customary for small boats. The handiest are the regulation boom and gaff and sprit rigs for mainsails, while it is well to have a small boom for the foot of the jib, because its proper manipulation and set are so important for the handling of the boat. The bowsprit is large and heavy, and projects from two and one-half to three feet beyond the hull. It is made removable, so that larger or smaller sticks can be substituted according to weather.

The sail spread of the scooter differs from that of common craft in that the canvas has its greatest extent laterally instead of in height. The scooter wants as much sail as possible astern and in the bow, because it is the canvas alone that steers her. Therefore, a scooter with a nine foot mast may carry a seven or eight foot gaff and a boom extending fifteen feet and more, although fourteen is the usual length for a nine and a-half foot mast. The leach of such a sail will be fourteen feet or a little more. The

Behind the Line, Ready for the Race.

In Front of the Line, About to Start.

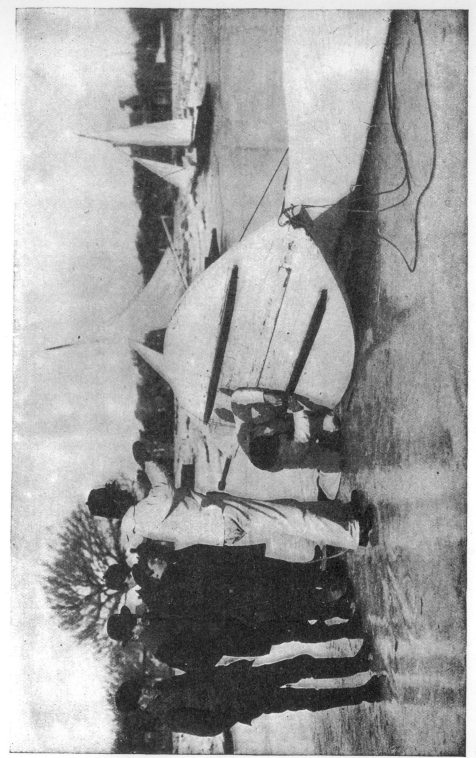

Sharpening the Runners.

foot of the jib will be at least seven feet and the leach about the same.

Most of the boats are built of pine with oak decks. They must be strong, to withstand the extremely violent wrenches and bumps due to the rough work in the broken ice. The equipment consists of a pair of oars and a pike pole with sharpened points. The latter is as vital to scootering as an anchor is to a yacht. It offers the only method by which the scooterer can work his way through bad mush ice if the wind is not strong enough to force him over or through it. It is needed, also, to bring the scooter around in extra heavy weather, in case the steering power of the jib should not be sufficient to do it quickly, or the sailor lose control of his craft temporarily, a contingency that is likely to happen with bewildering suddenness in the case of a two hundred pound craft with a forty mile wind behind projecting it over ice smooth as glass.

It is wonderful how well the jib steers the scooter, however. There being no tiller to demand the care of the sailor, he can handle his jib and mainsail alone and thus make them work in perfect harmony. Let go the jib sheet and haul taut the main, and the little boat will come around as sweetly as any deep-finned yacht minds her strong helm. She will reach and beat into the eye of the wind, and her runners will not make more leeway than most centerboards. If she is to come up in the wind in a particular hurry, the steersman steps swiftly toward the bow so that his weight makes the bearing fall on the keel forward, and the lightened stern comes right around. Thus, by nice adjustment of weight and close manipulation of sails, the scooter can be made to turn in her own length—spin around like a top. Practically, the man who can sail any small boat really well can sail a scooter. There are lots of "wrinkles;" but there is only one radically new thing to learn, and that is a queer one.

The scooter's poorest point of sailing is running free before the wind. Indeed, to be precise, the scooter can't sail at all before the wind. The moment the mainsail blankets the jib in a following wind, the steering power is totally gone.

The only way to sail a scooter before the wind is to beat down it. You've got to tack before a wind with a scooter just as you have to tack into one.

One or two make her crew. She can carry three, but it is better to have less. When she darts over smooth ice, the men perch on the combing aft to windward, as they do on catboats. When she nears rubble or hummocks, or prepares to dive into mush or water, all hands stand up, to relieve her of dead weight. To enter open water, she is driven straight at it. That is the time the hand at the "helm" must know what to do with that jib. Should she take it sideways, over she'll go. She must hit it true and be eased as much as may be by cunning play with the mainsail. Once over the first wild career of her plunge, which is almost identical with the gliding plunge of a "shoot-the-chutes" boat, she skims the water as neatly as she skims the ice. When approaching solid ice again, she must be headed straight into it. Her flaring bow goes up its edge, and if she has arrived with speed, she has slid up on it and is off again on her runners before you know it. If the wind is too light to drive her forcefully enough, she may have to be helped up with pike pole, or with another and unique implement specially devised, which looks as much like a hoe as anything.

Although the scooter has been in use for many years among the baymen and particularly the life savers, it was not until the winter of 1903 that its use for sport had become great enough to justify an attempt to sail a regular, organized race. On February 12th of last year the first really big race of this kind was sailed off Blue Point. Fourteen boats were entered. The course was a triangle, two miles to a leg, sailed over three times, making eighteen miles in all.

A Patchogue scooter, *Leader*, won the first prize, making the eighteen miles in 39 minutes, 38 seconds, thus sailing at the rate of twenty-seven miles an hour. This scooter was large, being eighteen feet over all, and five feet beam. Her sail spread was thirty yards of thirty-inch-wide canvas. The second boat, *Vamoose*, made her trip in 46 minutes, 41 seconds. She was fourteen feet, 6 inches long, four feet wide, and carried twenty-five yards of thirty-inch-wide canvas.

Better time than this has been made by scooters in stiff weather. In 1903, Albert Latham, a gold medal man of the Blue Point Life Saving Station, made five miles in six minutes, which would have been fifty miles an hour. But that speed is exceptional. The best scooters do not make more than thirty miles an hour at present under good conditions, and twenty-five miles is more usual. But who would sniff at the idea of skimming across ice, hummocks, mush, and into and out of open water, and over any old kind of surface at that rate of speed on a bright winter morning?

Accidents haven't been common, despite the great speed. A few "scooterers" have been capsized when diving into the water, and more have sailed their craft off the ice into the channel only to discover too late that they had a leak aboard as a silent but active passenger.

Thus two famous ice yachtsmen of New York "scootered" out of Bayport in January of last year with two young ladies. The scooter struck an air hole, and when she went into the water, she developed a leak. There was sunken ice under her keel, and it would have been easy to pole her to the ice-bank, but the good pike-pole had been forgotten. Finally the two men had to get out and stand in the water hip deep, to support the boat till help arrived.

But these accidents are rare; and against them stand the records of many lives saved by their aid. That they will live through a mighty gale was proved last winter when the schooner *George B. Cromwell* struck on the outer beach across from Bellport. So fierce was the storm that the lifeboat was thrown back, bow over stern, time and time again, when the men attempted to put her through the surf. Although many life-lines were shot over the wreck, the seas that washed her were so vast that her crew could not crawl to a single one, although they knew that to reach them meant the difference between life and death.

She struck at midnight. At seven o'clock the next morning nothing was left of the sturdy vessel except "kindling wood"—a term used so often that it has lost its expressive meaning, but that was just what the raving sea made out of the big schooner in seven hours. In the very midst of that gale, Lieutenant D. F. A. De Otte, Assistant Inspector of the Life Saving Service, crossed the Great South Bay from Patchogue to the scene of the wreck in a scooter, driving through everything from rolling open channels to steeley ice. He arrived in time to direct the rescue of all of the crew who were not washed away when the tide finally went down and the life savers could get their boat out.

Last winter saw the first extended scooter voyage, when Seward S. Wicks and Charles Gill, of Patchogue, sailed over the ice from that point to the head of the Great South Bay and thence on through East Bay into the Peconic Bay, finishing at New Suffolk, a round trip of almost one hundred miles. They returned with the information that their visit showed the "East Enders" for the first time what a scooter looked like.

That is a queer thing about the scooter. A few miles east or west of Great South Bay the craft is hardly known even by reputation. Yet the ice in front of Patchogue has been like a picnic ground for the past two years. Every variety of craft cruises its surface. Patchogue boys, awakening suddenly to their opportunity, have rigged sails on dry goods boxes and mounted them on runners. The owners of the heavy square wooden scows, used to transport oysters, mussels and ice in the summer, slide slowly and majestically along, under their lofty sails. Old flat-boats, with scrap-iron runners fastened to them, rasp around merrily, the occupants having almost as much fun as the sailors of the trim real scooters, which flit like white fairies everywhere, and dart in and out of even the most crowded spots with the ease and swiftness of birds.

But the Long Island bayman is slow to believe and slow to change. Only a month ago a Jamaica Bay oyster-man looked at me with quizzical wrinkles around his eyes when I said something to him about scooters.

"Scooters, eh?" said he, spitting with loving care at a piece of driftwood. "Scooters! And they jump off the ice into the water, do they? Well, well! What a lot of things there be on land and sea that a feller never would hear of at all if he didn't associate with any except them that tells the honest truth."

Richfield Springs
(1888)

RICHFIELD SPRINGS.

BY MRS. M. B. HEDGES.

SOUTH of the Mohawk River, and as near central as to its position in the State of New York as the shape of the State allows, is the beautiful County of Otsego. The scenery is such as is repeated in many portions of the Eastern and Middle States, pleasantly rural, with meadow land, hop fields, orchards, all well cared for and trim. Its high and sometimes thickly wooded hills, with limestone strata protruding from the rugged slopes and dark ravines, save the country from the charge of monotony. These wild features show the neighborhood of the great northern wilderness and Adirondacks on the northeast, and of the Helderbergs on the east. Its streams and lakes abound in fish, the forest and lake shores in small game. The glory of elk and deer has departed, but sufficient field remains for the sportsman who is not absolutely bent on malarious bogs and mosquitoes as concomitants of his sport, while here, at the altitude of 2,000 feet above tide-water, cool breezes temper the summer heat.

The inhabitants speak fondly of this pleasant region as "Old Otsego." In any other country "old" would be ill applied, for the first patent, which gave the lands where Richfield now stands to a yeoman proprietor, was dated 1754. His Gracious Majesty George II. was to receive the important consideration of one barleycorn for one thousand acres of the wild forest land, with streams and lakes yet unnamed and untamed. What the monarch did with the barleycorn is unrecorded. What the yeoman did with the land is a matter of history. He subdued its savagery and divided it into parcels, which he sold for tidy sums of sterling money. At present the wealthy New York or Boston gentlemen who attempt pitching their tents or building cottages on the pleasant slopes of Richfield hills, find that no barleycorn or peppercorn equivalent, not even with the addition of the "pair of fat fowles" annually, specified in so many old leases, will suffice, but that real estate, though not prohibitive in price, is sought for and valuable.

But all that has been said of the country so far, might be said as well of many another fair and fertile tract of hill and valley land. If it were all, the numerous fine hotels and cottages, the parks and drives, the steamers on the lakes would never have been rendered necessary. Nature bestowed a gift upon Richfield that enhanced her attractions a thousand times, which did not wait for a white discoverer. At the foot of an ancient pine-tree, in the heart of a dense forest, gushed from its bed of rock a "medicine" spring, to whose healing waters a dusky tribe of pilgrims trooped long before the advent of the fashionable crowds that now make it their resort. Priestcraft took possession of the "medicine waters," and a hoary old impostor made his dwelling upon one of the twin islands in the neighboring lake, one of the loveliest spots about Richfield. He did not allow the spring to be approached without suitable incantations, and we may be sure, propitiatory offerings of maize and furs for his own benefit. The rites are somewhat different now, incantations being out of fashion, but the votaries of the spring find approach to it expensive as of yore. It is a comfort to know that in the midst of a violent storm the island of the prophet went down into the crystal waves of Lake Canadarago, freighted with all its extorted treasures, and the spring was free for a while to work its marvelous cures. The remaining island in this beautiful lake, only three-fourths of a mile from the principal hotels, has become, partly in consequence of the disappearance of its twin, a popular object of pilgrimage. Divested of legend, it appears that within the memory of man, a robust little island of from seven to ten acres has actually sunk out of sight in the waters of the lake ; a fact from which geologists will draw their own deductions about caves and subterranean streams in the underlying strata.

The spring continued to be known to settlers and visitors long after the disappearance of the Wizard of Canadarago. In 1821 twenty-five persons spent the "season"

at Richfield, now famous for cures wrought on rheumatic subjects and others afflicted with diseases amenable to mineral water treatment. A gentleman prominent in political life just after the war, Gen. Frank E. Spinner, writes, in a private letter : "A little over fifty years ago, when Sheriff of Herkimer County, while riding from Little Lakes to Mohawk, I was attracted by a strong odor of sulphur. I dismounted, hitched my horse, climbed over a log-and-rail fence, and found the spring overlaid by rotten logs. The wood of the logs was as black as ebony. I put a piece in my overcoat pocket, and the coat was hung up at my home. After a few days I found the stick of wood lying on the floor. On investigation it was found that the sulphuric acid contained in the wood had eaten a great hole in my coat. At that time, as I now recollect it, there was no house within half a mile of the spring, and your beautiful lake, and your now far-famed spring were both called Canadarago. What a pity the name had not been continued for both ! "

A little boy was once sent with friends for a long summer's day at a resort noted for its sulphurous waters. When he returned at night his doting mother asked, "Well, Phil, what kind of a day have you had ? "

"A very bad-smelling day," was the emphatic reply.

At Richfield Springs they manage better. The healing springs are discreetly housed, and no votive crutches are hung above the fuming fountains. We have spoken all along of "the spring," because the Great White Sulphur is emphatically *the* spring ; but the whole country is rich in mineral waters. The White Sulphur is now the property of T. R. Proctor, the well-known proprietor of the famous Spring House. The spring

VAN HORNESVILLE FALLS,
NEAR RICHFIELD SPRINGS.

is enclosed, and its waters are taken according to medical prescription, hot or cold, as a beverage, or in the form of baths. The guest of a day would not suspect from the movement and gayety of the throngs around him that here invalids resort for health. The health seekers are only a fraction of the summer guests. Here are sportsmen with rod and gun, wheelmen with their spider-web steeds, and lovers of manly exercise, while, to give zest, here are found all the attractions of society. Richfield is too various to be vapid, but it cannot escape being fashionable. The wilderness has its charms, but it has also mosquitoes, coarse food, long tramps, more than a hint of malaria, and a bed of hemlock tips is as rheumatic as romantic. Richfield is one of the most attractive of our Northern resorts, its name is uttered in the same breath with Newport and Saratoga, and there is much here to draw these crowds besides the seductive sulphur cup for the invalid, and the attractions of the ball-room and opportunities to display her fine feathers for the society belle. Brief holidays are here our portion. I speak for men of business in crowded New York or intense Boston, and we are glad not to further abbreviate our play-time by a long and severe journey.

From Boston there is but one change, at Albany. From New York you have choice of two roads, and can breakfast at home and sup at Richfield. You can go to any one of many fine hotels, or you can invade a tidy and well-kept cottage, and there is no law to prevent your pitching gypsy tents upon the side of Waiontha, in the dark recesses of Panther Mountain, or in sight of the clear mirror of Lake Canadarago, if you refuse beds of down and the culinary triumphs of the *chef*.

Such campers will probably be at Richfield for the shooting and fishing, rather than the sulphur bath and german, so here are a few timely words about the sport they may expect to find. From the first there has been enterprise shown in stocking the numerous lakes and brooks. Twenty-five years ago Messrs. Lewis & Berthick stocked Canadarago with lake trout from the cool waters of Otsego Lake, and lake trout, white fish and black bass from the State hatchery were put in plentifully fifeeen years ago. A trout stream called the South Columbia was stocked with forty thousand brook trout two years ago. A group of lakes, called Little Lakes, three miles from Richfield, have a great variety of fish. Five brook-trout streams within eight miles is not bad. The fly-fisher finds his best grounds in the numerous streams of Miller's Mills, only eight miles away, while Fly Creek and others are nearer and almost as good. Lake Canadarago has a great variety of fish : trout, pickerel, perch, black bass, oswego, rock and strawberry bass, not to mention the tribe of suckers, sunfish *et id omne genus*. There are a few old fishermen here " to the manner born." These old hands will become familiar to the eye by looking over the shoulders of the artists busy in every romantic nook. As an amateur once said, " Get one of these fishing fellows in your foreground ; he stands still better than a cow." From these members of the

CRUGER MANSION.

THE OBSERVATORY.

patient craft, when you have made their acquaintance, you will hear stories that would have brought Izaak Walton to Richfield— stories of long summer days spent by the side of .a babbling trout stream, while your fly floats down amidst the light and shade, till, splash! and you have landed your struggling victim with more satisfaction than has been afforded by many a professional triumph.

The shooting for all our native species of grouse, duck, other water-fowl, and all small wood game is good. The whole region was a favorite hunting-ground of the Indian tribes, and after the war of the Revolution, one of the most striking characters in Richfield history, Panther John, returned to live and die in his old loved haunts. A savage of the sternest school of savagery was Panther John, and he has impressed his name upon the wild mountain that still, wooded to its top, overhangs the southern shore of the lake. In its proper place we should have said that the neighboring Lake Otsego boasts of a variety of bass said to be known in no other finny circle. It is the creed of Cooperstown that no other waters are cool and clear enough for this aristocrat of the lake. Certainly its flavor gives the epi-

cure a new sensation, and it affords good sport.

In your tramps about Richfield you may see what appears to be the silhouette of a gigantic cricket. It approaches rapidly; man and wheel separate themselves to the vision; it is a bicyclist, perhaps the veteran E. A. Hinds himself, the oldest bicyclist in old Otsego, and the president of the Cycling Club. The Waiontha Club are star riders, and have connection with the L. A. W. They have reorganized for 1888 strictly on a wheeling basis. The club has a membership of thirty, though only three years old. The captain is August Kinnie, another noted wheelman of that section of New York State. They are a strong club as to their record. E. A. Hinds is not only president of the local club, but local consul of the L. A. W. He spent last winter in San Francisco with his wheel, and had, to quote his own expression, "a royal time" in California and Colorado, riding all over those States. He rode his wheel from Denver to Colorado Springs, Manitou Springs, and through the Garden of the Gods, and came home through the Southern States, visiting all the principal cities. There are about sixty wheels and seventy riders in Richfield.

The roads around Richfield are good, and on the wheelman's favorite trails there are no more ascents than are needed to break the monotony. The run around Lake Canadarago, twelve miles, is very delightful and level, with the exception of two or three short, sharp hills. Another favorite run is to Cooperstown, via Warren and Otsego Lakes. Bicyclists are noted for their courtesy and readiness to make the roads pleasant to brother wheelmen, and the members of the Waiontha are no exception to the general rule.

As for other means of killing time, nowhere are they so plentiful. Lake Canadarago, of which the poet might have written:

> "On thy fair bosom, silver lake,
>   The wild swan spreads her snowy sail,"

is large enough not only for a steamboat, which plies its daily round, touching at the widowed Island, whose mate went down into the dark tide long ago, and conveying picnic parties to favored points, but for a whole fleet of little boats. You may charter one for fishing purposes, or a constitutional row, and explore quiet wooded bays and shady nooks choked with pond-lilies and blue pickerel weed with as much sense of solitude as if the little city of summer people were miles away. Many smaller lakes are dotted between this and Lake Otsego. There are no continuous

LAWN-TENNIS IN SPRING HOUSE PARK.

waterways for canoeing, but the last-named lake gives a good course for races. A brilliant regatta was held upon Lake Canadarago two years ago.

Coaching is greatly in vogue, and to see the earnestness with which this pleasant sport is pursued recalls what Dickens and De Quincey wrote of coaching when it had the serious dignity of a means of travel. What spirit and zest were in it then! what adventures, as one "traveled by mail" over these very hills! The ancient stage-coach lumbered along with Beauty inside and her baggage in the boot, no longer ago than the days of Cooper, for the main arterial road of the State, the Cherry Valley Turnpike, passed through this locality. The charms of the wayside scenery encourages cross-country driving. Every summer families from New York come here in their own carriages, realizing the pleasures celebrated in Black's "Adventures of a Phaeton." Drag-hunting, too, offers its charms to lovers of exercise, and the original American picnic flourishes under every green tree, and leaves, from season to season, its desolating traces of egg-shells and empty bottles in the fairest wood retreats.

To the sports of forest and field which we have been describing, must be added those which Richfield furnishes more particularly for her summer guests and the

OTSEGO LAKE.

occupants of the various hotels and cottages. Some enterprising New York gentlemen, who return here annually, have inaugurated races, which take place in July and August in the Driving Park, and draw numbers of transient visitors from Utica and the neighboring towns. The liberal management renders Richfield race-days attractive to the country round.

At the Spring House are well laid out tennis courts—indeed, all the hotels and cottages make provision for tennis, and clubs abound. A grand tennis tournament marks the culmination of the season, and rival clubs from Cooperstown and other places enter the lists. Some of the most experienced tennis players in this country gather laurels in these contests.

A good measure of the growth and improvements in Richfield is afforded by the changes that have taken place in her hotels. The first hotel to accommodate summer visitors was the Spring House, built in 1823. Its name arose naturally from the Great White Sulphur in its grounds, which, still without rival, was then the only spring spoken of. Its guests could scarcely exceed a score in number. It has been noted down to the present owner of that title, for the high character and position of its proprietors, and one of these early hosts, on becoming a member of Congress, leased the house for $500 a year. Now, not to note changes in detail, its forty feet of length has grown to six hundred! A beautiful lake surrounds it, enclosing grand old shade-trees, fountains, summer-houses and tennis courts ; croquet and archery grounds, with spring-house, bath-house and summer theatre grouped near by.

To every convenience and luxury known to the modern hotel the taste of the present proprietor has added many of the charms of an elegant home. The *New York Home Journal* says of the main drawing-room of the Spring House, that "it is probably the most beautiful to be seen in any summer hotel in America." And of its park, that it is "the beauty spot of Richfield." Its score of guests has swelled to annual hundreds, and the most distinguished men and women may be met here at some time during the season.

The New American, another of Richfield's best hotels, also possesses a spring, and the only one whose waters share with the White Sulphur the honor of complete analysis. It was discovered in 1865. The house has itself been considerably modernized. It has very recently passed from the ownership of Mr. Uriah Welch, of the Mitchell House, Thomasville, Ga., to that of Mr. E. M. Earle, of Earle's Hotel, New York. This enterprising boniface has thoroughly overhauled the premises, partly refurnished the house, provided it with an elevator, added a commodious billiard-room and attractive café, and it is said that he has only begun his improvements.

Many other hostelries there are. Cooperstown, with its legendary, literary and historical associations, is so near a neighbor, that the two places are frequently spoken of together. There is a constant interchange of visitors, whom Mr. Crittenden, of the Cooper House, receives on behalf of Cooperstown, with his well-known and widely enjoyed hospitality.

Only incidentally have the charms of scenery been mentioned. They are sufficiently powerful to draw the same nature lovers to these hills year after year. They have been celebrated by poets and artists. From the time when the silver flying shuttle of the April rain begins to weave violets, anemones, daisies, buttercups, into the grassy carpet of the meadows, till the graceful hop clusters swing from the tall poles like green banners heralding advancing autumn with its procession of fruits and flowers, every day offers its excursion, its drive, its row, or its shady places for sauntering with a book. From the heights of Otsego Mountain, where the observatory is placed, you may see a wide expanse of northern wilderness dark with forests and dotted with steely-gray lakes. Turning to the east the hills of Berkshire are before you, to the south the rich Otsego meadows. In Richfield September only turns a richly illuminated page and holds the guests enticed by the bright fresh days of earlier June. Once here for sport, or health, or holiday, you loiter, linger, go reluctantly, return surely : that is every one's experience at Richfield.

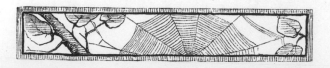

On the Harlem ,
Up to Pawling
and Beyond
(1891)

ON THE HARLEM, UP TO PAWLING AND BEYOND.

BY ERNEST INGERSOLL.

NO journey out of New York is pleasanter in point of what interests the eye and mind of a traveler than that along the Harlem.

Slowly but surely the city's widening domain is extending, and in the natural course of events at no very remote future we may expect to see the principal residential portion of the metropolis north of the Harlem River. Almost before the city is quit the country begins, and after the historic old town of White Plains has been passed the rural scenes are unbroken for a hundred miles. There is a charm, too, in this district, additional to its native beauty of landscape and excellence of climate — it is "far from the madding crowd," yet not too far.

The route trends through a north and south valley, or irregular depression, drained by the Bronx, the Croton and other small rivers, separated from the Hudson by the Fishkill range of "mountains," and from the Housatonic Valley eastward by a less distinct line of hills and ridges, written down in the books as the Taghkanick range. This spelling is an attempt to represent phonetically the rough, aspirated pronunciation of the Algonkin word, but the name has been more euphoniously familiarized in geology as Tacomic, and applied to a system of crystalline rocks, the type of which is found in the range. These mountains grow as they are followed northward, and finally blend with the Berkshire Hills of Western Massachusetts.

As in the Blue Ridge (of which, in fact, they are only a continuation) the old

rocks of which these hills are built decay into strong and fertile soils, and the farms which long ago swept the valleys clear of forest have been extended in strips and patches of rich grain fields up to the very tops of the highest ridges, interspersed with spaces of woodland, and interrupted here and there by some bold tor or rough escarpment, where the rocks are exposed in picturesque ledges, or the stony slope is too steep to hold anything except such sturdy and weather-warped trees as can thrust their roots far into crevices and defy both the gales and the washing of torrents to uproot them.

In this diversified landscape, the new and the old in architecture, the historical and the modern, are pleasingly mixed; and the people, to a great extent, correspond like chrysalids to the houses they live in — more precisely, perhaps, their houses, like cocoons, have been shaped by the occupants. One sees, fortunately, few angled "villas," looking like exaggerated toys, but plenty of substantial, simply decorated farm houses standing among great trees close beside the highway, attended by huge barns and stables, trim and erect, which attest the productivity of the broad acreage of which these establishments are the focus. Therein live men of account, who have kept pace with the times and are in touch with the city, yet have never abandoned the soil nor forgotten the worthiness of their calling.

Here and there, by the old post road in the edge of a village, or hidden away in some nook of the hills, you will find an old colonial manor house, stout of frame and retaining under careful hands the respectability, if not the importance, of its youth, when a kind of feudal proprietor sat in the warmest corner of its vast fireplace. Lastly, here and there still stands the old-time cottage, with its huge central chimney, or, perchance, one at the end, showing its broad stone foundation in the outer wall and its eaves sloping almost to the ground. One that I knew of measured only 32 by 24 feet, yet inclosed a chimney 14 by 12 feet square. Inquire at such a house and you will almost always find that its owner still bears a name which belongs to the earliest annals of the region.

The many villages scattered along the line are mainly mere hamlets, with now and then one like Katonah, Brewster's, Pawling, or, further north, Wassaic, Amenia, Sharon or Hillsdale rising to a thousand or fifteen hundred inhabitants. They are brisk, clean, pretty little places as a rule, and many of them contain hotels of a size and elegance surprising until one remembers that in summer they are filled with city people. A few special summer resorts exist, of which those at Lake Mahopac and the "Mizzentop" near Pawling are most widely known.

Lake Mahopac has for its convenience a branch line from Golden's Bridge northwest half a dozen miles ; and no more charming digression from the main line can be made than to follow it and spend a few days there. Putman County is full of ponds of deep water nestling among its hills. The Waccabuc lakes, four miles east of Golden's Bridge, Lake Geneida, upon whose shore stands Carmel, the county seat, Lake Oscawana and others are attractive in many ways ; but the largest and best of them all is Mahopac.

The short ride from Golden's Bridge is a fitting prelude to the scene.

The clear and rushing Croton, so interesting to all New Yorkers, is beside the track for a mile or two, shaded by willows, pursuing a strangely devious course in order to make its way through the barrier of the Fishkill range of mountains, which here begins to be of some account, though not so high and regular as it will appear when we get further north. Then the railroad leaves the Croton and climbs the open of Plumbrook. Here the grades are steep and the car windows often overlook a wide and most beautiful prospect of farms and dairy pastures, with quaint old houses, mossy stone walls and winding roads, bordered by lofty elms and maples, showing how long and peaceful has been

STREET IN PAWLING.

the occupation of these fertile valleys. The hamlet Somer's Centre is a stopping place which will attract every lover of rural scenery, and scores of families from the city here find summer homes with the farmers. Still climbing, other hills are passed, other valleys open charming vistas and Lake Mahopac comes into view.

The railway approaches its southeastern extremity, where the shore is dotted with hotels, cottages and prosperous dairy farms, and nearby is the village.

This beautiful lake lies 800 feet above the level of the Hudson, surrounded by rocky hills, many of which are still clothed with forest. It covers less than seven hundred acres, but it is so irregular in outline, so indented by points and headlands, and so broken by islands that its extent seems much greater, for nowhere can one on the bank or in a boat perceive the whole breadth of it at once. With every change of position some new and charming composition of blue water and dark forest, cultivated shore, rocky islet and pretty cottage or farm house, pleases the eye. The water is deep in many places—fifty to one hundred feet often— and always clear and pure, for it is fed wholly by springs. It is not surprising, therefore, that fine fish abound. Black bass of six or eight pounds' weight are taken every season from its depths, while pickerel and the humble but toothsome yellow perch are caught by the hundreds.

Mahopac is no new aspirant for the favor of the refugee from the heat of a summer in the city. As early as 1822 a character known as "Old Bolivar" Monk, who is still remembered for his eccentricities, set up a tavern on its borders, to which the "tourists" of that day resorted.

It is probable that a census of visitors at Lake Mahopac in August would count one thousand five hundred or two thousand boarders in hotels and cottages.

How do all these people amuse themselves? Well, when they are not on the lake they are having a good time on land.

Ashore there are always baseball and tennis and croquet. Baseball is especially affected at Mahopac, the different hotels playing against one another with great vim. This for the youngsters. The older people drive a great deal, for the roads are excellent and the scenery always interesting. It is only fourteen miles to Peekskill and the militia camp, only nine

THE DUTCHER HOUSE AT PAWLING.

QUAKER HILL, PAWLING.

miles to Croton Falls, five miles to Carmel and so on.

But to return to Pawling, which may be taken as a good type of the whole region. It is a little place sixty miles north of New York, which has had a position for more than one hundred and fifty years on the map, but held only a few scattered buildings until a dozen years or so ago, when John B. Dutcher established there the breeding and dairy farm of Holstein and other fine cattle which have made his place famous. His example was imitated, more or less intelligently, by his neighbors, many of whom were wealthy and had had long experience in dairying, and that part of Dutchess County became a district of milk and butter production second to none in the State.

Coincident with this growth of prosperity in dairying, the people of Pawling and vicinity were moved to special efforts toward making their hills and vales and lake shores attractive as places of summer residence for "city folks." In this they surely had a good basis to work upon. Pawling itself is seven hundred feet or more above the level of Long Island Sound, and the hills around it rise six or seven hundred feet higher. Mount Tom, a peak just west of the village, is the highest point in that part of the State—a huge knoll forested to its very cap. Half way up its side a medicinal mineral spring gushes out, the water of which is piped

down; and near its base is the pretty Green Mountain Lake.

Appreciating the attractiveness of the locality, Mr. Dutcher built in the centre of Pawling village the handsome brick hotel which bears his name. Though it is open all the year round its capacious rooms are only filled in summer, when a throng of happy people make it their residence. In its rear, facing the beautiful West Mountains and a pretty park, is a line of immense piazzas, and attached to the hotel is a small opera house, with all the apparatus needed for complete theatrical display.

Green Mountain Lake, to which reference was made in a preceding paragraph, is inclosed in a part of Mr. Dutcher's estate called Lakeside Park, and a club house has been built upon its shore, half a mile from Pawling station. Here boats can be secured and excellent fishing enjoyed by introduced guests, who bring back strings of pickerel, bass and perch. As the lake has been well stocked by the State Fish Commission there is no lack of sport. Next the club house is a half-mile track for exercising and speeding the fleet horses that have always divided, with the Holsteins, Mr. Dutcher's interest in thoroughbred animals, and a covered grand stand insures the comfort of spectators at these amateur races.

But this is only one of half a dozen lakes and ponds within easy reach, and nowhere is driving or riding more enjoyable than in seeking them out. The roads are fair, though necessarily hilly—better than the average of country roads, because the soil here is light and gravelly and there is everywhere some inclination to shed the rain. Up and down the valley runs the old New York and Albany post road, one of the oldest turnpikes in the State, maintained in excellent order.

This road was cleared and made fit for traveling by Lord Loudoun, in order that he and his troops might march northward this way to attack the French in Canada at the beginning of the long French and Indian war, which so taxed the endurance of the colonies previous to the struggle for independence. Even then—in fact

GREEN MOUNTAIN LAKE AND CLUB HOUSE.

LAKE HAMMERSLEY AND BOAT HOUSE.

as early as 1680—what is now Dutchess County had been explored by the Dutchmen, who reported that it was a region so rough, heavily timbered and full of swamps as to offer no attractions to settlers compared with other districts open to the squatters of that day. Consequently, although this immediate region was granted to Beekman and descended to his son-in-law (after whom Pawling is named), it was half a century later before many clearings let the light in upon the head waters of the Croton.

Meanwhile a curious bit of history was making among the Taghkanick hills along the boundary of Connecticut.

Every reader has noticed doubtless the extraordinary little projection at the southwest corner of the map of Connecticut, and some perhaps have felt a curiosity to know how it came about. This is the way: In 1662 a conflict of claims arose between the New Englanders of Connecticut and the Dutchmen of Manhattan, who claimed all territory east to the Connecticut River. Finally a compromise was effected by an agreement to run a boundary line parallel with the Hudson River and twenty miles east of it; but so bad was either the surveying or the geography that the line started at the mouth of the Byram River (where Portchester now stands) would have crossed the Hudson below West Point. When this error was discovered a new boundary was projected from a point on the Sound, just west of Stamford, to run due northward.

Meanwhile, however, a lot of good Calvinists had settled along the shore of the Sound, between Stamford and Portchester, and when these people found that they were to be cut off from the Land of Steady Habits and made citizens of ungodly New York they raised such a clamor as compelled a hearing. The result was that Connecticut bought a shore piece large enough to take her loving children into her fold, and paid for it by ceding to New York a strip two and a half miles in width, extending along her whole western edge.

The moment this transaction was settled land in the Oblong, as the ceded strip is still called locally, became very desirable, because it was not the property of any grantee (whose conveyances were sometimes disputable), but that of the colony of New York, which could give an unquestionable title. A number of Quaker families of means therefore bought large tracts of the choicest land, and settled all along these hills, where their descendants are still numerous.

The most influential, if not the first, settlement of these good and thrifty people was made upon the lofty ridge three miles east of Pawling, then called the Oblong purchase, but long past known as Quaker Hill, which now forms one of the most interesting and beautiful rural localities in the whole State. Some of the old houses are left, including a typical meeting house of the ancient order; but the wealthy descendants of the simple-hearted Friends who cleared the fertile slopes have erected houses which their grandfathers would have called palatial, while outsiders have come in and built among them such modern mansions for summer homes as would be imposing in a city. Finally, at the old " Toffey's Four Corners " has risen the huge Mizzentop Hotel and a group of expensive "cottages" which in summer are a scene of brilliant gaiety that would have turned Gran'ther Toffey's hair white with grief and dismay at the frivolity of mankind could he have foreseen it.

It is a delightful ride from Pawling over to and around Quaker Hill. For a mile or so the post road is followed southward, and a house, now modernized, is pointed out as having been long ago a tavern well known to travelers. As it stood at the intersection of the post road with the main road from Poughkeepsie to Danbury and Hartford, it enjoyed a plentiful custom, and was a favorite stopping place for army officers during the Revolution, Washington himself having once taken a meal under its roof. Back of it the valley slopes down in a long range of tilled fields and pastures to where the gables of John B. Dutcher's house are seen among a group of noble trees. The road then turns eastward and faces the southern extremity of Purgatory Hill, a long, wooded ridge of considerable height rising in the middle of the valley. Why " Purgatory ?" No one seems to know; but the writer hazards the guess that it was named by some irreverent wag from its half - way position between the heaven of Quaker Hill and the — well, the comparative deviltry of Pawling in the rough, old war days.

How hard life was among these dark hills in the turbulent days before and during the War of Independence one need read but little history or talk with someone learned in traditions only a short time to discover. Mr. Philip Smith's "History of Dutchess County" (published by himself at Pawling) is a repository of stories of bloody adventure and dark fanaticism or superstition, relieved here and there by some chronicle of noble heroism or romance that shows how human nature loved as well as hated in those lurid days. For some reason an extraordinary proportion of the people of this district were Tories, and their presence of course made the patriots only the more vehement in their patriotism. A constant internecine strife was therefore waged. Everyone went armed, suspected treachery and was prepared to engage in any adventure. This was the country that Enoch Crosby, the original of " The

LAKE MAHOPAC.

Spy," of J. Fenimore Cooper's story, ranged over, and this the society he sprang from and knew.

Families were divided between Tory and Continental doctrines, and the saddest consequences ensued. It was here that a woman named Butter lived with her husband in a log cabin. He was an intense American, and tireless in hunting Tories out of their hiding places, securing their arrest or their scalps. She, on the contrary, was not only a loyalist but the intimate of the captain of a British band ; and one night, when her husband was at home, she led the Tories to their house, herself pulled away the chinking from between the logs of the bed, and stood aside while they shot him as he lay asleep in the family couch.

As we approach Purgatory Hill, the road rising toward the right to wind around its southern shoulder, we admire the picture we are leaving behind, and where Pawling is embosomed in a little vale at the foot of Mount Tom, and farther beyond is the rounded mass of the West Mountain, or Fishkill Range, while at our right is a broad array of fine farms, dotted with sleepy cattle. On Purgatory Hill, during the summer of 1778, Washington's army was encamped for a considerable time. How many men were here I don't know, but certainly a large detachment spent three weeks or more on this ground and cut down a considerable extent of forest to use as fuel and in hut making. The remains of some of these huts are well remembered by many of the older people, and even now those who know where to look for them can find the rude ovens of masonry in which baking was done for the army. No intrenchments seem to have been thrown up, and no fighting is known to have occurred. Subsistence was largely derived by enforced purchase from the Quaker farmers, whom the quartermasters and commissary officers made requisitions upon without reluctance, since it was generally believed that they were sympathizers with the crown rather than with the colonies ; but there seems little evidence of this beyond their non-combatancy, which was a stumbling block to patriots in that hour of bitter struggle.

Purgatory Hill is now covered with second-growth brush, and it is said to be a good place to shoot woodcock in the fall. I presume a winter tramp with dogs there would put up a few foxes.

The road makes its way high up its southern slope, and, as it curves around toward the eastern declivity, the great Mizzentop Hotel suddenly comes into view, situated a mile in advance upon the crest of Quaker Hill and looking very admirable. A new road is to be built, which will reach it by curve around to the left upon an easier grade ; but the old road, though hard upon the horses that have to draw the coach loads of guests from the station, will retain a picturesque and historic interest.

Beside the road on their land is a tiny graveyard, perhaps a quarter of an acre in extent, shadowed by ancient trees and set thick with mossy tombstones, some of which have fallen down. Here, in unmarked and perhaps forgotten grave, lies buried the robber Vaughn, who was a famous "Cowboy"—one of that class of marauders who infested the outskirts of the American armies during the Revolution, ostensibly doing what damage they could to the soldiers and to anybody who sympathized with them, but in reality robbing right and left without any distinction as to their victims. The Cowboy of '76 was the prototype of the bushwhacker and jayhawker of the War of the Rebellion. Vaughn was a young man, naturally smart and fairly well educated. He came into especial notice by a descent with his gang one night upon the home of the Pearces, who were well known as a family active in the cause of American independence. The senior member of the family—Captain Pearce—was away, as no doubt they knew, but his brother Nathan was at home attending to farm work and living peaceably with his neighbors of whatever opinion. The band surprised him in the night, beat him half dead, then hung him to the rafters by his thumbs and whipped him again. When found in the morning he was dead.

Protected by Tories, Vaughn and his band were able to hide from vengeance for some months and to perpetrate many another black deed. Over at the right (south) of the hotel as you approach it you can see a deep ravine or rocky gash in the hill, shadowy with rock ledges and tangled woods. In those days it was in the centre of a wide forest, invisible and almost unapproachable, and there Vaughn made his lair in a small cavern. This was discovered at length, and Captain Pearce made haste to collect his friends and go upon his errand of vengeance. They

Drawn by Lincoln.

ON THE ROAD TO THE MIZZENTOP.

Engraved by Schoonmaker.

THE DRIVE ALONG LAKE MAHOPAC.

crept through the woods like cats until they were near enough to catch a glimmer of the fire the robbers had, in their fancied security, built upon the flat rock outside the cave mouth. Creeping nearer, with the Indian-like stealth of the practiced frontiersmen, they saw the gang clustered about the blaze, which lit up their evil faces and made them targets for the rifles whose long barrels were so near that they almost caught the firelight as each was pointed straight at a victim's heart. Crash! went their messages of death in dreadful unison, and through the smoke, bayonet and knife in hand, the avengers leaped amid the writhing bodies of their foes to finish the work. All were dead but Vaughn, who, horribly wounded, begged piteously for his life, and was answered by a thrust of Pearce's sword, literally pinning him to the ground.

'Tis a gruesome tale; but 'twill serve to spice with romance the picnics and rambles of light-hearted companies of guests who now go strolling gaily through that ravine, or climb again those rocks whose bloody stains were long since overgrown with lichens and hidden in saxifrage and columbine and the delicate petals of the windflower.

Just at the foot of Quaker Hill, on the right hand, stands a large farm house, the main front of which is comparatively modern. The back part belonged at the time of the Revolution to the finest building in the neighborhood. It was known as the Kirby house. Its owner, Mr. Reed Ferris, was apprised that Washington desired to make it his headquarters during the stay of the army there in 1778 and to this he proudly assented. The best chamber was set apart for the general's use, while the front parlor became his office, and the whole dooryard became the camp of his staff. Many pleasant traditions remain of that peaceful month, and of the great man who conferred immortality upon whatever he made use of. An additional interest attaches to this place, however, from the fact that it was in this house — and the fact is not generally known — that the trial of General Schuyler took place.

Gates, through jealousy and personal enmity, had succeeded in blackening the reputation of Schuyler before the Congress of the country by charging him with having neglected his duty and criminally mismanaged the Northern army during the disastrous campaign of 1776.

Schuyler had been deposed in favor of Gates, but for a wearily long time was unable to get a court martial to try his case and hear his defense. At last this was accomplished. A circle of high officers gathered in Mr. Ferris' parlor in October of 1778, and, to Washington's delight, Schuyler was acquitted and reinstated in his command.

The tortuous road brings us, step by step, to the summit of the hill, where a scene of gaiety awaits. A dozen large and beautiful cottages surround the great Mizzentop Hotel, situated in the midst of flowery lawns and scattered trees, overlooking a wide and beautiful expanse of valley land and range behind range of grandly proportioned hills. One can trace the windings of the Croton, whose springs are at his feet, far down behind Pawling into Paterson, and count farm houses and hamlets by the score.

This point is nearly fifteen hundred feet above the sea, and the air is clear and sweet and cool. It would be hard to find a better place to plant a hotel for summer guests and hard for summer guests to find a better hotel. There are immense verandas facing the south, and lawns by the acre full of shady nooks. There is music and dancing galore for the evenings and rainy days. Finally, to complete this catalogue of good things (in which the abundance of milk and home-made butter and country fare generally should not be forgotten), the proprietors have given the ladies a billiard room all to themselves, and over it is an opera house, with a stage and regular scenery, where private theatricals or any public entertainment can be given with ten times the comfort and good effect it would have in a crowded parlor. Where did it get the name Mizzentop is everyone's query. This is the explanation : Some distance northward the ridge swells upward into a knoll of a hundred feet or more higher than the site of the hotel. There Commodore Worden—the hero of the *Monitor*—built himself a cottage which he called the Maintop. As the hotel was somewhat lower, the idea was fancifully carried out by styling it Mizzentop. This point, where the roads cross, has always been called Toffey's Corners.

The old ridge road keeps on northward along the backbone of the hill, which is covered by park-like estates and fine houses—some new and fantastic, others with old-fashioned solidity and a dignity to which the modern country house rarely attains. The road is shaded for the most

DENIZENS OF THE DISTRICT.

MR. J. B. DUTCHER'S RESIDENCE, PAWLING, N. Y.

of the distance by magnificent maples and elms and forms a delightful walking place, at any rate as far as the old Quaker Meeting House at another cross-roads a mile north of the hotel. This is one of the first objects of pilgrimage for every new-comer. It is a two-story, square, un-painted building, as plain as a barn, with small-paned windows like a house, and two doors side by side in the middle of the front. There is no porch, nor cornice, nor the slightest attempt at ornament, much less steeple or bell. Inside is an equal absence of elegance—nothing but rows of straight-backed, unpainted benches, just alike on each side of the partition which, as in all the old-fashioned Friends' meeting houses, divides the men from the women during the silent hour of worship.

This interesting building was erected by the Oblong Meeting in 1764, and is still used on certain occasions for reli-gious meetings, though the "new" meet-ing house close by, itself nearly a century old, is the ordinary house of worship. Many an entertaining tradition clings about these quaint buildings and the col-ony of Hicksites of which they are the

centre, and the writer or artist who is for-tunate enough to spend a summer on Quaker Hill will find his note books filled with suggestive materials for work before his vacation has ended.

A more distant point for excursions is to a piece of water among the hills, three miles north of the Mizzentop, which al-ways used to be called Oblong Pond, but lately has received the more elegant ap-pellation — it would be inappropriate to say simply "finer name "—of Lake Ham-mersley after the family within whose pos-sessions it lies and which gave to an admiring world the present Duchess of Marlborough. Here a club house has been built for the use of the guests and cottagers of the Mizzentop, boating and sailing may be enjoyed, and the wily bass and pickerel can be lured from their weedy hiding places to take your treacherous hook.

On the whole, it would be difficult to find an inland spot which combines more of the advantages which one seeks in a rural residence during the hot weather than does the region around Pawling and Quaker Hill.

Among the
Thousand Islands
(1883)

AMONG THE THOUSAND ISLANDS.

By HOWARD PYLE.

THE terrific combat between Manabozho, the Indian hero, better known as the Hiawatha of Longfellow, and his father, the West Wind, was doubtless suggested to the first narrator of that memorable event by the lakes of northern New York upon the one hand, and those of the St. Lawrence chain upon the other, as marking the cavities from which those Titans might be supposed to have plucked the masses of rock they hurled at each other, the falling fragments of which formed that peculiar geological phenomenon known as the Thousand Islands, scattered through the St. Lawrence for a hundred miles or so of its course.

These islands, about eighteen hundred in number, stretching throughout that broad portion of the upper St. Lawrence extending from Lake Ontario to the Long Sault, are of all sizes and of all kinds; some not more than a yard or so in extent, and some covering many acres; some bare, rocky, and desolate; some thickly covered with a scraggy growth of scrub pines and hemlocks; some shaded with considerable forests of timber trees, and some cultivated here and there, producing such slight sustenance as the inhabitants can wring from an unfruitful soil.

In the old Indian days, this beautiful extent of the river from Clayton to Alexandria Bay, embracing an extent of sixteen miles, widening almost to a lake and crowded with a perfect maze of islands, went by the name of Manatoana, or Garden of the Great Spirit; and, indeed, in the time of Nature's undisputed empire, when the larger islands were covered with thick growths of pine, hemlock, white birch, and maple; when the wild deer swam from woody islet to woody islet, and each little lily-padded bay, nestling in among the hills and bluffs of the islands, teemed with water-fowl undisturbed by the report of a gun, it was worthy, to the semi-poetical mind of the Indian, to be an abode of Him who created all nature, and who had made this lovely region as an especial dwelling-place for himself. Even so late as fifty years ago, before the great tumult-creating steam-boats had disturbed these solitudes, the islands were the favorite retreat of deer; catamounts wailed in the tangled depths of the night-woods, and each cool nook and corner teemed with wild life.

Now, however, the inexorably rotating kaleidoscope of time has shaken away the savage scenes of old, never to be repeated, and new ones appear to the eye of the present. No longer in Alexan-

MAP OF
Part of the
THOUSAND ISLANDS
-of the-
St. Lawrence River
Near Alexandria Bay N. Y.
Corrected from an old Canada Map of 1815-16
[Names as known in 1874-5]
Rev. Geo. Rockwell

dria Bay—fortunately still beautiful—does Nature reign in silent majesty, for the constant flutter and bustle of the life and gayety of a summer resort have superseded her. But although Alexandria Bay is in this continual tumult of life, for some fortunate and almost unaccountable reason, the Thousand Islands are not in the least tinctured with the *blasé* air of an ordinary watering-place, nor are they likely to become so. There are hundreds—thousands of places, rugged and solitary, among which a boat can glide, while its occupant lies gloriously indolent, doing nothing, but reveling in the realization of life; little bays, almost land-locked, where the resinous odors of hemlock and pine fill the nostrils, and the whispers of nature's unseen life serves but to make the solitude more perceptible. Sometimes the vociferous cawing of crows sounds through the hol-

low woods, or a solitary eagle lifts from his perch on the top of a stark and dead pine and sails majestically across the blue arch of the sky. Such scenes occur in a beautiful sheet of water called the Lake of the Isle, lying placidly and balmily in the lap of the piney hills of Wells Island, reflecting their rugged crests in its glassy surface, dotted here and there by tiny islands.

In the stillest bays are spots that seem to lie in a Rip Van Winkle sleep, where one would scarcely be surprised to see an Indian

INLET TO THE LAKE.

canoe shoot from beneath the hemlocks of the shore into the open, freighted with a Natty Bumpo or a Chingachgook, breaking the placid surface of the water into slowly widening ripples. In such a spot, one evening, after a day spent in sketching, when paddling our boat about in an indolent, aimless way, looking down through the crystal clearness of the water to the jungle of weeds below, now frightening a pickerel from his haunt or startling a brood of wood-ducks from among the rushes and arrowheads, we found ourselves belated. As the sun set in a blaze of crimson and gold, two boatmen rowing homeward passed darkly along the glassy surface that caught the blazing light of the sky, and across the water came, in measured rhythm with the dip of their oars, the tune of a quaint, old, half-melancholy Methodist hymn that they sang. We listened as the song trailed after them until they turned into the inlet behind the dusky woods and were lost to view. From such romantic and secluded scenes one can watch the bustle and hurry of life as serenely as though one were the inhabitant of another planet.

About a quarter of a mile back of the Thousand Island House is a spring of mineral water strongly tinctured with iron, clear as a diamond of the first water and cold as ice. A little creek, a perfect conservatory of aquatic and amphibious plants, winding in and out

HEAD OF CREEK AND IRON SPRING.

with many abrupt turns, leads to within a few paces of it. On either side of the open water of its channel is an almost tropical tangle and profusion of vegetation; water-lilies, white as driven snow, with hearts of gold, reposing on their glossy, cool green pads; yellow-docks, arrowheads with purple clusters of tiny flowers, giant bulrushes, cat-tails and ferns,—all in a bewildering tangle of verdure, at times almost impassable. A rude wooden bridge spans it at one place, so close to the water that the boatman is obliged to bend nearly double in passing under it. Here one may occasionally see a chubby urchin angling in the glassy water for small pickerel or rock bass. The bottom of the creek is matted, and in some places fairly choked, with an exuberance of water-grasses of all descriptions.

Perhaps one of the best and easiest ways of becoming thoroughly acquainted with the various views, some of them extremely beautiful, that the islands present, is by means of a little steam-yacht which runs in daily trips around Wells Island. Starting from Alexandria Bay, she steams up the river among the group of islands lying there, past cottages and camping-tents nestling among the cool green shadows of the trees; past shallow lily-padded bays, at whose edge stands, sentinel-like, an ancient log-cabin or dilapidated barn; past a camp-meeting ground at the upper extremity of

FLOWERS FROM IRON
SPRING.

Wells Island, the so-called Thousand Island Park; and finally, taking a sudden turn, she seems to direct her course against an abrupt shore. As she advances, however, a little inlet gradually opens to view; a few rods further and the land seems to shift and change like a dissolving view, while the little craft glides into a narrow channel between two abrupt islands, the banks on either hand being shaded by overhanging pines and hemlocks. The channel, not more than six or seven feet deep, is thickly covered along the bottom with the usual tangle of waving water-grasses and weeds, long ribbons of eel-grass, feathery Carolina weed, and other varieties, purple, green, and brown. Now and then a startled pickerel darts from under the bows of the steamer, or a solitary heron flops heavily away from among the water-lilies along the bank. On past a shallow sheet of water, Eel Bay, where an occasional fisherman with his assistant may be seen; past the white towers of a stumpy light-house, perched upon the corner of a little island and defined against the dark green of the pines at its back; on, at last, into the Canadian channel. Here a bewildering maze of beautiful islands, north, south, east, and west, rises upon every hand. At times, the channel seems a lake surrounded by an amphitheater of thickly wooded hills and bluffs, with no outlet but that through which the boat has just entered; proceeding onward, it dissolves into a long channel, contracts into an abrupt inlet, or widens to an open bay. Further on is that sudden variation in the course of the channel known to all St. Lawrence voyagers and boatmen as the "Fiddler's Elbow." As the boat enters this portion of the channel, it seems to be directed by the helmsman point blank into an island. At the very moment, however, when a few rods of further progress in that direction would dash the boat against the rocks, she makes a sudden deviation to the left, another to the right, and lo! the Canadian channel lies before her a good mile and three-quarters broad, and Grenadier Light-house lifts in the far distance. After passing a number of curious Canadian lumber stations, perched high on the steep bank, the boat rounds the lower end of Wells Island, directs her course among the little isles on the American side, and finally stops at Alexandria Bay.

The islands in the Canadian channel of this part of the river are chiefly in possession of the Government of the Dominion. Among them are some of the most interesting of the whole group. Old Bluff raises his rugged front from a hundred feet of water to eighty feet of bare, perpendicular rock, his forehead closely matted with a thick growth of scrub pines. Through the center of the island runs a valley, almost a gorge, in which stands an uninhabited frame shanty for the accommodation of visitors. It is a rough, unfinished structure of the coarsest deal, but it looks picturesque and romantic enough, shaded and almost hidden as it is by maples and white birch. From the top of the high bluff, fronting down the river, a magnificent view is obtained of the islands lying beneath, both in the American and Canadian channels. Here the artist sat perched upon the sheer edge of the bluff, sketching diligently, in full view of the natives for a mile around, and vastly to their astonishment.

"Hulloa, Cap!" came faintly up from below. He looked down; a cockle-shell of a melon-boat was tossing on the waves below.

"Be ye needin' a watermillin?"

He thought not, unless the anxious fruit-vender would carry it up the hill at the rear of the bluff. While engaged in this colloquy, the artist's sketch-book slipped from his hand and landed after many gyrations about half-way down the face of the cliff. Two of the party were obliged to go below in a boat, one of them climbing the rocks to secure the lost book, while a third remained above to direct their movements.

One of the most curious of the American islands stands a short distance above Alexandria Bay,—a cubical block of granite having almost the appearance of being carved by human hands, rejoicing in the not very savory name of The Devil's Oven, its summit giving

THE DEVIL'S OVEN.

sustenance to a few gaunt cedars, and its sides perforated by an almost circular opening which at a distance does bear some resemblance to a gigantic baker's oven.

The upper extremity of Carleton's Island, some twenty-eight miles above Alexandria Bay, narrows into a contracted promontory of land ending in an abrupt bluff fifty or sixty feet high. Here, perched aloft, perceptible to all passers-by along the river, and distinctly visible for miles around, stand a number of toppling and half-ruined chimneys. Like so many sentinels standing solemn-faced, waiting for the blessed time of rest that will relieve them from duty, they watch over the ruins of an old French fort, so old that its history has been lost in the mists of the past. Attracted by that romantic glamour that hangs in the very air of the antiquated and dilapidated ruin, we were induced to pay it a visit, to the mild wonder of the natives, who seemed to look upon the artist as a species of harmless lunatic. So interested were we with the time-worn remains that a brief visit developed into a three days' stay.

The early history of the place is almost entirely lost, insomuch that it is supposed by some to be the ruin of old Fort Frontenac. It was, so far as existing data go to prove, commanded by the French about the year 1760; then fell into the hands of the English with the

GENERAL VIEW FROM BLUFF ISLAND.

French possessions, and was finally captured during the war of 1812 by a party of Americans under command of one Hubbard, an ex-Revolutionary soldier, who found this once large and important fortress under the immediate command of two women and three invalids; an Ichabod of forts, its glory had departed. The women and invalids were valorously attacked, and after a slight resistance they capitulated; the poor old fort, as if to accelerate its already progressing ruin, was fired, and the Americans with their prisoners retired to the main-land, where they were received with salutes, cheers, and the music of the Cape Vincent band,—one fife and a drum.

Since that day the fort has never been rebuilt, but has been allowed gradually to crumble away into ruin, producing, as fruit of its semi-mythical history, a rich crop of romantic stories and legends. An antiquated well, dug through the solid Trenton limestone to the level of the lake, has been converted by the vivid imaginations of the natives into a receptacle of the doubloons which the French upon evacuating the fort are said to have thrown therein, with the brass cannons on top of them: though why they threw their doubloons

37A

RUINS OF THE OLD FORT,
CARLETON'S ISLAND.

into the well instead of carrying them away, has, I believe, never been satisfactorily explained.

Upon either side, and immediately in front of the bluff upon which the old fort stands, is a pretty little bay, which once doubtless afforded pleasant and easy anchorage for the vessels that lay under its protecting guns. An innocent lumber craft, sunk many years ago in this harbor, has been, through the medium of the romantic atmosphere that hangs about the place, converted into an audacious smuggler that, blown ashore here, sank with a fabulous amount of moneys, silks, laces, and Canadian brandies hidden beneath the lumber.

Without doubt, the place was once of considerable importance. The fortress has been built in the most elaborate manner after the system of Vauban, and exhibits a skill of the very highest order in the art of constructing defenses. The fortifications in the rear are semicircular in form; the trench, four feet deep and twenty broad, is cut through the solid Trenton limestone; the glacis, which is approached by a gradual elevation, being constructed of the same material to the height of four feet. Directly on the river-front it is naturally impregnable, and at the precipitous side was probably defended merely by a stockade.

Numbers of graves lie in a flat field immediately back of the fort, many of which have been excavated by relic-seekers in search of French buttons or shoe and knee buckles. A number of ghost-like rose-bushes standing starkly here and there, long since past the lusty age of flower-bearing, probably marked out paths through this cemetery in the wilderness. Back in the island, in a copse, are the remains of an Indian burying-ground, where numbers of stone arrow-heads, tomahawks, etc., have been picked up at different times ; and to the right of the fortress, immediately upon the bluff overlooking the Canadian Channel, are still older graves, where, it is said, as the bluff slowly wears away, an occasional grinning skull or grisly bone is exposed to the long excluded light of heaven.

In this vicinity, numbers of excellent old-fashioned wrought nails are constantly being plowed up or otherwise collected, some buildings being almost completely joined with them.

While here, we had an excellent opportunity of gaining a practical knowledge of the daily life of the island farmers, being obliged to lodge for a time at a little farm-house that nestled beneath the brow of the old fortification, like a swallow's nest in a cannon's mouth.

The proprietor did not seem overzealous to accommodate us; for what sane man, of his own free choice, would sit day after day in the broiling sun sketching the old chimneys? The bill of fare of our supper with the farm hands consisted of stewed potatoes, bread and butter, and pie, with the addition of scalding tea. The tea was perhaps rather lacking in the titillating taste of the herb itself, but any weakness in that direction was fully compensated for by the thickness of the bread and the solidity of the pie. After this repast, we were solemnly shown to our apartment immediately above the kitchen, dining and reception room, and in consequence intensely hot on this midsummer's night. Our sleeping chamber was evidently the room of state, hung with wonderful wall-paper, the floor pierced by the arm of a stove-pipe from the room below. Here stood the wash-stand, without the usual accompaniments of ewer, basin, and looking-glass; and our couches,—one a trundle-bed, and the other a gigantic four-poster of antiquated date. The stove-pipe

RIVER CRAFT.

served as an excellent
telephone whereby to
hear our landlady in
the room beneath dis-
cussing with a crony the proper amount
of board to charge her guests.   "Well," said the crony, " I've a feller
a-stayen with me; I'm a-goin' to charge him two dollars a week,
and "—in a determined tone—" I'm a-goin' to git it, too ! "   Modern
luxuries should always be paid for at whatever price.

On some of the islands and along the main-land one sometimes
comes upon an antiquated group of Lombardy poplars, almost invari-
ably standing in the vicinity of some equally antiquated log-cabin or
farm-house. The poplar is the ancient sign of hospitality, and in the
old country was generally planted near an inn or hostelry.   These
trees doubtless were brought to this country by the old voyagers,
and served as a landmark by which many a traveler or sailor on the
St. Lawrence, making the long journey from Montreal to Toronto,

hailed the vicinity of Christian help and assistance indicated by these darkly colored trees.

Behind Lower Grenadier Island, and three or four miles from Alexandria Bay, upon the Canadian main-land, are a number of excavations with remains of chimneys which we were puzzled for a long time to account for. They were certainly under-ground dwellings, but what was their use we could not satisfactorily explain. At length, we met a fisherman who told us he recollected hearing from his grandmother that in the "English war" British troops were quartered there during the winter. Whether the English war was that of 1812 or the Revolution, we could not discover; probably the war of older date may be referred to, as in many instances trees of considerable size have grown up in the midst of the excavations.

Of late years, perhaps, no event caused such a stir of excitement in this region as the so-called Patriot war in 1838,—a revolt of certain Canadians dissatisfied with the government of Sir Francis Bond Head, then governor-general of Canada,— which was joined by a number of American agitators ever ripe for any disturbance. The first center of operations of these so-called patriots was Navy Island, in the middle of the Niagara River, where they congregated, employing the little steam-vessel *Caroline* in carrying arms and munitions of war to that point. At length the steamer was captured by some Canadians, fired, and run over the falls of Niagara. Considerable indignation was excited in the United States by this destruction of the property of American citizens, particularly along the border, where indignation meetings were held, and secret societies called "Hunter's Lodges" were formed, with pass-words, secret signals, and all due attendant mysteries, the express purpose of which was revenge upon the Canadian Government. The agitators were deceived by these signs into imagining that events were now ripe for a general border war, in which they hoped to free Canada from the rule of Great Britain.

It was a wild, insane affair altogether, and after some time consumed in petty threats of attack, finally reached a climax in the burning of the Canadian steamer *Sir Robert Peel,*— one of the finest vessels upon the St. Lawrence. The most prominent actor in this affair was Bill Johnston,—a name familiar to every one around this region,— whose career forms a series of romantic adventures, deeds, and escapes,—followed by his final capture,—which would fill a novel. Indeed, we understand that a novel has been written by a Canadian Frenchman on this theme, though we have not had the good fortune to find any one who has read it. The burning of the steamer *Peel*, which occurred on the 29th of May, 1838, remains, however, an act of inexcusable and stupid incendiarism, answering no conceivable good purpose.

For some time there had been mutterings among certain of the societies, and for a few days previous to the occurrence something mysterious was felt to be in progress. The night of the 29th was dark and rainy. About eleven o'clock, the *Peel*, then on her way from Prescott to Toronto, stopped at McDonald's Wharf, on the south side of Wellesley—now Wells—Island, for the purpose of replenishing her almost exhausted stock of wood. The passengers were all asleep in the cabin, and the crew busily engaged in their occupation, when a body of men, twenty in number, disguised as Indians and with blackened faces, yelling tumultuously and shouting, "Remember the *Caroline!*" ran quickly down the bank, armed with muskets and bayonets, led by a tall, strongly built man, in a red shirt—Bill Johnston himself. In a moment they overpowered the unsuspecting crew, while on board all was tumult and terror. Some of the ladies fainted, and several of the passengers fled to the shore through the rain, clad only in their night-clothes. A short opportunity was allowed for the passengers and crew to carry their baggage to the shore, but by far the greater part was lost when the vessel was subsequently burned.

Toward morning, the *Peel* was drawn off from the wharf, and after being run upon a point of shoal about thirty yards below, was set on fire and abandoned. For some time the flames blazed aloft, illuminating the shores for miles around; but about dawn in the morning she once more got adrift, and finally sank in about seventy feet of water. It was nominally the intention of the captors of the steamer to convert her into a gun-boat and use her against the Canadian Government; but upon finding that she was firmly aground and resisted all their efforts to get her free, they fired her to prevent her recapture. By some it is asserted that the vessel was deliberately robbed and then burned to prevent detection and throw an air of patriotism over the crime of the perpetrators.

DOCK WHERE THE STEAMER "PEEL" WAS BURNED.

Johnston was originally a British subject, but turned renegade, serving as a spy in the war of 1812, in which capacity he is said to have robbed the mails to gain intelligence. He hated his native country with all the bitterness which a renegade alone is capable of feeling. He was one of the earliest agitators upon the American side of the border, and was the one who instigated the destruction of the *Peel*. A reward was offered by the government of each country for his apprehension,—so he was compelled to take to the islands for safety. Here he continued for several months, though with numbers of hair-breadth escapes, in which he was assisted by his daughter, who seems to have been a noble girl, and who is still living at Clayton. Many stories are told of remarkable acts performed by him,—of his choking up the inlet of the Lake of the Isle with rocks, so as to prevent vessels of any size entering that sheet of water ; of his having a skiff in which he could outspeed any ordinary sailing craft, and which he carried bodily across necks of land when his enemies were in pursuit of him, and of his hiding in all manner of out-of-the-way spots, once especially in the Devil's Oven, previously described, to which his daughter, who alone was in his confidence, disguised as a boy, carried provisions. He was finally captured and sent to Albany, where, after suffering a slight penalty for his offense, he was subsequently released, although he was always very careful to keep out of the clutch of the indignant Canadians. His son, John Johnston, still resides at Clayton, and from him, after some pressure, a part of this information as to his father's adventures was extracted.

There is a certain breath of life about the northern United States and the neighboring region of Canada suggestive even in mid-summer of hard winters,—of long months when the face of the St. Lawrence is as adamant; of snow lying four feet deep all winter without intermission; an indescribable reminder of that season when a huge wood fire roars in the capacious fire-place, and when the bellowing wind dashes hissing snow wreaths in among the tossing and writhing pines and hemlocks. There is a rugged look about the landscape, as though Nature, not daring to expend her strength in the labor of growing,—save in little secret nooks here and there, —merely rested to gain fresh strength for her yearly tussle with grim winter. The inhabitants—generally fishermen—are an honest, rough, weather-beaten set, truthful,—with the exception of legends of buried treasure, or perchance wonderful stories of an eighty-pound muskallonge or two,—kind-hearted and hospitable. The fisherman is quaint in dialect, curious in manners, with the invariable story of the huge fish which he almost caught—and didn't. "Be ye a-goin' to skitch to-day?" inquires he, patronizingly, as he leans over the rail of the slip and looks down into the boat, where the artist is making some preparations. "Ye hadn't oughter lose so much time from fishin'." Or, "Where be ye ter dinner (take luncheon) to-day?" An island where it is customary to take picnic dinners is usually denominated a "dinnerin'-place."

Sometimes, rowing home at night, one passes by the blazing fire of a camping party, twinkling in the gloom of some thickly wooded islet. Around the fire move the dark forms of the boatmen or cook, preparing the evening meal. To one side, the campers themselves lie stretched at ease, smoking, or talking over the day's sport.

One of the great features of enjoyment to the casual visitor to the Thousand Islands consists in occasional picnic dinners—not the ordinary picnic dinner, where a table-cloth is spread upon the ground, and cold meats and sundries upon the table-cloth; where

CAMPING OUT.

long-legged spiders or centipedes career across the viands or drop into one's cup of lukewarm coffee; but dinners as luxurious in their bill of fare as any of the hotels can afford, combined with all the unfettered gayety incident to such an *al fresco* meal. A day's fishing is nominally the backbone of the expedition, around which the day's pleasure is actually built. We will suppose that the party of a dozen ladies and gentlemen is formed, and the day planned for the expedition arrived,—a clear, sunny one, with not a ripple stirring the glassy surface of the stream. Six boats are hired, a gentleman and lady going in each, under the superintendence of a fisherman, which fisherman, if he should happen to be George Campbell, one of the Patterson Brothers, McCue, or some such competent hand, may afford his lucky party a day's sport that of itself would fully satisfy the expectations of most people. Perhaps, if the fishing-ground be distant, a steam yacht is engaged, the boats, stretching in a long line, are taken in tow, and off the jolly party starts, with flags flying merrily.

A FISHING PARTY.

At length, the desired spot is reached and the sport begins, each party fishing as if their lives depended upon it, and all internally praying that, if a monster pickerel or muskallonge is caught,—of which there may be about one chance in five hundred,—they may be the particular ones selected by Fortune as the catchers thereof. But whether such a capture is made or not, the fishing is sure to be fine, and so exciting that the dinner hour approaches without notice until, warned by the shrill whistle of the little steam-yacht, the boats wend their way from all quarters to the " dinnerin'-place."

The luncheon, mind you, is not made up according to the simple bill of fare presented at the desk of the hotel, composed of mere necessaries, such as eggs, bread and butter, coffee, and fat pork ; but, under the supervision of Isaac, the overseer of the luncheon-room at the Thousand Island House, it crops out in various " extras " and " sundries," in the shape of a tender chicken or two, juicy steak and chops, green corn, tomatoes, and the like. The fishermen— excellent cooks, deft and cleanly—perform the task of preparing the meal with wonderful dispatch, and in a short time a royal repast is laid before the hungry anglers, whose appetites, whetted by health- ful exercise and invigorating air, do ample justice to the feast. After dinner, while the fishermen are packing away the dishes and other et ceteras, the ladies retire for a short nap and the gentlemen for a social cigar; then, as evening approaches, back to the hotel, there to doff the flannel shirts and fishing-dresses, and once more to assume society clothes and manners.

Many, however, prefer solitary sport, or with a company of two or three gentlemen only; and by starting in the early morning, long trips can be made, far down below Grenadier Island. There, in the more shallow portions of the river, striped with long beds of water-grasses, green and purple, undisturbed by the turmoil and commotion of passing steam-boats, the indolent pickerel lies tranquilly in the secluded tangle of his own especial retreat; or huge black bass, reaching sometimes to the weight of five or six pounds, stand guard along the edge of the grass, waiting for some unwary minnow or perch to pass. At rare intervals are spots where the savage mus-

COOKING A CAMP DINNER.

kallonge, the tiger of fresh-water fish, lies hidden among the water-grasses in solitary majesty. Sluggishly he lies, glaring with his savage eyes to right and left of him, watching for his prey. He sees a minnow in the distance, apparently twitching and wriggling in a very eccentric course; a moment the monarch poises himself, with waving fins, then, a sudden sweep of his majestic tail, and he darts like a thunder-bolt upon his intended victim. The next moment the sharp agony of the

CATCHING A MUSKALLONGE.

fisherman's hook is in his throat. For a moment he lies in motionless astonishment; then, as he feels the line tighten and discovers he is indeed caught, he struggles with rage, making the water eddy and swirl with the sweeps of his powerful tail, and causing the rod to bend almost double. This way and that he darts, mad with rage and pain, while the line hisses as it spins from the reel; but in vain; in spite of all his endeavors, he feels the tightening line drawing him nearer and nearer to the surface. Again and again he is brought to the side of the boat only to dart away once more, until at last, sullen, exhausted, and conquered, he lies motionless in the water beside the victorious fisherman's skiff. A moment more and the gaff strikes his side and he is landed safely in the bottom of the boat.

SPEARING EELS IN EEL BAY.

"Hurrah! a twenty-pounder!"

In the early spring, when the shallows of Eel Bay or other sheets of water of the same kind become free from ice, the water, not being deep, becomes warm much more quickly than elsewhere, and here the half-frozen fish congregate in great quantities. The professional fisherman in the bow of the boat holds a spear, in shape like a trident, but with an alternate sharp iron prong between each barbed shaft, the whole fixed upon a long, firm handle. Immediately upon seeing a fish, he darts this gig at him, fixing the barb so effectually in his victim that to strike is to capture him. The weapon used is called a jaw-spear, from its peculiar form, being a jaw-shaped piece of wood, with a sharp iron barb firmly fixed in the angle, against which the eels are forced and pinned fast until they are safely landed in the boat. Eel-spearing is generally pur-

38

sued at night, not only because the water is usually more quiet then than during the day-time, but also because the light of the blazing pine chunks in the "jack" or open brazier fixed in the bow of the skiff makes objects on the bottom more apparent by contrast with the surrounding gloom.

It is a picturesque sight to see the swarthy forms of the fishermen, lit up in the circumscribed circle of light, looking like phantoms or demons—the one in the bow bending eagerly forward, holding the spear and watching the bottom keenly for his victim; the one in the stern silently paddling the boat across the motionless water, not a sound breaking the stillness of night but the tremulous "Ho-o-o-o" of the screech-owl or the crackling of pine chunks in the jack. Suddenly the figure in the prow poises himself for a moment, drives his spear forward through the water with a splash, then draws it back with the wriggling victim gleaming in the blazing light of the pine.

In June there is fly-fishing, and fine sport it is to cast a fly so adroitly as to tempt a plump bass in the seclusion of his rocky retreat beneath the overhanging birches along the bank, and fine sport to land him, too; for the bass, lusty and strong through good living and pure water, will battle with the sportsman as vigorously as ever did dappled trout, struck in the pools of Maine.

Toward summer, the fish become more sluggish and refuse to strike at a fly, and then "still fishing," with live minnows for bait, or the less skillful sport of "trolling" take the place of fly-fishing. Of trolling, little is to be said. The lines are merely trolled from the stern of the boat; and if the fish bites, unless it be an extraordinary large one, nothing is required but to haul him in, hand over hand, and land him finally, without any skillful handling, in the bottom of the boat.

With still fishing, however, more skill is required. As a sport it occupies the intermediate point between trolling and fly-fishing, and, should very light rods be used, a great deal of sport may be obtained in playing and landing the fish. Nearly all the boatmen, upon the least encouragement, will recount stupendous stories of eighty-pound muskallonge, forty-pound pickerel, or eight-pound bass. The largest fish that I could find reliable record of as having been caught and landed were a muskallonge fifty-one pounds, a pickerel twenty-seven, and a black bass six and a quarter.

Numbers of ducks of different varieties frequent the bays and inlets of the Thousand Islands in the spring and autumn, and quantities of ruffed grouse are found upon the main-land, so that the shooting is said to be excellent in its season. While we were there, two or three deer were said to have come from the main-land to Wells Island, where they were diligently hunted, but, so far as we heard, without success.

The most interesting part of the development of this region as a watering-place is that which relates to the settlement of the islands by private residents. The islands have not been held at too high a price, and a multitude of men have bought them and built houses upon them for summer use. Some of these are little more than shelters or "shooting-boxes"; some are comfortable houses; and several are expensive and very splendid and showy places, so that a passenger on a river steamer, making his first trip down the stream, will find much of picturesque interest in glimpses of the architecture which greet him on every hand. There is no chance for fighting over boundary lines, and some of the lots with a liquid fence are so small that their owners can throw a fly from their front door-step to the bass they can plainly see in the clear water which is never disturbed by a freshet.

There are summer hotels at Clayton and other points along the shore, but Alexandria Bay is the grand center of the summer life. Of course, the Lake Ontario and St. Lawrence boats from all parts touch here, and there is a daily line between Ogdensburg and Alexandria Bay. Here are the great hotels, and here is the multitude. The village contains about five hundred people, with two churches — a Methodist and a Dutch Reformed Presbyterian. The latter is a mission church, and was founded by the late Rev. Dr. Bethune, who was a famous fisherman in his day, and who, in his summer recreations on the river, did not forget to fish for men. The Methodists have established the "Thousand Island Park," several miles above, where they come in great numbers every year for recreation and a camp-meeting. They have a fine dock and quite a number of private residences. Westminster Park is a new enterprise. An association has purchased five or six hundred acres of Wells Island, nearly opposite to the village of Alexandria Bay, and the enterprise is now in the full tide of development. Fourteen miles of road have

been laid out, five of which are already graded. A dock has been
built more than a thousand feet long; and hundreds of building lots
have been thrown into the market. Under the influence of this great
influx of visitors, the fishing is quite likely to suffer; but the pure
water and the pure air that sweep down the mighty channel are
enough for the drinking and the breathing of a continent.

Pleasant are the recollections of the place of which some aspects
are recorded here; pleasant for all reasons; pleasant as a center
of watering-place life; pleasant for hours of fishing under the skillful guidance of George Campbell; and doubly pleasant, delightful,
for hours of silent, solitary communion with Nature in tranquil
bays and spicy cedar woods,—communion sometimes as uninterrupted as though we belonged to a different sphere from this earthly
one of hurry and bustle; a place of legend and romance, of old associations—an unfailing fountain of interest both in itself and its
inhabitants.

BONNIE CASTLE. OWNED BY THE LATE DR. J. G. HOLLAND.

Three Hundred Years on the Hudson (1909)

HALF A THOUSAND SKY-SCRAPERS GUARD THE ENTRANCE TO THE RIVER WHICH
HUDSON FOUND FLOWING THROUGH A WILDERNESS.

THREE HUNDRED YEARS ON THE HUDSON

BY ARTHUR B. REEVE

F Henry Hudson could return from his last port and sail again up the river which bears his name in the reproduction of his old *Halve Maene,* which the Dutch have sent to the Hudson-Fulton celebration, he would find not a point, not a stream, not a valley, not a peak, but has acquired its story or romance in the three hundred years since he made his first voyage. He would find that history flows down the Hudson valley as freely as the water of the river itself. Let us "follow the river," as the steamboat captains on the Hudson say, by the same stages as Hudson did in his vain search for the Northwest Passage.

We shall find it more varied in scenery than even the Rhine. The Rhine has its great past; the Hudson has a past and a present and future as well. The Rhine is feudal; the Hudson democratic. The Hudson has everything from the sublime to the serviceable. It is one of the greatest highways of travel and commerce in the country, the river that has made the Empire State what it is. It has wild scenery, thrifty cities, fertile farms, splendid estates. At its mouth is the metropolis of the new world, and over five million people live along its banks.

"This is a very good land to fall in with and a pleasant land to see," is the entry in Hudson's journal on September 2, 1609, when he anchored in the lower bay of New York. Other navigators had been within the sharp, reëntrant angle of Sandy Hook, but Hudson was the first to explore the river and to make authentic records.

To-day if Hudson came sailing up the bay he would pass through the deep Ambrose Channel which the Government is building for the great liners, and he would see the white towers of Coney Island, the world's greatest amusement resort. On up he would go through the Narrows, with Staten Island to the west and Long Island to the east, past Quarantine, past the heroic Statue of Liberty, greater than the Colossus of Rhodes, past Ellis Island, the gateway of the nation where nearly a million newcomers enter each year, past Governor's Island, and then at the Battery he would pause in wonder.

Before him would lie Manhattan Island which was bought for $24 and to-day is assessed at $7\frac{1}{2}$ billions. After he had recovered from his surprise at the skyline of over half a thousand sky-scrapers, he would probably look across to Jersey City and Hoboken and then again up on the Manhattan side of the river perhaps to the foot of West Tenth Street whence, two centuries after his first visit, a boat named the *Clermont* was to travel his route to Albany and back, without sails and against the wind.

Here he would be introduced to Robert Fulton with whom jointly he must

steamboats, he perfected many warlike devices. He had a crude submarine boat, the *Nautilus,* in which he actually dived and stayed under water some time; he had a sort of submarine torpedo; and during the War of 1812 he built the first steam war vessel, the *Demologos.*

It is true that John Fitch ran the first steamboat in America on the Delaware in 1786, that Rumsey followed in

ON BOTH SIDES ARE THE STEEP HILLS OF THE HIGHLANDS, RISING WITH
JUTTING CRAGS AND WOODED SIDES.

share the honors of the river. Fulton was the first to be economically successful with steamboats, just as Hudson was the first navigator to be authentic in his exploration of the river. Each had forerunners, yet each overshadows those who went before.

Fulton was born in Pennsylvania. He early showed an artistic temperament and went abroad to study art under Benjamin West, but was soon persuaded to give up art for invention. It is not generally known that besides his

1787, that Fitch experimented later in 1796 on the old "Collect Pond" in New York, and that in 1804 Colonel John Stevens had a sort of steamboat on the Hudson itself. Then, as we shall see, Chancellor Robert R. Livingstone had done much more than remain an interested spectator of steam navigation before he met Fulton in Paris while he was American ambassador in 1801.

But, after all, the voyage of the *Clermont* on August 17, 1807, was the first practicable application of steam to navigation. In one day the reception of "Fulton's folly" changed from jeers to cheers. All this happened at the foot of West Tenth Street, not far from the dock where the boats now sail daily up the river. Fulton's vessel had its side paddle wheels absolutely uncovered, its engine was exposed, and it was steered by a tiller in the stern. Contrast the 74-foot *Half Moon* with the 150-foot *Clermont* and both with the 790-foot

Above Hoboken lies Weehawken, where Alexander Hamilton fought Aaron Burr and paid with his life for his adherence to the code.

The original monument marking the spot was so chipped by souvenir hunters that it had to be removed. Now a new one is protected by a strong fence. Just above this spot, where now are piers, is Castle Point where actually took place the events in the life of Mary Rogers

Detroit Publishing Co.

BEYOND WEST POINT LIES STORM KING, GRANDEST OF THE PEAKS THAT RISE
ABOVE THE RIVER'S SHORES.

Lusitania. It may be that this celebration of 1909, a century hence, will be remembered for its flying machine flights, completing the triad of locomotion—of steamboat on water, steam engine on land, and flying machine in the air.

Just below the Stevens house, at Paulus Hook which is now Jersey City, Stevens ran the first ferryboat to New York, the Cortlandt Street ferry, in 1811. The second John Stevens had the honor of building the *Savannah,* the first vessel to steam across the Atlantic.

which furnished the plot of Poe's "Murders in the Rue Morgue."

On the New York side is Riverside Drive, with the Soldier's and Sailor's monument at Eighty-ninth Street, Columbia University, "the Acropolis of the New World," at 116th Street, and the great $600,000 Grant's Tomb towering in white stateliness at 122d Street.

Opposite is the beginning of the Palisades, a great ribbed stone wall, twenty-three miles long with a sheer height of 250 to 600 feet. Where the river nar-

Photograph by Arthur Hewitt.

SCORES OF LITTLE BAYS BREAK THE SHORE LINE AND GIVE GLIMPSES OF HILLS
AND FIELDS IN THE DISTANCE.

rows, just above, were Forts Washington and Lee, the heights where, in 1776, after the disastrous battle of Long Island, the Continental forces stopped on their retreat.

Hudson would probably be in despair by this time of recognizing anything at all on the river, but around Spuyten Duyvil Creek he would find a part of New York City that has changed little since his day. The creek itself has altered since those days, when Anthony van Corlaer, "Anthony the Trumpeter," vowed he would swim its raging tide, *spuyt den duyvil,* and was never seen again. But the country about it remains much the same; here a great column to Hudson is being reared two hundred feet in the air.

Leaving Yonkers—*jonkheer's landt,* or the young gentleman's land, referring to Adriæn Van der Donck—the river widens into Tappan Zee. Indeed the Hudson, with its seas and bays, is more a fiord or an estuary than a river. It has tides as far north as Albany, where they rise over two feet. Salt water wedges its way at times under the fresh river water as far as the city of Hudson.

But to return to Tappan Zee—from the Palisades to Haverstraw. Here in this inland sea is the cruising place of ghosts and goblins, the haunt of the "Storm Ship," the "Flying Dutchman of the Hudson" which forebodes storm, riding over river and shoal.

Before you leave Tappan Zee, look across at Sunnyside. That was the home of the man who *really* discovered the Hudson, Washington Irving. There is no time to dwell on Ichabod Crane and Sleepy Hollow; where Irving's body rests, on the "Knickerbocker History" and on—well, that's Tarrytown just above, and back of it are the Pocantico Hills and John D. Rockefeller's place, you know, and lots of others. Here is where Major André was captured in 1780 by the three noble privates whose loyalty shamed the treason of the general, Arnold. What need is there of repeating the story? Across the river, and a little back, near Tappan, André was executed.

There is Sing Sing a few miles above Tarrytown, too. If you are not in the prison it is Ossining, however. The prison is full, too full, and farther up,

Photograph by Arthur Hewitt.

IN PLACES THE RIVER FRETS AROUND BOWLDERS AND RIPPLES OVER SHALLOWS
THAT HINDER ITS SMOOTH FLOW.

on the west shore of the river, after you have begun to enter the Highlands, you will see Bear Mountain. There they are beginning to build a new State prison to supplant Sing Sing.

Now we are well into Haverstraw bay. This is famous for the making of bricks. Indeed the lower Hudson is full of brickyards, the upper of icehouses. As the bay begins to narrow down at the north you come to a pair of incongruous spots—Treason Hill where Arnold and André haggled over the price of the United States, and Stony Point, the "Gibraltar of the Highlands," as Irving called it, where "Mad Anthony" Wayne covered himself with glory.

When the British had captured this entrance to the Highlands it was "Mad Anthony" who said to his commander, when asked if he could recapture it: "I'll storm hell, sir, if you will plan it." "Try Stony Point first," was the dry reply. Wayne did, and he won it, but the point could not be held by the Continental forces.

Hudson entered in his journal that he came to a "streight between two points," on this day. That must mean the river as it converges on Stony Point to the west and Verplanck's Point to the east. Here is where on his return journey he shed the first Indian blood in a battle with the natives. A little above Verplanck's one comes upon Peekskill where the State militia camp every summer. From Peekskill to New York old "Commodore" Vanderbilt himself once "followed the river" as a steamboat captain and a good one.

Opposite Peekskill and farther up are Dunderberg and Bear Mountain. Dunderberg—"thunder mountain"—is at least the second place so far where Captain Kidd is reputed to have buried his treasure. One promoter spent $22,000 —of other people's money—looking for it. The other place is near Tarrytown. A third place is just above the Highlands at Matteawan. There is also an asylum for insane criminals at Matteawan—which is probably more famous now as the residence of Harry Thaw than as the site of Kidd's treasure.

Dunderberg on the west and Manito Mountain on the east are what may be called the "southern gateway" to the famous "Highlands of the Hudson "—

" a very high and mountainous region,"
as the unimaginative Hudson journal
puts it. Now, the river narrows again.
On both sides are the steep hills of the
Highlands, rising with jutting crags and
wooded sides abruptly from the water.
With wide sweeping curves the river
winds its way among the mountains
which crowd down and almost overhang
the boat.

Next to Manito is Anthony's Nose—
named for the same old Anthony, the
Trumpeter. His nose, it is related, was
so red—usual cause—that once the reflection of the sun on it when he was
washing his face here killed a great
sturgeon outright. Thus the mountain
was immortalized. The Dutch peopled
the Highlands with all kinds of mischievous beings, the Indians with the
mighty spirit of Manito.

In the days of the Revolution this
southern gateway was guarded by a
heavy wooden boom across the river,
linked together by chains and floated
by rafts, from Bear Mountain to Anthony's Nose.

Here Hudson anchored on September
14, 1609.

The Nursery of Warriors

Passing Fort Clinton, Fort Montgomery, famous as the home of " Captain "
Molly Pitcher, the heroine of Mon-
mouth, Iona Island, and Highland Falls,
you come at last to West Point—cradle
of war. Since 1802 it has been turning
out Grants and Lees—a list too long
even to quote from.

At West Point the Americans carried a chain across the river to prevent
the British ships from passing up and
down. Pieces of it are yet preserved
in museums. To-day West Point is being made over. From its steep sides
rise new turreted castles; new buildings
for the great military academy crown
the top of this bold promontory, which
rises two hundred feet above the river.

Above the academy one of the picturesque spots is old Fort Putnam, while
out in the river, facing it, is Constitution
Island. This has been made famous as
the home of the two sisters Susan and
Anna Bartlett Warner. Susan Warner

died in 1885 and is the only woman
buried in the military cemetery at West
Point, but Anna Warner has continued
their literary work. Last year Mrs. Sage
bought the island from Miss Warner
for $150,000 and presented it to the
Government.

Beyond West Point lies Mount Taurus on the east, and Cro' Nest on the
west. Then comes Breakneck on the
east above Taurus and, paired off with
Breakneck, on the west side is grand
old Storm King. Here is the " northern
gateway " to the Highlands.

In the river at this point a busy dredge
is at work, trying to find the solid rock
that underlies the mud in the bottom of
the river, so that a huge siphon can be
tunneled through it. Water, six hundred million gallons of it a day, from an
area as large as the State of Rhode Island which will be drained in the Catskills, will be siphoned from Storm King
to Breakneck and thence down to the
five boroughs of New York City. They
have gone down six hundred feet already
without finding rock bottom—so deeply
hidden is that ancient rock-bed of the
old Hudson now covered with the mud
of millions of years.

You must have noticed as you travel
up the Hudson that a good deal of it
has been literally " skinned alive," that
many of its choicest forests lie in cordwood on the piers ready to be loaded
and shipped. How is this to be stopped?
The cost of making the Highlands a
forest preserve like those in the Catskills and Adirondacks would be prohibitive. Therefore, only a few months ago
a new State law was passed which for-
bids anything except scientific lumbering
on the private lands between Stony Point
and Cornwall, each point a little to
either side of the southern and northern
" gateways." The cordwood piles must
go.

Thus there will practically be a forest
reserve at only the cost of the few thousand dollars necessary to maintain adequate supervision. An awful example of
what the skinning of the mountains can
do is the cutting on Dunderberg which
has left much of it nothing but gray
rock and scrub trees. There are now
some seventy-five square miles of " forest

Photograph by Arthur Hewitt.

TROY IS THE HEAD OF TIDEWATER, SITE OF THE STATE DAM AND OF THE
TERMINALS OF THE HUDSON, ERIE, AND CHAMPLAIN CANALS.

preserves" about thirty miles north of New York City itself. Besides this tract there are the State tracts at Bear Mountain and the Government tracts of West Point. So the Highlands are in a fair way to be cared for in the matter of forests.

A Land of Beauty

Another feature of the Highlands is the new State road from Stony Point north to West Point. This is just being completed and will open up to tourists a new area of beautiful scenery. But the safety of the Highlands is not assured with scientific forestry alone. In fact it is menaced by an even greater danger, against which there seems as yet no defense. It is the inevitable stone-crusher.

Driven from the Palisades, it has taken refuge at Hook Mountain, a horrible example of the blasters' art. There are some crushers at work on the upper Hudson, and now they are invading the

Highlands! When the quarries on Breakneck and Cro' Nest were abandoned nature-lovers felt relieved. Now a new one has appeared on Storm King, the most notable of all the headlands.

Leaving the Highlands behind, the traveler comes to the beautiful town of Cornwall where E. P. Roe returned to write "Driven Back to Eden." It is Eden, indeed. A few miles above is the historic city of Newburgh. Here is the State museum of Revolutionary relics, here was Washington's headquarters during the days when the army was battling at various points along the middle and upper Hudson, here the Society of the Cincinnati was organized after the war was over.

In the hills about Newburgh were the haunts of the American spy, Enoch Crosby, whose exploits Cooper has immortalized in "The Spy." Opposite Newburgh is Fishkill, back of which is Beacon Hill where the signal fires during the war could be seen from the one direction in the Catskills and from the other in the Berkshires.

Gradually the river changes its aspect from rugged hills to low, rolling country with fertile farms and orchards and here and there a busy city. Far ahead you see a spidery line stretching across— the Poughkeepsie Bridge and as you near the huge cantalever a toy train crawls across, high overhead. This bridge was built to put Pennsylvania coal straight into the heart of the New England manufacturing region. From it Poughkeepsie gets its name of "The Bridge City."

Poughkeepsie sticks in your mind as the home of Vassar College, one of the oldest and largest of the women's colleges. It may come as a surprise to you to see the sign along the river front " M. Vassar & Co.'s Brewery." Matthew Vassar came to this country as a boy with his father in the last decade of the eighteenth century. His father and uncle founded a brewery which later he himself carried on.

Back in the sixties he decided to erect a great monument along the river as one way of perpetuating his name, so he announced that he would build one to Henry Hudson. No one seemed to care much about it, so he abandoned the idea and decided to establish a woman's college instead and show the world that higher education for women was not a bugbear. People have cared a great deal about that. Truly the monument could wait. Two miles east of the city the great institution lies.

Poughkeepsie is also noted as the scene of the intercollegiate races every summer. There are a hundred or more oarsmen in the various contests followed by gay flotillas on the water and immense crowds on the observation trains on the west shore—one of the gala events of the college world. In this region of the Hudson, also, such writers as John Bigelow and Joel Benton have helped to add fame to the river; here also Morse invented the telegraph. A little farther up John Burroughs surveys the world from " Slabsides."

Cropping up above the horizon to the west beyond Poughkeepsie are the Catskills, " other mountains which lie from the river's side," said Hudson. Through this region he went slowly, taking two whole days. Well he might. Even Charles Dickens who was impressed with the unusual in man rather than nature, while on his way to visit the Shakers, noted: " And for many miles the Kaatskill Mountains towered in the blue distance like stately clouds."

Here among the peaks and down the valleys of the misty mountains is the domain of all that is fanciful and supernatural. Rip Van Winkle slept his twenty-year sleep here. The thunder still echoes the grave game of ninepins of the queer little Dutchmen. Here survives the pretty Indian legend of Minnewa-wa. In the olden days the little Dutch children were taught to believe that good St. Nicholas dwelt among these mountains and across the river at Claverack, looking out on them, Clement Moore wrote: " 'Twas the night before Christmas and all through the house."

No Longer an Angler's Paradise

While the scenery along the Hudson has suffered some slight impairment, the sport has been practically destroyed. Once along these broad river reaches there was shad fishing that was world famous. It's about gone now—how can a respectable shad get past the 500,000,-000 gallons of sewage poured daily into the waters about New York The sportsmen were the first to find it out; reluctantly the rivermen are finding it out, too. Once, also, the striped bass, a sporty fish, was the fisherman's delight in these waters; it's only a tradition now.

Once even, the Indians used to catch oysters—the shell heaps prove it. Also, as " The Culprit Fay " tells, there was the uncouth sturgeon. Herring, perch, white fish, and " snappers," or little bluefish, abounded. Nowadays the Fish Commission is making a frantic effort to stock the river with thousands of salmon and other likely fry, but it's no use. The Hudson is no longer the fisherman's paradise. Pollution has killed it. The sewage of many cities and the waste of many mills above do not make a good habitat for fish.

Rondout and Kingston are next. At

Photograph by Arthur Hewitt.

"TEAR OF THE CLOUDS" THE INDIANS CALLED THE RIVER AT ITS SOURCE
WHERE ONE MAY CROSS THE TINY STREAM ON STEPPING STONES.

Kingston Point there is an amusement park that is quite a sight, and here, too, the convention of the representatives of the State of New York fled in 1776 and 1777, when they were making the State constitution. From New York to Harlem, to White Plains, to Poughkeepsie, to Fishkill, and finally to Kingston they went. Beyond is the little Huguenot settlement of New Paltz. In this region, too, are more stone crushers.

"It was a monster moving up the river defying wind and tide and breathing flames and smoke," said one witness of the voyage of the *Clermont* in 1807. One and a half miles from Tivoli, and about 110 from New York, is Clermont Manor, home of the old Livingston family, where Chancellor Livingstone lived. Here Fulton's boat, which was named after the manor, arrived after twenty-four hours and spent the night. Setting out again in the morning, she arrived in Albany, a total of thirty-six hours on the way. One does it now in less than nine and a half hours. The fare then was fourteen dollars for the round trip; now it is three and a half dollars.

A Robber Baron of the Hudson

Diagonally across the river, and up, is the inland seaport of Hudson. Near here Henry Hudson became discouraged and stopped. It was not far from this city that his men plied the Indians with liquor and got them all drunk, an incident usually placed on Manhattan. At the jutting rock of Barren Island, just above, old Nicholas Koren in the days of the Dutch rule was wont to exact tribute from passing ships, after the fashion of the robber barons on the old Rhine. It is related that when William the Testy sent our old friend Anthony the Trumpeter to demand that it be stopped, Anthony came back to Manhattan with a derisive message, and the tribute-taking went gayly on.

On the west side is the stream and vale of Tawasentha, the home of the Indian singer Nawadaha, who gave Longfellow the theme of the Songs of Hiawatha. At Norman's Kill in 1618 the Dutch made a treaty with the Iroquois which was not broken until after the English came in 1674. The very next month after the Dutch treaty, Champlain fought and defeated the Five Nations at the head of Lake Champlain, and so these Indians hated the French and loved the Dutch. Across, to the east, is Schodack Heights where was the ever-burning council fire of the Mohicans.

Setting sail, Henry Hudson proceeded as far as a few miles below Albany. There he stopped on the 19th, thoroughly discouraged by the freshening of the water. Nevertheless he sent a small boat on up in a last vain hope that the river would widen, the islands disappear, and the way open to China and India.

As you thread the islands, at last, around a bend in the river, you sight the great State Capitol building rising boldly from its hill above the city of Albany, almost like a mirage, its base seeming to lie among the steeple tops. Albany is one of the oldest of the permanent settlements made in America. The obliteration of Jamestown leaves only St. Augustine, Santa Fé, and Quebec to antedate it.

Hudson's men went up as far as Waterford, twenty-seven miles from the stopping place of the *Half Moon*, returning to their ship on September 22. So the traveler in search of the romance of the Hudson might go on up, past Glens Falls, the retreat of Cooper's Leather-stocking, where the water drops eighty feet over masses of black marble, on up into the very heart of the Adirondacks in Essex County, where between Mount Marcy and Mount McIntyre, nearly five thousand feet above sea level, in silken skeins of mist and amid the bubbling icy springs, the Hudson takes its real rise. "Tear of the clouds," the Indians called its source. And so ends the panorama of the Hudson.

As for Henry Hudson himself, whose progress we have followed up the river, he must start down on September 23, arriving off Manhattan by October 3. Then his shade must set sail on October 4 to report to the shadowy Dutch East India Company what has happened to the great river they paid him 800 guilders—$320—to discover.

Hunting the Adirondack Grouse (1909)

HUNTING THE ADIRONDACK GROUSE

BY TODD RUSSELL

A GREAT light that broke some years ago on New York's lawmakers at Albany led them to establish, in the name of the State, the Adirondack Forest Preserve, with the idea of making the territory included therein, to which the State took title through its right of eminent domain, a great park and playground for those who sought the out-of-doors for health and pleasure.

The territory taken has been increased from year to year, and is still being increased, until the boundaries of the State lands now run from McKeever on the west to within a few miles of Lakes George and Champlain on the east, and from Loon Lake on the north to a point some twenty miles north of the Mohawk River on the south.

To the sportsman, this country of hundreds of lakes and thousands of acres of woods is one of infinite attraction. Most varieties of our fresh-water game fish are found in profusion within its boundaries, and deer, bear, squirrels, and coons furnish sport for the rifle, while for the shotgun enthusiast, all parts of this territory provide grouse and many parts woodcock. But over the shooting of feathered game, for a reason traceable with some probability to the inhabitants of the country, a blight has been cast, for the last legislature has enacted a law prohibiting the taking of dogs into the State preserves. This law is intended to make more effective the very proper regulations against the hounding of deer, but to the bird-dog enthusiast, a more unjust piece of legislation could not be imagined.

The natives of the country, who in the fall make up its coterie of guides, have not, in large part, ever seen a trained bird-dog. If they have ever used a dog in partridge hunting, it has been of the spaniel type, which barked the birds into trees, there to be potted. Wing shooting is but little practiced, for almost without exception the people are hunters of deer (and there are none better), and the only grouse that fall to their guns are such birds as cross the trail home and foolishly take to a nearby limb.

In a country where grouse are so plentiful, it seems strange that they have been so little pursued and in such ways and are treated generally as of such small value for sport. Grouse shooting during the very dry times when still-hunting deer is so unproductive may save many a trip from failure.

The State Fish, Forest, and Game Commission, in a letter to the writer, states "that the loyalty to a law by the citizens produces better results when there are no exceptions made, and taking bird-dogs into the Adirondacks makes the residents of this locality ask the question, 'Why can't we keep hounds to run foxes?'"

Leaving out the question of ethics, we come to the questions of the natives and of the hounds and foxes. These are best answered by recalling that a good fox pelt is worth three dollars, of which a good hunter may collect three or four a season, and that a good partridge shooter is worth three dollars a day to his hotel, as much more to his guide, and usually stays two weeks a season. It is a financial calculation, that the guide and hotel man can make or should have made for him.

Point two is that hounds will run deer and that bird-dogs are physically incapable of trailing them. The bird hunters had better look after their own, and possibly if they asked a "question" or two of their representatives at Albany, there might be a disposition to treat all residents of the State who contribute to the maintenance of the State lands to a more equitable division of the hunting chances.

But the law, being as it is, must be observed, and therefore, to the practical sportsman who goes for feathered game within the park limits, certain advice as to methods of hunting without dogs may be of interest, while further on we will take up the hunting grounds on the out-skirts of the sacred territory where pos-sibly for a few years the pointer or set-ter may have a chance still to pit his in-telligence against the wariest and sportiest of all our game birds.

No Hunting Without a License

The game law of the State requires each citizen who goes shooting to obtain an annual hunter's license, from any county, city, or town clerk, without re-gard to where used; the charge is $1.10, and for non-residents $20.50. Owners or lessees of land within the State need pay no license for hunting on their own territory. Grouse and woodcock may not be sold, nor may they be carried without the State.

The open season for both birds is from October 1 to November 30, both inclu-sive, and in this period is embraced the open season on all the snipe and the waders and shore birds which are occa-sionally found in the grouse country.

The equipment need not vary from that for similar shooting anywhere, but it is well to remember that there is cold weather in the Adirondacks before the end of November and a thermometer searching for the zero mark o' nights makes woolen underwear a desirable thing. The writer has found that very light wool is to be preferred; when the need comes, the doubling of suits is not only warmer but more convenient than the packing of heavy apparel through warm days.

A hammerless gun is absolutely essen-tial in those sections where a dog may not be used because of the method of hunting, for the hammer gun must be carried at full cock or many shots will be lost and life presents risks enough without adding this one. Presuming the gun to be a twelve gauge, the right bar-rel bored to a cylinder, and the left slightly modified, a standard load of an ounce and an eighth of chilled number seven shot is about the proper outfit. Soft, comfortable shoes, moccasins being avoided, and dark woolen trousers are most comfortable.

The territory shot over divides itself naturally into three classes within the limits of the State preserves, consisting of beech and maple woods, old burnings overgrown with briars, and the edges of cleared land where sumach and other food for birds may be found. This year there is every evidence of an excellent crop of beechnuts which promises not only the most pleasant phase of this shooting but a finer flavor in the game.

The hunter, set down in beech terri-tory, must quarter it after the fashion of the English bird-dog. There is little use looking for likely places, though an occa-sional detour to the edges of a swamp lined with small spruce and hemlock is sometimes productive in the middle of the day. The most effective method is to take a straight line across the territory selected and work back and forth across it in zigzag lines, giving careful atten-tion to fallen treetops and bits of brush.

Noiselessness is not necessary, for the birds must literally be frightened out of cover and picked off as they rise. Drum-ming birds may be located by ear, though the direction of the sound is at first con-fusing. A bird once raised will fly in al-most a straight line and can almost cer-tainly be walked up for the second or even the third shot.

A straight eye and the habit of getting an exact line by two trees or other marks on the bird's first flight are great aids in filling the bag, for though there may be shooters who will get many birds on the first rise in this kind of shooting, experi-ence seems to show that they have many a day when they are "off" in the game. Constant alertness is of the greatest help, and the gun must be carried constantly so that it can be swung into position at the first whir and rush of the frightened bird, which goes straight up for some feet and coaxes the too-impetuous to undershoot him time and again.

In cover along ravines and gullies, birds have a habit of crossing the hollow before lighting. In any kind of hunting without a dog the bird will seldom light in the trees, while a bird flushed by a dog, if not fired at, usually takes refuge on a nearby limb. Sufficient data for definite conclusions are not at hand, but in shooting both grouse and quail, it is noticeable that birds which the dog has put up will more frequently light on the ground if the gun be discharged. This is presented more as a personal observation than as an unvarying fact.

The ruffed grouse does not take long flights through the timber, a couple of hundred yards being about the average, though he can undoubtedly go farther. The longest flight subject to actual measurement that the writer has seen, was from a projecting point across an arm of a lake over a measured distance of half a mile. This bird was hidden at the water's edge and was afterwards shot not twenty feet inland from the farther shore where the cover was so sparse as to give rise to the idea that he was too exhausted after his trip to hunt the deeper woods immediately beyond.

The bag limit of grouse is six birds to each day and thirty-six during the season to each hunter. The fair shot should have little difficulty in reaching this limit in any of the Adirondack country where the deer-hunters, not searching for this game and going very quietly, raise from six to a dozen birds a day.

An additional precaution for the grouse hunter, which sometimes shows a profit in venison, is the carrying of two or three shells loaded with buckshot in a handy waistcoat pocket. It is a good idea to have them of a different color from the shells loaded with small shot to permit their being easily distinguished; it is needless to add that a deer, no matter how close, nor how great the temptation, should never be fired at with the small shot charge.

A wise precaution in the deer country is the wearing of a broad red band around the hat. There are accidents every year because of deer hunters firing at half-seen objects, and while these are growing creditably less, it is not necessary that they should occur at all.

Within the limits of the Adirondack Park preserve the country about Fulton Chain, Big Moose, Lake Clear, and Loon Lake on the New York Central, offer both grouse and deer shooting, while the Central and the Delaware and Hudson touch the country on the west, south, and

east of the preserve where dogs may be used. Such places as Lyons Falls, Glenfield, and Benson Mines may be suggested on the west and any of the stations on the Delaware and Hudson on the east between Saratoga, Plattsburg, and beyond.

Within the limits of the State lands the hunting is open to all carrying proper licenses. Temporary camps may be built, but tents only are allowed for this purpose. In unsettled territory outside the preserve limits the farmers usually make no objection to shooting and the local guide or hotel-keeper is always well acquainted with the possibilities.

How to Carry Your Dogs

In carrying dogs into the country where they are not prohibited, it is far better to ship them in crates by express than otherwise. The railroad companies will take them, at a valuation not exceeding twenty-five dollars, at excess baggage rates, but it is somewhat of a nuisance to check and look after them in this way. Dog food need not be taken beyond that necessary for the trip as all the hotels and boarding-houses will provide ample table scraps for feeding. Very fast dogs are not suitable, thoroughly stanch ones are necessary, and a dog that is a good retriever is as valuable here as elsewhere, for the winged grouse is a confirmed runner and skillful in hiding.

Grouse do not always lie close to a dog but will run from in front of him in a way that makes the veteran often tried on quail look extremely puzzled at times. It is perhaps as effective a method as any to walk rapidly ahead of the dog which is puzzled and roading slowly, steadying him with a word of command and expecting the bird to get up anywhere, frequently twenty yards ahead.

It has been said that ruffed grouse shooting is the most difficult known. Certainly it requires a quick eye, a steady hand, and a judgment not so often needed in the pursuit of quail; the country traversed in the Adirondacks offers a diversity of scenery, a variety of game, an appetite at meals, and a soundness of sleep at nights that cannot be excelled.

By Canoe from Lake George to the Atlantic (1893)

BY CANOE FROM LAKE GEORGE TO THE ATLANTIC.

BY WILLIAM JOHN WARBURTON.

ON the eighth of September, a certain humble canoeist turned his back regretfully upon the well-known points and islands about Hulett's Landing, Lake George, intent on a two hundred and fifty mile voyage to New York. His tiny craft found ample acommodation under its after-hatch for the waterproof dunnage-bag, while a rolled blanket and two or three cushions stuffed with corkdust offered an inviting seat in the cockpit. Under the deck, forward of the foot steering-gear, was a genuine *multum in parvo*, for there reposed the necessary assortment of cooking utensils, with store of coffee, bacon, and canned meats, leaving room for such additional edibles as the cast-iron laws of trampdom might permit. For the cruiser had determined to rough it in the most approved "tramp" style—to abjure boiled shirts and feather beds and dainty food, and even good grammar, until such time as the wheel of Fortune might perambulate him into the metropolis. And the cruise would lead for a score of miles through lovely Lake George waters, then between the green banks of the Northern Canal, and so to the seaward-rolling Hudson. Such would be the fitting end to a month of delightful camp-life—to journey homeward, not by train or steamer or any such modern improvement, but by the most primitive method of travel, a frail canoe, propelled only by the paddle-wielding arms of its lone occupant.

It was about an hour before sundown, though Old Sol was creeping to his rest, unobserved, behind ominous clouds. The fresh autumn breeze blew steadily toward the north, soon to return bearing winter on its pinions. Far up on the hillsides the bright yellow and scarlet of the maples, distinct against a dark pine forest, repeated the tale that deserted hotels had already told, of a departure too long delayed and of the gloomy days that were to come. So the lone voyager headed southward for a ten-mile race with fast approaching darkness. Who that has known Lake George in all its changing moods, cannot remember when the darkened waters, tumbling and white-crested, have lost their wondrous iridescent blue ; when the pine boughs bend and sough in the breeze, and the shadows lie deep between the rugged shore and the islands with their bare rocks and scraggy bushes? And then the night comes down intense and heavy, so that beneath its weight the wind is crushed into stillness. Across the unruffled waters comes the chorus of forest sounds, and sometimes a glint from a distant light on the shore, the cheering tones of the human voice, or the bark of a watchful dog. And in unison sounds the steady dip, dip of the double-bladed paddle, with its tireless sweep, till Bolton lights shine out in glad welcome through the darkness. To moor beneath the tempting gleam of those cheerful lamps and seek the hospitality of some hotel, would be to violate the canoeist's principles at the very beginning ; so the Tramp peered again into the night, to find an inviting retreat in a waterside summerhouse. And then the rains descended and the floods came and beat upon his bed of blankets, but the weary sailorman, retreating, head and all, into his nest, fell into deep slumber.

"Wall, it hain't got no call to rain for three weeks yit, but there's no tellin'," reckoned the weather-wise villager next morning, and with this uncertain information the canoe was launched, and then away, breakfastless, for Caldwell. Not that there was any approaching darkness to race with this time, but the morning steamer would soon be treading on one's heels, and with its arrival at the head of the lake the train would take departure, passing through Fort Edward, the nearest accessible point on the canal. It may be valuable experience, but it is very poor fun, this long, hungry paddle through a permeating drizzle, with the vast lungs of one's steam-propelled rival puffing away close in the wake. But the train was in no particular hurry that morning, and delayed until the *Jay-Jay* and its crew

frightened, now desperate prisoner, like the lightning's flash, out into the deeper water. Less line then, and more resilient force from the rod, a firmer suggestion of limitation from the reel, and a stronger insistence upon more perfect subjection.

"Steady, boy," spoke the General, as his beaming glance rested upon the swaying rod and his ears caught the music of the swishing silk as it sliced the water right and left. "Steady; he's well hooked; look to it that he does not smash your tackle or steal your slack. Steady! This is worth tramping for all the way from the Divide and back. Look out!"

"I'd resign my internal-revenue collectorship for one minute at the big end of that pole," broke in the General; "but for the Lord's sake don't let that fish get away! If you do, and old Ouray hears of it, over the range yonder, this commission's jig is up. Swing it around here and I'll yank it in for you."

"Friend, doesn't thee think thee had better reel in a little more line, and hadn't thee better set the butt a little more firmly 'gainst thy forearm? There! And now he might break thy line with his devious devices and sinewy tail. That was beautiful!"

As the earnest, now enthusiastic Quaker spoke the words there was another scintillation and prismatic panorama, another futile effort to escape. Next came a struggle, right, left, left, right, then sounding the depths, the click reel holding its advantage, now yielding inch by inch to the stubborn tugging of the fish. What furious, forceful rushes, yet how strong the hold upon the watery giant of that fragile, pliant tool! What curves it took, and yet how resolutely, how unfailing it asserted its integrity.

But what was that? A swifter sweep of the fish, a louder swish of the loyal silken tether, a momentary relaxation of the telling strain, and *two* great shapes vaulted into air, circled like dolphins at play, and clove the troubled, foam-flecked pool.

"A double, by all that's good!" yelled the Governor.

"Two of 'em, by all that's wonderful!" shouted the General, jumping down the embankment and landing in two feet of water.

"Thee has twain, but pray keep thy hand true and thy good pole firm!" came the warning from Maine.

"A fine pair to draw to," broke in the Lieutenant, "and they're aces at that!"

Indeed there was a pair of as fine trout as the eye of angler ever rested upon, tugging, straining, using every artifice known to trout to gain their freedom.

"One of 'em's a yard long," said the General, as the water squirted out of his shoes.

"They'll weigh thirty pounds, if an ounce," suggested the Lieutenant.

"Friend, thee'd better let them have a little more of the butt," significantly remarked the Quaker; "it would, indeed, be a pity to lose such excellent fish."

It was the work of a good half-hour to bring the pair under moderate control. The current, the danger of doubling a log that lay not far down the stream, the anxiety of the situation, the desire to save both, the fear of flaw in tackle—all these gave zest to the occasion. But when at last the muscular tails had weakened through brave efforts to escape, and the belly of each turned toward the sky, it was found that the landing net was not at hand, and there was no gaff. What was to be done? A private solved the problem by jumping forward with a tent-fly, which he and two others unrolled, and as the fish were slowly, surely drawn out of the current into the quieter water within a dozen feet of shore, the soldiers deftly jumped outside, slipped the canvas behind the captives, and the next moment lifted them on to the bank.

As they lay gasping on the shingly shore we gathered round the pair of mountain trout, whose dark spots and chromatic sides made them most beautiful to behold. The trusty steelyards of the soldier cook gave the gratifying assurance of five and a half pounds for one and three pounds four and a half ounces for its mate.

"I'll not cast a fly there to-night," said the Governor, with dignified courtesy. "Such record is good enough for an entire journey of the continent. We'll let it stand as it is, and not be so particular about flies when we reach the Saguache to-morrow."

And he wasn't.

This was my first and only cast in the Rio Grande. The sun had not lifted itself above Sierra Blanca, next morning, when we were on the march.

were safe on board. Then a silent fare-well to Lake George and to all the jol-lities of a summer vacation, and away through the few miles of uninteresting scenery that must intervene before a second launching of the ship. Ac-cording to the lord-high-something of the D. & H. road at Albany, canoes are carried as the baggage of their ac-companying owners. But according to the presiding genius of that particu-lar train, that particular canoe should not go as baggage unless his private greed was satisfied. Of course, a sop of coins was thrown to Cerberus, but these petty extortions leave a bad taste in one's mouth.

Afloat at last in the canal, paddling in and out among the huge boats that lie moored by the town, with the high tow-path bounding the horizon on one side and the rank eel-grass on the other, and the rain as enthusiastic as ever! A vivid recollection remains that when the canal began externally, the "blues" began internally ; and as cheerfulness is essential on a cruise, the Tramp pro-ceeded to indulge in an analysis of his emotions, while the canoe never paused in its onward gliding. He could look back to an exceptionally bright past, the future promised fair, and the inter-vening present, *i.e.*, the cruise, was the result of a longing for hermetic pleasure, muscle, and—yes, the gratifi-cation of obstinacy. The pleasure would come when the rain ceased, the muscle would come rain or shine, and as for the obstinacy—stay, fair voyager, 'tis high afternoon, and appetite should call a halt. But no, the wind on the canal's bank would not suffer an alcohol flame to heat the coffee, so a scant crust of bread and again *en voyage*.

As the rain cleared away before even-ing, the canal scenery proved not un-interesting. There were grassy slopes and harvested fields, many a group of solemn-faced cows, and many a red barn, as red as the traditional red barn of every rural sketch. Occasionally one can catch a glimpse, over the bank, of the river below, the shallow picturesque stream of the upper Hudson. Beyond are low hills, densely wooded, and further westward fields and pastures to the horizon. Here is the first lock, and the "captain"—every man on the canal has attained to that commanding rank—proceeds with alacrity and good

will to open his sluices and lower us to the interior level. He doesn't often handle such small canal-boats, he admits, and he peers curiously over the edge as we sink slowly down, down, with the bubbling water. It is an odd sensation one experiences sitting there in so tiny a craft, while the great wet walls seem to rise up above like grow-ing things, and little streams spout out from their crevices. Only in such a way can one appreciate the awful death of Rogue Riderhood and the desperate schoolmaster, as they fell struggling in-to the smooth pit, where no answer would come to a despairing cry. The lower gates open slowly, and the green canal banks appear beyond, and then for a steady paddle over the next level until another lock is reached, with four or five more at irregular distances beyond. Again night closes down black and threatening, but the Schuylersville lights are already shining cheerily across the dark still water.

Throughout the experience of this and of other trips, the "canalers" were found to be a good-natured and kind-hearted set of men. Every captain had spoken a pleasant word, and every lock-keeper had wished good luck as the craft went out through the gates with the seething water. But when our canoeist paused in the darkness by the towing-line barn at Schuylersville, and the agent himself came out and helped to carry the canoe within doors, and built a big fire in his stove and drove nails in the wall to hang up the Tramp's wet clothes and bade him wel-come to the office, that dripping worthy concluded that canal-life turns out some of the best of good fellows. Only clothe yourself in the garment of de-mocracy, and you may find a sure approach to their hearts. So a pie from the baker's made a good supper, and well-warmed blankets made a good bed on the floor, and then came old Joe, the wooden-legged driver, who had been out after Custer, and lulled to slumber with his weird tales of war.

Dawn came, gray and cheerless, with never-ceasing rain, but the glowing stove and well-filled coffee-pot and fry-ing-pan made life worth living, never-theless. The agent, after his all-night vigil, was relieved and departed, but his successor was also a good fellow, who kept the welcome warm, and discussed breakfast and points of English history with equal apparent interest. Occasionally a driver would come in from the outer barn and obtain from the agent a pair of boots, an oil-skin suit, a paper of tobacco, or some such requisite, for all of which the company, or rather its canal superintendent, charges the most extravagant prices, often more than double the value. But there is no help for the penniless drivers, for this is their only means of obtaining credit. The sum of these items is subtracted from their wages, which are paid in a "lump" at the end of the towing season. At each meal time, eating-tickets were doled out to all hands in the stable, and the men wended their way to a neighboring boarding-house. These drivers are a most peculiar set of men. Rough, frightfully profane, and intoxicated at every opportunity, they are yet light-hearted and good-natured, and in many cases possessed of an unfailing fund of humor. They have actually graduated from the whiskey stage of drunkenness, and now prefer alcohol diluted with water, a fiery compound, the effectiveness of which can be imagined. It is very amusing to hear the men addressing their mules, as they move from stall to stall, now commanding, now remonstrating, now pleading, more often overwhelming with invectives. Their remarkable skill in the use of expletives is probably due to the peculiar nature of this treacherous beast—their most frequent companion. Indeed, it is a hard life these drivers lead, walking with their animals for five or six hours at a stretch, alike night or day, rain or shine. But there is a reward for temperance, perseverance and efficiency, for the driver possessed of these traits may find himself presently in the comfortable position of a station agent, perhaps to rise yet higher in the service. Indeed, the most important officers of the company are men who have served their time behind the mules. There are cripples of all kinds on the tow-path, but among them one-legged men form the great majority. Actually, at one time there were five wooden legs gathered in an amicable group by the office door. It may be said that a wooden leg is of advantage to its possessor, for when some unruly mule delivers a sudden kick, the fortunate driver, using his artificial member as a pivot, can swing himself into safety. Old Joe will show you a deep indentation in his "off" leg, recently made when his long-eared pet was mistaken in its aim.

Amused by the queer sayings of these singular men, and by their oddly-told tales of canal life, the Tramp heeded not the passing hours, until, late in the afternoon, the pertinacity of that rain exhausted his patience, and the *Jay-Jay* was launched in the midst of a very hard downpour. Two hours before, a "liner" had passed southward, a boat towed by the company's mule-relays, and traveling day and night. Once having overtaken the boat the voyager would be sure of a comfortable bunk, but meanwhile there was a wet bit of paddling to be performed. There were still similar green slopes and harvested fields, red barns, and solemn bovines, but through a veil of raindrops the landscape was very cheerless. At the end of a five-mile chase the slow-moving canal boat was overtaken, and two miles further on was another barn, where the boat would pause for fresh mules. Naturally enough the canoe got there first, and its crew was warming his chilled body by the fire when the yellow oilskins of that precocious young driver, "the Jersey Lily," loomed up through the darkness, and the boat's lights appeared not far behind. It was but the work of a moment to drag the canoe upon the path and raise it thence to the *Crippen's* deck, where the captain stood, with a hearty word of welcome on his lips. The cabin was well-filled with his numerous family, but a smoky glow shone from the tiny hatchway forward, and easy was the descent to that Avernus. The fo'castle was certainly rather small, not quite five feet high, and there was just room for the stove, the deck-hand and the Tramp, if the two latter were content not to move about much. So coffee was made and clothes were dried, and thanks were returned that one could proceed on his way without regard to the detestable weather. Captain H., it appeared from conversation, was "own cousin" to another canal man of the passenger's acquaintance, on whose boat he had received hospitality during a northward cruise in early August. Oh, the memory of those balmy starlit nights, when "Brutus" and "Cassius" might lie upon the deck in jolly fellowship, smoking the pipe of peace or indulging in some wonderful duets. But old Pluvius wouldn't permit such familiarities a second time, and these equinoctial rains made firelight a welcome substitute for starlight. Emile, the deckhand, was a native of lower Canada ; so the fo'castle contingent learnedly compared *patois* and " France French " until bedtime, and after a long slumber awoke to find the bright sun stealing through chinks in the hatch. A glorious morning, indeed, and our energetic captain had passed the canal and was locking down into the river at Troy. Incidentally, we find that a canal captain displays much more celerity when paid by the trip than when drawing a regular stipend per diem. By noon, with a clear sky and a fast steam tug, the *Crippen* made Albany, and some letters at the post-office came like a whiff of metropolitan civilization. After rain and roughing-it, culinary operations and queer sleeping places, the wanderer's clothes did not warrant a hotel dinner. He was invited, however, into a small waterside hostelry, and seated at a long table among a party of horny-handed sons of toil. So good digestion waited on appetite, and a stout lady of great antiquity waited on table, dispensing nutritive dishes.

When the big tow to which our hospitable barge was attached left Albany at seven o'clock, the water-works were again in full play, and the Tramp looked gloomily forward to the prospect of a wet paddle ashore at Catskill. For there the little *Jay-Jay* was to await an expected addition to its crew. After a frugal meal in the cabin and an interesting conversation on the dangers of canaling, the captain set his alarm clock for his guest's benefit, and sought the arms of Morpheus, while the Tramp followed suit on a bench in the fo'castle. About half-past two a resounding summons down the hatchway brought the *Jay-Jay's* sleepy crew on deck. The tow was then, our captain judged, eyeing certain eastward lights through the incessant drizzle, about opposite Hudson and, therefore, Catskill could not be far distant. So the canoe was carried across an intervening lumber-boat, and shot off into the foaming water. The crew descended with some difficulty, the painter was cast off, and the tow rapidly disappeared in the night.

Out on the great dark river, with shore lights but dimly visible through the rain, one could imagine himself a veritable Ancient Mariner, " alone on a wide, wide sea." So a long pull and a strong pull, cleaving the darkness and the dampness, while the western lights twinkled cheerily nearer and nearer. As good luck would have it, there was a little boat house on the shore, half hidden in the shadow of a huge ice-house. The dim lamp in the living room discovered a tumbled bed, but no occupant, and all was as still as still could be. Is there not an Eastern tale that tells of some wandering prince dropped at night into an unknown city ? Well, this modern adventurer, equally ignorant of the local geography, tramped the wet streets in vain, meeting no belated citizen to enlighten him as to his whereabouts. But the boatman, who had regained his shanty when the fruitless search was ended, ventured the information that this town was Athens, and offered the floor to me for a resting-place.

Up with the misty dawn and five miles run down to Catskill as an appetizer. The lighthouse lamps flickered with sickly yellow against a gray morning, and the huge ice-houses, familiar to every traveler on the Hudson, loomed up darkly, like deserted castles. A chilly wind was moaning through the sedges along Catskill creek, and the clouds, awakening to a sense of duty delayed, began again their tireless labor. Catskill will be memorable for a disappointing telegram from the expected recruit, and for a long day of rain, wearily witnessed by the little group in the boat-house.

When night had drawn down, and culinary labors and pleasures were over, the lamplight peered out at the white mist on the creek, and discovered blue pipe-smoke curling lazily upward from the doorway and losing itself in the darkness. Now comes a belated duck hunter, weary and disgusted with abundance of wetting and scarcity of shooting. The shoreward doors of the boat-house are locked, so, unable to pass through, he paddles his skiff to land ; but wishing something from the house, endeavors to swing over to the float on the Tramp's outstretched hand. Alas for human miscalculations ! As he careened wildly backward, fortune placed in his way a duck-boat about half-filled with rain water, and in it he lay down incontinently. The Tramp, following somewhat precipitately, by a desperate leap spread himself over the prostrate huntsman. Little is required to amuse a solitary, only wishing for something to support his spirits, and the old boat-house rang with laughter.

On Saturday morning old Sol had his watch on deck, and a stiff southerly wind was rolling the clouds over and over each other in precipitate flight. Then away with a steady swing down the river, past low-lying islands with their crop of rank grass, past ice-houses and yet other ice-houses, past hovels on the waterside and mansions on the hill-tops, yet always accompanied by that interminable line of black railway. What though the day proved faithless to its bright promises, and sent down shower after shower, with brief spaces of burning sunshine between? What though the strong head-wind grew stronger and stronger as the day advanced, and its big white-caps broke remorselessly against the bow? On and on, against wind or tide, rain or sun, for we have delayed too long already. On and on, for eleven consecutive hours of steady paddling, lying low in the canoe to escape the force of the head-wind. Sweeping around a beautiful bend in the river, with one backward glance, we find the northerly passage hid in gloomy gray. Nearer at hand the great columns of rain are drawing rapidly across the river, bending and swaying like sand pillars in a Sahara simoon.. The sun sinks westward in a glory of crimson and purple, but night spreads a pall of intense black over the waters. A single star peers anxiously out between the sweeping clouds that threaten to quench its light. But cold comfort is that gleam, and the shore lights ahead, though they seem equally distant, offer more incentive to a toil that must not be relaxed, for the wind has freshened to a gale. Occasionally a flash of lightning breaks from the clouds and reveals the dark, heaving waters, and we see a great wave, huge it seems in the momentary light, rolling forward with foamy crest. So on and on through the darkness until Rhinecliff is reached, and kind-hearted ferrymen pull the voyager and his craft ashore.

Next morning, with a gale lashing the river into foam, a gloomy, threatening sky, and a badly strained muscle to back these substantial arguments, the Tramp concluded that discretion was the better part of valor, and headed across the river. A dull morning aboard the brick barges off Kingston Point made it painfully apparent that the big Albany tows had already passed, so there was nothing for it but to bid farewell to beloved trampdom, and conclude the voyage on that evening's steamer. Rondout, with its deserted streets and piers, does not present an enlivening scene on the first day of the week, though the rickety little tub of a ferryboat, drawn by cable across the creek, might amuse a humorously-inclined visitor for hours. The pretty but seldom-used house of the Rondout Canoe Club was opened for inspection by its aged janitor, who bewailed the bygone days of cruises and regattas.

Down the night-shrouded river steamed the ex-Tramp, gradually habituating himself to the usages of civilized society. And so under the long Poughkeepsie bridge, and past the occasional shore lights, and past bed-time; and then, nestling in the unwonted comfort of a mattress, through the highways and byways of dreamland, until gray dawn made the world conscious of more mist and rain—nothing but mist and rain in every direction from that downtown pier. But we must hasten to catch the last hour of flood-tide, so the paddle swings boldly out into the fog. The ferry-boats and tugs are whistling their notes of warning in all the gamut of hoarse sounds, and churning into foam those never quiet waters. Then on past the long, black docks, not yet roused to the day's activity, and we count the streets as they number higher and higher. There are the great anchored men of war, looming up like gray ghosts through the fog, while their bells toll mournfully over the waters, as it were a knell for the dead. To the west there is nothing but the gray veil; but to the east, docks, and docks, and docks, until we hail with delight the hospitable Columbia Yacht Club, from whose float a well-remembered northward cruise had taken its beginning seven weeks before. A backward glance at the gray Hudson and the pleasures of the past, and the tramp cruise was over; but the rain—ah, the rain !

The Atlantic Yacht Club:
Its Origin and History
(1898)

Photo by T. C. Turner.

THE NEW HOME OF THE ATLANTIC YACHT CLUB
AT SEA GATE, GRAVESEND BAY, N. Y.

THE ATLANTIC YACHT CLUB.

ITS ORIGIN AND HISTORY.

BY A. J. KENEALY.

YACHT CLUB requires more care to develop so as to win the crown of success than any other assemblage of men banded together for social purposes and sport. Internal dissensions that would only disturb an athletic club would in all probability totally wreck a yacht club. Why this is I do not attempt to explain, but there is no doubt of its truth. The Atlantic tars have had their ups and their downs; but the club though occasionally caught in a heavy squall or even beset by a cyclone has safely weathered the storms like a stout and seaworthy vessel, and has reached port at last, with spars, sails and rigging unscathed by the gale and the grand old hull never so much as strained.

One of the chief reasons of its success is that it has always been run by the right men. From its very start its members have been practical boat-sailers, lovers of the sea for the health and joyous sport it freely offers its devotees. The young men who built up the club brought to it youth, enthusiasm and zeal —three attributes that both deserve and command the palm of victory. All the

original incorporators in 1866 were young and enthusiastic yachtsmen, and they determined that it should not be their fault if success did not perch on their snowy burgee inscribed with the bright red letter A. According to its charter the object of the club is " to encourage yacht-building and naval architecture, social recreation in yachting, and the cultivation of naval science," and right well has it lived up to its mission.

Only two of the charter members, Henry A. Gouge and J. Rogers Maxwell, are now on the roll of the club. It was at Mr. Gouge's house in Washington street, Brooklyn, that the club was formed, and for that reason Mr. Gouge is known as the father of the club.

The encouragement accorded to the smaller classes of yachts no doubt did much to enhance the club's popularity. Any yacht not less than sixteen feet length on the load water-line enrolled in the club entitles its owner to a vote, and this is one reason why owners of small craft hasten to join the Atlantic's fleet. In the New York Yacht Club the line is drawn at yachts under fifteen tons, old measurement, and only by a special dispensation are the popular 30-footers permitted to take part in the club regattas.

The percentage of actual yacht-owners

MODEL ROOM, SEA GATE.

sloop, designed by Herreshoff. She was the first yacht seen hereabouts to carry a club-topsail and a balloon jib-topsail. Though of rather crude design compared with the modern artistic "creations" of the down-to-date sail-makers, these flying kites made a great sensation wherever seen.

The second regatta, in 1867, had sixteen starters, Mr. Sheppard Homans' 55-footer, *White Wings*, being the largest craft. Since then a successful regatta has been held every year.

is larger in the Atlantic Club than in many others, the purpose being not to encourage too many members to join for social purposes only.

The formal opening of the club has taken place every year on Decoration Day, when the fleet at the proper signal from the gun ashore, weighs anchor and starts out on the "opening sail." The course used to be from the club-house off Bay Ridge down through the Narrows and down the bay as far as the Southwest Spit. These opening sails were very enjoyable events, and there was keen rivalry in every class in the squadron, although the affair did not attain the dignity of a formal regatta until 1895. Each boat, however, picked out her pet opponent, and went at her, hammer and tongs, from start to finish. Private match-races were frequent and added to the interest of the exciting day.

The first regatta of the club was sailed on June 11, 1866, the year the club was founded. Fourteen yachts started, the race being sailed without time allowance. The *Hector*, owned by Mr. William Peet, and *Psyche*, owned by Mr. F. B. Taylor, were the winners. *Psyche* was a fast

In the all-important matter of commodores the club has had reason to congratulate itself. They have been: T. C. Lyman, sloop *Lois*, 1866–67; Sheppard Homans, sloop *White Wings*, 1868; William Voorhis, sloop *Addie V.*, 1869–70; William Peet, sloop *Nimbus*, 1871–72; J. Rogers Maxwell, sloop *Peerless*, 1873–74; George A. Taylor, schooner *Triton*, 1875–78; Latham A. Fish, schooner *Agnes*, 1879–81; W. R. Vermilye, schooner *Atalanta*, 1882–83; H. H. Hogins, schooner *Agnes*, 1884–86; Frank C. Swan, sloop *Rover*, 1887; J. Lawrence Marcellus, sloop *Stella*, 1888; Jefferson Hogan, schooner *Cavalier*, 1889; Newbury D. Lawton, sloop *Chispa*, 1890–91; David Banks, schooner

ENTRANCE HALL, SEA GATE.

Water Witch, 1892–94; George J. Gould, 1895–97.

Fred. T. Adams, who was vice-commodore since 1895, is the present commodore, his flagship being the schooner *Sachem*, a famous vessel, designed by Edward Burgess, and winner of the Goelet Cup in 1887–88. Mr. Adams has acted as commodore during Mr. Gould's absence in Europe, and is in every way qualified for the position. No better sailor ever walked a deck. He is a navigator as well as a seaman, and popular to boot among his brother yachtsmen. The other officers for the present year are : Vice-commodore, Harrison B. Moore, steamer *Marietta ;* rear-commodore, J. Herbert Ballantine, steamer *Juanita ;* secretary, David E. Austen ; treasurer, George H. Church ; measurer, George Hill. Trustees : J.

Larchmont, on a Friday afternoon ; and then to make a start early on Saturday for Black Rock, where the fleet passed a quiet Sunday, the only events being divine worship on board one of the larger schooners and the dressing of the squadron with flags. On Monday the cruise would be resumed down the Sound, Port Morris, Stonington and New London being the ports stopped at. Then from New London through Plum Gut to Shelter Island, where the fleet generally disbanded.

Sometimes the fleet has gone as far East as Newport, and once Martha's Vineyard was the boundary reached.

Much interest has always attended the cruise from start to finish, every run from port to port being a race with prizes for the winners in each class. Aside from the attraction of cup-hunt-

VIEW FROM THE CLUB ROOF, LOOKING NORTH.
A. Fort Hamilton.   B. Fort Wadsworth.

Rogers Maxwell, George J. Gould, Newbury D. Lawton, Philip G. Sanford, Thomas L. Watson and J. F. Ackerman. Committee on Membership : Howard P. Frothingnam, J. M. Ceballos and Henry B. Howell. Regatta Committee : David E. Austen, George W. McNulty and Henry C. Barnet.

The club has always made a feature of its annual cruise, which is sailed in the month of July. The first occurred in 1866, William Peet's *Hector*, 26 feet in length, and Sheppard Homans' *Nameless*, 28 feet in length, cruising together to Newport and Bristol, R. I. Ever since that year there has been a regular squadron cruise.

The usual course in past years has been for the fleet to rendezvous at Glen Cove or some point on the other side of the Sound, such as New Rochelle or

ing, social visits from one yacht to another, dinner and card parties, hops at the George Hotel, Black Rock ; the Manhansett House, at Shelter Island, and the Edgecombe House, at New London, enhance the enjoyment of the cruise. Ladies are always made welcome by the Atlantic members, and many of the yachts have as guests aboard the wives, sisters, and daughters of their owners.

One of the pleasantest cruises in the history of the club was that of 1880. The squadron mustered at Whitestone, L. I., on July 31, under command of Commodore Latham A. Fish. The fleet was composed of seven schooners and seventeen sloops, the flag-ship being the schooner *Agnes*. The first run was to Black Rock, where Sunday was spent, New London being made on the following day. A grand ball was held at the

THE FIRST CLUB-HOUSE.

where it disbanded, having hugely enjoyed the cruise.

It is on record that the Atlantic squadron was the first to discover the advantages of Greenport harbor as a yachting resort, and the club was at one time so vividly and favorably impressed by it that a scheme was conceived of establishing the headquarters there. One of the members presented a plot of ground on which to build a house, and another member headed the list of subscriptions with a $500 donation. The plan was quite dazzling, for the club was then located in the old canal-boat at the foot of Court street, Brooklyn. But the idea of

Edgecombe House in honor of the visitors. On Tuesday the yachts, for the first time in the career of the club, sailed to Block Island, but found the anchorage and the harbor unsatisfactory, and determined never to repeat the trip. The next port touched at was New Bedford, where, in spite of stormy weather, the usual good time was had. Next Cottage City was made, and the yachtsmen were feted there to their hearts' content, after the custom of that most hospitable summer colony. The beat thence back to Newport was enjoyable and exciting. Next day the squadron sailed over to Greenport,

THE THIRD CLUB-HOUSE.

THE SECOND CLUB-HOUSE.

shifting so far from Brooklyn did not find favor in the sight of the more sagacious members, and the project was never heard of after, though Greenport still remains a favorite harbor for the fleet to touch at occasionally during its annual cruises. Sometimes the squadron anchors in Deering Cove, Shelter Island, opposite the Prospect

ler, H. H. Hogins and many others. The requisite funds were subscribed, and Mr. Philip R. Elsworth was engaged to design the boat.

EMERALD."

House, while at other times it makes the Manhansett House its headquarters.

The cruise of the club in 1889 will always be remembered for the bad weather encountered in the Sound between Black Rock and New London. In that year Jefferson Hogan was commodore, and I was the guest of Vice-Commodore E. B. Havens on his stout sloop *Athlone* for twelve hours of the toughest fighting it has ever been my lot to thrash through. Commodore Hogan, in the *Cavalier*, could have easily made the passage, but he felt it his duty to stick to the bulk of the fleet, a most commendable sacrifice. *Athlone* made the record heavy-weather run in her history.

But we must hark back a year or two for one of the brightest pages of the club's history.

When Lieutenant Henn challenged for the *America's* Cup with his cutter *Galatea*, the Atlantic Yacht Club determined to be represented in the international race of 1886. A syndicate was accordingly formed, the leading members of which were Messrs. Latham A. Fish, J. Rogers Maxwell, John G. Prague, John M. Sawyer, William Zieg-

Mr. Elsworth was somewhat slightingly looked upon by the "scientific set" of Boston and New York, because he was what they termed a "rule-of-thumb" designer. His method, they declared, was to take a chunk of soft wood, whittle out a model of the desired craft, and then turn it over to a naval architect to produce the necessary drawings for the construction of the vessel. This process was, from their point of view, crude and unscientific.

The numerous friends of Mr. Elsworth, on the other hand, pointed with pride to the many excellent records made by yachts from his designs, including the schooners *Montauk* and *Grayling* and the sloops *Fanita*, *Crocodile*, *Anaconda*, *Sasqua* and others.

Mr. John F. Mumm, of Bay Ridge, built the craft, and as she carried thirty-three tons of lead on her keel her construction was necessarily very strong, particularly the center-board trunk. The keel, stem and sternpost were of white oak, the frames of oak and hackmatack, and the planking of pine. Her fastenings below the waterline were of copper; above, of galvanized iron.

EX-COMMODORE GEORGE GOULD.

The *Atlantic* was an exclusive product of the Atlantic Yacht Club. She was known in South Brooklyn as the "Pride of Bay Ridge." In Brooklyn it was thought she would prove an easy victor over her opponents, *Priscilla*, *Puritan* and *Mayflower*. She was launched on the afternoon of May 1st, 1886, a large crowd of enthusiastic yachtsmen witnessing the ceremony.

HOWARD GOULD.

Columns descriptive of her were published in the Brooklyn newspapers. on the following morning, and it may be said that the whole water-front of New York's sister city exulted with flamboyant haughtiness.

A picked crew of yacht sailors was shipped, and to Captain Joe Elsworth, the brother of Philip Elsworth, her designer, was entrusted the task of "tuning up" the *Atlantic* for the trial races. Captain Joe is one of our best amateur yachtsmen, his talents in sailing racing craft to victory having been demonstrated in many a hard-fought contest. He had given Mr. Malcolm Forbes the benefit of his counsel on the *Puritan* in her races with the *Genesta* the previous year, and no doubt existed about his yachting ability. He generously devoted the greater part of his time to getting the big Brooklyn sloop in shape for the fray, and in this he was assisted by the leading lights of the Atlantic Yacht Club, all of whom took a deep interest in the success of their namesake.

It is not my purpose to tell the story of *Atlantic's* struggles as a prospective cup defender. She was undoubtedly a capital boat, but *Mayflower* was evidently superior in speed to *Atlantic*, *Puritan* and *Priscilla*, and, as a matter of course, was chosen to meet *Galatea*.

It is worthy of record that in the yachting season of the following year *Atlantic*, under the management of Commodore Latham A. Fish, beat *Galatea* on more than one occasion. Yachtsmen hailing from Brooklyn still hold to the opinion that the *America's* cup would have remained in this country if its defense had been intrusted to the "Pride of Bay Ridge." I fully believe it, too. It may be added that *Atlantic*, now rigged as a schooner, is an excellent craft, looking well and sailing well. Like most of Elsworth's yachts, she is at her best in heavy weather.

In 1887 it was announced that the British intended to challenge for the *America's* Cup with a crack cutter about 70 feet on the water-line. Former Commodore J. Rogers Maxwell, one of the original incorporators of the club, a thorough yachtsman to whom the club owes much of its prosperity, and a designer as well as a sailor, designed the sloop *Shamrock*, 81 feet over all, 68 feet

5 inches on the water-line, 20 feet beam and 8 feet 5 inches draught. Mr. C. Oliver Iselin commissioned Mr. Burgess to design the 70-footer, *Titania* under the same expectation. The information respecting a British challenge turned out to be erroneous, but *Shamrock* and *Titania* sailed many splendid races with varying results in 1887 and in the following year, when *Katrina*, another 70-footer, designed by Cary Smith for Messrs. E. S. and H. D. Auchincloss, also appeared on the scene. To meet this new opponent, *Shamrock* was hipped out and otherwise improved; and these three smart "seventies" enlivened the season with a series of match-races and other contests, *Titania* proving herself the

the *Peerless*, the result being close and exciting tussles. It is good for posterity that Mr. Maxwell has two sturdy sons, true "chips of the old block," who are as fond of the sport as their father and have learned the art of boat-sailing in a capital school. Both are members of the club.

Ladies' day, a comparatively recent innovation, has met with popular approval from those for whom it was chiefly designed. Prizes worth $25 are given to each class winner, and each lady on the winning craft is presented with a handsome gold pin enameled with the club's burgee. A reception and entertainment, followed by a dance, wind up the evening. That Brooklyn

ATALANTA, THE FLAGSHIP OF EX-COMMODORE GEORGE GOULD.—NOW IN SERVICE OF U. S. NAVY.

fastest of the three. *Shamrock* was sold by her owner, and was transformed into a schooner. The same fate befell *Titania*, while *Katrina* is now rigged as a yawl and has done a good deal of off-shore cruising, proving like all Smith's yachts an able and seaworthy vessel. Mr. Maxwell's next boat was the 46-footer *Nautilus*, a handsome craft but not quite speedy enough for her crack competitors.

One of Mr. Maxwell's keenest opponents in the olden time was Former Commodore George A. Thayer, who sailed his sloop *Orion* against the *Daphne* with varying success; it was often nip and tuck. Mr. Thayer afterward built the *Triton* especially to beat

girls appreciate the Atlantic Yacht Club and that the feeling is reciprocated by the members is shown by the number of pretty women who flock to the house upon every occasion when the rustle of silken petticoats is permitted to be heard.

Although the club has ever been noted for its gallant attentions to the fair sex, both afloat and ashore, it has not yet allowed women to join as flag-members. This is a privilege extended to the better half of humanity by two such organizations only, namely, the New York and the Seawanhaka Corinthian Yacht Clubs. There is a tendency, however, in the younger element to follow the excellent example of the two clubs cited, and it will surprise me much if the necessary legislation to admit lady yacht-owners as flag-members is not soon enacted by the marine jurists of the club.

Truth to tell, there is a strong conservative, nay almost Puritanical, element in the club, a survival of its early days, when yachtsmen were more serious than they are now. For instance, not so very many years ago nothing stronger than lemonade was served on the club's steamers during regatta days. On the annual cruises grog and cards were frowned down upon, and the sparkling exuberance of youth was discouraged. The club chaplain, too, has always been a cherished "feature" or institution of the Atlantic. Doubtless the club imagined that it required a large and intellectual force of what sailors irreverently call "sky-pilots." Other yacht clubs, while glad to enroll the reverend clergy on their books, have given no official recognition to the club chaplain. There are no less than ten of them on the present Atlantic muster-roll. Two of them are old and dear friends of mine and I can vouch for them as true Christians as well as bold and skillful sailors.

COMMODORE FRED. T. ADAMS.

I refer to Dr. George Hepworth, of New York, and the Rev. William H. Thomas. They are "sky-pilots" whom any storm-tossed mariner might be glad to take aboard to guide him safe to port. I have been shipmates with both, and know whereof I speak. The others are the Revs. J. T. Duryea, H. M. Gallaher, W. L. Moore, R. Heber Newton, Lindsay Parker, Jos. J. Reynolds, E. Van Slyke and A. A. Willets, truly a remarkable array of divines.

The lessons learned from the Larchmont brethren in 1895 were accentuated during the cruise of 1896, when Commodore George Gould was personally in command of the squadron. He and

Mrs. Gould dispensed bounteous hospitality on the flagship *Atalanta*, winning all hearts by their kindly courtesy. This cruise will always be remembered as one of the most brilliant social and sporting events in the annals of the club. George Gould joined the Atlantic Yacht Club on November 13, 1882, and has taken sincere and practical interest in its welfare. No other member has brought so many strong and influential recruits to the club as he. He did some dashing racing and bold cruising on the smart sloop *Fanita*, and later purchased the fine schooner *Hildegarde*, once the property of the Prince of Wales. How he and his brother, Howard Gould, bought the *Vigilant*, sailed her over to England and raced her in British waters during the season of 1894, is part of American yachting history to which I have space for only a passing reference, but which reflects great credit on the enterprising and sportsmanlike brothers. Howard Gould became a member of the Atlantic Yacht Club on May 10, 1894. His plucky and successful racing career abroad for two seasons with the Herreshoff 20-rater *Niagara* established securely his fame as a thoroughly clever yachtsman. His recent presentation of his new and costly steam-yacht *Niagara* to the Government for use in the war against Spain is sufficient proof of his patriotism.

The imposing contrast between the first humble home of the club in a canal-boat and its present commanding and magnificent quarters, as shown in the illustrations presented here with, tells the whole story of the club's wonderful progress, pictorially, and in a more striking way than by words alone. One can imagine how hard the leading spirits of the organization must have worked to produce such splendid results. With

"SACHEM," THE FLAGSHIP OF COMMODORE ADAMS

what pride must the surviving veterans who were identified with its origin now look upon the giant of 1898 whom they cradled and cherished with such tender care in the days of its infancy, more than thirty years ago.

In 1880 the old canal boat at Court street was abandoned, and an old farm and farm house at the foot of Fifty-fifth street, South Brooklyn, were bought and fitted up as a club-house. A basin was dredged out for the fleet. In these rather rude but useful quarters the club remained until 1891. In that year extensive improvements were made and a new house was built at the end of a pier erected for the purpose, Mr. J. G. Prague, an old member of the club and an architect by profession, making the design.

This house, a view of which is given on page 288, was

attractive nooks for yachtsmen swelter-ing in the fierce midsummer heat. The basin itself was dredged out and en-larged, forming a fine sheltered harbor for the yachts in both winter and sum-mer, a capital place for fitting-out and laying-up. The club soon learned to love the house and its bright and cheer-ful surroundings.

The only possible objection to Bay Ridge as a yachting station is the scar-city of wind when a breeze is most need-ed, I mean on regatta days. There are too many "bald spots" to the northward of the Narrows to suit the down-to-date yachtsmen; and in the breezy vicinity of Sea Gate they will not suffer so much from flat calms and ex-asperating doldrums as was often their wont when at a

"SHAMROCK."

opened with appropriate ceremonies and rejoicing on Decoration Day, 1891. It was then considered the finest quar-ters for yachtsmen in the vicinity of New York, the house being commodious and spacious, and especially cool in sum-mer time, as Lord Dunraven—an honor-ary member—who was a guest of the club when he came here cup-hunting with his *Valkyrie*, was glad to admit. The pier on which the house was con-structed projected well out from the shore, catching every breath of air, and the well-shaded verandas offered many

further distance from the heaving ocean. If there is any breeze about, one gener-ally feels it off Norton's Point.

Early in 1897, after due consideration the club decided to move to Sea Gate, formerly known as Norton's Point, Coney Island. The report of the com-mittee appointed to investigate the feasibility of the scheme was approved by Commodore Gould and adopted by the club, as was also the financial scheme for obtaining possession of the necessary real estate.

The plot of ground secured by the club

JOSEPH ELSWORTH, WHO SAILED "ATLANTIC."

is 650 feet by 250 feet facing Gravesend Bay. The location is in every way adapted for a yachting station. Open to the breezes of bay and ocean, healthful and picturesque, the members rightly look upon the site as an ideal one. When the Government builds the long-promised and much-needed breakwater the anchorage will be equally desirable.

The new house designed by Mr. Frank Tallman Cornell is a handsome building of the English colonial style of architecture, three stories in height, with broad piazzas on the north, south and west sides. On the same sides on the second floor a spacious balcony is built, and on the roof is a roomy promenade. The interior is admirably arranged. The ground floor is divided into commodious apartments consisting of a large dining-room, ladies' parlor, hall, model-room, billiard-room and café, cloak-room and office. There are seventeen rooms for members on the second floor and numerous bath-rooms. The third floor is similarly arranged.

The eastern end of the house contains the kitchen and servants' quarters. It is also of three stories. On the first floor are a store-room and refrigerator-room, laundry and drying-room, the kitchen proper, servants' dining-room, engine and boiler rooms, and storage place for wood and coal. The servants' dormitories are on the second and third floors.

The grounds by next year will assume a pleasing appearance, when the lawns and the shrubs and the flowers have had time to establish themselves. Outside and inside, nothing but praise can be uttered by the most fastidious of critics.

While stationed at Bay Ridge the club enjoyed many of its most glorious triumphs. During the memorable days of the three international cup contests, the anchorage of the club was used by an immense fleet of visiting yachts, to whose owners all the facilities and hospitalities of the house were fraternally tendered. It will be remembered what busy scenes the float presented during those exciting times, with its flotilla of gigs, dinghies and launches landing and embarking gay parties to and from the squadron.

The Bay Ridge station was always popular with the fair sex because of the frequent "hops" given during the season, in honor of sweethearts and wives, after the good and time-honored custom of mariners. The jolly luncheons and dinners on the cool and shady piazzas were always appreciated by the lady contingent of the club—for be it known to all men, and women, too, for that matter, that the Atlantic members glory in their *cuisine* and have always exercised due

"ATLANTIC."

PHILIP R. ELSWORTH, WHO DESIGNED "ATLANTIC."

TRUSTEE
J. F. ACKERMAN.

TRUSTEE
GENERAL THOS. L. WATSON.

EX-VICE-COMMODORE
E. B. HAVENS.

skill and discrimination in their choice of a *chef*.

It will be a cause of perennial joy to the veteran members that the Bay Ridge club-house, that hospitable building in which so many jocund hours were passed, the scene of so many festivities, the center where matches were made, contests arranged, and best of all, marine battles were fought over and over again in those pleasant evenings in the fall of the year, with the grateful accompaniments of the blue smoke of fragrant tobacco and the petulant pop of corks, still remains the property of the club. It was placed on a raft, towed down to Sea Gate, landed, and placed in position beside the new main building. It was fitted up with forty rooms for members, many of which have been rented for the season. Thus the old quarters have been utilized, and they

will doubtless furnish a considerable source of revenue to the club, as well as afford a fund of pleasant reminiscences of happy days now gone.

Such was the origin and rise of the Atlantic Yacht Club. That its liberal policy, its wise and enlightened government, together with its spirited sportsmanship, will command success in the future as in the past, is as assured as anything in this sphere of uncertainties can be. Long may the Atlantic Yacht Club flourish as the home of good fellows and the cradle of all that is worth cultivating in the domain of yachting, is the hope and prayer of every son of Neptune. Worthy sons of worthy sires are on hand to carry on the good work, and the lesson of the year, that yachting can materially aid the nation's safeguarding, will be an additional incentive to its promotion as a pastime.

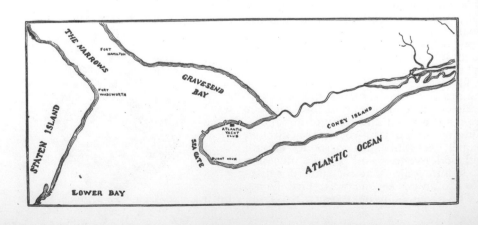

Bluefishing at Montauk
(1898)

BLUEFISHING AT MONTAUK.

BY E. M. S.

IS daybreak at Wapague, a small harbor on the east end of Long Island, and the old oil works show in sharp silhouette against the eastern sky. The fishing boats lie quietly at anchor, with their riding lights still burning brightly.

As the dawn grows brighter, signs of life begin to show. A cock crows ashore, and the cry of a yellow-leg plover falls from the sky. A man with his head well sprinkled with gray, appears from the cabin of a small yacht, anchored near the other boats. He rubs his eyes, and carefully scans the sky.

A beautiful morning it gives promise of. There is not a ripple on the water lying so black and cold around him, while the air has a crisp suggestive freshness.

While Captain Sanford, for this is the man's name, standing in the companionway, is making his almanac for the day, and before his crew wake up, perhaps we should explain matters a little.

The boat, to begin with, is the *Bessie Earl*, a thirty-foot sloop. She is not a

255

modern racing machine, with a lead mine hanging from her keel, and drawing as much water as an ocean steamer, but a good comfortable center-board craft. Her paint is white and clean, and the bright work about her shows care and attention. Her cabin is roomy, with a cook-room forward, and an ice-chest aft under the cockpit floor. She carries, besides her mainsail and jib, a club-topsail and jib-topsail for use in light weather. A light skiff is fastened to her stern.

Her owner, Capt. John Sanford, is a tough, rugged man of about sixty years of age, and forty of these years have been spent at sea. When he left the ocean and took up his abode with his family ashore, he found that he had contracted a habit, or disease, that nothing but water would cure. In the winter, when everything is frozen up and covered with snow, he is contented to stay home with his family, but when warm weather comes he begins to grow uneasy, and nothing will quiet him but the blue water. The *Bessie Earl* is his pet and darling; in fact she is his summer home, and most of his time from May to October is spent on board of her.

In the cozy cabin are four boys, on their vacation. Tom Sanford, the captain's nephew, has been with his uncle often, and feels quite competent to sail the yacht anywhere. With his comrades, Joe Rogers and Harry and Jack Goddard, he has been out three days on a bluefishing trip, with little luck. The fish at Plum Gut were scarce, and in the Race there was none. But all the fleet told great stories of the fish at Montauk, and this point, twelve miles away, is where our young friends are bound this morning.

"What are we going to have for weather to-day, captain?" inquires Joe, as his curly black head appears by the captain's side.

"The weather will be all right," replied the captain, "when we get a little wind to make a start with. You get the boys up, while I start a fire, and we will have something to eat."

The morning meal is soon disposed of, the dishes washed, and the cabin put in order. A gentle ripple on the water shows a breath of wind from the southwest. From over the water comes the rattle of jib-hanks as another of the fleet trips her anchor and moves down the bay.

Soon we, too, are ready, and with the jib to help, the bow slowly swings off. The captain takes the wheel, and the pretty craft starts for the open sea.

There is barely enough wind to fill the sails, and the boys watch with interest the other boats. A big white schooner-yacht lies down near the mouth of the harbor with not a sign of life aboard. Her white canvas and yellow spars show clear against the sky as she rides quietly at her anchor. A lone clammer from his hut on the shore is rowing his dingy little boat over to the opposite point, while a fleet of boats is floating slowly down the harbor.

At the spar buoy, they separate; the little lobster smacks go to the Race, a Connecticut River boat and others head for Plum Gut, while Capt. Sanford swings his boom to port and points for Montauk.

The wind freshens as we clear the point. The club-topsail is swung aloft, and Tom casts the jib-topsail loose and sets it. With this additional sail, the *Bessie Earl* leans gracefully to it, and with her bowsprit pointing due east, she glides quietly through the water.

This is the poetry of sailing — a smooth sea, with the white sands and stunted bushes of Long Island on one side, and the open Sound on the other. There are few sails in sight, as Wapague is an unfrequented part of the island. A bunker fisherman from the factory at the Promised Land is starting out for his day's work, while far out a solitary schooner is pointing up for the Race.

The boys make themselves comfortable and listen to the captain as he tells them tales of his past life: stories of long voyages to the Orient, around Cape Horn to the Pacific coast, trips to South American ports, and, in fact, nearly all over the world.

Three years of his life were spent in a whaler. From this cruise alone come stories almost without limit: tales of Arctic ice, and days with no night, and months of unending darkness.

All this time the white sails have been quietly at work, and the lighthouse at Montauk is now plainly visible. The lines and jigs are taken out and examined; new hooks are put on to replace any broken or rusted.

Bluefish are caught by trolling, and

the jig, or bait, is simply a round piece of bone, or wood, shaped something like your finger, with a stout hook in the end.

"Tom," calls the captain, "you boys get that skiff up and lay it across the cockpit out of the way; shut the cabin doors, and fix this box to put the fish in. I can see gulls at work, and we should be in the fish soon."

The wind had slowly increased since the start, and the light sails will have to come in. This is soon accomplished, and under mainsail and jib the sloop is swiftly nearing the gulls, now in plain sight.

"Have you seen a fish whip, captain?" says Joe.

"No, but we will shortly. They are in that rough water just out from the point; there one goes. Now get your lines over and make them fast."

The boys had been so interested in the fishing, that they had not noticed the different nature of the water where the fish are. Under the land it had been smooth, but now as they get out from the point they feel for the first time the long ocean roll, coming in perhaps from some gale far out at sea.

The boys have all confidence in the captain, but when the little yacht slides down one watery hill to meet another directly at the foot of it, why they hold on and wonder where they will fetch up. But this feeling all leaves them as Tom's line suddenly straightens, and a bluefish leaves the water far astern, with the jig in his mouth.

"Pull, Tom; don't give him any slack," says the captain, and the boy does pull, and with one last dash of salt water from the tail of the fish, it is safely boated. A lusty big one it is, too.

Joe takes his turn, and another is soon hauled in to keep the first one company. We get four this time across.

"Ready to go about!" calls the captain. The helm is put down, and the sails flap wildly in the wind, then fill,

and back we go over the same ground. This time we get three.

We work and work hard. The fish are hungry and savage, and after a few trips through the school, the fish-box is one mass of struggling victims. The cabin doors and seats in the cockpit are covered with blood and gurry. The boys are soaked, their fingers cut and bleeding, but wild enthusiasm still prevails.

Bluefish, however, have their regular hours for meals; and an hour is spent in a hunt for another school, but with no further success.

"It is of no use, Tom," says the captain; "we might as well give it up." And with that we flatten sheets down and start for home.

The crew wash down and clean up aft. The wind is just a good topsail breeze, and the *Bessie Earl* lies over until her lee-rail is just awash, while over her sharp bows there comes now and then a dash of spray. It is a good long pull to New London, and the boys are hungry. It is too rough to cook much, so they content themselves with a cold bite, and the sandwiches and cold beans taste good.

There are more craft than were seen in the morning. The fishing steamers have found fish, and are hard at work. One gang almost in our path has just finished passing up the net, while the oar up-ended in one of the boats, tells the steamer to come and take the fish. A big four-masted schooner, with every sail set, is coming down, bound out to sea, while farther away there are a dozen or more white sails showing plain on the water.

The *Bessie Earl* makes a straight wake for the Race, up by the Middle Ground buoy, through the Rip and by the Race Rock light. Here we have the wind more on the quarter, and the seven miles to New London are soon covered, and just as the sun sank back of Fort Trumbull the anchor found the bottom.

The Helderbergs
(1869)

THE HELDERBERGS.

THE HELDERBERGS, AT THE INDIAN LADDER.

IN the State of New York are three principal mountain chains. The Adirondacks cover the northern, granite region of the State, of rock which has been violently heated, if not melted, by the earth's internal fires. They are igneous, plutonic mountains, with peaks perhaps six thousand feet above tide-level. The Catskills are an isolated group of peaks on the Hudson, more than a hundred miles south of their granite elder brethren of the Adirondack. They are principally of the old red sandstones and shales which underlie the coal formation. These are sedimentary rocks, the silt of ancient ocean currents; their peaks exceed three thousand feet in height.

Between these, north of the Catskills, not twenty miles distant, is a line of small mountains known as the Helderbergs, the third though not the least of the mountain systems of New York. They are a long angular range of solid blue limestone cliffs, running nearly east and west. Their geographical name exists only in Albany County; but, geologically, they are over three hundred miles in length, their unbroken strata reaching from the Hudson to Niagara and on into Canada. Their greatest altitude is one thousand two hundred feet.

These calcareous cliffs, filled with fossil, petrified sea-shells, answer to the European Silurian and Devonian ages. By its peculiar fossil shells the Helderberg, like other rock, is known when met with in distant regions. In subterranean darkness it stretches, a hidden, undulating sheet of strata, an inner mantle to the continent, cropping out here and there, and leaving its wooded "Silurian ruins" to render picturesque the scenery of many a State.

In the far West a geologist picks up a fossil shell, examines it, and says, "Helderberg"—surmises that good limestone may thereabout be found, and gypsum for the plasterer's art, and iron pyrites—fool's gold—useful for sulphur and sulphuric acid manufacture. Caves also may be expected, and sulphur springs, strontian, or barytes, if not more valuable deposits, may be near.

A Tennessee geologist also picks up a petrifaction, and makes note of it as "Helderberg." In Britain Sir Roderick Murchison, mentioning the existence of his favorite Siluria in America, will not fail to speak of the Helderberg formation. Yet it is possible that of these three not one had ever seen the Helderberg.

"Helderberg" is a Dutch corruption of the old German *Helle-berg*, meaning "Clear Mountain." This name was given by the first settlers of Schoharie County, who had the bold and distinct *berg* constantly in view during their first day's journey westward into the then wilderness. Though plainly visible, and but ten or fifteen miles from the ancient city of Albany, few of its citizens appear even to know of their existence, let alone their traditions and their beauties. Helderberg to many Albanians means "anti-rent," "sheriff's posse," military, blue uniforms, bright muskets and bayonets, and shackled prisoners, against whom no crime being proved they are always released.

Most of the farms on these hills were what was once called "manor land." It had its feudal lord and manor-house after the fashion in England prior to our Revolution. The farmers were peasantry, of whom feudal rents in the shape of wheat, chickens, and "days' service" were exacted, though the land was indentured, or deeded, to them, their heirs and assigns forever. Ignorant emigrants were led to purchase, invest their all, clear and improve the land, and give it value, not dreaming that they would have to pay the interest on their own improvements.

Alas! they found that they had exchanged the hard lot of a Holland "boor" for one even harder. Shrewd Yankees, living on free soil, jeered at them as slaves.

The Revolution came, the battles of liberty were fought, and down went Tory and Royalist. After that feudal exactions seemed hard and oppressive, as well as unrepublican and monarchical. Some now refused to pay the "quarter sale"—one quarter of the price received by the farmer each time a place was sold. If the farm was sold four times the "Lord" received the cash value of the farm, and still pretended to own it! Threats not sufficing, they were called "Anti-renters," and war was levied upon them. But since then the conflict has raged, nor is it ended yet; but quarter sales are abolished.

The Susquehanna Railroad trains, as they leave Albany crowded with tourists bound for Sharon Springs, the beauteous Susquehanna River Valley, or distant Pennsylvania, are forced to follow the wall-like precipices facing the Helderberg almost along their whole extent, far to the north and west, before they are able to climb it. It is its romantic wooded rock scenery, dark caverns, and sprayey waterfalls, its varied landscape and accessible mountain grandeur, that render the Helderberg interesting to artist, author, poet, tourist, or rusticator.

The traditions herein written are at least as true as traditions ever are, and I tell them substantially as they were told to me. The sketches may give some idea of the scenery.

To those who desire to escape for a day from the oven-like city in summer; who wish to enjoy a scramble among romantic cliffs, in shady

MOUNTAIN SPURS.

woods, beside cool mountain brooks and water-falls; to view spots sacred to legends of wild Revolutionary days, of Tory and Indian depredation, naming place, precipice, and mountain; to gather the fossil corals and shells (univalves, bivalves, and brachipods) which, forming the very soil the farmer tills, cropping from out the sod, are reared as farm walls or burned to lime; to visit and explore known caves, and search for new ones, possibly existing unknown and unexplored, among the cliff ledges, the "Indian Ladder" region of the Helderbergs offers superior inducements.

Taking an early train on the Susquehanna Railroad and stopping at Guilderland Station brings one within a mile of the Indian Ladder Gap. Even from that distance the mountain spurs are visible. Wondrous are the deep, black shadows that they cast early in the day. A scarcely discernible zigzag ascending line, not unresembling a military siege-approach, shows the Indian Ladder Road crawling up the mountain and along and beneath the precipices.

It is but an easy two hours' drive, however, from Albany, and many may prefer to visit it in the saddle or with a pleasant party. If the weather be dry and not very sultry the jaunt will well repay you. If your horses are brave and steady you may drive up the mountain road—it is a mile to the summit—or you may lead your horses up, the party walking leisurely after. Still some descending team may be met, and it is ill passing on that narrow cliff road. Notwithstanding many accidents this road is the highway, winter and summer, of the country folk.

If, however, you have a desire to "foot it," and wish to see the wildest, most romantic scenery the place affords, abandon the road and follow the stream, called by some Black Creek, up the valley to the foot of the gorge—a savage stairway up the mountain slope, of broken rock-fragments and great water-worn boulders. Then, if your heart fail you not—for any place more difficult to climb is impassable—you will ascend for a breathless, dangerous, exciting three or four hours to the foot of the cliffs and the falls—an escalade which will bear comparison with any thing climbable.

But you should not return without mementoes of your visit. Carry then a satchel, unless you have capacious pockets; for curiosities will meet you on every side. Besides the fossil medals of creation—petrifactions and minerals—the collector will find a thousand objects of interest. If he have keen eyes he may note some curious grafts, great hemlocks on huge pine-trees, perhaps of Indian handicraft. Large slow-worms, unknown lizards, insects, perhaps black-snakes, toads, and eels, mingled in strange confusion, swarm amidst the rocks. The place was once renowned for the multitude, size, and venom of its rattlesnakes.

The damp, thick woods of oak, hickory, red (slippery) elm, basswood (linden), butternut, ash, beech, and birch, with white pine, hemlock, and some spruce, give color to the scenery, heightened by the green, graceful frondage of the scarlet-fruited sumac, the trailing cordage of the wild grape-vines, and the numberless other rarer wild plants—annuals, biennials, perennials, every where luxuriant.

Your satchel may contain some luncheon; a geological hammer and a chisel would not be inappropriate; your sketch-book by all means. Gun or fishing-tackle here are useless; hunting there is none save foxes, "coons," some ruffled grouse (partridge), and at times wild pigeons. The fishing is also poor, except for pickerel, perch, sunfish, and the like, in lakes and brooks amidst the hills back from the summit.

What is this Indian Ladder so often mentioned? In 1710 this Helderberg region was a wilderness; nay, all westward of the Hudson River settlements was unknown. Albany was a frontier town, a trading post, a place where annuities were paid, and blankets exchanged with Indians for beaver pelts. From Albany over the sand plains—Schen-ec-ta-da (pine-barrens) of the Indians—led an Indian trail westward. Straight as the wild bee or the crow the wild Indian made his course from the white man's settlement to his own home in the beauteous Schoharie Valley. The stern cliffs of these hills opposed his progress; his hatchet fells a tree against them, the stumps of the branches which he trimmed away formed the rounds of the Indian Ladder.

That Indian trail, then, led up this valley, up yonder mountain slope, to a cave now known

GULCH VIEW.

THE SMALL FALL.

as the "Tory House." The cave gained that name during the Revolution: of that more anon. The trail ended in a corner of the cliffs where the precipice did not exceed 20 feet in height. Here stood the tree—the old Ladder. In 1820 this ancient ladder was yet in daily use. There are one or two yet living who have climbed it. Greater convenience became necessary, and the road was constructed during the next summer. It followed the old trail up the mountain. The ladder was torn away, and a passage through the cliffs blasted for the roadway. The rock-walled pass at the head of the road is where the Indian Ladder stood. The Indians had once a similar ladder near Niagara Falls. There were probably many such among the cliffs. It was possibly the resemblance of this wild mount-ain scenery to that of father-land far away that induced its early settlement by the Swiss, and gave the name of Berne to the neighboring town.

You have followed the rapid brook up the valley through the shadowy woods, and have reached a little prairie—an opening surrounded almost on every side by the great mountain slopes which rise grandly to the impregnable cliffs walling the summits. It seems a window whereby the crag-climber may observe the whole extent of his labors. This spot was known as the "Tory Hook" or Plat, and in days gone by was their rendezvous—a lone, se-questered glade of the savage forest. Above you, in front and to right and left, is a colossal natural amphitheatre, the long, wooded slopes rising tier on tier to the base of the circling precipices. Two rocky gorges, which ascend like the diverging aisles of an amphitheatre, part the wilderness of green. The steep slopes have four-fifths of the mountain height.

Towering above the uppermost tree-tops are the gray, battlement-like cliffs. Many a dark opening, gloomy recess, and inaccessible ledge can be seen which human foot has never trod; once, probably, the pathway and home of that blood-thirsty savage, the nimble and stealthy-footed cougar. Two lofty waterfalls stream down, milk-white, from the cliff-top at the head of each dry, rock-filled gorge. Your way lies to the right, up the gorge to the smaller of the two falls.

Following the stream and entering the opposite woods you commence the ascent of the gorge. It is no light undertaking. The bed of the stream is your best road; keep to the right. Difficulties begin; you are frequently compelled to cross the rapid stream on stepping-stones. At length you reach what may be termed the foot of the gorge. The stream rushes down in a number of little cascades—above it is lost amidst the huge rocks. Look upward, your labor lies before you.

Up, then! Up! Ah—it is fatiguing? Look below! It seems easier to climb up than down. Retreat appears impossible, if not recreant. Upward, then! no longer over fallen rocks merely, but over prostrate cliffs rather. Huge blocks as large as little cottages or backwoods log-cabins are heaped in wild confusion; up them and over them! More toilsome, nay, dangerous, becomes the ascent; but now the novelty and danger give new zest, and "Forward!" shouts one. Whereat you all, with vigorous competition hurrying, climb and scramble upward; sometimes on foot, oftener upon hands and knees, and frequently prone, with aid of fingers and toe of boot making slow progress up the face of some fallen mountain.

To climb, some aid themselves with sticks snatched up from where they were cast by the last great freshet that foamed down the wild gorge. The barkless pole, dry and withered, often fails the user, who scarce has time to drop the worthless fragments, snatch a firm grip upon immovable rock, and thank his stars that he has not followed the fragments of his staff that rattle down half a hundred feet before they reach a cranny large enough to hold them. Do not take each wriggling thing among the rocks to be a snake. Once thinking to capture what I took to be a serpent sunning himself on the rocks, I found I had a sleek, fat eel! An eel there on those dry rocks? Assuredly. For, hark! do you hear that steady rushing sound, as of a subterranean waterfall? Hours of toilsome climbing have passed. Look upward, the falls are before you at last.

From the brink of the dark cliff drops a spray-white stream, about eighty feet, unbroken. Lost for a moment to sight it issues from a rocky basin, and ripples down in two streams bright-

ly over a series of little stone steps, the angular parallel edges of abraded schist strata, seldom over an inch in thickness. Suddenly the smooth descent ceases; the rock drops perpendicularly fifteen or eighteen feet. Down the face of this wall or "fault" dash two little cascades; they fall upon another series of the miniature rock steps, and, glittering and shining like a magic stream of crystal, hurry down to lose their waters among the huge rocks of the gorge; lost for a thousand feet of that dread mountain slope ere coming forth to light again as the stream in the valley below. At last beneath the precipice you stand in the cool shadow of the dark dripping rocks, at the foot of the falls, the top of the gorge—that goal for which you have so arduously labored.

This is the Small Fall, sometimes called the "Dry Falls." The latter name you will hardly appreciate should you visit it when swollen by recent rains. Here you may enjoy an unequaled shower-bath; but the stream carries pebbles, and the dashing water itself stings like a shower of shot.

Below (and on the cliffs above) this fall is one of the best localities for Helderberg fossils or petrifactions. Among these fossil shells of ancient seas are many peculiar to the Helderbergs. The names and features of these shells once mastered, two of the most important of geological ages are known to you. On the Pacific slope, amidst the Sierras, throughout the North American continent, even in foreign lands, knowing these fossils you will be able to recognize the Silurian and Devonian rocks. The Helderbergs are principally Silurian; above this, on the summit of the hills and on their southern slopes, Devonian rocks are found.

When, years ago, Lyell in his geological travels visited these hills, he was struck with amazement. It seemed a new, a forgotten world. There is a stratum of the cliff rock, sometimes fifty feet in thickness, entirely composed of one variety of fossil shell—the *Pentamerus galeatus*—the shells massed together in a way astounding. This, once the shell-covered bed of an ocean, is now a portion of a mountain cliff. It is this that gives such interest to Helderberg precipices, more than to basalt Palisades, or even dread Wall-Face of the Adirondacks.

If you are fortunate you may find the outcrop of that stratum and bring away a "chunk" of shells. Besides the *Pentamerus* a dozen or more varieties of fossils may here be found. *Spirifer* and *Athyris*, whose delicate internal spirals art has brought to light. The well-named *Platyceras dumosum*, a flat horn covered with spikes, as its name implies. The beautiful minute *Tentaculites*, that resemble little petrified minnows or fishes just hatched—they fairly swarm on the thin, clinking fragments of the water-lime stone. *Encrinoids* (stone lilies), ancient *Trilobites* (*dalmania*), with their numberless eyes, perhaps a rare, odd-looking thing called a *Cystad*, a beautiful little *Euomphalus*,

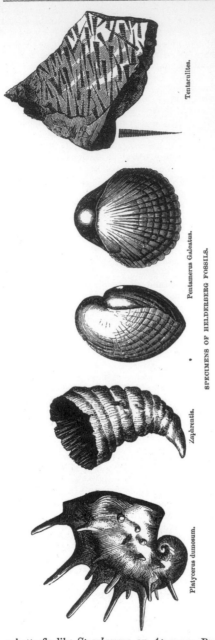

Tentaculites.

Pentamerus Galeatus.

Zaphrentis.

Platyceras dumosum.

SPECIMENS OF HELDERBERG FOSSILS.

Along beneath the cliffs runs a narrow path. The débris of the mountain drops on one side (a steep wooded slope); on the other the overhanging precipice forms a wall. Westward this path leads to the Indian Ladder road; and, going that way, you pass a curious scene. At the base of the cliff is a dark opening, about three feet high by six or eight in width, narrowing inward. From the dark interior of the cliff a clear, sparkling stream issues, constant summer and winter. This place I once explored in a boat built for the purpose, narrow and coffin-like, carried thither from the road along the ledges. I found a black, narrow passage—no deep water, lakes, or large rooms—nothing to reward me for my pains.

Eastward the path leads to the "Big," "Mine Lot," or "Indian Ladder Falls." Have a care when following this path; the overhanging rocks are often loose and trembling. Sometimes your mere approaching tramp will be sufficient to cause their rattling fall. Suddenly you turn a corner of the cliff, and pause in admiration of the scene before you.

From the edge of the overhanging precipice, more than a hundred feet above your head, streams down a silvery rope of spray, with a whispering rush, sweeping before it damp, chilly eddies of fugitive air, that sway the watery cable to and fro. Back, beneath the rocky shelf from off which the fall precipitates its unceasing stream, is a black, cavernous semicircle of rock, its gloomy darkness in deep contrast with the snow-white fall. Below, to the left, the woods are swept away to the base of the mountains, and in their place a wild and desolate descent of broken rocks falls sharply —rendered more savage to the eye by the shattered trunks of dead trees mingled.

Back of the fall at the base of the precipice is a low, horizontal cavity in the rock, from four to six feet in height, fifty or sixty feet in length, by fifteen in depth. Stooping and clambering in over a low heap of rubbish—probably the old waste of the mine—you enter. Mine, strictly, there is none; but the marks of mining implements and the excavation show that operations of some kind have been carried on. Here is a massive vein of iron pyrites (bisulphide of iron), fine-grained and solid, and well suited for sulphuric acid manufacture. The bed or vein of pyrites has evidently been much thicker, but it has decomposed, a yellow oxyd of iron and sulphate of lime (gypsum) resulting.

The particular appearance of the bed is interesting. At the bottom of the excavation can be seen the glittering masses of pyrites, above them calcareous incrustations, over which appears the yellow oxyd of iron, resulting from the decomposition of former pyrites, seamed and segregated with veins of gypsum—misnamed "plaster of Paris." There is no sulphate of iron (proper) or green copperas resulting, but a white, acid, crumbling substance answering to *Coquimbite* (white copperas) may be found; and a yellow incrustation, in one place

a butterfly-like *Strophomena*, an *Atrypa* or *Rynchonella*, cornucopia-like *Zaphrentis* — Corals (favorites), *Bryozoans*, *Fucoids*, and others valuable to the geologist, surprising and interesting to any one.

These rocks (or rather the rocks of this age) were till within a year called *Palæozoic*, as containing "the most ancient life." Fossils have since been found in the older, granite *Azoic* (without life) rock. Those names, having lost their meaning, are now obsolete.

at least, resembling sulphur flowers. The oxydized sulphur of the pyrites, as sulphuric acid, has united with the limestones to form the gypsum, of which there are sufficient indications to warrant a search. As the limestones are frequently magnesian, another result has been the formation of sulphate of magnesia, and beautiful acicular crystals of the Epsom or "hair" salt have here been found. Almost all the "plaster" used in the State comes from the western Helderberg limestones. California is said to have imported from New York in 1868 nearly 25,000 barrels of gypsum.

Long years ago wild stories were told about this mine and its workers; of two strange, taciturn, foreign men who frequented the spot, who kept their mouths shut, and minded their own business in a way astonishing and irritating to the country people around. Nay, more incomprehensible, they lived there beneath those silent rocks, and often in dark nights strange lights were seen flashing and moving among the dangerous precipices — wild, heathenish shouts and noises heard among the cavernous recesses of the cliffs. At times in the misty haze of early morning they had been met upon the road with heavy packs upon their sturdy shoulders, wending their way toward some mart, and all who saw them muttered "a good riddance." But suddenly some night lights would again be seen flashing far above the farm-houses among the gloomy, night-hidden rocks. At length they vanished, never to return. The object of their labors is unknown; the ruinous remains of a stone structure resembling a vat, said to be of their construction, yet exists; it is called "The Leach." The mine is known as the "Red-Paint Mine," and it is asserted that the miners were engaged in the manufacture of a red paint from the yellow,

THE HANGING ROCK.

THE DOME.

ochery oxyd of iron there existing. How they managed it seems now among the lost arts.

Were the Helderberg rock but slightly metamorphosed, with here and there a dyke of trap or basalt, what minerals might it not contain? The Almaden mercury mines of Spain (red cinnabar, vermilion, "paint") are in metamorphic Silurian limestones. The White Pine and Treasure Hill silver mines of Nevada are in a metamorphosed, crinoidal limestone of the Silurian age, the quartz veins containing the familiar fossils silicified. Old Dutch Colonial Governor Kieft protested that there was gold in this region. Nay, it is said that he found it; and doughty Van Der Donck, the histori-

ographer of the New Netherlands, swears to it.

You may reach the cliff top from here by going further east, where the precipices decrease in height. Search till you find the ascent to a narrow ledge that leads to a square embrasure-like break in the cliff; it seems as though a huge block twenty feet square had been quarried out. In one corner you will discover the crumbling fragments of a tree-ladder; it can not exceed twenty-five feet to the summit. Ascend, and you will have an idea of the Indian Ladder.

Westward now along the cliff tops, back toward the falls again, and the Indian Ladder road. You reach the stream which forms the Big or Mine Lot Fall, and, stepping through the bushes which obscure your view, stand upon the verge of the precipice. To your left, from the lowest ledge below, the fall leaps the cliff brink, and pours in a steady stream.

Recline here and rest. Six inches beyond your feet is the mossy, weather-worn, blackened cliff edge. A wild flower growing in some cliff below, never once trodden by now living man or beast, raises its unpretending head just above the precipice brink. Out beyond is empty air; below, the dark afternoon shadows of the perpendicular mountains are already casting the valley in shade. The wild, rock-filled gorges seem but tiny gutters; the forests shrubbery; all below miniature.

Leaning head and shoulders over as you recline, you see that the rock on which you rest is a projecting shelf but a foot or so in thickness. Should the table-rock yield beneath your weight, rushing with it through mid-air you might light upon the cruel jagged tops of those dead hemlocks, thrust upward from below, whose withered points, lightning-scarred, and broken moss-wreathed limbs, seem waiting, bristling, to receive your fall.

It is grand, thus reclining on the cliff brink, to view the wide-spread landscape to the north of the mountains—the joint basin of the Hudson and the Mohawk—a deep valley more than sixty-miles in width. From here you see a wide-spread level country, a true basin, bounded by distant mountain chains; not the bewildering sea of lesser peaks and hills visible from Tahawus. You see, nearest, the deep savage valley, with shades predominating, mountain-walled; the checkered fields and woods beyond, in vast perspective; the distant white farmhouse and the red barns, and half forest-hidden steeple of the village church—all vanishing in hazy distance; last, the blue, ragged outline of the northern granite mountains, a bright sky flecked with feathery cirro-cumuli, ever changing, lit with a rich, warm, mellow North American sunlight, brighter than which can not shine either in Italy or on South Sea palm groves.

The cliff, measured by cord and plummet, is here about one hundred and twenty-six feet in height; that of the waterfall may be estimated at one hundred and sixteen feet. Here you may lunch beside the brook, and gaze out past the Hanging Rock, across the valley, to the opposite mountain spur, where a faint ascending line shows the Indian Ladder road again; by it you will soon descend the mountain. Amidst the bushes back from the falls is a deep, narrow crevice. A stone dropped in rattles and clatters and hops till lost to hearing. To what gloomy cavern is this the sky-light? Some careless person may yet tumble in and learn; yet no one else would ever be the wiser. Such crevices account for the numerous springs at the cliff base. The rock must be ramified with caverns.

Leaving the fall, westward again along the cliff tops, brings you to the Small Fall and a road; following this you come out upon another road. Look to your right: that deep angular cut through the rock is the Pass, the head of the Indian Ladder road.

Descend the defile; you are below the cliffs again in gloomy shadow. Here stood the Indian Ladder. Observe the semi-Alpine character of the road; off this built-up, wharf-like way more than one team has dashed. The trees on the long, steep slope beneath have their history: "The horse struck that one; the man was found just here."

As you descend the road the cliffs increase in height, and the Dome, a mantle-piece-like projection, fairly overhangs and threatens it. Climb the débris beneath the Dome and you will find a path. Follow it. It leads to a cave, the resort of Tories and Indians during the Revolution.

"The Tory House" is a large circular or semicircular cavity in the cliff, just above the road, a good view of which it commands. It is a single room, perhaps twenty-five or thirty feet in diameter, open on one side; looking out over a block of fallen stone—an imperfect rampart—down the wooded slope to the road, and beyond, into the deep valley between the mountain spurs.

Here Jacob Salisbury, a notorious royalist spy, is said to have been captured, about the time that Burgoyne was marching his army toward the now historic plains of Saratoga, visible from the mountain-top. The capture of this spy was deemed of considerable importance. It was with difficulty that his lurking-place was discovered and his projects frustrated.

No road then climbed these cliffs. In those wild, unsafe days the wolves were left in undisturbed possession, and the cave was almost unknown. Imagine the darkness of night enveloping the scene. Within the cave, the dusky figure of a man who kneels before a feeble and smoking fire, which ever and anon gives forth a lurid flash—lights for a moment the dungeon-like cave—shines from the brass-bound butts of the huge pistols decorating his belt; then disappears in more mysterious shadow. The thick smoke irritates, he sneezes, how melancholy and hollow is the echo! how quick suppressed the sound! Hark! a twig snaps without; the rattling fall of a stone is heard! The flame leaps up once more as he turns his savage, bearded face; mark the knit brows, the glaring eyes—a desperate *spy*. His right hand reaches toward his musket, yet he hesitates. A heavy tread outside; the rattling of many stones; a brushing through the bushes. He starts defiantly to his feet; though trembling, cocks his musket—at bay! There is a muttering of human voices in the impenetrable darkness without; an ominous clicking as of many rifle-locks; and suddenly some one cries out, "Jacob Salisbury, lay down your arms! You are surrounded and can not escape. A dozen rifles are leveled at your breast." He hesitates.

THE TORY HOUSE.

"Down with your musket!" shouts one without. "Do you love treason better than life?" As he dashes his musket, with a curse, to the ground, the flame leaps brightly up and shows the shadowy forms of his foemen; their leveled rifles, steady aim; their leader, sword in hand, in front. Disarmed and bound, the spy is hurried down the mountain, and the lonely cavern abandoned to wild beasts again.

In the roof of the Tory House is a dark, tubular or spire-like cavity, which has, apparently, no connection with any other chamber or cavern. You may, returning, descend the mountain by the road, having seen the more prominent places of interest of the Indian Ladder region.

I will now locate and slightly describe a few of the numberless Helderberg caves. Indeed, without such guidance, the visitor might never find any of them; for to discover caves appears to require a cave-hunting instinct, a learned eye. The under-world has its peculiarities. It differs from the upper-world. Its rivers run at right angles beneath the surface torrents, and are generally little influenced by surface storms and changes. Some run a clear, cold, unaltering, constant stream; others ebb and flow with the seasons; are impassable, muddy, furious in spring flood-time; and the waters vanish, dry up, and are lost in seasons of drought.

The limestone rock of the Helderberg is the cave rock of the world. Other names it may have beyond the oceans; but the rock is of the same age, and contains fossils similar to those found here. Only in Silurian limestones is there space for a region of extensive caves— "Silurian," on this continent, carries Helderberg with it. The Mammoth Cave of Kentucky appears to be in the corniferous, upper Helderberg limestone, which is, however, Devonian. In England, on the Continent, in Palestine, are caverns in limestone, and some in other rock, but rock which has been changed, having by heat been metamorphosed into marbles and the like.

Within thirty miles of the Indian Ladder one may count twenty caverns large and small. Among them, in Schoharie County, Ball's or Gebhard's Cave—brightest of alabaster caverns—whose gloomy portal drops perpendicularly over a hundred feet to a region of large lakes and wondrous waterfalls; and Howe's or the Otsgaragee Cavern, which strives to rival Kentucky's Mammoth Cave.

The caves of the Helderberg are not glittering crystal grottoes. Though often extensive, they are dark and dungeon-like, damp and muddy; on every side they show the means which made them. The hollow, constant rushing of the water also tells the story of their formation.

Among the cliffs, however, are some caves comparatively or quite dry. Many a dark hole and crevice may be seen on the face of the impregnable precipices; and the water-worn appearance of the rock just below these openings proves them the entrance of unknown caves. None have explored, none save the fool-hardy will explore, their passages.

Sutphen's Cave, near the Indian Ladder, is reached by descending a narrow crevice through the rock to a ledge a few inches wide. Along this you crawl, the cliff above and below you, a dangerous path in winter, ice and snow covered. Reaching a chill recess beneath overhanging cliffs, you are at the cave entrance. The cave is said to be of some extent, and perhaps it is— under water. A short distance in, after wading

THE CLIFFS.

at one place knee-deep, icy cold, the cave becomes spacious, and you reach a deep, clear body of water. It is said that in a heavy rain-storm this cave fills up suddenly, and pours a perfect torrent from its mouth. One of those savage, rock-filled gorges descends from this cave's mouth down the water-worn mountain slope.

Westward, among the cliffs, above the village of Knowersville, is Livingston's Cave, a small, dry, and romantic cavern. Should you happen to be near, it is worth a visit. West and east there are many more caves which you may find by seeking. Near the Hudson, toward Coeyman's, there are several.

At Clarksville, twelve miles from Albany, and eight or ten miles southeast from the Indian Ladder, are more caves. Two of these are well known; the entrance of one is in the back-yard of one of the village houses. The subterranean river is the house well; a pair of steps lead down into a crevice in the rock. They have no other water. For drinking it is unsurpassed; but it issues from lime rock,

and is therefore hard and unfit for washing. This same river bursts forth near by in the bed of the Oniskethau, and aids that stream to run a saw and paper mill. Chaff thrown upon the river in the cave is soon found floating on the mill-pond. The stream empties into the Hudson at Coeyman's. I once heard it remarked that an amphibious animal might make its way through the caverns from Hudson River to Niagara Falls without once coming forth to daylight!

These two caves are said to be respectively one-eighth and one-half a mile in length. They should not be called two caves, however, for the "river" seems to flow from one to the other, and forms a connection which a person who likes ice-water baths might explore. Taken as one cave they may exceed a mile in length. The smaller cave is dry and airy, and has some spacious corridors. Squeezing your way down through the narrow entrance you reach a sort of room—the vestibule—faintly lit with the few white rays of daylight which glimmer down through the entrance. You have suddenly passed into a dim region of silence, only broken by the faint tinkling and murmuring of the subterranean stream below. You light your lanterns, and the red flame guides your footsteps. A short way through a narrow passage and you ascend into a lofty chamber—the "Room of the Gallery." Should you visit it in winter, as I once did, you may start horrified back. Two or three ghostly, white columns rise here and there from the floor! There are no such stalagmites in this cave. What, then, are these white columns gathered in a spectral circle? You approach; they move not. Nearer, nearer still, and the white columns resolve themselves into fantastic stalagmites of ice—beautiful yet fragile. The water dropping from the roof, the frost which reaches in thus far, account for them.

That dark hole plunging downward to the right is the continuation of the cave; descend, and turn in at and climb the first side passage to your left, and you will reach the "Gallery."

It is related that a villager, venturing in to pass a hot summer night, having but a solitary tallow-candle, his light became extinguished, and he thought himself all but lost. Feeling along in the dark to find some means of exit, he was suddenly precipitated into a dark pit. A while after, as he sought to ascend, he fell again, deeper, receiving severe injuries. Dreadfully alarmed, he rushed hither and thither, only to fall a third time, and still deeper. He swooned from terror; and when he awoke he observed a faint light opposite. Scrambling toward it, he entered a room; it was the cave entrance! Some assert that he mistook the passage in re-

turning, and merely climbed to and fell from the gallery three several times.

There are other large rooms and corridors in this cave, but there are few stalactites or stalagmites, if any. In one place are some beautiful incrustations of spar; and in another spot a vein of the massive calc-spar, with large crystals, is found. The latter sometimes contains the Silurian anthracite, supposed to have had its origin in the organic animal life of that age. The rock inclosing the calc-spar is a granular or sub-crystalline limestone—the Upper Helderberg.

A singular feature of the cave are the water-worn pot-holes in the rock ceiling. Every one knows that rational, common-sense brooks or rivers of the surface world make them according to law of gravitation in their water-worn beds. Here natural laws seem laughed to scorn; and these pot-holes, as though from very perverseness, are set inverted in the roof. They were formed undoubtedly when the cave was filled with water, whirling and rushing against the roof.

A narrow passage leads to the extremity of the cave. Where it enlarges is a steep and rather slippery descent to water. This is called by some a lake; the rock roof comes so close to the surface that its lateral extent can not be seen. Naptha poured upon the water and ignited, though it makes a singular sight, burning with a blue, lambent flame, shows nothing, and the darkness is deeper when it dies away. The water is very clear and still, and increases in depth, gradually, off the shore. There are here no "eyeless fishes."

The "Half-mile Cave"—the larger cave, or

THE STAIRWAY—CAVE ENTRANCE.

THE STYX.

the longer end of the cave, if they are but one —is about a quarter of a mile from the hotel in Clarksville. This cave is often visited, and has a large, wooden, cellar-like door, and wet, slippery steps, which lead in winter down into warm, steaming darkness.

Mind your steps; I speak literally. Now go down the dark hole on your right; it is a steep descent. You are in darkness again, and your lights but feebly illuminate the place. There is a sickening damp warmth; it is not unlike a charnel-house, a catacomb. This mouldy earth beneath your feet, lixiviated, would probably yield much nitre; the earth of caves generally contains it. Notice those black strata veins of flinty hornstone; they may have served their time in the days of flint-lock rifles. Here is flint, there saltpetre; pyrites through heat will yield sulphur; the alders and willows from beside mountain brooks give choice charcoal. Here is gunpowder in the raw, for those adepts in its manufacture!

It was these veins of brittle, translucent flint, called hornstone, which gave the name of "corniferous limestone" to this rock, from the Latin cornu—horn. It was not the fossil shell, the cow-horn shaped *zaphrentis*, which originated the name; though that is the most prominent of the many brown, weathered shells incrusting the roof and walls of the cave. These same shells—*zaphrentis*—project similarly from the walls of the great Kentucky cavern. This corniferous (upper Helderberg) limestone is peculiar as being the oldest rock in which the fossil remains of fishes have been found.

You may have a mile or more of clambering in and out from this cave, and that is as good, though not quite so bad, as twenty-five miles. There are long passages where you might drive a team of horses and a wagon; narrow, muddy passages in profusion; bats, overhead and fluttering past you, every where.

The bats hang from the ceilings separately, and from one another in curious festoons. They are now hibernating. Aroused by your approach, some take wing and occasionally strike against your lantern, shattering the glass. On all sides you hear them squeaking and chattering and grinding with their teeth; it is horrid. How they live there is a mystery; no suitable food is visible, and the door of the cavern is kept closed. Some of the bats seem withered and

BAT HIBERNATING.

half dead; others are more lively. The gray or frosty bat is sometimes found here. The *cheiroptera* of this cave have been described in Goodman's "Natural History;" for this is the one therein mentioned as "an extensive cavern about twelve miles south of Albany, New York." They have quite changed their habits since sketches were made of them by that reliable naturalist. In his time, it is evident from the engravings, all bats hung themselves cozily head up; now the contrary vampires all hang head down, in a way that could not fail to be alarming to apoplectics—a vile rebellion against the naturalist. Bats, sleeping, hang then with their heads downward, holding fast by the little paws they have behind, and not by the hooks attached to their membranous wings. In their flight near the roof they stop and flutter for a moment, then hang correctly. It is thought that they catch by their hooks, and, if the place suit them, assume the upside-down posture. If they fall to the ground they are for the while helpless; however, with the aid of their front hooks, they climb to some little eminence from which, by turning a sort of somersault, they fall down, and, as they fall, take wing and search for better quarters. Nature has given them instinct so to repose that, when disturbed, they may be able to take to flight and escape.

If you determine to see the end of the cave and the lake, and are not afraid of mud and low, flat passages, you will go further, perhaps fare worse. Again the cavern enlarges, a black emptiness is before you. Approach. You stand upon the shores of "Styx." A vaulted roof of dripping rock, a silent, echoing cavity, scarcely illuminated by dim lantern-light. Unruffled are the still, deep waters, green, though clear. The silence only broken by the sudden, occasional tinkling of a drop of water falling somewhere in one of the dark side passages, only to be explored in a boat. The boat is wrecked.

In returning you have to repeat the crawling and scrambling through the low, narrow, or wet and muddy passages: it seems endless. You

halt to await the approach of a loitering companion. His lantern is seen, in distant perspective, far down the dark corridor. You shout for him to hurry. Hark to the distant, echoing answer, "Coming!" Turn your lantern this way, and look down the long, shadowy passage of the cavern; in the dim vista he seems an imp, dancing along with a fire-brand. Suddenly, while you think him yet at a distance, he seems to enlarge, and is close to you.

I once fired a pistol-shot in this cave to hear the echoes; instead of the sharp crack which should have followed the flash came a volley of deep, echoing, hollow thunders, a rolling and swelling roar, a musical, harmonious earthquake, deafening. One of our party who was on ahead took it for heavy, celestial thundering.

Cave explorations are interesting to those who love to see the wonders of nature—things before unseen, new and surprising. Who knows, some one thus exploring may discover a great, subterranean, transcontinental river; an underground, round-the-world canal, cheapening freightage between New York and San Fran-

MINE LOT FALLS IN WINTER.

cisco. Whether you should find this wondrous stream or not, a visit to the under-world will not be forgotten; the hornstone and the fossils collected, nay, the grimy, shattered lantern that you carried, will ever remain objects of interest.

Winter is the best time to visit caves; it is certainly the most healthy season, for it is dangerous to enter a cold, damp cave in hot weather. Nevertheless, ice closes the entrance of some caves in winter, and, if among the cliffs, the climbing is dangerous.

In winter the Indian Ladder or Mine Lot Fall is one huge icicle from the cliff brink to its base; the water pours down—an unceasing stream—through the huge frost-proof conduit it has formed for itself. A pyramid of pure green-white ice, glittering, resplendent with icicles, which in fringed sheets, strange and fantastic shapes, adorn the translucent column, one hundred and sixteen feet in height. Have a care how you climb up among the rocks in winter; it is almost impossible to descend again, and dread indeed is the ascent. Upward may prove your only path to safety over slippery ice and snow-capped rocks; below you the cliff, the tree-tops, the dread craggy mountain slope! Hands icy and stiffened, useless and bleeding, my only reward for the climb depicted was a bit of rare moss (the *Hamelia gracilis*) which I found on the rock above.

Frequently upon the brow of the mountain you will see a ruined tower perched; surprised, you draw near. The door is low and narrow, and seems to be almost closed by the débris; it has a very ancient look, and resembles some old feudal watch-tower you may have seen in Europe. The slope below is white with rubbish, and covered with fallen stone—the tower itself blackened with fire. It is a Helderberg lime-kiln. The lime made here is the best known; many of the poorer farmers burn lime in the winter. It replaces the charcoal burning of other regions, and though quite as laborious and scorching, is more remunerative. The fuel used is wood, and the great heaps of ashes thus obtained are greedily sought by agriculturists and potash makers. The kilns are of refractory rock; blocks of clay-slate are preferred; and they are generally built near the quarry where the limestone is blasted out. These lime-burners will tell you curious stories of the "animals" they have seen in the rocks; some of them have singular collections of the fossils.

The limestone, when blasted, breaks into large, regular blocks, well suited for building purposes. This is generally owing to the cleavage, but frequently huge blocks are quarried which are perfectly loose and need no blasting. These owe their origin to "shrinkage clefts," which, as another singular feature of Helderberg scenery, is worth explanation.

Often the roads on the summit of Helderberg are of solid, level rock; the mountain top is a plateau as smooth as a table. Cantering along on horseback the constant ringing clatter of iron against stone is painful. In

CLIMBING AMIDST ICICLES.

places the rock is jointed and in small blocks, and resembles a Belgian pavement; again it changes, and a singular sight meets your eyes.

The rock plateau is split by numberless parallel crevices, stretching on either side in perspective; if you view them with half-closed eyes the dark clefts resemble railroad tracks. The sutures between the long blocks or trunks of stone are often twenty feet or more in depth, though sometimes choked with rubbish, and generally six, eight, or ten inches wide. In storms the water rushes down into the caves below. On the mountain (above the village of New Salem) these clefts extend perfectly parallel for miles. At times rectangular or diagonal sutures cross the main ones; then the rock is cut in blocks a yard square on the surface; downward—twenty feet, more or less—it is a pillar; you may teeter it where it is; a thousand like you could not lift it out. These barren, arid rocks refuse to grow aught save stunted cedars, ground-hemlocks, and white birches, though now and then a larger kind of tree supports itself in a rock cleft. The foxes also find excellent hiding-places in these clefts.

Near Clarksville, on the slope of Copeland Hill, the clefts are two, three, or four feet wide; sometimes black, bottomless looking pits, unexplored. Below are often other subterraneous rivers, flowing no one knows where from or whither. A robber once had a boat there, and in a cavern deposited stolen goods; his secret was discovered, and himself and plunder captured. The sudden and mysterious disappearance of obnoxious men is mentioned in connection with these dark pits. There is a stream which dashes, full-bodied, into a great pit or sink-hole in the rock, travels an unknown course, and issues at once from a cliff three quarters of a mile distant.

The slippery or red elm (*Ulmus fulva*) is, or used to be, very abundant, and tons of the bark have from hence been brought to market. Maple-sugar making is another industry common here. In frosty spring, smoke rising here and there over the woods tells of the fires crackling and flaming under the great iron kettles in the open forest, or—as at old Peter Ball's, near Berne, on the slope of Mount Uhi—in a well-built sap-house. In early frosty mornings the "Sugar Bush" is a bright scene; the sunlight streams down over the mountain, and the old trees cast long shadows. The sugar-maker hurries hither and thither, collecting the buckets of clear, colorless sap, throwing out the ice which has frozen on the surface overnight (for experience has taught him that in freezing it has lost its sugar), placing empty buckets under the taps—ever busy.

But there is not space to mention every thing of interest in this forgotten range of hills—the numerous waterfalls and caverns and mountain-split gulfs.

If but a few learn from these scant notes that there is something new to be seen at home as well as abroad I am satisfied.

A Canoe Camp Mid' Hudson Highlands (1884)

ON THE MOODNA.

OUTING.

VOL. V.   DECEMBER, 1884.   No. 3.

A CANOE CAMP 'MID HUDSON HIGHLANDS.

LOW work, this towing."

"Wal, some might think so, an' ag'in others mightn't. It's fast enough for me, and it beats sloopin' all holler. Time was, when I was a boy, that we might be a couple of weeks running up the river. Now we aint never mor'n forty-eight hours at the most. Yaas, it beats sloopin'."

"I suppose it does beat slooping; and it certainly beats the time made by old Hudson himself, for he took thirty days to sail up sixty miles of the river; but it doesn't beat canoeing, and I shall be glad when we reach Newburgh Bay."

The last speaker was a stalwart young canoeist on his way from New York to the annual meet of Hudson River canoeists, which was held this year on the shores of Newburgh Bay. For the sake of adding to his experiences of travel he had engaged deck passage, for himself and his canoe, on a canal-boat that formed one of an im-mense up-river tow, bound to Albany, and had left New York at five o'clock that afternoon. His companion on deck was the captain of the craft with which he had, for the present, cast his fortunes. While keeping his guest company, and resenting his somewhat disparaging remarks upon their rate of progress, the "canaller" smoked a cutty pipe, and leaned mechanically against the clumsy helm which, from constant association, seemed to have almost become a part of himself. It was still early in the evening when the canoeist assumed his blankets, and laid down on deck beside his canoe to sleep, and the "canaller" turned in to his stuffy little bunk below. While they slept, the long tow of nearly fifty boats steadily ascended the mighty river, now buried in the black shadows of its Palisades or wooded headlands, and then bathed in the moonlight of its broad, open reaches. Its motive power was the huge skeleton of a steamer that had once done service as a palatial passenger packet; but now, stripped to its very bones, was reduced to the slow drudgery of towing. As if conscious of its former station, and realizing the obligations of rank even in its degradation, the powerful tow-boat performed its task with a dignified silence, that offered a strong contrast to the fussy little tugs which occasionally passed her with their lighter burdens, and which had been nothing but tugs all

their lives. The swift night-boats, laden with throngs of passengers, and gay with lights and music, swept scornfully past her, nor once proffered the friendly salute of whistle blasts with which they greeted their equals. But the poor old tow-boat, now stripped of her gilded saloons and gaudy fittings, knew that she had once been as fine as they, and that they in their turn would in time be reduced to her level. Thus comforted she strained bravely at the great hawsers, and compelled the reluctant fleet of ice-barges, canal-boats, hay-barges, and brick-sloops, to follow her through the long watches of the night; until, in the dim twilight of morning, she led them into the enchanted waters that mirror the Hudson Highlands.

The morning air was chill, and the river flowed gray and sullen between its sombre walls. Night still lingered in the valleys and in the deep ravines that seam the hill-sides; and the bald heads of the Highlands were still enveloped in misty nightcaps when the first signs of life began to appear on the tow. Unkempt men stretched and yawned at the openings that led down into the close little cabins, sickly flames were extinguished in the blackened signal lanterns, and uncertain puffs of smoke from the galley fires gave faint promise of breakfast. As the "canaller" added his to the group of frowsy heads appearing from the several compan-

ion-ways, the canoeist, still wrapped in his blankets, sat up, gazed about him and listened. The regular throb of the steamer was nearly drowned by the floods of melody that came bubbling from the throats of hundreds of little feathered highlanders. It was the grand opening chorus, an ecstasy of music over the birth of a day. For a moment the trills and warblings were hushed by the thunder-roll of the sunrise gun at West Point. It was hurled back and forth from one mountain giant to another, until, faint and exhausted, its distant reverberations sank into silence. Then was echoed the cheery music of the bugles, and the noisy *reveillé* of the drums. Then a sunbeam kissed the gloomy brow of Dunderberg, glanced across the river to Anthony's Nose, flashed back among the shadows still lurking about Bear Hill, and at last slipped down into the river to give it a morning kiss, and change its sullen gray into a glory of blue and gold.

As they passed West Point the captain of the canal-boat said to the canoeist, "This here bit of water is what we old sloopers used to call the ' Blow Holl,' and it's the awkwardest stretch between New York and Albany. The wind'll blow a dozen different ways to once here, and many's the sloop that's been dismasted or turned turtle betwixt this and Newburgh Bay. ' Wey Gat' the old Dutchmen called it, and I spose that means ' Blow Holl'; if it don't it ought to."

Slowly the tow wended its way among the iron-ribbed hills, past Cro' Nest and Mt. Taurus, Break-Neck, Storm-King and Beacon Hill, until at last it floated in the open waters of Newburgh Bay. Here off Polipell's Island, the canoeist bade adieu to his friend the "canaller," dropped his light craft into the water, and, impelled by her outspread wings, sped away towards the western shore, to join his fellows who were already gathered there.

Although the Highlands of the Hudson extend along less than twenty miles of its length, they form the most noteworthy, features of the river. To them it owes, in a large measure, its world-wide reputation; and among them, more than along any other portion of its course, linger the romance legend and poetry, that are immediately associated with its name. It is safe to say that no other area of equal extent on the continent is so replete with historic associations, or can so thrill the patriot's heart with tales of his country's struggle for freedom, as these hills. Here, in the shadow of these hallowed hills of the " Shattemuc," as the Indians named the Hudson, during the last days of spring and the first of summer, were met the canoeists who dwell on the banks of the great river, from its source to its mouth. To the number of fifty they camped in and around the earthworks of old Fort Meacham, which once defended the western end of the *chevaux-de-frise* that was extended across the river from Plum Point to Polipell's Island, as a barrier to the upward progress of British ships. Several of its iron-tipped, worm-eaten timbers may still be seen amid the stored revolutionary relics of the museum, in the Washington Head-quarters at Newburgh.

The tents of the camping canoeists, of all shapes and sizes, were scattered in the most picturesque confusion, behind the old earthworks, and along the beach. Above them hung the flags of the New York and Knickerbocker clubs of New York city, the Mohicans of Albany, the Newburgh, Rondout, Amsterdam and Middletown clubs, their bright colors making bits of vivid contrast to the green of the surrounding foliage. Among the tiny flags fluttering from the mast-heads of the canoes drawn up along the shore, were also to be seen those of the Lake George and Rochester clubs, and the St. John's Canoe Club of Florida.

At night the ruddy camp-fires threw the gleaming tents into strong relief against the inky background of the trees, and cast strange shadows far out over the placid waters. Around the fires song, story, and merry jest woke echoes that had slumbered for a century ; and above their dying midnight embers floated the spirits of those who knew the place long years ago. Among them were dusky canoe-men who encamped here when pale-faced intruders were still unknown, round-bellied Dutchmen, who made this a resting-place after braving the perils of the " Wey Gat," and

> ... "Old Continentals,
> In their ragged regimentals,"

who here spent years of anxious watching for the advance of a dreaded foe, and here, in the glare of beacon fires from the surrounding hill-tops, celebrated the glorious consummation of their struggle.

To the left of the camp-ground, between it and Cornwall, flows the placid Moodna, bordered by sedges and lily-pads, and narrowing as it retreats from the river until it is spanned by a green arch of dense foliage. Here a rustic bridge leads a shaded woodland road from bank to bank, and affords vantage ground for patient angling. The wild duck brings forth her downy brood from hidden Moodna coverts ; and in its shallow sedges the great blue heron seeks his prey. To those canoes whose sharp prows unlocked the secrets of its guarded treasures, the Moodna proved a dreamy idyl, full of calm content and quiet beauty. That the gentle stream does

THE OLD FURNACE.

not still bear the ghastly name of "Murderer's Creek," we owe to N. P. Willis, whose Idlewild rises from its western bank, near its confluence with Hudson waters. Between the house and the river is the rugged gorge that gave the place its name, and in whose depths laughs and brawls a riotous mountain stream, that is only subdued by the quieting influences of the Moodna, into which it plunges. The oft-repeated story of the origin of the name Idlewild is that as Willis was negotiating for the property with its rural owner, he inquired what value was set upon the deep gorge and its brawling brook. "Hoot," said the farmer, "ye'll not want that, 'tis naught but an idle wild." But Willis did want it, and purchased it, and to-day it adds tenfold to the value of the property.

From Idlewild the village of Cornwall lines the semicircle of the bay, which sweeps in a gentle curve from Plum Point on the north, to Storm-King on the south. "Cornwall-on-Hudson," it is called. Ever since Cornwall was brought into prominence by Willis's writings, it has been a favorite resort of literary people, several of whom have made permanent homes there. Among these are Lyman Abbott, editor of the *Christian Union*, and E. P. Roe, the novelist, and successful cultivator of small fruits, who from Cornwall and its vicinity has drawn most of the material for his latest story "Nature's Serial."

Many of Cornwall's summer eyries are perched high above the river among the northern spurs of the Storm-King hills, where the glorious outlook afforded them more than compensates for their difficulty of access. The summit of Storm-King can only be reached by a rough two hours' scramble, up vaguely defined foot-paths encumbered by logs and boulders. Halfway up is a spring of deliciously cool water where the invitation to rest is rarely declined. The summit once attained, exhaustion gives way to exaltation, and fatigue is forgotten, as the glory outspread around and below bursts into view. Lost to all else you gaze and gaze, and drink in the ever-unfolding beauties of the scene as thirstily as a while ago you quaffed long draughts from the spring on the mountain side.

Boter Berg, Butter Hill, or Storm-King, is but sixteen hundred feet high; but, owing to its position and its surroundings, it proves a more satisfactory eminence from which to view the world beneath than many a more pretentious mountain; and, as you become familiar with its varying aspects, you willingly concede its domination and acknowledge it king of the Highlands.

"Stand there alone for a little while;
   And, with gentle approaches, it grows sublime,
   Dilating slowly, as you win
   A sense, from the silence, to take it in.
   So wide the loneness, so lucid the air,
   The granite beneath you so savagely bare.
   You well might think you were looking down
   From some sky-silenced mountain's crown:
   Whose far-down pines are wont to tear
   Locks of wool from the topmost cloud."

Far to the north, in misty outlines, rise the Catskills, haunts of Rip Van Winkle and of Hendrick Hudson's merry men; to them Storm-King is joined by the grand inland-sweeping curve of the Shawangunks, gemmed with many a dimpling lake and flashing stream. On the west reigns the tumult of Ramapo Hills, and the Schunemunks, rich in iron ore and abounding in mines and furnaces. To the south stretch the Western Highlands of the Hudson, which extend from Storm-King to Dunderberg, with Cro' Nest and Bear Hill rising boldly between them. Cro' Nest proper is a depression in the mountain top just beyond Storm-King, which has been immortalized by Joseph Rodman Drake, who here locates the scene of his exquisite poem, "The Culprit Fay," who dwelt where—

"The moon looks down on old Cro' Nest;
   She mellows the shades on his shaggy breast;
   And seems his huge gray form to throw
   In a silver cone, on the wave below."

Midway up the scarred and storm-beaten front of granite, that the Boter Berg advances so defiantly into the river, is a cliff bearing the curious name of "Kidd's Plug." It is so called from the fact that, high up on its face, a huge rock juts forth in so peculiar a fashion as to at once suggest its use in closing some aperture or cave. The ignorant superstition, which attaches to the half-mythical buccaneer, and invests him with supernatural powers, relates a legend of fabulous wealth buried in such a cave by Captain Kidd, who closed, or plugged, the entrance with a great boulder of such weight that no man, save himself, should ever move it. Tradition assigns to the Highlands a goodly share of the innumerable localities in which the bold pirate is supposed to have arranged his safe deposit vaults. Some of these tales have borne such impress of truth as to induce active and costly search to be made for treasure at certain points thus named. In this manner small fortunes have been squandered at Caldwell's landing, and on Iona and Polipell's islands. The former of these islands is just inside the southern gate-way of the Highlands,

the island, where there didn't ought to be no light, and, after watching it awhile, my curiosity got considerably riled. Finally I rousted out the cook, and him an' me took the dinkey and pulled over to the island, to see who it was a'spooking round that time o' night. We could hear men a'talking afore we landed, and when we

NORTHERN ENTRANCE TO THE HIGHLANDS.

and is a popular picnic resort. On its lower end may still be seen relics of the misdirected labors of the treasure-seekers.

Polipell's Island lies close to the Northern entrance to the "Wey Gat," and directly at the feet of him who looks down on it from Storm-King's summit. It is but a little rocky islet, and was for years only inhabited by a solitary fisherman and his crazy wife, whom he tenderly cared for. She fancied herself to be the Queen of England, in which delusion she was carefully humored by her husband and his few acquaintances, who always addressed her as "Your Majesty." The mate of a river schooner recently told the following story of his experience with treasure-seekers on Polipell's Island : —

"'Twas in the latter part of June, about three years ago, when we dropped anchor one night off Polipell's, waiting for the tide to turn afore we tried to go down through the Highlands. 'Bout eleven o'clock in my watch on deck I seed a light over on

clim' over the rocks and looked down into a little holler, we seen five of 'em a'diggin' for old Kidd's treasure : one stood up, fast asleep, kind o' mesmerized like, and told the others where to dig. Thinking I might have some fun out of 'em, I slipped back to the dinkey for an old fog-horn, that we kep' in her, an' brought it back to the diggin's. 'Twas a ghostly kind of a night and the moon was tearin' through the clouds, dead afore the wind, with ev'ry rag set and drawin'. I felt kind o' scary myself, when I remembered the stories I'd heard of the speerits that allers guards old Kidd's gold, an' every now and then I gin a look over my shoulder into the bushes, more'n half expecting to see some of them spiritooal gardeens of the treasure put in an appearance an' stop the proceedings. The diggin' fellers seemed to need to keep their courage up, too; for every few minutes they'd stop work to take a swig from a big jug of Jamaicy, that stood on the edge of the hole.

" Bimeby, after we'd watched 'em 'bout an hour or so, one of 'em struck something hard with his spade, a bit of old iron or a tomato can I reckon, and they all gathered round to examine what it was. Just then I up with the old horn and giv a blast, that must have sounded like Gabriel's trumpet to them fellows ; for you oughter have seen 'em scatter. Sich a gittin' I never see afore or sence — Helter-skelter, lickitty split, they went for their boat, leaving their tools and the jug behind 'em. I collared the jug, and me and the cook made tracks for the dinkey. Sence that time I've never heard of anybody's diggin' for Kidd's gold on Polipell's ; but it's considered a powerful hanted place, and has got a big reputation for speerits."

From Cornwall a capital road leads over the mountains, back of Storm-King and Cro' Nest, to West Point ; and, in the early summer, when one is jubilant over his first outing, and the woods are sweet with the perfumes of the wild grape-vines ; or in autumn, when the crisp air sends the blood tingling through every vein, and when the woods are aglow with the gorgeous coloring of a year's accumulation of gold and precious dyes, and heavy with the scent of ripened leaves, it offers a walk that is well worth the taking

West Point, lapped in the very bosom of the Highlands, is their *chef-d'œuvre* as an attraction. Probably more of sentiment and romance centres about it than about any other spot in the country. It is the military stronghold of the Hudson, and, in a certain sense, of the nation ; for from here come the trained leaders to whom in times of danger the nation looks for guidance. That sentiment flourishes amid the beautiful scenery and bewitching accessories of West Point can easily be imagined ; and that its reputation as a lover's paradise is world-wide may be gained from the following anecdote of an incident of travel, that occurred to a young Bostonian in Paris last summer.

He had just been introduced to a sprightly French girl, who showed a decided partiality towards Americans, and who was very proud of the intimate knowledge of their country that she had acquired in the course of numerous conversations with them.

YOUNG BOSTONIAN. — "Yes, I am from the East, New England we call it."

MADEMOISELLE. — " Ah ! ze East, vat you call New England. Mais vere you haf no sentiment, no affaires du cœur."

" No sentiment, mademoiselle ? I beg pardon, but really you are mistaken ; why, in Boston we abound in sentiment."

" Ah non. Not ze true sentiment, not l'amour. Zat est réservé for ze west, ze extreme point of ze West, ou est la promenade de l'amour."

" The promenade de l'amour ! Really, mademoiselle, I am ashamed to say that I never even heard of such a place in my country."

" Oui, oui, so I haf tell you. In ze Boston you haf no such promenade de l'amour, de la coquetterie, as in ze West, in ze point of ze West."

With its Flirtation Walk, its monuments and relics, its battle-flags, its cemetery, in which lie many of the country's bravest and best, its traditions and history, its music, its living heroes, and fledgeling cadets, its exquisite scenery, and with the military glamour that surrounds it like a halo. West Point is certainly a fascinating place to visit, and one of which Americans may feel justly proud.

Leaving the Academy grounds, the road winds through the woods along the high river bank, affording every now and then bits of delicious scenery, glancing waters, white sails, and distant mountains. It passes Cranston's great summer hostelry, perched high above the river on the verge of a stupendous cliff, through the villages of Highland Falls and Fort Montgomery, crosses the restless Popolopen, skirts Bloody Pond, guarded by ghosts of Hessian soldiers, winds around the base of Bear Hill, makes an inland detour to avoid the Doodletown marshes, and finally, upborne on the broad flanks of Dunderberg, passes from the Highlands into the more level country beyond.

Next to West Point the most important and interesting place in the Western Highlands is Fort Montgomery. During the Revolution it and Fort Clinton on the opposite side of Popolopen Creek were erected for the protection of the huge iron chain which, buoyed by rafts of logs, was stretched across the river to Anthony's Nose, and so formed the first of the three barriers thus opposed to British navigation of the Hudson. Now, shorn of its military importance, Fort Montgomery is only notable as being a dumping-point for iron ore, and the river terminus of a road leading far back in the mountains, to the Forest of Dean mine, one of the most famous iron mines in the country. It was worked long before the Revolution, and

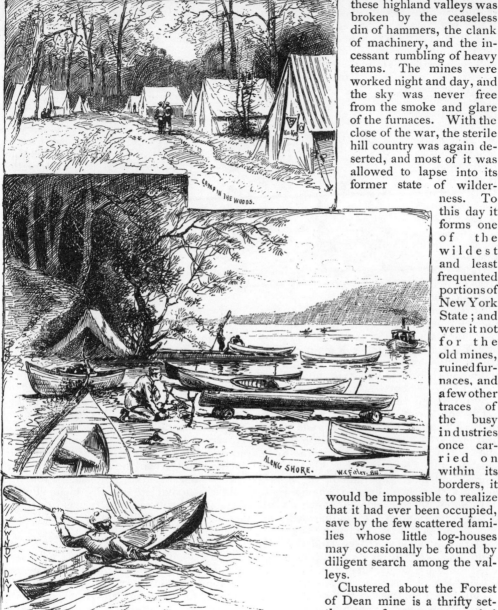

CAMP IN THE WOODS.

ALONG SHORE.

A WINDY DAY.

these highland valleys was broken by the ceaseless din of hammers, the clank of machinery, and the incessant rumbling of heavy teams. The mines were worked night and day, and the sky was never free from the smoke and glare of the furnaces. With the close of the war, the sterile hill country was again deserted, and most of it was allowed to lapse into its former state of wilderness. To this day it forms one of the wildest and least frequented portions of New York State; and were it not for the old mines, ruined furnaces, and a few other traces of the busy industries once carried on within its borders, it would be impossible to realize that it had ever been occupied, save by the few scattered families whose little log-houses may occasionally be found by diligent search among the valleys.

Clustered about the Forest of Dean mine is a thrifty settlement of cottages occupied by those employed about the works, and in this vicinity are several good farms; but farther back in the hills the dwellers are a rude and savage race, whose knowledge of the world is often limited by the mountains that bound their horizon. Here, in primitive structures of logs, poles, and bark, whole families live in a single room. At the approach of a stranger the children, who are often as naked as though born in the interior of Africa, scuttle away

from it came much of the material employed in the manufacture of guns for the American army. During the war, government engineers from West Point erected furnaces for the reduction of ore all through the hills, and many new mines were opened. Roads were built to the river, and for eight years the solitude of

into the underbrush like so many partridges, while their elders regard the intruder with an air of mixed apprehension and curiosity. They make a scanty living by burning charcoal, cutting hoop-poles, gathering berries, hunting, and, very rarely, working in the mines. Here is presented the curious spectacle of the semi-barbarism of the remotest frontier rampant within forty miles of the metropolis of the country. So easy of access is this remarkable and little known section, that the explorer may run out from New York on an early morning train over the Erie Railway, stop at any of the stations in the Ramapo valley, tramp fifteen or twenty miles through the wilderness to the Hudson, and there, taking a West Shore train, be back in the city in time for a late dinner.

5. A.M.

On the direct road from Fort Montgomery to the Ramapo valley, and about four miles back from the Hudson, stands one of the most picturesque ruins to be seen in this country. It is that of the largest and most important of the several furnaces that were erected among these ferruginous hills, and is well worth a visit. It stands in an open field by the road-side, and is about thirty feet high; its gray walls are mantled with ivy, and from its crumbling crest springs a clump of good-sized forest-trees. Its arched entrance and interior dome are as clean-cut and unbroken as when the builders left them, and are beautiful specimens of the stone-mason's art. It is known as the old furnace *par excellence*, and is said to have been erected under the personal supervision of Kosciusko, the gallant Pole, whose love for liberty brought him to the assistance of the struggling colonies. From this furnace came the metal for the links of the most southerly of the Hudson-river chains, for the making of many cannon, and tons of shot and shell. Its present peaceful occupation is to afford shelter to a farmer's cattle.

The visitor will find the greater part of the way from Fort Montgomery to the old furnace deeply rutted and horribly dusty, from the passage of the never-ending procession of ore-laden wagons from the iron mines; but, if he can only discover them, a series of charming by-paths through the woods will lead him to his destination by a route much shorter than the travelled road.

Although the Western Highlands of the Hudson offer, in every direction, more attractions than their neighbors across the river, the latter are by no means devoid of interesting features. To one ascending the river, the Eastern Highlands proper begin with Anthony's Nose, although the very considerable height of Manitou Mountain rises between it and Peekskill on the south. According to the legend related by Washington Irving, Anthony's Nose received its name from no less a person than Governor Peter Stuyvesant himself, while, accompanied by his favorite trumpeter Anthony Van Corlear, he was on his memorable voyage up the Hudson. From the subtle pen that so skilfully blended prosy facts and quaint conceits, we have the following account of how it came to pass: —

"And now I am going to tell a fact, which I doubt much my readers will hesitate to believe; but if they do they are welcome not to believe a word in this whole history, for nothing which it contains is more true. It must be known then that the nose of Antony the trumpeter was of a very lusty size, strutting boldly forth from his countenance like a mountain of Golconda; being sumptuously bedecked with rubies and other precious stones, the true regalia of a king of good fellows, which jolly Bacchus grants to all who bowse it heartily at the flagon. Now thus it happened that bright and early in the morning the good Antony, having washed his burly visage, was leaning over the quarter railing of the galley, contemplating it in the glassy wave below. Just at this moment the illustrious sun, breaking in all its splendor from behind a high bluff of the Highlands, did dart one of his most potent beams full upon the refulgent nose of the sounder of brass — the reflection of which shot straightway down, hissing-hot into the water, and killed a mighty sturgeon that was sporting beside the vessel! This huge monster, being with infinite labor hoisted on board, furnished a luxurious repast to all of the crew, being accounted of excellent flavor, excepting about the wound, where it smacked a little of brimstone; and this, on my veracity, was the first time that ever sturgeon was eaten in these parts by Christian people. When this astonishing miracle came to be made known to Peter Stuyvesant, and that he tasted of the unknown fish, he, as may well be supposed, marvelled exceedingly; and, as a monument thereof, he gave the name of *Antony's Nose* to a stout promontory in the neighborhood; and it has continued to be called Antony's Nose ever since that time."

On the top of this mountain is a copper mine, the only one in operation in the Highlands, and from this same summit may be obtained a view equal in interest,

and more extended, than that offered from Storm-King. On the south from the Highlands to the distant blue Palisades it embraces the broad Hudson valley, with its cities and villages, its fertile farms, and many teeming hives of industry. Included in this view on the south-east, lies the village of Dover Plains, the home of Lossing the historian. In the immediate foreground glisten in the sunlight the tents of the State encampment of the National Guard, and close beyond, Peekskill, where Henry Ward Beecher has his summer house, straggles up its hill side. In the dim distance, across Westchester farms, and beyond the hazy hills of Connecticut, may be caught an occasional gleam of the salt waters of Long Island Sound.

To the north of Anthony's Nose the hills retire somewhat from the river, so as to leave an irregular terrace between them and it, which has been utilized as the site of a number of fine residences, among which, at Garrison's, opposite West Point, is that of the Hon. Hamilton Fish. Back of these, clean-cut and sharp as an obelisk, rises Sugar Loaf, the best known of the Highlands; for its peculiar shape betrays its identity, even to him who sees it for the first time. The first summit north of

CAMP AT PLUMB ISLAND.

Sugar-Loaf is crowned by a peculiar and incongruous architectural pile known as " Osborne's Castle," from which the view is superb ; but its extreme isolation must be depressing.

Beyond Garrison's, still to the north, lies Constitution Island, of which the westernmost rocks are but a hand's throw from West Point. Here are the " Narrows" of the Hudson ; for here its channel is more contracted than at any other point south of Troy. On Constitution Island, in quiet retirement, dwell the Warner sisters, whose " Wide Wide World " has gained for them an enviable literary reputation. Hidden by the island from the view of the up-river traveller until he is abreast of it, in a peaceful valley at the foot of Mt. Taurus, lies the pretty village of Cold Spring, famous for its foundries from which, during our civil war, came the great Parrot guns that were served with such terrible precision in Union batteries. Nestled at the feet of Taurus is Undercliff, once the home of the poet Morris ; and beyond rises sharply the naked wall of Break-Neck, which is flanked on the opposite side by the dome of Beacon Hill, most northerly of the Eastern Highlands, and forming one of the pillars that guard their upper gateway. From here the Fishkill Hills — called by the Indians " Matteawan," or good fur — sweep away to the north-east, and are soon merged in the Berkshires of Massachusetts. The country between them and Newburgh Bay was the scene of many of the exploits of Enoch Crosby, the " Harvey Birch " of Fennimore Cooper's " Spy."

Having hurried down through the Western Highlands, taken a flying trip up the river again among their neighbors on the east, and thus glanced at the most salient features of the scenery amid which the canoeists of the Hudson have pitched their tents, we have arrived once more at the shore of Newburgh Bay opposite the camp on Plum Point. Crossing the bay we shall find the canoeists, whom we left sleeping near the flickering embers of the camp-fires, awakening to the duties and pleasures of another day, and remonstrating against the provoking shortness of the hours allotted to sleep, and the undesirable promptness of the sun's rising. On one side may be seen a hungry Mohican who has coaxed a small fire into a blaze, and is preparing for himself a slight ante-breakfast repast, with which to fortify himself against the morning air. An-

other of the tribe which sails under the totem of the turtle, sleeps near by and dreams of breakfasts other than those prepared by himself.

Beyond the Mohicans, among their canoes, are camped the New York men, one of whom, still enveloped in his midnight blanket, gazes ruefully at the little pile of damp sticks from which he has vainly endeavored to evolve a cheerful blaze. The pensive silhouette, standing on the end of the landing-float and gazing wistfully out over the waters, is another member from New York, who is wondering if there are any fish in the river, and if he could catch them if there were, and if not, what he shall do for breakfast. Back in the woods, their columns of smoke reveal the camp of the provident Knickerbockers, who have already begun those culinary operations which will be continued during the day for their own entertainment and that of the hungry stragglers who are sure to be attracted to these tents of proverbial hospitality.

The sun has hardly risen when a series of shrill whistle-blasts from the river, announce the arrival of the " bumboat," a diminutive steam launch that acts as tender to that peculiar river institution, a floating grocery. The " bumboat" has hardly come to anchor when she is surrounded by a swarm of canoes of all models, propelled by hungry and dishevelled paddlers, who clamor for bread, butter, eggs, sugar, coffee, and the score of articles that come under the general head of morning supplies.

After breakfast comes dinner, and after dinner comes supper ; of course with intervals of much loafing and some racing. At this meet the racing was not particularly good, as the waters of the bay either slumbered in calms, or were lashed to fury by blasts from out the " Wey Gat," during the hours devoted to the sport. Amid one of these periods of turmoil, the " Dot " of New York, and the " Snake " of Albany, attempted to sail their great match race ; but, as neither could get over the course within the time limit, they exchanged flags, and agreed to try conclusions another time.

This Hudson River Canoe Meet, which proved an eminently successful affair, was but one of a series of similar local gatherings which, as the natural result of the rapid spread of canoeing, have been held in various sections of the country, during the summer. Thus, in addition to the

great annual meet of the American Canoe Association held at the Thousand Islands the first two weeks of August, meets have been held on the Merrimac, on the Connecticut, at Lake George, on Esopus Island in the Hudson, at Chicago, and at other places. Another season we shall, doubtless, in addition to others, hear of a Canadian Meet, a Pacific Coast Meet, a Western, and a Southern Meet, and of branch associations growing out of these meets. Such associations are already needed, and will prove of great benefit to canoeists living so remote from the place of holding the A. C. A. Meet, that they are unable to attend it. They will bear the same relations to the parent organization, that State Divisions do to the League of American Wheelmen, and will be similarly governed.

So thoroughly enjoyable and pleasant are these local gatherings of kindred spirits, united by ties of a common interest, that those of us who attended the first Hudson River Meet are already looking forward with bright anticipations to its repetition in 1885. Although we have been compelled to house our canoes for the winter our camp-fires still burn brightly, and around them we revive delightful memories of that summer camp beside Hudson waters, and await impatiently the time when we may again pitch our tents in the shadows of its Highlands.

Kirk Munroe.

The Catskills
(1883)

THE CATSKILLS.

IN a faded letter lying before me, and which is dated from Greenwich Street, in New York, fifty years ago, the writer says:

"I could wish the Hudson were in better condition for my trip to Catskill. I shall be four or five days in going, but I will start well prepared for the journey."

I wonder what the anxious gentleman of that day would say were he to sit in his own library on this morning, and listen to and observe the changes in his beloved Catskill since that period of green fields and wide-spreading orchards, fine old country estates and farms that stretched down to the very water's edge? Where the Indians grew their corn, and the Duboises and Van Vechtens built their homes, a great arena of summer traffic has developed. Boats and trains are coming and going, the bustle of arrival and departure stirs all the "Point," animating the village in the way peculiar to American towns near a "resort," and the whole community to a new-comer seems to be on the alert for signs of travel.

But to the right of this provincial crowd and clatter one sees, directly on landing, a vista of very fair and quiet country. The river curves about the greenest of banks,

A RIFT IN THE MIST.

the sky shines above a rim of close dark foliage, and the flight of the bird is across a peaceful stretch of land and water. But this is not the Catskill of Indian romance and one's imagination. One longs to

293

leave the concentration of the village life, the bustle of the wharves and station behind one, and be up and away to the hills, whose everlasting beauty is the background for this picture of activity, thrift, and speculative lounging.

I recall my first visit twenty years ago to these grand old mountains. It seems only the other day, yet such trips were then matters of much more calculation as well as duration. We took the night boat, and though it was a rather poor affair, I am afraid, to my childish eyes it seemed a floating palace, and the ladies' cabin a mingling of the fascination of the theatre with the luxuries of real life. The cabin was presided over by a colored woman, portly and affable, and full of a rather weird sort of anecdote which charmed me greatly. She impressed me as being about as old as people ever were, but I presume she was not over fifty. And she told me stories of slave times in the Northern States, which seemed to me ghastly traditions, I remember, for that peaceful moon-lit country.

She had been brought up in the mountains, and loved the suggestions of old Rip and of the Indian period with a fervor worthy of a larger intelligence than she owned, and from her I first heard any of the romance of the region about which I am writing.

When our boat landed we took a large lumbering old coach, which stopped at all the public houses and various private ones, deposited and took up letters, packages, and messages. Our driver was a man of amiable though meagre physiognomy, and he idled over his employment in a way that gave the child beside him ample opportunity to fill her eyes and heart—indeed, perhaps, to touch some glimmerings of her soul—with the majesty, the gigantic wonders, of the scene before her. High upon every side rose the mountains, their pathways cleft with gorge and ravine, their indomitable silence broken only by the rushing of their many waters, or the quiet summer wind moving through the pines. God's grace and bounty spoke through it all, in the green splendor of their height and depth, their width and vastness.

Those old days have passed away. Progress has come sweeping over the country, setting much at defiance, but it can never destroy what nature has reared there. To this hour the message of the Catskills may be read as reverently and as awfully as when their depths echoed Indian voices, or their waters carried the Indian's canoe.

And herein I find the greatest charm of this country. Nothing seems to take away the fearless beauty of the hill. No intrusion seems to disturb the solemnity of the peaks and gorges, the sweetness of the mountain streams, the innumerable brooks and torrents.

The Catskill of to-day is a large, active place, characterized by the usual appearance of the American village. A long main street with shops and hotels and idly speculative loungers, and almost nothing to indicate what the place once was, unless it be in the names which have descended through many generations since Dutch and colonial and provincial times. Around about, in a sort of stately indifference to the activity of the place as a "resort," are the houses of olden time, belonging to families who have authorized Americans in their feeling that pride of race may be consistent with the most simply republican sentiment. And these old places give a dignity to the town. He who runs may read their story, since in few instances have the original forms been altered. They preserve their Dutch symbols, the heavy cross-beams, the generous fire-places, or the English architecture of the last century so perfectly that their tale is assuredly written in stone and wood work, and I will be pardoned, I am sure, for returning to some mention of these later.

But what would the writer of the letter before me say were he to arrive at the "Point" in Catskill on a summer's morning of 1882? Everything bespeaks not only bustle and enterprise, but the exhilaration of something very new, since a railroad has been established from the Landing up to Laurenceville, just at the mountain's foot. Surely this is something to awaken the Van Vechtens and Van Dusens and Livingstons and Fieros from their slumbers, but, as is sure to be the case in all American enterprises, it has been received with the most matter-of-course thankfulness and patronage. Is it, we question, possible to overcome the American tourist with any contrivance for his comfort or luxury? I believe he is not to be moved to surprise in any such direction, and certainly the manner in which the travellers leave the boat and

HAINES'S FALLS.

step on to the brand-new little train await-ing them is worthy of study.*

The train rushes down into the placid loveliness of the shore where the boat lands, with little shrieks and starts and various signs of its being new to this ex-

* The first trip on the mountain railroad was made in July, 1882.

istence, and I think it is disappointing to most people to be met with so much bustle and crudity when their destination is such an old and grand region. But once away from the bank and you will find that the trip can include the romance of the hills, for the route is well chosen, and leads you away over a country full of richness and peace, of idly growing things, great fields

LEEDS BRIDGE.

of corn, stretches of buckwheat with the bloom of August on it; into ravines where the water rushes, with an ancient melody in its movement, and out and over a plain beyond which the mountains rise, relegating all smaller things to insignificance.

I think nothing can be more perfect than the slow evolution of the dusk and change to moonlight over this country: then arises some understanding of the lore which all old Catskillians cling to, and which, let us hope, no strength of enterprise, no congregation of the "summer boarder," can ever take away.

The train takes us up around Catskill proper and into Leeds, and Leeds was really old Catskill—in very truth the place which gave this part of the country a name. Whence comes the name, I believe the most faithful chronicler can not say. It is found in various old records. In a letter dated over one hundred years ago,

and which the present owner kindly allowed me to read, "Catskill Village" is mentioned, but the place now known by that name was then referred to as the "Strand," or the "Landing," for, as I have said, the village of Leeds was then Catskill proper.

I think it nurtured in men a curious feeling of permanence, proprietorship, of desire to keep Nature unchanged, glorious, and true to her first, best impulses, for there at Leeds one finds so few marks of the impress of destroying man, so little which could jar the student of form and color as God has laid it upon His earth. Whether this has come from jealousy, listlessness, or perhaps the appreciation of vastness, one can not say. All that can be reduced to fact is that Leeds village, the old Catskill, lies simply embosomed by the hills and vales which the Indians and Dutch must have known, and it seemed to me a most perfect relic of the past, which is fast becoming too traditional to seem our own.

In 1678 a solemn company of Dutch gentlemen, at the Stadt Huis in Albany, effected the purchase of Catskill. They bought the "plain and land" for four miles around.

I think the picture of that morning an intensely significant and American one. There was the old room in that quaint Dutch town, and there were his Majesty's humble though enterprising and shrewd servants, Robert Livingston and Marten Gerritsen Van Bergen and Sylvester Salisbury, Esquires, and with them the magistrates of the jurisdiction, and those strongly pathetic figures of the time, Mahak-Neminaw and his six head-men, representatives of an Indian tribe who were, as they had been for years, in possession of the solemnly beautiful Catskills, where their corn grew, and their camp fires burned.

The Dutch and English gentlemen bought the Indian country; the deed was executed with writing and hieroglyphics. If the Indians were stoical, the purchasers cared but little for tradition, since we can find no records of the original occupants of old Catskill valuable enough to give them a place. They disappeared, wandering we know not where, and the only tradition worth preserving is of a handful of the tribe who sometimes came quite peacefully to the new settlement, simply from a desire to visit their forefathers' ground. They never lingered long; finally they disappeared entirely; and then descendants of that 8th of July, 1678, woke up to the fact that the Indians' idea of the hills must have been picturesque and colored strongly enough by romance to bear comparison with the print and canvas of their own more varied, progressive period.

I think no one is quite certain what was at first done with the new purchase, yet this last example of enterprise, the mountain railroad, leads past the very houses which were built by the sons or grandsons of the earliest Dutch and English owners. In those days Albany was a thriving town, and certain smaller settlements had gained reputation as being habitable, sociable, and "worthy of domicile"; but this new settlement in the country of the Indians must have had its origin in the merest speculation, since the few who gathered there seem to have made almost no effort to found or encourage a community.

Francis Salisbury built in 1705 the fine house still standing. One of the Van Vechtens had a dwelling deeper in the hills, and we are told that here and there houses were built, but there could scarcely have been anything like the feeling of an active community in a region that was all wilderness, silence, and the impenetrable grandeur of mountain, clove, and forest.

Gerritsen Van Bergen's house is still upright, and one can not but wonder what was the story of those early buildings. Tiles and bricks imported from Holland, wood-work put in with slow and patient hands—what a picture one can conjure up as the train goes rushing by, past Leeds, into the dim silence of the real mountain country, where one waits for the stages up the grand old hills!

Of all the old landmarks just at this point, the Salisbury house is, I think, most interesting. We drove to it one sunshiny day when the mountains were like great purpling monuments ahead of us, the greener country looking strangely fresh and young for that old country; and as we went past corn fields and buckwheat meadows we talked of the Indian and Dutch traditions of the land almost as though we had all of us the associations with them to which one of our party could lay hereditary claim, and the story of the Salisbury house was told as I faithfully give it here.

Francis Salisbury built it, on his share of the land purchased from Mahak-Neminaw, in 1705, when it must have been a very stately dwelling. After his occupancy there lived in it a man whose life included a romance which Hawthorne would have illumined with his weirdest fancies. He was a person of strange and arbitrary temper, and so ill-used a slave or bound girl in his service that she fled from the old house, aided, it was supposed, by her lover, a young Dutch settler. Infuriated by her escape, her master rode up the mountains in search of her, discovering the girl at night-fall. He tied her to the tail of his horse, and started furiously back to Catskill. As might be expected, the horse dashed the unfortunate girl to pieces on the rocks; and slight as was the law of the land, it found means to arrest the murderer and put him on public trial. His family united political power with great wealth, and when the man was brought to trial, and justly condemned to death, they obtained a respite of the sentence. But herein lies the curious part of the story. The decree of the magistrates

IN THE SALISBURY HOUSE.

was that he should be publicly hung in his *ninety-ninth year*, and meanwhile he was condemned to wear about his neck a halter, that all might know him to be a murderer doomed to death.

From this time forth the criminal lived in a strange and gloomy seclusion, rarely coming into the village of Catskill, isolating himself from his fellow-creatures, but doggedly wearing his halter, which on certain occasions had to be shown in public. Until quite recently there lived in Catskill aged people who could remember having seen this strange recluse wearing his halter, and, singular as it seems, he actually lived to complete his hundredth year! But times had changed. King George's rule gone, the new order of things seems to have swept into oblivion the curious decree of that colonial magistrate, and the unhappy owner of the Salisbury house was left to die in his bed; but his singular story affected the neighborhood, as might be expected, with a belief that the house was haunted, and strange tales used to be told of a spectral horse and rider, with the shrieking figure of a

girl flung from it. One old lady told me that when a child she used to live in terror of the peaceful spot where the Salisbury house stands, firmly believing that its ghostly occupant, with a halter about his shrivelled neck, could at any moment appear.

DATE ON THE SALISBURY HOUSE.

Certainly any such ideas were dispelled by the sunny look of things about it the day we spent at the old house. It is a large two-story building, with walls of sandstone and regular windows, and the date 1705 in iron letters along the upper ledge of stone. There is not much shade about it, yet enough to shut out all glare, and the garden and orchards are a pretty tangle of growing things, which give it an air of homely comfort rather than any ghostly dread. Within, on entering, is a hallway running the length of the house, with a quaint staircase to the left, and on either side doors open into living-rooms which are treasures for the antiquarian. The ceilings are supported by heavy beams, the windows are deep, and the panes of glass small and old, while the fire-places are the deep caverns of the early eighteenth century. At present these rooms, the scene of much festivity in the early Salisbury days, are furnished quietly, but in quaint enough style to suggest the origin of the house: a suggestion of lavender and dried roses lingers in the drawing-room as of summers long gone by ; and the low footed chairs, the old brass and Chippendale book-cases, might have been there when the Salisbury house was very young, and the orchards without mere striplings. Our hospitable hostess showed us a genuine old Dutch Bible, which stood on a table near one of the fire-places, and there was nothing in the house to my mind more pathetically suggestive than that book—the queer characters, the bits of faded writing interspersed, the pages thinned by use and age, and the heavy binding, all conjured up pictures of by-gone Van Dusens, or Van Bergens, or perhaps Salisburys, who sat in the long low room with the book held open before them, dreaming, let us wonder of what, as they read, or perhaps looking out across the rich and silent country which they had just entered upon, foreseeing so little —oh, let us hope so very little—of what the æsthetic development of the present hour were to demand of this lovely uncultured region.

When we had wandered about the house, and in its many suggestions of calmer lives forgotten its period of horror, we went out around the sleepy garden to the rear, where we looked at the little loopholes pierced in the walls in days when the tribes of Iroquois were considered dangerous. From these quite a stout resistance could be maintained, and the Catskill region abounds in Indian stories which show that such fears as our ancestors entertained of certain tribes were not groundless. Not far from Salisbury there is a house where a most daring capture was once made by the Indians, and nearer to the present village of Catskill is a small stone cottage which was the scene of a cruel invasion one moonlight night by a party of Indians who crossed the river for the purpose.

Yet how all this has been changed! The only recent traditions of fear are of wolves found not so many years ago in the bosom of the hills, and some tales of hunters thirty years ago are fresh in the minds of many. But now, "Trains for Laurenceville to connect with the stages," etc., are the announcements eagerly scanned by the new arrival. Paterfamilias with his wife and daughters, and perhaps (how often, alas! it is perhaps) sons, who intend to sojourn for a time in the mountains before resuming their customary occupations. The summer boarder has descended upon that fair tract of country so solemnly sold and purchased in 1678, and we have only to watch the arrival and departure of the stages to understand what to expect on reaching the mountain's summit.

A curious scene presents itself at the railway terminus. Although nothing is finished yet, the traveller demands swift locomotion, and so things have been put in working order in advance of their actual completion. With High Peak rising grandly at his back, with the rush of a mountain torrent in his ears, with a stretch of richly rolling country to right and left, silent with the silence of majestic supremacy, the ticket agent of the railroad sits out-of-doors, with a little pine table before him whence he distributes tickets. And round about are the travellers: young ladies in the latest style of summer costume, young men with alpenstock and Knickerbockers, elderly people in search of health or quiet, or amusement for their younger ones—all either waiting for the mountain stages or the train down to Catskill Landing; and the fragments of conversation at this point in the journey are keenly interesting. I wonder if the day will ever come when the American summer boarder in all of his and her phases will have been entirely written out! Here is one party, consisting of an easy-going, good-looking man, with a mixture of the soldier and the merchant in his bearing; not distinctly *bourgeois*, and yet decidedly not patrician; rich, one may judge by his wife's apparel and his own contented air, but in no special way ambitious. His wife is handsome, and thin, and if not exactly cross, yet habitually complaining, and superbly dressed, and fine in her manner; and with them is "Georgie," the inevitable small boy, who ought to be bottled, or casked, or buried, while the family are at summer resorts.

In the stage there are, of course, the dumb, awe-struck people new to the journey, and who seem to wonder what they came for; the people who have been so often before that at every point they are able to give accurate information about everything to every one else with endless repetitions of the pronoun "I"; and the gay young people who are wondering whether the hotel band is good, and who there will be up there to dance the racquet and play at tennis.

The stage is well enough now and again, but for a genuinely happy journey up the eternal hills I think one should have one's own conveyance, starting from Catskill village itself, and taking the journey slowly enough to know the country at least by sight, and appreciate in some fashion its sublimity.

There are many roads up to the mountain's summit, and all are worthy of experience. The Clove Road shuts in the more delicate variations of tree and shadow, of brook and ravine, and its history is full of romantic interest. Twenty-five years ago few pedestrians really knew anything of this country, and a story is related of an ardent New-Yorker who visited the region with an old Catskillian, and who was thoroughly enchanted by all he saw. The guide, though loving his rugged, beautiful native land, was rather bored by the visitor's enthusiasm, especially when he was forced to wait while nobly sounding verses rose to the tourist's lips. Finally he turned upon him with, "Come from New York, don't you, sir?"

"Yes," was the answer.

"Wa'al, I'd like t' know what *you'd* say if I went down thar and *gawked* around like you do up yere."

The Cloves are many, and I think that known as the Platterkill is the wildest and most picturesque, but only hardy walkers should attempt its ascent. Eighteen water-falls may be counted in a walk up this Clove, and the wild grandeur of the scene has defied almost every pen and pencil. The Kaaterskill and Stony Cloves are more frequented and less hazardous than the grand old Platterkill, and almost as beautiful, yet with the latter we must feel the sympathy that one gives a defiant conqueror. It rests—captive if you like by the present day in one sense, but boldly suggestive of the days when its first inhabitants lived in it without touching one stone or curve, one stream or angle, that nature had set there, and the steady stream of progress, or perhaps I should say tourist, may go on another fifty years before the Platterkill will succumb to the imperious claims of man.

The Kaaterskill Clove still carries with it the fascination of Indian story and tradition, and I think the legend which dear old Diedrich Knickerbocker gives of the stream bearing its name is sufficient to make one feel that the great depths of the mountains, the ravines and gorges, belong to the region of fable and Indian lore. In olden times he tells us there existed a spirit, or, as the Indians called it, Manitou, who inhabited the very wildest recesses of the mountains. What he was like none knew, yet the charm of his life or existence seemed to be in playing endless pranks upon the red man. An Indian patiently ascending the mountain in search of game would find him moving as a bear, or panther, or wolf. A chase would ensue, and suddenly the wild beast would disappear, leaving the hunter wearied and torn in some most forlorn part of the hills.

Now in the mountains there is shown at this time a great rock, high in air, and with its base softened by the growth of vines and wild flowers,* and this in those days was known as the place where the Manitou dwelt. It is even now looked upon as lonely and inaccessible, and before Mahak-Neminaw sold the ground to the white man the Indians of his tribe feared to approach this place. It is said that the most venturesome hunter never pursued his game so far as this lonely, defiant, flower-grown height.

There is, however, always a break in such persistency. We always find in such traditions one lonely figure uprising against a background of doubt and dread,

---

* This is now called the "Garden Rock."

ON THE KAATERSKILL.

of superstition and perhaps romance. So in this story comes the picture of a young hunter who penetrated the Kaaterskill Clove beyond this awful point, and there to his amazement he beheld ranged in the trees a number of gourds. They seemed to him to indicate some special, subtle meaning, and, impressed only by the spirit of his enterprise, he pressed forward and grasped one of them, turning to make his retreat quickly. But the fatal moment had come. The gourd burst open; from its orange source rushed a stream which beat upon the rocks and carried him headlong, and speedily dead, with it, and leaping and falling, turning the still ravine into movement and the poetry of dropping water, it goes on to this day, known as the Kaaterskill.

I have taken no liberties with this curious old story but to put the simple legend into my own language, and, I think, as one leans over the bridge above the eddying torrent, one feels assured that somewhere or somehow a romance must lie within its depths, perhaps in the great solemn heights of mountain that form its horizon.

At all events, who can regret contributing to the legendary lore of our country? No one can, I think, who takes one journey up that mountain path, and sees the vague-eyed conventional summer boarder enjoying himself or herself on the piazza of every house, or along the roads dividing the sumacs and the fair "sweet parsley" that border all these vagrant, wandering hedge-rows. Be it known, however, that not always is the animate creature an incumbrance, for there are to be found any number of eager, active pedestrians of both sexes who love the fresh pure air, the green fields, the blue sky, and the grand old hills, and who spend their summers inspired by all these elements, content to feel America may have a Switzerland wherein health of body and vigor of mind are to be obtained from the simple sources of out-door active and even *dolce far niente* life. Such tourists one meets all along the journey, dressed in the garb that befits them—the young women in charming red petticoats and blue flannels, the young men in the stoutest Knickerbocker suits—and one may prophesy bloom and vigor therefrom for the coming season of balls and racquets. But the people who painfully emphasize one element in the country are those who insist on taking it in its ultra-fashionable meaning —those who occupy the farm-houses along the road, and who are to be found straying among some beautiful wilderness of ferns and bramble, of tall sumac and stateliest oak, in muslins and laces, high-heeled boots and gossamer parasols! The horrible incongruity of such pictures makes one glad to turn away, continuing our journey by clove or level road up toward the high peak of the hills.

The word *clove*, we know, means only *cleft*, and these clefts occur frequently in the mountains, never marring their grandeur, rather adding to it, like deep inflections of some rich and sonorous voice, emphasizing the heights beyond or about each deep ravine. Names, of course, have been given to every point—Overlook, High Peak, Grand View, Mountain Summit, Round Top—these occur, while the lesser points have their own dignity of cognomen; and one learns, I think, to cherish certain places in such a region all the more when a name has seemed to characterize it, or usher it, as it were, into the world of title and familiarity.

The Kaaterskill Clove winds in and out and up and down with every variety of mountain and forest scenery, breaking off where the roads somewhat sternly divide, going up to the various points or peaks occupied by hotels, and here and there forcibly reminding the most casual tourist of the land he is in by such breaks as occur at the Rip Van Winkle house.

It seems to me that the early spring and late autumn are the seasons when this mythically historic spot should be seen to its best advantage, for the shifting elements of the summer-time force upon it too business-like an aspect. In the very mildest part of one October I remember driving up the hilly curve that brings on to the brief sweep of land which is a sort of halt before the mountain's final ascent. There, to the right, stands the dilapidated old house, bearing a historic picture of Rip and his flagon, and to the left is a terrific gorge, crowded by trees and ferns, and which in its lavish break westward shows one of those rich and smiling valleys which meet one at every opening in this luxurious country. Dale meets forest, and the sweep of meadow-land is broken by beltings of darkest foliage, while here and there purpling shadows lie dense and close, almost to the brink of the waters that seem to catch every gleam of the sunlight pouring down from a universal, joyous heaven. The rush and feeling of the air seems to speak only of the mountain height, while all about are those unfathomable, cool, dark recesses either of stone or impenetrable greens where one can pause, fancying the mystery of the hills to be borne on here finally to be forever hidden. Nothing seems to indicate change, yet all is variety, and the human voice of gayety and laughter seems only to stir some outer atmosphere, some thin vapor inclosing what is essential and real in the scene before us. I think that in spite of all that is done to pervert this region into a speculative country, nowhere can one feel so entirely, wholly, and undividedly a humble worshipper of nature. It confronts us in forms that defy man and decay, and it is for us to behold and revere in honest silence.

The Rip Van Winkle house, it seems to me, is only a shell to bear on its outer side the cracked and worn picture of the dear old sleeper of these hills. Turning away from the gorge, we asked a man lounging about where the picture came from, and he informed us it had been there

SLEEPY HOLLOW, FROM THE ROAD.

over forty years, and no one seemed to know its origin. It is not altogether bad in color, and the drawing is not worse than the best sort of a sign-board, while it has a certain charm of antiquity which gives it character. It hangs just above the tumble-down little doorway of the house, and to the left, high up among the rocks and their underbrush, is the spot where Rip was supposed to take his sleep of twenty years. I do not like to profane so sacred a place by an idle jest, yet I must own the inscription which blazons forth this fact might be mistaken anywhere for that of any patent medicine, and gave us the uncomfortable feeling that Rip and his doings had degenerated into the medium whereby some one's pills and

STONY CLOVE.

powders might be advertised. However, from such lowering reflections one may turn to the final ascent of the mountain; and if the hour be nearing twilight, I can think of no more enchanting drive. From the moment the real heights are entered upon. there comes a new feeling in the air—a consciousness, dim at first, but fast growing into exhilaration, that we are reaching the final uplands of the world. The roads are now almost perfect, and the tales of overturned stages and runaway horses are fast growing mythical. These last miles up the mountain are at twilight full of melancholy charm; and I think that as we go on and upward the sense of isolation even from humanity so grows that the darkness falls as though a shrouding of nature were only what one might expect. Sounds are few; movement is, as it were, only part of the still-life about one, and the green to right and left darkens into impenetrable night. Then suddenly comes a revelation. Here on the very summit of the highest mountain-peak we come upon a great lawn and terrace illumined by electric light, a hotel all doors and windows and vivid animation. A band is playing; there is a vista of a long room with whirling figures, while everything round and about is suggestive of youth and brilliancy, fashion and luxury. What a surprising change is this! and yet nothing could be more characteristic of this country. Here we find the young and old who desire to make their summer flitting profitable in various ways—fashionable, diverting, and piquant with the piquancy of novelty and easily adjusted change. The idea of a hotel set on these mountains, with electric lights, two elevators, gas, steam heat, and the usual every-day luxuries of civilization, is, we must admit, repellent until we learn to appreciate the creature comforts offered; for man must be sustained in various ways, and woman needs more than a comprehension of the divine side of nature to make even the Catskills enjoyable.

Once up on the mountain-top, the traveller feels impelled or urged on into the ordinary stream of summer action at a summer resort. Before one stretches a view of hill and dale, of valley land, which is beautiful enough to bear every analysis, but the ordinary impulse of life, once the mountain height is reached, is toward humanity, and I must say, at a house accommodating very comfortably eleven hundred souls, humanity may be diversely studied. The occupations are dressing, dining, and flirting, of course; the amusements, tennis, croquet, the delicious racquet of evenings, and reading the newest novels and magazines. What spice is lent to the day by gossip one dares not ask, but there is the usual "I hear," or "Would you believe it?" or "I was saying to my husband," which is the floating coin of all summer hotel piazzas, and each new-comer is scanned as critically as if he or she were of real importance, instead of being only one of the moving, gayly colored, eager eleven hundred. And just here I want to comment on one fact, brought to my mind by a somewhat lengthy experience of hotel life. Let any one study the first appearance of new guests. They descend from the carriage or stage with an indescribably nervous consciousness of the eyes that are upon them, and this sense of being intrusive usually lingers until late the next day, when a new stage-load of passengers is deposited, with the same sense of timidity, and last night's arrivals rise into a consciousness that they are masters of the field. I like to observe the gradations of this change from the first walk down the dining-room to the period, twenty-four hours later, when the guest

fairly flutters with a consciousness of having become quite at home even with the subtleties of the hotel existence. Being up unusually early one morning, I studied with great interest the gathering together of one family party who had come by the late train the night before, and who were evidently uneasily conscious of the exact hour for breakfast. They were of the class which even in America one may denominate as *bourgeois*, since no word, I think, can so well express the elements of comfortable, half-educated, good-humored commonplaceness which make up this character, and there was an elderly lady rather loudly called "grandma" by all the others, and about whom there was much openly expressed concern, a mother with a very handsome black silk dress and perfectly dull expression, and three daughters growing to womanhood, and one thin, clean-looking little girl, whom all the family commended or reproved, or pushed or jostled, as they stood about discussing breakfast.

"Well, I guess grandma's ready to go in," was suggested by the oldest daughter. "Ain't you, grandma?" in a louder key.

"Well, yes. Well, yes, I am," came slowly from the old lady.

"Well," said the mother, with a little sigh, "I don't see as there's any use in our standing about, then."

But another pause of indecision occurred, during which grandma gathered her spectacles and handkerchief together, first in one hand, then in the other, and looked out patiently at the lovely stretch of country below the cliff.

"Well," one of the girls said, in a moment; "come, shall we go in?"

"I'd as lief," said grandma.

"Well," said the mother, "we may as well. I don't see but what we'd better."

And the party carefully entered the house, passing with anxious regard to right and left down the hall, and into the dining-room, where superb Mr. Johnson seemed to frighten them into their seats.

One wondered if all the events of the day were as timidly undertaken, or subject to as many halting remarks. The girls seemed to enjoy themselves. They had a great many fine dresses, and went out most conventionally equipped for the mountain rambles, which, in spite of fashion and luxury within-doors, still retain their charm for all visitors to the hills.

The variety seems almost endless, and new pathways are opening on every side. For a time we hesitated about revisiting the Kaaterskill Falls, dear to our childhood, since they are so completely under business management; but, after all, we were entirely repaid even for the laborious climbing up and down the cleft, at the foot of which one can see the falls in all their glory leaping and tumbling over the finely irregular rock; and in spite of the business-like manner in which the visit must be made, there is some interest and amusement to be derived even from the spirit of speculation and "sight-seeing" of the native and the visitor. There is a little summer-house at the entrance to the falls, where you pay your twenty-five cents, and may invest still further if you like in candy—the real old-fashioned sticks of candy—or such beverages as root-beer, lemonade, or soda-water, and there are always interesting and entertaining fragments of conversation floating about. A country couple came there one day, evidently desirous of seeing something of the wonders of nature, yet also prudent about the investment of their money.

"Could we have lemonade if we didn't see the falls?" she inquired, anxiously.

"Oh yes," he answered, quite cheerfully, and we could see a suspicion of relieved feelings in his glance—"oh yes, of course we could."

"Well," she said, after a brief reflection —"well, I think I'd rather have lemonade, or perhaps root-beer."

And we left them to the placid enjoyment of this drink while we slowly made our way down the gorge to the rocks below the falls. It certainly is not inspiring to have the falls "turned on" to order, but those in authority declare that this is done by no means simply from speculation, for there has been long felt a danger of the water giving out if not held in check.

Soon, however, the scene itself dispels the commonplace feeling which came first. Surely this might well be the scene of that old tradition of the hunter and his gourd. And upon the rocks, even in the noisy waters, high up on either side, seems the spell of the mountain's magic—the peculiar loneliness and sense of each rock, each stream, each tall fir, communing with itself, repeating over and again the strange stories of the past.

The various scenes worthy of many days' journey in the mountain seem to stretch like an irregular chain down through clove and valley land to the "new" Catskill once again, and here and there, against the background of sociable, fashionable summer animation, start up one or two genuine mountain characters. It was a deep satisfaction to me to find near Stony Clove an old friend, a man whose habitation has been so long in the very heart of the hills that something almost fantastically like old Rip seems to tinge his whole bearing—his shrewd, weather-beaten countenance, his kindly faded blue eyes, thin flowing gray locks, and dress half corduroy, half a sort of rough cloth which is discolored by the suns and rains of many a season. His little dwelling looked so precisely as we remembered it, except that its dimensions seemed dwarfed since our childish eyes had rested upon it, but the windows were decorated as before with rows of glass jars in which were sticks of striped candy, the half-moist peppermint and the brown sugary squares just such as he used to sell nearly twenty years ago. It was a slight dash to our friendly spirits to find the old man had not even the vaguest sort of recollection of us.

"But, dear me, miss," he said, with his smile like a net-work all over his face, "such a crowd comes and goes, and some say they're *sp'ilin'* the mountain. There! I do think so myself sometimes. But I don't see as they're much account," he said in a moment. "I say let 'em come if it suits 'em. They want a change, I don't doubt, and let 'em come."

We asked him if he remembered telling us once that when he was young he had always religiously believed the story of Rip.

"Oh," he said, "there's some as does now, some as believes it all, and I d' know myself just what to think—just what to think; I railly don't."

He looked forth from his door with a curiously speculative gaze, and it seemed possible that as old age descended he was going back to the simpler faiths of his childhood, as he repeated, "I d' know now just what it *railly* all come from."

Then he settled down to some of his favorite traditions. He retold the story of a house lower down in the hills where in the last century a daring capture was made by the Indians; and if he had forgotten our chats in the old times, we re-

VIEW FROM NORTH MOUNTAIN.

membered at once his ver-
nacular. It seemed to em-
phasize the quiet and peace
of the country, I thought,
to hear our old friend relate
his well-worn anecdotes with almost the
same inflections as twenty years ago. He
seemed, before we left, rather impressed
by the visit, and said we must come
again; and he shouldn't wonder, now 'at
he *looked*, as he did sorter remember
suthin' or other; but then so many came!
Well, he wouldn't forgit agin anyhow,
even ef times changed more'n they had,
and things got the wuss for wear, which
somehow never seemed as if they *did* up
yere: wa'n't it so? And standing in his
doorway looking up at the arch and
strength and fierce grandeur of the hills
about us, it seemed as if no, they never
could. Wear, time, change, what do they
mean to those rugged mountain heights?

I shall always be glad that just before
we left I remembered a little patient dog
he used to have, named, so far as I could
understand, "So-so." And speaking of it
brought a quick smile to the man's face,
and he said, in a most happy though low
key of voice, "Why, yes, did we remember
little Yoeyoe?"—it was named by a Spanish gentleman who gave it to him—"why,
yes, of course, little Yoeyoe, who died
blind and lame with old age." I doubt
not that memories would have crowded

INTERIOR OF THE "STONE JUG."

thickly about the chance mention of this long-ago little favorite, but we had to go away, leaving our old friend in the twilight, still standing in his doorway, speculating over the clouds that were darkening the hills.

Nearer to the Point, as I said in the beginning, there are many fine old relics of the early architecture of this region, perhaps no house more romantically interesting than the fine stone mansion just at the water's edge, known as "Dies's Folly," or the "Stone Jug." The house is large, and built of gray stone, with a fine porch and generous entrance and hallway, and although so near the town and the varying elements of the shore, it seems set in a certain seclusion of its own, and gives a tinge of dignity to its surroundings. The story of the house begins in the last century, when Major John Dies, a British officer, married Miss Jane Goelet, and at the same time deserted and "fled" to Catskill. Here he spent lavish sums upon the stone mansion still known as "Dies's Folly"; but in spite of his gay and reckless life, he lived in constant fear of being arrest-

ed as a deserter. At the first appearance of British troops Major Dies would betake himself to the garret, where he hid in a hollow of the chimney-stack, whose existence was known only to his wife, and to which she brought him food and drink in secret until the danger was over. When Madame Dies's father died he left his money in such a way that her reprobate husband could not squander it, and so after his death the lady lived in quiet comfort and much dignity of state; and as in those days the Folly overlooked a rich stretch of country, undisfigured as now by wharves and kilns, it is no wonder that it acquired a solid reputation of elegance and luxurious seclusion.*

Madame Dies lived until 1799, and I was told by a resident of Catskill that in his boyhood he well remembered talking to old people who had known her, and who spoke of her elegant accomplishments, her piety, and the stateliness of her manner.

* I am indebted for the history of this old house to Mr. Henry Brace, whose family now occupy it, and in whose possession is the old mill of Jacob Goelet, Madame Dies's father.

Wandering about the fine rooms of the old house, it was easy enough to people it with figures of the dashing major's period; for it, like many other famous dwellings

Madame Dies's descendants were the Duboises, of varied memory, and I think that I may be permitted to give here portions of a letter written by the old lady to her daughter Catherine, and which is still in the possession of the Duboises:

"CATTS KILL TOWN, *March* 15, 1796.

"DEAR CATE,—I received all you sent and for wich Receive my harty Thanks. Your Brother tells me of your suffering for wich I am sorry. I have you and all your sisters and brothers with me in my aproches at the Throne of Grace......Cate sent me last fall 2 Viols. 1 she said was Lavandar. I did not smell the Lavandar. The Other was for Weekness but she did not say how it was to be taken. Dear Cate I send you Eggs as you Desired. I gave 3 shillings a Dozen and you must counte them and pay for the 2 Viols and let me know how I am to take the midcine for weakness.

"Hope this may meet you in Better Health and our Blessed Jesus grant you Some Longer time on earth with the under aged children.

BITS ON SOUTH MOUNTAIN.

in the neighborhood, has not suffered much from change. The heavy rafters are untouched, the walls and windows unchanged, and one has only to regret the very curious old tiled fire-place which once occupied the southwest parlor, and which has been described to me as representing Bible characters with the most amiably patriotic Dutch symbols!

Inclosed you have 5 Dollers wich with the Eggs for which I was obliged to give 3 shilling a dozen please to pay the post for the 2 Viols and send twelve shilling Kag corn Hams and Buiskets. Mark it J. D. and the Remainder send in Sugar Candy and Candied Oranges.

My Cate joins me in tender Regard to self and all the family and after my best wishes for your better healt Believe me your sinciar Friud "JANE DIES."

And in a postscript the old-time lady adds a request for "5 *pound Pepper mint Lozingis.*"

Madame Dies having had an education partially Dutch and partially English, her doubtful orthography may be forgiven.

This is all in old new Catskill—the Catskill of the last century of Dutch and English times—but as the boat swings out upon the twilight waters, we lift our eyes, and far beyond the bustle of the town and wharf, the stately quiet of the old houses, rise the hills of Mahak-Neminaw's old possession, from North and South Mountains to the Overlook, their eternal heights speaking, as it were, some solemn tale to the sky that meets them, and across which a banner of vibrating colors has been unfurled. Something rests there so strongly willful in its secret of olden time, so repellent of all that can take height or breadth or solemnity away, that we feel, in spite of all that is new, the old will remain forever, and the hills of Catskill bear always "Everlasting" written on their brow.

Picknicking in the Adirondacks (1889)

PICNICKING IN THE ADIRONDACKS.

BY J. OSGOOD.

E had made many excursions on lake and river and up mountain tops; there was still a fortnight of August tempting us to life in the open air. How and where should we spend it? How could it be made most delightful and unique? We were floating in our boat on Lake Champlain, with the Adirondack peaks rising in sky-blue grandeur before us.

"Let's spend our two weeks in the Adirondacks," said I.

"Won't it be awfully expensive?" asked Sweetbrier. "How much would it cost?"

"Why, just what you wanted to spend," I responded.

"Could we have a good time and see whatever we wanted to, and spend not more than—not more than $40 apiece?" questioned Sweetbrier, as if the proposition were the wildest possible.

"Why, of course," said I. "We can make one long picnic of it. We can ride and walk and bask in the sun all day and sleep in a new place each night, just as we used to the three months we traveled in England. We will cut the big hotels, except when they seem really inviting, and sleep at 'wayside inns'—if there be any to find."

So it was settled that we should leave trunks behind and take only hand baggage, which included a change of lightest underwear, warm outside wraps, one book apiece, and we each had a lunch basket and folding cup.

We made our point of departure the steamboat landing at Port Kent. Oh, how glorious the day was! And we, mounted on the topmost seats of a six-horse Concord coach, felt as if we commanded the universe. We were in haste to have our first picnic meal, and ate it as we rode along on the coach top. Would you like to peep into our lunch baskets, and find out what dainties contributed to that delicious meal? We had a loaf of bread (no butter), a box of graham crackers, plenty of cookies, some cheese, and fresh peaches. When the stage stopped at the Lake View House all alighted, and our traps were taken down with the rest. But while our fellow passengers lost an hour of that perfect day in the close hotel dining room, we were in readiness to start directly for the chasm. For two miles the Au Sable winds through rocky walls that rise in places nearly two hundred feet above the dashing stream.

A narrow plank walk with rough railing clings to the precipice midway of its steep side, and rises or falls as the exigencies demand. "Here we go up, up, up; and there we go down, down, down." Here we turn aside to explore a fern-fringed

and abuse and insult the judge. It is many chances that he knows more about it than you do, and that your dog was properly placed. Of course I am speaking to the novice, not to the old exhibitor and "authority," who is frequently horrified by the judge's placing of his dogs.

Bitches, as a rule, come in season once every six months, the approach of the "heat" being evidenced by her desire to play with the dogs she meets in the street. The vagina swells and, after a day or two, discharges a blood-like matter. This will flow for probably two weeks or more, when it ceases. Then is the time to allow her to visit the dog.

In selecting a sire do not blindly rush after the dog that is winning the greatest number of prizes. Study the good and bad points of your bitch, and endeavor to procure a mate for her who is strong in the points that she is weak in. Select the dog for his progeny rather than for his individual merits, but consider well what his opportunities in the stud have been. A grand dog bred to unsuitable bitches cannot get high-class stock.

It is well to breed the bitch twice to the dog, a day intervening betwixt the services. She will whelp in between sixty and sixty-five days, dating from either of the connections. During the period of gestation she should be regularly exercised and liberally fed. She should be rather low in flesh when served.

When from her actions she seems to be in labor, administer a liberal dose of castor oil and put her in her bed. This should be made in a warm, dry corner that is well sheltered from draughts, and must consist of straw—not carpet—for the bitch always scrapes the straw from underneath her, making a sort of nest about her, and will only lie upon bare boards. She does this to enable her to clean the puppies after their birth, and to keep them so more easily. She should be kept in a retired place, where she runs no risk of being disturbed. Plenty of water must be placed beside her within easy reach. She is better left alone. Some bitches will not be satisfied unless their master or mistress stays beside them in their trouble ; one especially that I know of insists upon her paw being held throughout ; but these are isolated cases.

After all the puppies are born a strong milk gruel should be given and the mother must be fed upon "slops" only for a day or two, when the most nourishing of food must be given and in abundance.

If the puppies are spaniels or terriers whose tails must be cut, the operation should be performed when they are about a fortnight old. Have someone to assist you in the work, and make him hold the puppies upon a block of wood on their backs, so that if any contraction of the muscle takes place consequent upon the operation, the tail will hang down instead of sticking up. Your instrument should be a razor free from rust, a short, heavy stick, a lighted lamp and a piece of iron heated until red in the flame.

Hold the razor at the point in the tail where you wish to cut it through, and give it a sharp rap with the stick ; then sear the wound with the hot iron and return the puppy to the maternal nest. If an hour or two later you find any of the wounds still bleeding, tie a piece of twine tightly round the tail as near the end as it will hold. This will prevent further loss of blood.

Cropping ears I know nothing of, and therefore will not describe the operation, though I would not if I could, for I consider it a useless and a cruel practice. The flaps are provided to the organs of hearing for the exclusion of injurious matter, while tails protect no supersensitive parts. In spaniels used for covert shooting it is cruel *not* to dock the tails, for from their always being in motion from side to side they become sore, and even "raw," from contact with the undergrowth. Indeed, some owners of pointers and setters, who use them for work in covert, find it necessary to remove portions of their dogs' tails for this very reason.

In the days of dog fighting it was found necessary to remove the ears of bulldogs because they afforded a hold to their adversaries in the conflict, but, thank heaven, that brutality has virtually been done away with, and there is now no cogent reason to be argued in favor of cropping.

If you are fortunate enough to be the owner of a dog that has made a mark in the canine world and are desirous of profiting pecuniarily by his successes, advertise him as being in the stud in the kennel journals. Remember, in stating the stud fee to be charged, that it is better to place the sum too low than too high. Have a neat stud card printed, with a photograph or "cut" of your dog displayed upon it, and give his description,

cavern, and now we seat ourselves on a moss bank and look back on the glories we have left behind. The walls of the chasm are curtained with ferns and vines, and capped with forest trees. The water below, the sky above, the marvelous architecture of the chasm, form a scene of enchantment, gallery, pier and buttress looking as if chiseled by a band of giants. "It is worth a journey from Europe" was the verdict of Fredrika Bremer.

One party of tourists after another passed us; the fat, pouting mamma; the tall, fidgety papa; the irrepressible boy; the inevitable and interesting lovers. They were "doing" the chasm; we were enjoying it to the bottom of our souls. An odd genius who seemed less pressed for time than the others watched us curiously for a while, and then said good naturedly in passing: "You seem to be taking in all the side shows!" And so we were. Entering the last boat, we were skillfully guided through the rapids, touching the foam with our hands as we dashed past the rocks, and enjoying that part of the trip more than the shooting of the famous Lachine Rapids, now made tame by frequent repetition and the size and security of the steamers employed.

Returned to the hotel, we took our traps and started in search of wayside inn No. 1. We found it without trouble, an old-fashioned stone dwelling with piazza extending to the second story. The hostess said she asked 50 cents a night for rooms; they were as clean and comfortable as those we had later at the $3 and $4 hotels. We engaged them with satisfaction, and went to enjoy our evening meal. Choosing a cedar-sheltered spot on a hillside overlooking the Au Sable River, and having bought a quart of new milk at a farm house, we spread our repast on leafy plates garnished with ferns and red berries, and ate like epicures; delighting in each mouthful, loafing, looking, chatting, happy as two orioles in June. Then packing up, ready for removal, we adjourned, when the stars came out, to the piazza of our inn, where we watched the moon rise, and then went to good beds and sound sleep.

We breakfasted under pine trees, giving an hour to the morning meal; then Sweetbrier, leaving the traps to go with me in the buggy, walked freehanded to the steamboat landing, three miles away, where we took passage for Plattsburg, purchasing a ticket to the end of the Chateaugay Railroad, with stop-over privileges along the whole route.

We intended to go to the Chateaugay Chasm and accordingly left the train at Lyon Mountain, but Lyon Mountain looked very uninviting; we learned that the captain of the boat on the lakes had been drowned a few days before and the steamer was not running. I looked into Sweetbrier's eyes and wanted to say, "Oh, don't stop in this dismal place!" and she, interpreting, said: "No, we won't stay here," and rushing for the train, which had made an unaccountably long stop, we regained our former seats, feeling like two flies that had almost been drawn into Mr. Spider's parlor.

Along the line of the Chateaugay the timber has been ruthlessly burnt and cut off; the charcoal burners have devastated the region, and their poor huts are to the lover of woodland scenery anything but compensation for the giants of the forest. The next place which offered any attraction was Inman, the station for Loon Lake. We left the train and proceeded to make inquiries about the neighborhood from a handsome, courteous young fellow who was handling express matter. "Yes," he said, "you can get rooms at that big unpainted house. I board there, and the people are 'kind' and the eating is good."

As he walked along with us, carrying some of the lighter bundles, his cough told a sad story, supplemented, however, by cheerful words spoken in a cheery tone. "Yes, I have consumption. My home is in Virginia. I spent last winter in Saranac, at the Sanatorium. Perhaps I shall get better in these spruce woods; I can't live anywhere else."

We found at the house recommended, the only dwelling in sight except charcoal burners' huts, clean beds in uncarpeted rooms and farmer's fare for 25 cents a meal.

We went to the woods to prepare our supper, buying from the country folk, as we were nearly always able to, fresh, sweet milk to take with us. We found in an opening, skirting the woods, a luxuriant growth of red raspberries; we made leafy cups and filled them with the delicious fruit, and going farther up the hillside found a profusion of ripe blueberries, which we also gathered to add to our repast, eating by the way as if there were no limit to mountain appetite.

The variety and beauty of the ferns

were bewildering, and the clustering cor-
nel berries seemed to glow with a richer
hue than was their wont.

On a bed of moss, with garniture of
ferns and mountain blooms and berries,
was spread a tempting repast, but no
sooner were we seated than our delight
changed to discomfiture. An army of
mosquitoes and midges settled down upon
us, making life miserable and dissipating
appetite. To eat sitting was impossible ;
we rose simultaneously to our feet, and
by dint of vigorously flourishing pocket-
handkerchiefs managed to eat something
of the substantials, the berries and their
æsthetic accompaniments being out of
harmony with our aggravating conditions
and consequently neglected. The bitter-
est pang lay in the probability of finding the same disturbers of the peace in
all parts of the mountains, a foreboding
which was not realized. We had no second visitation from either variety of the
insect pests which came down upon us in
armed squadrons at " Midge Camp," as
we christened the spot where we ate the
peripatetic supper just described.

Returning to our lodgings we passed a
baby's grave, decorated with remnants of
wild-flower wreaths that could not have
been placed there many months before,
yet the white headstone told us that the
little one had lain there nearly half a century. Sweetbrier and I speculated about
the baby and the flower offerings as we
walked on, and entering the house asked
the grandmother what she knew about
the solitary mound, the little sleeper and
the faded wreaths.

" Oh " she said, " our May put the
flowers there. She's a queer girl. She
does it every summer. The dead baby
was a stranger here ; no one of that name
ever lived in these parts. Perhaps the
folks were emigrants moving and the
child died on the way—that's what we
think, but no one knows."

The next morning we awoke to a driving storm of wind and rain. A spotlessly
clean, uncarpeted sitting room, cheerful
with house plants and warmed with a
wood fire, was given up to us. We opened
the windows and enjoyed the fresh mois-
ture-laden air, wrote letters and read
aloud ; and when the storm cleared at
sunset tramped off over the muddy roads,
and returned triumphant with delicious
fall violets, white, with pinky lilac tints—
the canadensis, I believe.

Next day, having obtained a good lunch

from our hostess, we walked three and a
half miles to Loon Lake and its attractive hotel. Entering the very large parlor,
with polished floor, we took seats on the
carpeted dais surrounding the room, and
entered heartily into the scene before us.
The blazing wood fire in the generous
fireplace did not heat the air, but simply
modified the fresh morning breeze that
came through open doors. Two ladies
presided at violin and piano, and on the
floor were young girls in tasteful mountain costumes, dancing with the freedom
and vigor of peasants. It was a pretty
sight and held us there till the music
stopped and the musicians adjourned to
the tennis ground.

Then we strolled along the lakeside,
admiring the camps that, following in
close succession, vied with each other in
attractiveness. Rustic lodges open toward the lake, floating flags, light boats
drawn up on the bank, crackling camp
fires, with groups of picturesque loungers,
from which children were not absent ;
madam, with fancy work ; girls, with
book or pen ; young fellows busy with
tools or sketching block : all these we
saw grouped in a series of charming open-
air tableaux.

We wanted to sit down by every camp
fire, to laugh at the jokes that went
round, to peep into the books that could
engross attention 'mid such jollity and
good fellowship. And for a moment we
fancied we had a faint touch of the pangs
which the homeless wanderer at Christmas feels who stands outside of the glittering shops and hungrily sees what he
cannot share. May the memory stand by
us when jolly Yuletide comes again ! yes,
and whenever a bright interior smiles upon us while friendless ones stand without !

But to return to the alluring camp fires.
We kept a courteous distance from them,
and did not gaze too curiously at the picturesque loungers, and in due time floated in our own (hired) boat on the blue
waters, and, mooring under the shadow
of overhanging branches, browsed in our
own chosen books till it was almost too
late to catch the return stage to the railroad station.

Our next stop was at Bloomingdale,
from whence a brisk coach ride of six
miles brought us to Paul Smith's renowned caravansary. Here we spent the
evening in watching the children's games
in the large parlor devoted to them, and

then adjourned to the ballroom, where the dancers whirled merrily hour after hour.

Those Adirondack days were idyllic ; spent in the open air, walking through fresh woods, rolling along through new scenes viewed from the coach top, or exploring the bays and islands of a new lake. We visited, in our fortnight's trip, Loon, St. Regis, Saranac, Placid and Mirror lakes, and Edmond's and Au Sable ponds, and rowed on five different bodies of water.

The coach lurched from side to side most violently, it seemed, when we skirted steep and unprotected precipices. The road was new and very rough and rock lined. The lurches became exaggerated. The passengers, so gay in starting, relapsed into silence, watching anxiously every movement of the whip, which was maliciously used at the most inopportune times. Some of the men got out and walked. Some of the women went inside, that they might escape the sight of the driver's cruelty to his horses. The few remarks made on top seemed to gather impressiveness from the general silence, and attached themselves to the memory with comical force. An English couple on their wedding tour thought the whole thing " nasty," railroads, hotels and coaches. Said my lord the Briton to madam : " There's something in my eye ; get it out, won't you ? " " Ha ! ha ! " laughed the bride. " Fancy ! with my veil and gloves on ! " And nothing more was heard from that quarter.

When we traveled by coach, of course we always wanted outside seats ; so did most of the tourists, and up they piled, while the driver looked around and said, nonchalantly, " There are too many on top already, but it's your own lookout ! " and one laggard after another climbed up on the top-heavy vehicle, till finally those who had come half an hour early to secure good seats were forced to dismount for prudence sake and go inside.

We started from Saranac for Placid one superb afternoon with a top-heavy load. The driver remarked he didn't know what was to become of us, but he was all right. The latter statement we doubted, as he dismounted after a heavy pull and rewarded the intelligent but tired leader with a series of brutal kicks.

" It's worse than anything in Nevada or the Yellowstone," growled a stout, rusty old chap, who said he had been " everywhere."

A native tried to discuss crops with a commercial traveler on his vacation. Said the native, eyeing a field of scanty, stunted corn : " The season here is too short for the crop."

" Ah ! " responded the C. T., " I thought the crop seemed short for the season ! "

Then darkness was added to silence, and in this manner we finished the longest eight miles of road in the United States of America.

Of Mirror and Placid, with their indescribably beautiful surrounding of mountains, we caught our first glimpse the following morning from the hotel windows, and if a choice can be made from such an embarrassment of riches as the Adirondacks offer, this was perhaps the most beautiful spot we visited.

Making Mirror Lake headquarters, and engaging a comfortable vehicle with driver and well-fed horses for $16 for three days, we planned and executed a series of delightful excursions. First, to Wilmington Gap, following a fork of the Au Sable, from one waterfall to another, snatching raspberries from the branches as we drove along, and finally dismounting when the profusion of the fruit became irresistible. At the falls we climbed out on overhanging rocks, reclining on the ledges, and watched the upward rising clouds of opaline spray framed in by spruce boughs. Here was a place to read Wordsworth's Tintern Abbey lines, and the joyous, life-giving description of the Easter morning walk in " Faust." And we did read them, and felt that life was almost too full with this complete response of the outward world to the sense of power and beauty swelling in heart and mind.

Such woods, such moss banks, such exquisite greenery as we saw that day we found nowhere else ! Do you know that daintiest of all leafiness—the network of fairy foliage that the linnæa spreads along the wayside in this region ? Have you seen the sprays of the creeping snowberry (chiogenes), embedded in moss banks where it ripens its aromatic berries ? Have you gathered the spikes of metallic, silvery-blue balls of the clintonia ? Have you tasted the cymes of the gorgeously-colored fruit of the bush cranberry ? You know the ground hemlock (American yew), with sturdy horizontal branches radiating in every direction close to the earth ; but have you seen its deep-dimpled scarlet berries scattered like jewels mid its dark foliage ? If so, you know some of the treasures of Wilmington Pass. We found in all, in the mountains, seven varieties of edible wild fruits—raspberries, blueberries, blackberries, gooseberries, cranberries, cherries and wintergreen—and ate them with such apparent relish that we were forced to contradict the bookworm's aphorism, that "Only children and birds know how cherries and berries taste."

The following day we penetrated the depths of the forest leading to the picturesque Adirondack Lodge, where we dined and rowed and loafed till the sun commenced to withdraw and light up the walls of Indian Pass.

Starting from Plattsburg without definite plan, almost forgetting that John Brown's grave lay in the heart of the Adirondacks, memories of the old hero crowded upon us till, as we approached the North Elba farm, where he lived and matured his plans and now lies buried, our whole journey seemed to shape itself into a pilgrimage to that spot. Our thoughts ran in rhythm to the music of the "Battle Hymn of the Republic:"

> John Brown's body lies a-mouldering in the grave;
> His soul is marching on.

In these solemn, snow-draped woods he wrought and thought in the fierce winter weather; in these sunny intervals, from the air of spring laden with fragrance of spruce and balsam, he breathed in inspiration as he ploughed and planned. And in midsummer, in the shadow of the great rock which stands a stone's throw from his cottage door, he sat and read in his beloved Bible the history of God's saints who did the Lord's work with fire and sword. And the Lord's work John Brown of Ossawatomie did with fire and sword, and was brought back here in midwinter, according to his request, and laid in a grave cut in the frozen ground in the shadow of the great rock where he loved " to sit and read the Word of God." "John Brown " is carved in huge letters on the gray pile. We laid our wreaths of goldenrod and evergreen twined with scarlet berries on the honored grave and went on our way, our hearts surging with the hero's greatness, yet acknowledging that John Brown was not without reproach, though not to be judged by us. His were the faults of a Brutus who struck that king rather than the country should perish ; of a Bayard who turned his strength to the liberation of the oppressed.

A beautiful drive leading through the narrow, rocky pass confining Edmond's ponds brought us from North Elba to Beede's, with its outlying cottages, where year after year one finds the same old familiar faces and some charming phases of social life, together with that unique paradise known as "Putnam's Camp." Here we supped with one circle of friends and dined with another. In one cottage discussed "Robert Elsmere" and Gladstone's review, and in another joined the attentive audience who listened to a lecture from Thomas Davidson on "Mediæval Interpretations of Aristotle." Best of all, with a chosen few read Epictetus beneath the big tree that shelters the tiny hermitage, where one after another the pure-minded disciples of ethics have drawn inspiration in summer hours from book and nature to be given to the world in winter in crystalized form.

The hours at Beede's flew only too quickly. An afternoon at the Au Sable ponds was followed by many cheery goodbyes, and at sunrise next morning we were off for Westport, the railroad and the wide world beyond.

We have told almost nothing of our little adventures, or what we saw, only how we saw it. Breathing the tonic air of those northern forests whose fragrance is beyond description, so many spicy plants are concealed in their green depths, we had walked and rowed in rain as well as sun without a single cold.

Our two weeks' trip was ended ; the sum playfully proposed in the beginning as the limit of expenses was not quite exhausted, and we had denied ourselves nothing that would have added to comfort, health or pleasure.

Summer Days in the Catskills (1884)

THE IRON DUKE.

OUTING.

VOL. IV. JULY, 1884. No. 4.

SUMMER DAYS IN THE CATSKILLS.

AST summer as an artist and a young art-student sat sketching together in one of the cool valleys that adorn the blue hills we see looking westward from the Hudson, the busy silence was suddenly broken by the younger man : —

"Mr. Vandyke, what do you think of the Catskills as a sketching-ground?"

"Think!" said he of the brush. "Why look here, and here, and here," and he signalled with his pipe — "a perfect picture on every side."

"Yes, but," a little doubtfully, "before I left New York I asked Mr. Umber" (and here he named a well-known painter) "the same question, and he said, 'Oh, don't go to the Catskills! they are so conventional, — quite in the style of the early American painters.'"

Thenceforward the friends had much merriment over the phrase ; and, when the sunlight danced on the lucid shallows of some wild brook, or touched with good-night caress the curved summits, they shouted, "Conventional!" till the phrase was called into universal service for morning mists and evening shadows, and all the beautiful and picturesque possibilities of summer time in the hills. Perhaps a train of thought scarcely less absurd has infected the general public.

"Oh, we can't go to the Catskills, you know, any more!" people say ; "they are too crowded."

Seventy thousand guests, say the newspapers ; and one feels afraid to venture thither lest peace and seclusion should

SLIDE MOUNTAIN.

have vanished utterly. Yet still they rise, green and gracious, with cool glens and mighty forests and far heights, not yet exhausted for artist or mountain lover. Neither railroad whistle nor electric light can wholly spoil the sense of stillness and rest in the deep valleys, or the distant splendors of the outward views; and for those who are pained by these innovations there remain quiet regions where they cannot come.

The approach by rail from Catskill is not a loss to the traveller. The drive across the plain was, on the whole, a tedious one. In the freshness of a dewy morning, or the strong lights of a late afternoon, there are many pleasant stretches and lovely glimpses of the blue hills drawing nearer; but under the heat of a burning sun, and over sandy grades, each mile seemed an enemy to be conquered. For the first few miles the pictures from the car-windows are charming. The creek has some fine ledges, and the track follows its shores so closely that you can enjoy them and the sparkling water and the graceful foliage upon its rocky borders. The later miles lose this brook comrade; but the hills are rising before you, and you do not miss it. At the little stations you may choose between the drives up to the mountain houses, or approach their level through the Clove. Here the railway cannot enter, and here, let us hope, it will never intrude. For in these winding, shaded roads, bordered with arching trees, or following the mountain watercourses, giving here and there, as they rise, brief glimpses of the sea-blue plain, dwells one great charm of the mountains.

If you choose the Clove road, as you

leave the last house in Palenville behind you, the spell begins. Suddenly you are in the deep heart of the hills; soon your carriage-way, in its gradual ascent, has left the bed of the Kaaterskill far below; but you hear its laughing welcome, and can see it springing and dancing through the narrow glen. Many hundred feet above you the green woods rise before they reach the level which you are seeking.

But, without delay, the peaceful hush of the scene takes possession of you. If you are returning, you note the old landmarks, the beautiful rock forms of Church's Ledge, the cool, shelving seats at the head of the Fawn's Leap, the mossy birch that plays it is a beech-tree, the nook where you read a poem years ago to the wild music of the rushing stream.

If it is your first visit you will try in vain to take it all in, — the fresh sweet smell of the forest earth and leafage, the green, restful tints of fern and moss and mountainside, and the glimpses of the far hill-tops. Half way up the valley widens a little; there are bits of fields and traces of ruined houses where the old tannery made a little settlement.

Here, fronting the wooded slope through whose deep verdure the Buttermilk and the Westbrook come leaping and singing from the great shoulder-like level far above, is a little plateau, raised just above the roadside dust, and bright with a scattered growth of hemlock and maple and ferns and vines, where the ideal hostelry of this region will yet be built, — not, we will hope, a great, bare, white barn, obtruding its glaring front and harsh angles upon the eye, but a rambling structure, with outlines quaint and graceful, with soft and sombre tints, with rustic porches overrun with vines, and home-like little cottages here and there through the grounds, for families or groups who choose to carry with them an atmosphere of seclusion.

Here is the home of the pedestrian and the wheelman, amongst these cool, unnamed glens, the sequestered walks, the deep forest. But we must go onward. Half a mile more of this peaceful valley, with the wider curves of circling hills about it, and we cross the stream that comes down the Kaaterskill ravine with song and shout and many a merry leap. The little path that turns here to follow up its banks affords a delightful ramble, with a bit of climbing on the way, but the carriage-road climbs slowly and steadily up to the westward. At our left a deep and heavily-wooded ravine slopes down from our side, and in its deepest recesses sometimes a silver presence shines and sings, and far up, over its topmost cliff, slides the upper cascade of Haines's Falls, too plainly evident to us who used to delight in its deep, arching bowers, sacrificed now for this effect. As we near the top of the long pull we turn for the beautiful view down the Clove. Most lovely is the outline of the curving hills that encircle it on the south. Here the steam-whistle greets us again; we have come out of the sylvan depths into a land of stations and boarding-houses, and sights to be seen for a quarter. Here, about Tannersville, extending on to Hunter, the large boarding-houses and smaller

save for the unusual preponderance of big white houses, differing but little in its general surface from any rolling country; but peaks and ridges rise about it, the fine terraced slope of Hunter Mountain illuminates it on the west, and a serrated chain stretches from the Stony Clove to High Peak. From these hills fine views are gained in all directions. The drives and excursions are charming everywhere, but the pedestrian must usually plod for a mile or two along dusty roads before he can lose himself in the forest paths and feel himself fairly upon his " native heath."

Hunter is a pretty little village at the foot of its namesake mountain, with some life of its own apart from the summer

EAGLE CLIFF, AUSTIN GLEN.

hotels most do congregate. The elevation of the plateau gives the bracing air and the cool nights so much desired and needed by city people, and the comfortable quarters reconcile them to the ugly exteriors. Here, too, these new railroads furnish that direct access from the city so desirable for families temporarily separated, and for those with brief vacations.

These odd little trains approach almost to the Kaaterskill Falls and the two large mountain houses, to which we can drive by turning to our right. The view straight before us is farm-like in its general effect,

boarder. Its people rejoice in the little thread of railway, that, slipping through the wild and narrow defile of the Stony Clove, links it to the great world beyond. It is from this level that the Plaaterkill ravine, and the road from its head to the Overlook Mountain House, are reached.

Now let us imagine ourselves at Palenville again, *en route* for the Hotel Kaaterskill. Before we reach the entrance of the Clove our driver turns to the right, and we begin a steady ascent. Soon the Clove road lies far below us. We curve and wind, always steadily, but always easily, upward, along great ledges, over parapets of logs and stone-work; and, as we rise, the opposite mountain seems to rise also with its exquisite curves, one sweep of living verdure to the Balsam crown of High Peak.

This wonderful road is a perpetual surprise to the old mountaineer. The cliffs and gorges it traverses were the least accessible to the wanderer on foot, and the picturesque view is a revelation of delight. But the summit comes at last, and you

GRAND GORGE.

sweep up to the entrance of the great hotel there — a little world in itself, with its electric lights and bells, and its crowds of gay people.

The whole seems like a piece of society life with its flower-beds and croquet and tennis grounds, set down here, island-like, amid the wild growth wisely left to surge up to the smooth lawn and tell how it overran all this level four years ago, while its neighbor, High Peak, looks down grandly on all this petty pomp.

Near this hotel is the Sunset Rock, and the charming path along the mountain's brow, where the view of the Clove, and the plateau westward towards Hunter is unequalled. From the Sunset Rock especially, on a warm August afternoon, you may gain those delicious, hazy tints that make Gifford's pictures truest truth. They are exceptional, those quivering opaline mists, but they do come, and the poet-painters love to interpret them.

The beauty and delight of any clear summer afternoon spent on Sunset Rock are

CATSKILL MT. HOUSE, FROM NORTH MT.

not exceptional, but permanent. As the sun sinks, the great valley of the Clove overbrims with rich and tremulous shadow, to which the brilliant light over the western distance offers a radiant contrast. In the bower-like recesses of Haines' ravine the falls used to glimmer and shine like jewels. The denuding process which has opened those sylvan glens too broadly to the open daylight has lessened the peculiar charm of this effect, but the hills still hold the shadows, the sun still shines down on the broad slope of Hunter Mountain till it glows with light and color. As of old, too, when all this beauty was framed by young trees (which were swept away by fire a few years ago, leaving the ledges open), the leafy shadows trembled above us as we watched and read, and waited for the end of the daily pageant. Oh, if life were only long enough for a summer of such sunsets!

There are two or three, perhaps more, drives and paths from the Hotel Kaaterskill to the Laurel House, which was opened many years ago, but is greatly enlarged now. Its owner is also the proprietor of the Kaaterskill Falls, and has earned much money and much execration by making a show of them, being the first to " let on " the water and charge admittance. The first feeling about such a tax is certainly an injured and unpleasant one, but the dry summers have so pinched the springs everywhere in our land, shorn of its water guarding forests, that the chance comer would never know the beauty of this wonderful fall but for Mr. Schutt's thrift. The charge is trifling, made but once in a season, and giving the use of the steps and walks, without which few would gain the depths of the cool glen below, whence the finest views are obtained.

One warm summer day it was my good

ories! — the fatigue, the tight shoe, the briers that scratched, the ill-chosen companion that fretted us, and seemed to spoil our day, these are evanescent, soon we forget them, but the pictures of such a ramble, — the young moon curving above a purple hill-crest against a golden sky,

CHURCH'S LEDGE.

fortune, after paying our little toll, and descending to the foot of the falls, to spend with a friend some hours there. Exquisite mists rose and played lovingly about the great amphitheatre, softening its barren walls with a rainbow-garlanded veil. The waters plunged and roared about us in gladness and delight. I must forgive the toll-gatherers when I recall that day. Ah, these glorious mountain mem-

the shadowy vista, the radiant transition from forest gloom to sunlit splendor, the perfect sunrise — these are forevermore our own.

The Catskill Mountain House, poised upon its vast outreaching ledges, is, as of old, a dignified hotel, with an impression of peace and repose. The sudden descent from this ledge gives a certain individuality to its view of the plain.

This spot was formerly the tourist's Catskills and his road to "The Falls." Perhaps, coming or going, he took the Clove road; a little strolling on the north and south mountain, and the hours on the piazzas, completed his visit. If he were a writer, he told the outer world his impressions from this stand-point. So Bryant, Cooper, Miss Sedgwick, and most charmingly, in later days, Curtis, wrote. Twenty-five years ago these two last-named hotels afforded the chief, almost the only, accommodation to the public. At that time our artists sought quieter and less expensive homes. They found, for instance, a tiny farm-house in the Clove, where they obtained quarters, and taught the goodwife to " broil a steak, and make a cup of coffee," as I once heard Mr. M'Entee say, adding, somewhat ruefully, that it was the artist's lot to find charming nooks, and then to be elbowed out of them.

To Brockett's, then, came in those early war times many of our well-known painters. Some brought their wives or sisters; a few people who longed for the hill, but did not like hotel life, followed them, and kindred spirits gathered in the little cottage, whose walls seemed elastic, so were their limits taxed.

Blithe days were those, and comical are the legends of the little house. How good-humoredly were its deficiencies endured on the part of the guests! How cheerfully, on the other hand, were meals served by the hosts at all sorts of impossible hours that the vagaries of pedestrians made necessary! Scarce a trace of Brockett's remains. The pioneer hostelry of the summer boarder has vanished utterly; the too odorous hen-feather pillow, which migrated from one complaining guest to another, till the merriment it caused half atoned for the discomfort, is a thing of the past, but many glad memories linger around the little glade whose grassy sods cover its ashes. I am sure that its life of simple excursions and quiet enjoyment was an ideal one for those who truly loved the hills. Soon a few houses in the little hamlet of Palenville opened their doors, where so many find pleasant homes now. Various families of Haineses, on the plateau, caught the infection. Gray's, now Roggins', was already established. These were the preluding chords to the great orchestra of welcome to the Catskills. Now seventy thousand people are said to enter this enchanted region in a season. The Plaaterkill was a favorite all-day pilgrimage from Brock-

ett's. Sometimes more than a wagon-load would start off together, the pedestrians exchanging places from time to time with those who were driving; but it was not unusual for two or three of the best walkers to make the whole distance of twenty-two or three miles on foot. The climb up the stream, which all took together, counted for more than double its distance. It was a delightful exertion. A certain quality of peculiar clearness in the water in this land of crystal streams made its pools and rippling stretches unequalled, and the upper cascades were exquisite. The harebells were very abundant there, nodding on the spray-washed crests of the great ledges in delightful inaccessibility, tempting rash girls to covet, and rash youths to gather them. Now the quarrying has greatly injured the lower part of this ravine, and at times it is unsafe to attempt the ascent.

But it is not difficult to go down from above to the glen at the head of the fourth fall, which is one of the most beautiful I know. The rocky floor near the brow of the fall is almost level; the stream has hollowed for itself a little channel, over which you can spring lightly. Here and there upon this surface lie flat stones, with a marvellous upholstery of ferny mosses; on either hand the forest rises far above, upborne on giant ledges; the eastern outlook gives you the plain and river, or so much of them as the hills at the lower entrance of the ravine will let you see between their graceful curves and crested summits, in a glimmering azure vista.

These enfolding hills have just enough distance from you to wear a soft, purplish tint against which the trees that spring from the varying depths below are clearly outlined, while the great birches and maples that rise from our own level over-arch and frame the whole outlook. But no picture can give you all the charm, the exhilarating rush of cool air that follows such a stream in its flight, the forest sounds and odors.

At your foot the stream leaps out for its plunge of eighty feet into one of those deep, mysterious, fathomless, emerald pools, then races along another brief level, and then again falls out of sight in a glen that seems from this height all soft, waving verdure.

You turn and walk a few paces up the stream. The great cliffs confront you, the falling water widens into a silver cascade, the wild fissures of the Cross Clove on your right hold their own tiny streamlet,

LAUREL HOUSE AND KAATERSKILL FALLS.

and, amid the distant foliage that trembles far against the upper heaven, shines another silver presence of living light and water,

" Like a white soul flung out to Eternity."

Again the plateau, with open fields and bright sunlight! We pause for the view through the ravine to the plain, — a wider vision, but very beautiful. We cross the little brook that sings along its way to turn the mill, with no thought of the wild splendors that await it, and find ourselves on the new road to the Overlook House. It gives us a delightful drive of five miles through the dense woods, stretching eastward and outward at first, and giving frequent glimpses of the plain or the hills across the Plaaterkill. This road links the old region on which I have dwelt so long, with the less known.

Twenty years ago the Woodstock Overlook was a far-off realm whose charms were seen only by more adventurous pedestrians: and the record of their delight had a rather tantalizing quality. When the Overlook Mountain House, and the Ulster and Delaware Railroad were built, this noble view became more accessible to the outer world. To reach it from the upper Catskills was no easy matter. Now, however, it is a charming drive.

The great river plain, as seen from the Overlook, sweeps away in long stretches to the extreme southern limit of vision. The northern view across the shoulders of the Plaaterkill, from the hill above the house, is very fine, but it is the westward view which gives the new-comer his great surprise. From the river he has thought this point the limit of the Catskills ; and lo ! beyond him, reaching away into the sunset, rise range after range, peak upon peak, higher, he is told, than any he has known. As the day wanes and the exquisite gradations of the afternoon light shimmer through a gentle haze upon the beautiful mountain forms, he looks, and lingers, and praises, and longs to explore that fairy land. And he will not cavil when he hears this enchanting vision called the most perfect extended view in the whole range.

The mountain rising to the north of the house is full of fine rock forms and delightful surprises, where graceful trees and magnificent ledges frame in or accent the glimpses which its narrow crest makes possible, now to the east, now to the west, as the paths wind. The Iron Duke one of these profile-like ledges is named, and how superbly its dark masses outline the soft tints of the distance, our artist tells you. [See frontispiece.] There is one westward picture from this point that I enjoy almost as much as the wider vistas.

Far below, behind this summit, is a deep valley, in which nestles a little lake, — a bit of sapphire, — and from its farther shore rises a most magnificent wall of forest, so directly facing the outlook as to give an unequalled display of foliage. I have

OLD BRIDGE AT LEEDS.

always seen it in June ; but in October how glorious it must be !

We can drive from the Overlook to West Hurley, and take the train there for the Shandakin Range, but perhaps it would be as well to imagine ourselves once more in the outer world, away from the breath of the hills. The new West Shore Road, with its fresh and comfortable appointments, seems, by its close connections with the Ulster and the Delaware, the fitting pathway to these newer resorts. To my mind the view, all the way from Rondout to Catskill, of the face of the upper range, is one of its claims to patronage.

But we leave it now at Kingston, and take the train into the hills. What an approach it is ! — the gradual ascent among the foot-hills, the mountain wall that rises before you as if to bar your entrance, the narrow gorges that open suddenly, through which you glide beside a sparkling stream that has taken the same way outward. At Phœnicia the connection is made for the Tannersville Plateau, the narrow-gauge road from this point to Hunter connecting at Tannersville Junction with the Kaaterskill Railway, which turns to the eastward and reaches very near the old Mountain House, as I have already mentioned, — thus affording, by the West Shore and its connections, a direct railroad route to all the places I have described. The passage through the Stony Clove is very wild, and the passengers enjoy it exceedingly ; but to one who has taken it on foot or in leisurely drives it is an unsatisfactory pleasure. The ledges and the steep opposing cliffs here are grand in their abrupt elevation, and no amount of personal convenience can quite console us for the havoc the railway has made in its intrusion. From Phœnicia our Ulster and Delaware train rushes onward and upward, among valleys themselves so far above sea level that the heights seem low, and suggested to me the lesser slopes of the Berkshires, the more so that the same cruel process of charcoaling has destroyed the older forest, and the same young growth of birch and soft maple is trying hard to repair man's ravages.

Beyond Shandakin the ascending grade is very evident, and the downward view along the line beautiful. The country beyond the summit, when the road begins to descend again, is more open, the Halcott valley widens to the right, — a peaceful, pastoral scene, — and the Drybrook valley has a unique charm. The Grand Gorge

rises in strong lines, seeming a gateway into the hills from the west. But the chief interest of the summer tourist in these Shandakin Catskills centres in the region about Summit. Pine Hill lies just below in a little valley circled about with hill-tops, a little street of hotels and boarding-houses, gay and bright in the season, with young faces and pretty costumes, glad with blithe social life.

Pine Hill and Hunter, in the Green County range, have each the same level, sixteen hundred feet above the sea, and seem to have many points in common. Above Pine Hill, on the Birch Creek Road, two or three city folks have made summer homes, — an enviable and delightful custom. It is a pleasant walk from Pine Hill to the Grand Hotel at Summit Station, a most unhappy name, to my fancy, for a summer home in the hills. Why could not its sponsors have recognized the native resonance of Shokan and Shandakin, or the musical càdence of Ontiora? But we half forgive them as we gaze on the superb picture framed in the slender pillars and arches as we look outward.

There are no new phrases to use ; even the artist's pencil, in the limits of illustration, is scarcely adequate to present the charm of these far-reaching views, so much does this depend upon the atmospheric color. Shall we ever forget an October morning spent on this piazza, when the house was all silent, the last summer guest flown, and the glow of the autumnal foliage and perfect sunshine suffused through all the hill country? The lines of the Slide, the Balsam, and the Panther mountains form, as seen from this point, a faultless mountain landscape. The view from the hill above the house is rather more extended, but not so picturesque. The walk from Grand Hotel to Monkey Hill — as this elevation above it is called — gives you an agreeable sense of climbing, with very little fatigue, and from the fine ledges, the Halcott valley smiles up at you, — a visible poem of peaceful fields and farms.

Coming out of the woods on this October day, as we came down from the hill to the hotel grounds we found, on a sunny knoll, built against a great rock, a child's playhouse, — an old-fashioned playhouse, made of bits of board, and gay with broken dishes, its roof adorned with that ambition of a child's heart in the olden time, a real stove-pipe. It was refreshing, in these days of elaborate toys, to think of children having such a good time amid the gayety

VIEW FROM SUMMIT HILL, NEAR
GRAND HOTEL.

of this great hotel. One has pitied the little, over-dressed creatures so often in summer resorts.

Leaving the last train one Saturday night at Pine Hill, we inquired at the station about quarters. We knew the larger houses would be closed, but had not supposed there would be any difficulty in finding room for two in one of the smaller ones. But the agent answered rather gloomily, "They are cleaning house. The boarders are all gone and everybody is cleaning house," as if there were something pestilential about the summer boarder which made instant purification necessary.

In this emergency we ventured to apply at a little farm-house that looked as if people went on living when summer boarders were no more. Fortunately for us it was the ideal farm-house of the seeker for country fare. We were served with genuine kindness, and found here the abundant milk and cream, the dainty breakfast cakes, the white clover honey, that one dreams of in farm life, but does not always find. Everywhere were pleasant drives, and we longed to linger here through the golden October weather.

But we had promised ourselves to climb Slide Mountain ere our return, and so one bright afternoon we drove through the Shandakin Valley, rich in fine mountain forms, blithe streams, and tree-bordered roads, to the unexplored haunt of the Big Indian. We had enjoyed Pine Hill and our pleasant home there, and the quiet walks and drives, and the grand prospect from Summit, but had been just a little homesick, after all, for the real mountains, —the deep, shadowy forests climbing to far heights, holding mysterious, gloomy vistas, and deep glens, and mighty ledges. Here

we came suddenly upon them all. This narrow valley of the Big Indian is closed at one end by the sombre dome of the Balsam Mountain. Through its depths brawls the Esopus; there is room beside it for a few fields of varying size, and the road, a farm-house here and there, or a saw-mill; but these are scattered, and seem but to emphasize its expression of lonely and unsubdued wildness.

Far, far above rise the crests of Big Indian and the Hemlock Mountain, clothed all the way with stately forests. Great curving basins, where the springs meet to leap outward and downward in silver cascades, hold the afternoon shadows; around these the higher ranks of foliage catch the golden lights, wood roads start upward with a vista, tempting to the pedestrian, of overarching boughs and a carpet of moss and pine needles, and the elastic odorous forest earth.

Panther Mountain stretches its giant length along the opposite side of the valley, less richly wooded and watered than its neighbor, comparing in this with the northern and southern walls of the Kaaterskill Clove, of which we find a reminder here, and we must own also something of unsubdued wildness and solitude not to be found there. The accommodations in the Big Indian are limited, and Pine Hill and many other points do certainly offer more comfort for families or invalids; but he who loves the veritable breath of the hills, the feeling of exploration, the wild ramble, the sombre magnificence of the unbroken forest, will cheerfully accept some denials in exchange for these.

Over all these mighty slopes dominates

Slide Mountain, which we were to climb on the morrow. The radiant sunset and clear starlight promised us a perfect morning. But, as we peered from the little windows in the early dawn, a mist we knew too well had settled over all, the heights had vanished, the nearer terraces glimmered dimly through at first, but soon the rain, solid and gray, closed down about us, cold and dispiriting. How helpless we felt! We tried to console ourselves as best we might with Black's Sunrise and the renewed fascinations of ·Charles Auchester. It was a long, dull day; but at last, in very despair, we sallied forth into the rain, which, apparently daunted by our audacity, paused, hesitated, and finally ceased. Before our walk was done the last gleam flung a rich color upon the heights, and we sighed softly "At eventide there shall be light."

But to the mountain lover less hurried than we these rainy days have their own charm. Faintly and with a glowing softness the woods shine in successive ranks through tender mists. You know the streams are rising, and will greet you to-morrow with fresh beauty: and the dusty weeds by the roadside will rejoice anew, while you find time for needful stitches, writing letters, or an unfinished story. Once, long ago, I found a merry party at Brockett's playing croquet in rubbers and water-proofs. Such blithe spirits can spare a day now and then for in-door diversions.

Then how beautifully the clearing mists draw themselves together and hurry along the hill-side, tearing apart upon the tree-tops, and rising onward and upward till they float in light against the evening sky, and the sunlight touches with farewell the mountain-tops, and to-morrow's promise makes the hills more beautiful than ever!

So to us, after this delay, the next morning came unclouded, and in its early sunlight we were driving upward, the first half of our ascent being on a rough mountain-road. As it winds it affords such beautiful views down the valley, that we turned again and again for them. Some most magnificent old trees rise from the borders of the stream far below us; and, as we neared the upper curves, the trunks of mighty maples lay prone beside the road-way, and we grew sad to think how, a year before, the birds sang in their branches, and how ere long these their comrades might be stricken also. Some great iron company has bought vast tracts of forest here,

and has built comfortable log-houses for its workmen, who are to carry on this cruel slaughter. Some of these houses were standing, new and empty, just where the outlook was superb; and I could imagine what a perfect summer two or three congenial families might have there, who could secure the homely shelter, and were not afraid of a primitive way of living.

One sudden curve which the road makes to gain an opposite height revealed to us a wonderful picture of interfolding hills, and the peaceful valley between them.

Near the spot where we take the foot-path there is a depression in the mountain-side where, within a short distance, four wild streams rise and flow by merry leaps and dancing rapids, in widely opposing courses, to far distant rivers in the world below. The ascent of Slide, after we leave the road, is not by any means a difficult one, with three miles of steady walking, — scarcely any portion of the way requiring what one might really call climbing; and the path is well blazed and easy to follow if one is accustomed to the woods. The fallen leaves obscured it a little, but we followed our guide and his prattling little maid cheerily.

The ferns had been very rich and beautiful along the roadside; the frost had not yet climbed so high, and they stood in gay crowds along the way in every shade of fading splendor. When we entered the deep woods we found only the evergreen plume-ferns, but they were unusually fine, and very green, and great mantles of the soft, warm-tinted moss that loves these high places covered the rocks and ledges everywhere.

The birches grew large on the upper slopes and took all manner of fantastic shapes, arching, twisting, overleaning, with soft, fine embroidery of daintiest mosses on their silver stems. Till we neared the summit we could see only the forest about us; but, on the last plateau, a cleared outlook here and there gave us a hint of promise. The balsams took possession of the soil, and their rich, strong breath made the air delicious. And then, suddenly, a purple distance shone through their sombre trunks, and we knew that we had reached the crown of all these mighty summits. Before us, beyond the lofty peaks and ridges, and seeming far away, smiled the well-known river plain; around us on all sides was the wide tumultuous upheaval of the everlasting hills, in lessening peaks and curves, far as the eye could see. A strange and weird prospect, seen from the rude tower, built of poles lashed and nailed to the trunks of four balsam trees, standing as they have stood on the mountain for ages. It swayed slightly in the autumnal wind and I was fain to cling to the rough railing as I gazed. There was something very fascinating in this sense of supremacy. Above all I stood in the centre of the visible earth, while below me lay the kingdoms of the world and the glory thereof. An unbroken horizon tempted the vision on every side. The guide named the points and ranges about us, and at first we listened with some interest. Far in the north-east shines the Overlook Mountain House, and just over the twin shoulders behind it, a rounded knot of paler blue, is the High Peak.

It seems from its distance almost insignificant, and if you have once believed it the monarch of the Catskills, and have loved and revered it, you feel half jealous and incredulous. Another starlike point in the south-west is the Grand Hotel at Summit, and you almost forgive the glaring paint of these great houses when you see them sparkle thus in the sun. The strange contour of the Panther Mountain, the curious bulwark of Cornell and the Wittemburg, and many others, were pointed out; but I was glad when the guide left us, and we could ignore these details and strive in silence to take in the strange splendor of these billowy hills. The cloud-shadows chased each other up and down their sides, purple-dark against the October colors of the sunlit woods, and over all an indescribable thin blue veil of air. We watched the Esopus as it slid through the Shokan Pass, and again glistened far out upon the plain, to join the shining river. Ah, how perfect would a sunrise be on Slide Mountain! How the morning lights would play about these lofty crests, these giant ridges!

The August moon should not be quite full, that it might set in splendor ere daylight, and leave the world in darkness to await the coming of the dawn; but weird and wonderful should be its silver shining through the night, worth an unbroken vigil. But one cannot look so long; the brain wearies and the eyes droop, even here at high noon; yet when the guide called us, we turned again and again to each enchanting distance, and descended reluctantly. If the descent to Avernus is easy, not so the path down the mountain-side. We started bravely, but the steady downward-gait is far harder than climbing, and the way seemed long, and we were very glad to clamber into the old wagon and rest, and remember, and welcome anew, the pictures of differing charm which our curving road revealed.

One recalls, as we talk of them, the effort of the tourists in the Sandwich Islands, who, becoming weary of the innumerable exclamations of "Lovely! — superb! — glorious!" as each new wonder rewarded their explorations, resolved to adopt a numerical scale, of which one hundred should be the supreme commendation, while for a graceful tree or pretty cascade twenty should express the modified approbation, and so on.

Yet neither feeble adjectives nor commonplace admirers can exhaust the gifts these green hills hold, and the old words come back anew: "I will lift up mine eyes unto the hills, from whence cometh my help."

Abbie C. Percy.

Summertime Among the Thousand Islands (1881)

LOTOS LAND.

WE found Lotos Land at last. Up and down through many strange lands we had wandered, like Homer's Great Tramp, looking for some spot around which, during a brief vacation, we might draw the charmed circle which should shut out all the fretting incidents and crushing cares of yesterday, and where we might forget all the toil and turmoil and multiplied burdens of the great bustling world in which we lived and struggled the rest of the year.

Vain was the search. Business and not rest, politics and not quiet, ethics and not peace, fashion and not contentment, heart-burnings and not heart's-ease, entered still the daily rounds of life, and the din of the world's ceaseless conflict struck heavily upon our ears. Is there no place, then, where we may live in dreamy forgetfulness of this great thundering machine which we call the world? Must a man die and be buried before he can forget, even for one delicious hour, what State and city he lives in, what business he follows, what interests yield him his bread and butter?

Season after season, as the dog-days came on, these thoughts pressed heavily upon us, while the winds of chance or perversity drove us hither and yon, until one year the summer breezes blew us, not like Ulysses upon the Libyan shores, but upon the broad bosom of the River St. Lawrence; and here we found our rest. Between these shores we float and fish, we sing and sleep amid the wondrous beauties of this lovely archipelago, until we forget that once we knew other scenes and other men, until every day seems like a new and separate life, and we have almost to pinch ourselves to realize that beyond this river is another world, where there are loved ones waiting our return, business that soon will be crying for our care, vulgar dollars and cents to be reckoned, or scrambled for.

And so Lotos Land is, to us, no longer a creation of old Homer's fervid imagination. For three delightful summers we have seen and touched the real land of dreamy forgetfulness. We know, by grace of the geologists, whence it is, and that it was evolved from some grand convulsion of Nature's mighty forces, when thousands of islands pushed their heads above the waters, and rocks were rent asunder, and upward through ten thousand narrow, sinuous rifts the volcanic substances rose from their fiery beds to cool their hot faces in the light of day, and bathe their shapeless forms in the limpid waters of the lakes. Mighty river and inland sea, mountain and plain, island and continent, Nature in her sweet and placid aspect, and in her dark and awful mood, all are blended here to form that singular combination of elements which the Iroquois Indians so appropriately named *Man-a-to-ana*—"the Garden of the Great Father."

My first knowledge of the Thousand Islands was, like almost all good things, obtained without any thanks being due therefor to my own perceptions or wise forethought. Among the many royal good fellows who live and move and have their being in that longest and narrowest, richest and poorest, most Christian and most heathen city west of the Atlantic, was my friend John. His search in life was, not for forgetfulness, but for the health which had been shattered years before by too assiduous a pursuit of business. Together John and I had been all the spring planning for our vacation. Now the scheme embraced two weeks in the saddle among the White Mountains; again it took the form of a rough trip to the Newfoundland Banks with a mackerel fleet; and later, of a yachting cruise up the Sound and along the coast to Mount Desert.

But as the weeks slipped by, and the time drew nearer, John's cheeks grew more pinched and his hacking cough worse, until it was plain that these vigorous pursuits must be abandoned, and he must seek quiet surroundings and healing air. Some one suggested the Thousand Islands, and because we knew nothing against them, and not because we knew the first fact in their favor, except their reputation for ozone, there we decided to go. Accordingly there was an exodus from Gotham, and one steaming hot night four of us were tucked away in that modern sweat-box denominated by common courtesy a sleeping-car, en route for Cape Vincent, viâ the New York Central. One of our sleeping-car companions was a silk-merchant, who could tell the whole interesting story of silk-culture in the Orient, and knew the entire St. Lawrence region intimately. I became deeply interested in his silk narrative, and could not help overhearing afterward his gossip with two young men from Ottawa, which displayed a knowledge of Canadian genealogy most creditable to his memory. Here was the man, thought I, who could direct me to the spots most desirable to see, and save no end of dreary hunting after interesting facts. To my anxious inquiry what there was to see, and was there any special point a visitor ought to see, he thoughtfully and hesitatingly replied, "Nothing but the islands." The dog-days had departed: it was chilly as November. This man had seen the whole world, he knew all the ins and outs of business, his early home was on the St. Lawrence, and all *he* had seen about the Thousand Islands was their plurality. Not very encouraging that to a man who had given up the glories of a two weeks' gallop through the mountains!

But the chill was yet to be deepened. I confess to a disappointment in my first view of the Thousand Islands from the deck of the mail-steamer from Cape Vincent. She rushed along the main American channel, past points, and coves, and islands great and small, but too distant to display their wild and varied beauty. A cold storm was coming on, and I stood shivering in a light overcoat, and cross-legged to keep my knees warm at high noon, while the noon before I had trodden the hot pavements of Wall Street mopping my reeking brow under a dog-day sky. That weather was exceptional, however, and while it is never hot to us Gothamites—except occasionally at mid-day—it is generally about like early June in New York, except that the nights are always cool enough for comfortable sleeping.

From Cape Vincent, where we took the little river steamer, there is little to engage the eye except the broad and magnificent expanse of river widening just beyond the cape into the grander expanse of Lake Ontario. We stopped at Clayton, at which point the Utica and Black River Railroad has its terminus, and then steamed away for Round Island, where a large hotel has recently been built upon a small island, which is designed specially as a resting-place for the Baptists. Indeed, the various religious denominations are vying with each other in the establishment of watering-places in this Garden of the Great Father. A

THOUSAND ISLAND PARK—BOAT-HOUSES AND COTTAGES.

few miles below we stopped again at Thousand Island Park, where the Methodists have erected a thousand-acre plot at the head of Wells' Island into a resort after the general plan of Ocean Grove. It is the most advanced, in many respects, of any summering place among the islands, except that it as yet lacks good hotels. The number of cottages is considerable, and some are very handsome, while hundreds of tents are leased during the season to transient parties. One feature at this pretty location, however, strikes the visitor most strangely, and that is the untimely thrift of the association, which imposes an admittance fee of fifteen cents for every passenger entering the grounds. Even the regular cottagers and lot owners are required to pay every day they leave the park and return, though they may purchase monthly tickets at a reduced rate. Directly opposite, upon the American mainland, is Fisher's Landing, which has a hotel well filled through the season, and glories in a telegraph station. Hub Island, lying close to Wells', is a little bare rock, upon which is a hotel almost entirely covering it. We saw skiffs lying at the kitchen door unloading milk, fish, and vegetables directly upon the kitchen floor—Venice on a small scale. Near by is Grinnell's Island, which is very little larger than the hotel it supports; and off further toward the Canadian shore stands yet another hotel upon the dark steep sides of Hemlock Island, accessible only from the

ALEXANDRIA BAY.

river, and then by long flights of wooden steps.

The stop at Thousand Island Park was barely long enough to grasp these facts as the obliging engineer pointed them out, and we were again on our way. Now we were running nearer the shores, and the passengers began to lean over the rail, and show their delight at the beauties of nature unfolding to view. Presently we pass four white cottages nestling among the oak-trees side by side, which their owners have christened the "Jolly Oaks." And they look jolly. Hammocks are swung beneath the ample branches of the oaks; below the bank their pretty skiffs rest at the water's edge; and the inmates of all four houses stand on their piazzas, waving a welcome to our snorting little propeller as she passes. Such were the Jolly Oaks when first I saw them; such they have been every time we have passed their hospitable doors since. We have steamed by early and late, on the mail-steamer and in one of those pretty St. Lawrence steam-yachts; but never yet has the puff of our engine failed to bring the

Jolly Oaks settlement to the front in full force, waving hats, handkerchiefs, flags, and on one particularly inspiring occasion giving to the ozone - charged breeze what bore suspicious resemblance to a table-cloth. And now the islands thicken in the channel. Islands to right of us, islands to left of us, islands in front of us, lift up their heads, crowned here with jutting rocks, there with forest trees, and again flanked by grassy slopes extending to the water's edge, and fringed with trees whose drooping branches reach down their leafy tips to drink the clear green waters of the river. The view grows more charming as we proceed. Channels open between the islands in every direction, and as our little steamer drives swiftly along the main and broadest channel, the shifting scenes go by us like a panorama. To our left still lies Wells' Island, nine miles long, shutting out all view beyond, while off to the right we catch through the rock-bound channels an occasional glimpse of the American mainland. A run of half an hour more brings us to Alexandria Bay. This is the central point of interest. For ten miles up and an equal distance down the river the islands lie thickest, the cottages are most numerous, and the fishing most alluring. The village, which takes its name from the bay, is perched upon a rocky headland on the American shore. Little can be said concerning the attractiveness of the little town itself, but it is surrounded by some of the finest scenery in the world, and has two very comfortable hotels.

Every day at Alexandria Bay witnesses a comical scene. Each of the principal hotels intrusts its interests with the travelling public, so far as choice of house is concerned, to "men and brudders" of sable hue, and the rivalry of these dusky runners, each clad in the livery of his house, and wearing a broad gold-lace band upon his cap, is of a deadly bitterness. Before the plank is thrown to the dock the entertainment begins. The representative of the older house is rather slender and short of stature, and scorns to ask an ally in his daily warfare. The rival house sends down two mighty champions. One is tall and distinguished - looking, with Burnside whiskers and an eagle eye, and his assistant is one of the fattest, oiliest negroes out of Congo land. Aldermanic in his measure between the suspender buttons, epicurean in the development of neck

and jowl, intensely economical in the proportions of the upper part of the head, and lavish to a fault in the matter of feet, he provokes a smile from all beholders as he rolls himself to his place beside his chief at the head of the plank, and clears his always husky throat for action. Their rival calls out from the opposite side of the plank, in shrill clarion notes, "This way to the C—— House"; and the moment the first word has escaped his lips, Burnside strikes in with his deep trombone, determined to spoil the rest of his rival's sentence by his overwhelming, "This way to the T—— House." Burnside is dramatic, too. He stands erect, as a commanding officer should; his manly head is tilted back to allow his stentorian voice free exit, and his gold-laced arm moves first toward the moving column of passengers, and then is brought with majestic sweep across his manly breast, with index finger extended toward his left shoulder. At this point the alderman takes up the last note of his chief, and in cracked and husky thunder tones bellows, "To de right fo' de T—— House." Not till the last passenger has left the plank do these worthies cease their almost superhuman efforts to drown the clarion notes of the opposition runner; and then our alderman strips off his coat to handle baggage, and battle afresh with the minion of the rival house. Each was trying one morning to get his baggage first from the great pile of trunks, and after sundry vigorous elbowings and hunchings of each other, the alderman brought a prolonged dispute to a summary termination by bursting out with: "Wot's mine's mine; wot's yourn's yourn. Dat's all 'bout it, now."

Opposite Alexandria Bay, at the foot of Wells' Island, lies Westminster Park, founded four years ago by a Presbyterian association, of which the Rev. Dr. Herrick Johnson was president. To call it, however, a denominational watering - place, would be now incorrect, for it differs from the other resorts among the Thousand Islands only in the facts that the unsold lots are owned by the Westminster Park Association, that Sunday excursion parties are not permitted to land or disturb the quiet of its peaceful Sabbaths, and that the liquor traffic is entirely prohibited. The association has erected a chapel upon the summit of Mount Beulah, just behind the hotel, and its tower, rising

CHAPEL ON MOUNT BEULAH, WESTMINSTER PARK.

and imposing hotels of Alexandria Bay, and to the left, beyond the rocky points of La Rue and Club islands, are the eight houses clustered upon the Canadian mainland, which international courtesy requires us to recognize as the village and custom-house station of Rockport. At our feet, just clear of the lines of trees, stands our hotel, the "Westminster," and here was our summer home. The location is unquestionably the finest in the Thousand Islands. For over a century a lovely little bay, jutting into the lower end of Wells' Island, has been marked by the river pilots by a group of five poplar-trees upon its banks, and hence took the name of Poplar Bay. It looks out upon a great sheet of water, three miles wide and several miles long, studded with islands, whose craggy sides are gray with lichen, spangled with mossy cushions, and belted fantastically across with long seams, out of which grow ferns and wild flowers that none can ever hope to touch with human fingers. At the head of Poplar Bay, and close to the group of poplars, the location of this hotel was settled upon. From one piazza the guests may watch the distant form of an occasional steamer toiling slowly along near the Canadian shore on her long journey from Montreal to Toronto, and wonder at the strange and rapid prismatic changes constantly taking place in the appearance of the waters of the bay. From the two other piazzas he gets a view of the American shore, and Alexandria Bay with its beautifully improved islands. One of these islands, now called "Fairy-land," has more than ordinary interest, not only for its beauty and the adornment which the taste of its owners has added, but for the circumstances connected with its adornment. The story was told me as follows: A wealthy family from Columbus, Ohio, brought an invalid

above the dense mass of forest trees crowning the eminence, is a landmark for many miles around. From this tower is one of the finest views to be had anywhere. Over one hundred islands may be seen from this point dotting the broad expanse of water. Down the river the sweep of vision extends till the woody sides of Dark Island and the high flat top of Corn Island shut off the view. Behind lies that singular and lovely sheet of water, the "Lake of the Isles"—a lake within a river, of which we shall see more presently. To the right are the white houses

POPLAR BAY.

daughter to the islands in an almost hopeless search for health. She was so weak that friends were required to carry her in arms, but before the season was over she had experienced so marked an improvement from this remarkably ozone-laden air that an island summer home was decided upon. This island was purchased, and two brothers built upon it each his house. The invalid began a systematic and carefully considered course of exercise in rowing. By degrees her strength came back. Everything that love could suggest and wealth purchase was added to her island home to make it beautiful. Grounds were tastefully laid out; summer-houses, observatories, and rambles were built; docks, boat-houses, and bathing-houses were constructed. By courtesy of the occupants a party of us was permitted to land, and roam over the island. It was a fairy-land. Art had gone just far enough. Nature had been adapted to man just far enough, and left unmolested for the rest. A trim little steam-yacht, the property of the two families, was lying at the little dock. Nothing was lacking to make her complete, not even an organ, which we fancied we could hear accompanying the chorus of happy voices as the boat ploughed the water. And all this outlay and loving care had brought its full recompense and reward, for the daughter was well again; and now every summer brings these families back, and each season sees "Fairy-land" grow more and more suggestive of its even now appropriate name.

Near by is Manhattan Island, and very near is Hart's, and down the river a little is Packer's, and over on the American shore, upon a headland, behind which just enough water flows to make it an island, is Bonnie Castle, the summer home of the celebrated author Dr. J. G. Holland. The symmetry and beauty of his home are suggestive of the grace and tenderness of "Bittersweet," while its solidity and practical air call back the stanch virility of "Timothy Titcomb's Letters to Young Men." Dr. Holland has the prettiest place among the Thousand Islands. Manhattan Island is composed of three islands, if you will pardon the Hibernicism. Three little islands are joined together by pretty rustic bridges thrown across the dividing channels, and these form the settlement known as Manhattan Island. At Packer's Island three insular fragments make a unit in a similar manner. The latter is owned by the family of the late Judge Packer, whose beneficent life and munificent testamentary disposition of his vast estate have won such proud and just distinction. At night the islands which are built upon present a beautiful spectacle. Many of them have adopted devices contrived by means of colored lights. One is a heart, others are anchors, crosses, stars, and circles, and their effect is extremely beautiful, reflected upon the smooth surface of the river. A little further up the river is Pullman's Island, where the palace-car inventor has erected a handsome chalet. Opposite Clayton is Governor's Island, the summer home of ex-Lieutenant-Governor Alvord.

Three miles below Cape Vincent is Carleton Island, where a number of stone chimneys attract the attention. These are the ruins of a fort built by the British troops during the Revolution. The stone parapet, and the ditch cut in the limestone rock, still mark the outlines of the fort. Three more historic incidents of minor interest are connected with these islands. Grenadier Island, nearly opposite Alexandria Bay, became during the war of 1812 a refuge in storm for the un-

lucky expedition fitted out at Sackett's Harbor, under General Wilkinson, for the proposed capture of Montreal. It was an ill-advised affair. The expedition was storm-stayed on Grenadier some time, and finally proceeded down the river to Chrysler's Farm, near the Long Sault, where the undertaking terminated with the defeat of the American army. The guide-books point out the battle-ground, which may be seen from the steamer's deck. The second was the war of Grindstone Island, a boundary dispute in 1823, at which time an earth-work, yet visible, was thrown up at the foot of that island. And the third was the burning of the Canadian steamer *Sir Robert Peel*, in 1838, by Bill Johnson and a lot of "patriots." Everybody who comes here must hear this story, with all its apocryphal incidents, and take a look at the dock on Wells' Island where the vessel was burned—and therefore I forbear.

Many tourists rush through the Thousand Islands by daylight, in true American style, on a big steamer, drop the morning paper or latest novel just long enough to glance over the rail at a pretty vista of channel or a cozy island home, and imagine they have seen the Thousand Islands. Just so the swift Yankee spends fifteen mortal minutes by the watch in "doing" the Louvre, or St. Peter's, or the galleries at Munich. Whoever does that loses one of the most inspiring opportunities of a lifetime. There is only one such archipelago in the world, and no man looking for the gems of nature's handiwork can afford to sail through the Thousand Islands and not know what they are.

To really know what the Thousand Islands are, one should stop among them for at least a week or two, put up at a good hotel, secure a skiff for the term of his stay, and then paddle, paddle, paddle in and out of these beautiful coves and bays, across and through these winding and rock-bound channels, and visit island and promontory and cliff. He must float slowly over this clearest of all water on a calm day, and see the vast aquarium beneath his keel, where six, eight, twelve feet down through the green sparkling river is such an under-water garden as the wildest fancy never dared to picture on God's footstool.

The flora of the river-bed is most luxuriant and beautiful. No aquarium was ever constructed by the hand of man equal to

DR. J. G. HOLLAND.

that over which we sail here for miles and miles. The water must be smooth, and the sun needs to shine, but, with these primary conditions, there is offered to a lover of nature a feast of delights that he will remember for many a day. The first aquarium I found among the islands was in the Lake of the Isles. This is located partly in Westminster Park, and is some three miles long and a mile in extreme width. It opens out of Muscalonge Bay, just above the Hotel Westminster, by an outlet so narrow that, except at a given range, it seems as though the high woody hills formed a continuous chain. As our little skiff nears it, a scene of strange wild beauty reveals itself. Straight ahead is the narrow cleft, through which we catch a glimpse of the lake beyond. On one side the crags stand out bare in all their solid roughness, and away up near the top a square jutting rock overhangs like a sentry-box upon a wall. The other side is less precipitous, and we ran our boat alongside, and picked from the face of the rock a huge cushion of moss set richly with delicate ferns and wild flowers that defied our botanical vocabulary. This narrow water-pass is several hundred yards in length, and then we find ourselves in the lake, and shut in on every side with rocky cliffs or heavily wooded hills. The lake is entirely within Wells' Island, except for three-fourths of a mile at its

THE RIFT—ENTRANCE TO THE LAKE OF THE ISLES.

mouth, where La Rue Island crowds up toward its larger sister, and forms the western boundary of its outlet. Thus is formed a lake within a river, while within the lake are a number of small islands. Upon one little rocky island we saw a curious outline, which, on closer approach, proved to be a solitary tree, whose double trunk had divided and shot upward, then died, and all the branches dropped away, leaving a perfect stringless lyre, around whose frame the wild vines had twined themselves. We forthwith held a solemn conference, and, with all the gravity of the ancient discoverers, said, "We name this, Lyre Island." This lovely lake has always been to us a favorite resort. One bright day we took our little skiff, a huge hamper of provisions, plenty of reading matter, and last, but not least, our trusty oarsman, Jackson, and went up the lake for a family picnic. A quiet little farm-house stands upon the western shore, whose air of seclusion from and absolute indifference to the rest of this busy world had excited our envy. John, who, like most little men, is nothing if not bold, resolved to pierce the

solitude of this Canadian homestead; and so our boat was pulled up to the shore, and John, with Jackson as a body-guard, proceeded to reconnoitre, while I remained behind with the girls. John and Jackson were gone so long that we had begun to fear that they had fallen among the Anthropophagi before they returned with the intelligence that they had actually rented the farmer's log-cabin for the day, and he and his family were to domicile themselves meantime in the adjoining frame house. The boat was drawn up to the Bailey family mooring, our hamper of goodies carried to the log-house, and we took formal possession. Jackson, who was an excellent plain cook, set himself at work to prepare our repast, and the girls spread the table, while John and I went over to talk with Farmer Bailey. The girls had finished their work, and Jackson his cooking, when we returned to the log-house, and sat down to an excellent dinner, with the cool breezes from the lake blowing through the open doors and windows. It was a repast and an occasion long to be remembered. We were at home in a Canadian farm-house, sitting down to broiled chicken, fresh corn, real cream, and all the intermediates that these imply, looking out upon the glassy surface of the lake, with no sign of human existence visible except immediately about us. The robins were singing merrily in the woods above us, and upon the lake rested a stillness and solitude unbroken except by the screaming of a distant bird of prey, and the low hum of the invisible life about us. Human conception can scarcely equal the visible reality of beauty at the bottom of the Lake of the Isles. Now we look down upon tangled grasses of a hundred rich varieties; again

much-prized black bass is visible. The diversity of scenery under water is equalled only by that of the islands themselves. Further up the lake, behind a headland, stands another log-cabin, which we visited one day. It is owned by a mason named Knell, who works at his trade upon the various islands or at "the Bay," while his broad-shouldered wife conducts family af-

THE SENTINEL—ENTRANCE TO THE LAKE OF THE ISLES.

on slender, graceful ferns; again on mosses that look like pale green coral; and then on tall waving weeds that reach up from their alluvial beds almost to the water's surface, and nod a welcome to our oar-blades just above their heads. Countless fish, which a quiet boatman may watch for hours, roam among these lovely gardens, and in the high weeds the swift pickerel hides, waiting the approach of a tinier fish, at which he darts, and makes a breakfast at one snap of his wide jaws. Anon our boat glides over a vast subaqueous desert, covered with brown rocks, through whose fissures the short dark form of the

fairs. Mrs. Knell thinks nothing of rowing six miles, in any kind of a sea, after a pound of tea, and as her brawny arms pull the heavy skiff, she improves the time by trolling for pickerel, with her line held in her teeth. Remote from settlements, and having no access to the world except by water, there are many weeks in winter when communication is cut off by floating ice or snow too heavy upon the river for a single traveller to make his way, and so this hardy family lay in three months' provisions in the fall, and nothing short of the heavens falling can disturb their equanimity.

A PICNIC.

One of the great attractions of the Thousand Islands is the good fishing. The principal catch is pickerel, which can be taken even by an unskillful fisherman, and is very plentiful. Pickerel are usually taken with a trolling-line from seventy-five to one hundred and fifty feet in length, terminating with what the fishermen call a trolling-spoon. This consists of a stout brass wire to which a spoon-shaped piece of polished metal is fastened so that it can revolve around the wire. Just at the end of the spoon are three stout barbs. The boat being kept in constant motion by the oarsman, the line drags astern its full length, and this motion causes the spoon to spin around its wire axis, and

present the appearance of a little fish swimming. The pickerel from his hiding-place sees his supposed victim flashing through the water, and with one quick plunge seizes the spoon, barbs and all, in his capacious mouth. It is an exciting moment in the boat. The rod bends almost double as the enraged and terrified fish dives, with that infernal machine in his jaws, back to his refuge among the tall weeds. He plunges madly about, lashing the water furiously in his wild struggles for freedom. Often rising to the surface, he bounds clear from the water many feet into the air. Will we land him? If the hooks are not securely fastened, the fierce plunges will free him, as his powerful muscles work against the line which slowly and steadily draws him in. Sometimes he swims with lightning speed up the line, and getting slack line faster than the fisher can take it up, turns suddenly in the opposite direction, and gets a momentum which snaps everything, and restores him to liberty with a bad case of face-ache. As he nears the boat his struggles become more desperate; he darts under it, and beats his body against the keel in sullen rage. Now the work must be carefully done, or he will escape. Slowly and steadily he is drawn to the front, and in a moment more the gaff has struck his side, and he is safe. It is no uncommon record for a skiff containing two persons besides the oarsman to come in, after a day's fishing, with a hundred-weight or more of fish. Excellent still-fishing can be had in almost any of these waters, and by this means most of the black bass are caught. But sitting still, in a small boat at anchor, holding a pole, and watching a "bob," is poor sport compared with trolling for pickerel in and out of bay and cove, skirting rocky cliffs and grassy slopes, and drinking in the rare and ever-changing beauties of nature in this Garden of the Great Father. This may be a sorry confession that I am an unscientific fisherman, but the world nowadays gives its thirsty children such immense draughts of science and such tiny sips of nature that some of us enjoy an occasional mixture of nature and science more than taking the latter unadulterated —especially in the matter of fish.

One of the best of days' sport is to be had upon a fishing picnic. These enjoyable affairs come off from Westminster Park every few days. A party of ten to twenty-five ladies and gentlemen set off in a steam-yacht for some distant fishing-ground, taking liberal supplies from the hotel, and half as many oarsmen as there are excursionists. Each oarsman takes his own skiff and fishing-tackle, the skiffs being towed in single file behind the yacht, presenting the appearance of a marine kite with a very long tail. On one of these picnics we went some ten miles up the river to Stave Island. Here the yacht was run up to the shore, and the party separated, each skiff taking a different direction, with the understanding that we should rendezvous again at the yacht at half past twelve. At the appointed hour the fishers returned, and the oarsmen set at work preparing dinner. The yacht carried boards for tables, and

IN CANADIAN WATERS.

the island furnished rocks to support them, as well as for seats. A fire-place was quickly improvised out of more rocks, and the savory odors of a hot dinner for a hungry company soon mingled with the piny odors from the woods.

Meanwhile one of the young ladies and I set off on an exploring expedition. Opposite Stave Island is a little wild-looking island, covered with tangled undergrowth, and seeming to defy the inquisitiveness of man. Running our skiff upon the rocks, and climbing up the bowlders that fringed its shores, we found shells among the bushes, which seemed so strangely out of place that we resolved to push exploration still further. Over beds of moss and fallen trees and crags of rock we slowly made our way, till, at the upper end of the little island, beneath a group of taller trees, we came upon the ruins of a little log-cabin. We could distinctly trace the dimensions of the hut. The logs, with bark unpeeled, lay in crumbling lines to mark the sides and ends; the stones of the fireplace were thrown down on the spot where once they had stood erect; but there was no pathway to the hut, and no landing-place anywhere upon the island. Why had this mysterious being built his house in so forbidding a spot, when Stave Island, close by, furnished sites more eligible? Why this seclusion? What was the secret of this strange abode? Was it some smuggler, some fugitive from justice, or only some man aweary of the wicked world, who had lived in this solitude? We debated these questions at dinner, without further result than to respectfully refer them to the readers of the Magazine, and to change the name of the island from Little Stave to Hermit Island.

The afternoon was spent by many lovers of the sport in fishing, while others had their picnic in the woods, or took a siesta in the cabin of the yacht. When the slanting rays gave warning of the close of day, the yacht's whistle called back the scattered boating parties, and we were off for home. The homeward course lay through the minor Canadian channels, where the islands are thicker than at any other point. Nothing I ever saw equalled the beauty of this scene. Hundreds of islands lay along and across our winding and zigzag course, no two of which were alike. It was an intricate labyrinth of channels, out of which none but an experienced pilot could steer. At times our little craft seemed to be in a lake but a few acres in extent, tightly hemmed in by sloping hills. The next minute she would be running between two rocky cliffs whose sides could almost be touched from the deck, while just ahead the land shut off further progress. Suddenly a channel opened to our left behind a rocky headland, and we were again upon a broad expanse of water, with islands clustering about us, and a dozen different channels, like so many noble rivers, disclosed to our delighted eyes. In this labyrinth are "Lost Channel"—most appropriately named—and "Fiddler's Elbow," a channel which turns sharply between the rocks.

Land days at Westminster Park are scarcely less delightful than water days. The grounds embrace a great variety of woodland, where forest trees grow tall and thick, and deer run wild, and game abounds, while nearer the haunts of men numerous groves of maple and oak and birch flutter their invitation to swing a hammock, or organize a picnic in their alluring shade. Thirty miles of drives have been laid out, and more are in progress. Under the trees near Mount Beulah is the spot where Captain Kidd was supposed to have buried his treasure, and so firmly was this conviction implanted in the native breast that it is but a few years since they ceased digging for his mythical loot. The grounds contain a crystal spring, whose waters are far superior to those of the river, which alone furnishes the drinking water for most other resorts in this region.

The air of the Thousand Islands is heavily charged with ozone, whose first effect is to induce a delicious drowsiness, helping us amazingly to forget the harassing cares of the business we left behind. The acknowledged wholesome effect of this air upon consumptives is due, however, not only to the ozone, but also to the piny breezes blowing across the vast Canadian forests, and gathering new richness from the woods of the islands themselves. The island air is, moreover, remarkable for its dryness. The ladies may play croquet, in slippers, in the early morning without gathering any dampness from the grass; and neither piazzas nor hammocks threaten their occupants, even at night, with rheumatism or ague. Excellent bathing can be had at many points where sandy beaches are found;

and as for boats, fifty cents a day will hire a first-class skiff, fitted with comfortable arm-chairs and cushioned seats. In the season there is good duck-shooting upon the river, the birds being mostly of the teal variety. Another water-fowl, passing here under the name of loon, but probably misnamed, frequents these waters in the fall of the year, and stories are told of the immense quantities a skillful sportsman may bag, which need to be taken, as the birds are, *cum grano salis.*

In many cases these are no more than bare rocks of half or even a quarter of an acre in extent, and range upward to nine miles in length. Their foundations are mostly granite overlaid with limestone, and in many places with Potsdam sandstone, through which long fissures have been made by some great upheaval, and these are filled with molten rock, coal, quartz, and copper and iron ore. The volcanic matter is, in many cases, imperfectly fused, and excellent specimens

LIGHT-HOUSE AT THE ENTRANCE TO LOST CHANNEL.

These make complete the charms of the spot. We have seen many people come and go these three years. We have seen them come for a day, and spend a fortnight, or come to spend a week, and stay the season through. Season after season witnesses their return, until it has passed into a proverb that he who comes for one season to the Thousand Islands becomes a resident. A clergyman from Indiana passes scores of new watering-places along the great lakes, and spends $150 in railroad fares to bring his family here, and this he has done every year since the park was opened. Whoever gave to this magnificent archipelago the name of the Thousand Islands I do not know, but of his nationality one thing is certain—he was not an American. No typical Yankee was ever yet guilty of such an underestimate of any treasure over which the American eagle had spread its wings.

Common tradition puts the number of islands at 1800, but the official charts show 1692 islands, if we count everything appearing above the surface of the river.

of coal, and copper and iron ore, can be easily obtained. Frequently where the face of a rock thus cleft has been long exposed to the elements, the original sandstone has worn away more rapidly than the volcanic matter, which thus protrudes beyond the edges of the fissure, and at a short distance presents the appearance of a great serpent basking upon the rock. The action of the glacial drift is plainly traceable among these islands. Great drift-grooves are cut into the solid granite many yards in length, several feet deep, and almost always as straight as an arrow, showing where the towering iceplane of centuries ago had caught some huge rock in its under surface, and rasped it with incalculable pressure across the face of its larger sisters. Many of the smaller islands are bare rock, others are covered with a thin earth deposit, which yields a scanty sustenance to the hardier species of tree and plant.

Some rocky islands rise perpendicularly from the water to a considerable height, and yet have a good depth of soil, while

INDIAN CAMP.

health and strength, of happiness and rest, of increased opportunities and capacities for usefulness. Do you wonder that we think we have found the real Lotos Land?

It would be too bad for one to spend a summer among these peaceful shores, where picturesqueness and rest are the traits written over all the land and water, rather than pomp and sublimity, and not see the strongly contrasted features of the river one day's sail below. Here the St. Lawrence holds its Thousand Islands upon a bosom calm and currentless, reflecting back their rocks and trees like a vast mirror. If there be aught but peace and quiet in its clear green tide, it gives no sign thereof to the dwellers among these islands. There is no suggestion here of power or

most, and notably the larger ones, are well covered with arable land, and yield reasonable returns for the slight care which the island farmer bestows upon his agriculture. Hundreds upon hundreds of desirable islands are yet uninhabited, and of those which are improved as summer homes almost all are in American waters. For forty miles along the River St. Lawrence the islands extend, beginning at the outlet of Lake Ontario. The international boundary line divides them into two unequal portions, giving the larger share to our Canadian cousins. The American islands are owned by private citizens, but the Canadian government holds titles to almost all those situated on its side of the line. The water of the dividing channels is in some cases one hundred and twenty feet in depth, and ordinary soundings show from thirty to sixty feet. This is the land we call our Lotos Land. Such, briefly and inadequately described, are its manifold attractions. Every season we bring a widening circle of friends within their influence, and every succeeding season they too become missionaries in the same good cause—the cause of

purpose in the flood. But, fifty miles below us, all this aspect changes. Here, presumptuous man imagines himself master of the sluggish tide which invites his lazy dreams; there, he knows what pigmies men and their proudest inventions are in the grip of Nature's mighty forces, when they have once roused from their habitual slumber to do her bidding.

Twenty-eight miles below Ogdensburg we enter the Long Sault, nine miles in length, through which the mighty flood runs at the rate of twenty miles an hour. During part of this distance the descent is so rapid that you enjoy the sensation of perceptibly sailing down hill on a big steamer at a tremendous speed. The water is quite smooth, except at four or five places; but there it rushes and eddies and whirls till the angry waters are dashed in massive, foamy billows straight up into the air twelve or fifteen feet, and, unlike the ocean waves, which "travel" and smite a ship with all their strength, these thick and formidable masses of seething water stand there immovable across the steamer's path. When the vessel nears these spots, steam is turned off, four men stand at the wheel in the pilot-house, four more affix an iron tiller to the rudder post to provide against the breaking of the rudder chains, and, propelled only by the current, she plunges in among those heaving snow heaps, where she sways and shivers and careens till you cling to the rail and shout with enthusiasm, or hold your breath for fear, according to the sort of nerves which Providence and your own habits have given you. Comparatively few people are afflicted with fear, however, the sensation caused by the stanch and trusty steamer buffeting with the angry waves being usually exhilarating, aside from the impression created by the grandeur of the waters.

Around each rapid a canal is built, by means of which the large steamers return, and through which smaller craft proceed both ways. Indeed, no vessels venture through the rapids, I believe, except the large passenger steamers carrying tourists.

Between the Long Sault and Montreal the river twice widens into a lake. One of these, Lake St. Francis, is thirty miles long and twelve miles wide. The other, Lake St. Louis, not so large, is just above the Lachine Rapids, which are the most difficult and dangerous of the entire series. Between Lake St. Francis and Lake St. Louis are three rapids, named respectively the Coteau, Cedars, and Cascades, all of which are very grand, though similar in aspect to the Long Sault.

Excursion trains run from Montreal twice daily connecting with the rapids steamer, the round trip consuming an hour and a half.

An Indian pilot is taken on board the large steamers at Lachine, ostensibly for the purpose of guiding the vessel through the dangerous channel, but really for the purpose of making an impression upon the traveller. The fall of the river here is much greater than at any of the preceding rapids, and the channel is so narrow that at one point the steamer passes between two low walls of black rock, plainly visible beneath a thin covering of rushing water, and but a few feet from her sides. Within these narrow limits the water rushes and surges with appalling

RUNNING THE RAPIDS.

speed, estimated by some authorities at forty miles an hour, while the surface of the river beyond is several feet higher than the channel along which we are being whirled at a dizzy speed, as through a veritable valley in the water. So rapid is our speed that only a few minutes elapse before we are again in smooth water; and as the steamer passes beneath the great spans of Victoria Bridge, we look back upon the mad waves of that mighty flood, rolling onward as it has through all the centuries, the safety-valve and overflow of vast inland seas and water-courses, feeling that we have seen the most stupendous system of water-works ever devised.

A GLIMPSE OF MONTREAL.

The Orange Lake
Ice-Yacht Club
(1899)

THE ORANGE LAKE ICE-YACHT CLUB
AND ITS RIVALS.

BY H. PERCY ASHLEY.

ORANGE LAKE I.Y.C.

DARK, cold and glistening looked Orange Lake as we followed the winding path, and on Pine Point the club-house, with its coronet of electric lights, loomed in sight. To the eastward lay the ice-yacht fleet in their brave panoply of gleaming spars and silver-plated iron-work, reflected in the rising moon's rays. Away to the northeastward it is dark, except for the bright lights of the Oak Point Club and an occasional gleam from the watchman's lantern as he makes his rounds of the now deserted summer cottages and hotels. To the northward, outside of the ice-yacht racing course, there is a shining and flickering light on the polished surface of the lake that can be no other than "Monk," the unfreezable, clad in his white flannel suit, making his nightly rounds of his fishing tip-ups.

I am aroused from my reverie by Boxer's genial voice: "Come in, old man. It is the Squire's evening at home, and the ice-yachts will keep until to-morrow morning." How natural and inviting the old place looks: the oak-paneled hall, with the dining-room to the right, shining with spotless damask, cut glass and electric lights; to the left, the grill-room, with its bright log fire.

The old racing crowd are all there, ready to make a daring and gamy struggle to defend their trophies; and as the hearty hand-shake is extended, and the celebrated Orange punch is served, and the fragrant tobacco smoke curls ceilingward to the strum, strum of Frank Taylor's banjo, I see the tried and true racing ice-yachtsmen, "Esquire" Boxer, "Doc" Woddie, "Steb," "Captain Bob," "Trum," H. S. R. and a score of others.

But I have not come to pass so cozy a night; I want to see the boats. So, clad in a pair of rubber hip-boots, corduroy breeches, a heavy sweater and reefing-jacket, I cross the board-walk to the lake front. Straight to the east by south I follow the path cut on the ice by Luna; and with creepers firmly strapped to my feet, I pass the three-quarters of a mile of patches of black shell-ice and slight snow-reefs to where the fleet lie, closely huddled under Oak Point bluff.

Stark and gaunt is the big *Windward*, the flagship of the fleet. She carries nearly seven hundred square feet of duck, and her scientifically curved back-bone of forty-eight feet in one stick substantiates her reputation of being one of the most powerful boats on the ice.

SOME OF THE ORANGE LAKE ICE-YACHT CLUB MEMBERS.

Near her, five runner spans to starboard, is the new *Cold Wave*, rigged as a sloop. Both boats are in the pink of perfection, as their gleaming spars, silvered iron-work, tuned-up shrouds with tightly-laced sail-covers and steering-box awnings show.

Around them are gathered the flower of the fleet in the same perfect condition; and as the big oaks from the bluff cast their shadows over the patch of black ice, I see as clearly as engraved on steel Vice-Commodore Willett Kidd's pennant-winner *Snowdrift*, four hundred and eighty-six square feet; Frank Woods' smart *Flying Jib*, of three hundred and eighty-five square feet; Capt. Bob Kernahan's (one of the most hardy ice-boat sailors) *Troubler*, carrying five hundred and twenty-three square feet; Charles M. Stebbins' *Ice King*, five hundred and thirty-eight square feet, and the lateen *Graziella*, with her wish-bone saucily raked forward, sitting well up on the horses. Here, too, are two new and yet thoroughly untried boats, one of

"BREEZE," OF THE KINGSTON, ONTARIO, ICE-YACHT CLUB. (*p. 412.*)

Buckhout's production, the slick *Æolus*, owned by the thorough sportsman George E. Trimble, carrying three hundred square feet, with her new backbone (shaped like a spar), and by E. Walsh's new boat, the *Arctic*, designed by the owner, with four hundred and eighty square feet of duck to her credit; and closely to port is H. S. Ramsdell's *Esquimaux*, surrounded by a galaxy of lesser stars.

The *Æolus* is a very handsome boat for her size, with selected pine backbone and runner-plank. Her dimensions are, back-bone twenty-eight feet; height at runner-plank ten inches, at ends five inches; length of steering-box eight feet, of Hudson River design; mainsail: on boom twenty feet, hoist eleven feet, gaff eleven feet, leech twenty-three and three-quarters; jib: hoist twelve feet, foot ten feet, on stay sixteen feet.

As I recline on the starboard butternut runner-plank of my favorite, the *Cold Wave*, I wonder why,

a few miles of Orange Lake. Then there are the New Hamburg Club and Carthage, both on the Hudson, and within short distance. The North Shrewsbury is not far away with her crack fleet of twenty-eight yachts, including the champion lateen *Georgie*. Over in Canada, too, are a score of clubs, the most prominent being the Kingston, Ontario; and in the West is the Lake Pepin, Wis., including Commodore Anderson's crack ice-yachts *Lorna* and *Irene*, which have made the fastest official time over a twenty-mile course for third class and Eastern records.

A gathering from these sources on Orange Lake would test, and mayhap settle, many of the new ideas of sail, rig and improvements; and, though each club claims to have the fastest yachts, there has not yet been a race between competitive organizations since 1893, when Commodore Archibald Rogers' first-

"ÆOLUS."

with the poor ice on the Hudson and Shrewsbury in the past few years, the owners of the boats of those districts do not come up to Orange Lake, where they are sure of the ice, and where there are brother sportsmen always ready for a friendly brush for cup or fun.

The classes most suited to the lake are the second or third: the second class carrying four hundred and fifty and under six hundred square feet; the third class carrying three hundred and under four hundred and fifty. The Hudson River I. Y. C. alone has twenty-one boats in these two classes, all within

class yacht *Jack Frost*, of Hudson River I. Y. C., on their course, won from the challenger, *Shadow*, of Orange Lake I. Y. C., over the Hudson River course, the ice challenge pennant of America. This boat won the same prize in 1887. In 1888, 1889, 1892 it was won by the *Icicle*, with her owner, J. A. Roosevelt. at the stick.

This champion challenge of the world means to ice yachtsmen what the *America's* Cup signifies to salt-water yachtsmen. It is the emblem of supremacy on the ice. Many and sturdy have aforetime been the battles for its possession

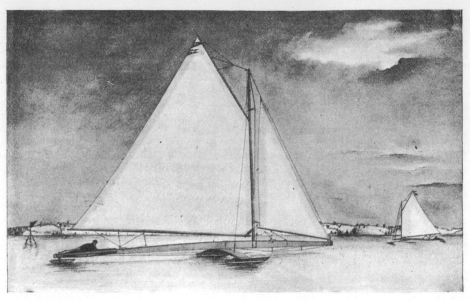

"WINDWARD."   (p. 408.)

between the devotees of the sport on the Hudson, between the Shrewsbury and Orange Lake Clubs and their brethren of the Hudson River I. Y. C. Commodore Rogers has won it three times with the *Jack Frost*, and Mr. Roosevelt three times with *Icicle*. (See table of OUTING, January, 1898, page 399.)

The prospect of such a renewal of contest leads me to remark that there are several bad rules governing this pennant. For instance, suppose a boat challenges for a certain class, why in the name of common sense should a dozen or a few less boats sail against her? If the champion pennant is again raced for, the Hudson River Club, I hope, will select only one boat, provided the challenging club enters one boat. Notice of the selection should be given twelve hours before the time fixed for the start, otherwise the defender will have a chance to select either a light or heavy weather boat against the challenger.

Other questions than actual superiority of one boat over another would be settled by a united meeting, for instance, that of actual speed. The *Jack Frost*, of the Hudson River I. Y. C., owned by Richard Rogers, is champion of the world, and carrying seven hundred and sixteen square feet of canvas, made the twenty miles of Hudson River

Photo by R. W. Brigstocke.

"WHISTLEWING" SAILING FORTY MILES AN HOUR.

course in 49 minutes 30 seconds, although the actual distance sailed was 31.38 at an apparent rate per mile of 2 minutes 28 seconds, equal to a calculated and actual rate per mile of 1 minute and 34 seconds. Against this time the little *Lorna*, at Lake Pepin, carrying four hundred and four feet of sail, made twenty miles in 39 minutes 7 seconds; actual distance sailed, in light wind, forty-one miles. When this time is applied to such large yachts as *Jack Frost*, *Icicle* and *Windward*, it must be remembered that they have never had a course with long enough legs to determine their true speed. For instance, take the *Reindeer*, which carries seven hundred and thirty-one square feet of sail. When she was taken from the Hudson River to the first-class course at Lake Minnetonka, Minn., her speed was apparently greatly increased; for the simple reason that to make the twenty miles on the Hudson the course has to be sailed over five times, whereas on the Western courses of twenty miles, two or three times around is sufficient, and every time a large boat goes about so much more is added to her time in covering the course. Then, too, the

questions of rigging, back-bone, runner-plank, and sail area would all receive valuable elucidation.

Among the Canadian boats which we would like to see at Orange is Howard Folger's new *Breeze*, an up-to-date Canadian ice-yacht hailing from the Kingston I. Y. C. She has a perfect-fitting suit of sails with Hudson-River runners. Then we should see the champion of the Kingston I. Y. C., ex-Vice-Commodore W. C. Kent's *Whistlewing*, carrying three hundred and ninety-five square feet of sail. Sanford Calvin might send his slick boat the *Blizzard;* she is a fair representative of the up-to-date Canadian racing ice-yacht of bridge up-plank and elliptical cockpit, with Canadian runners.

There are two important trophies of the Orange Lake Club; one is the Walker International Challenge Cup, now held by the *Spook*, of Cape Vincent I. Y. C., and the other is the new trophy yet unraced for, presented to the club by Commodore Calvin and Vice-Commodore Macnee. It is known as the Calvin-Macnee Trophy, and is a handsome and massive silver plate. Others would be quickly forthcoming.

A Former Bit of
New England
(1903)

FISHER'S ISLAND
a former bit of NEW ENGLAND

BY
HENRY
ROBINSON
PALMER

lies within three miles of the Connecticut shore, but belongs to the state of New York. The three states of Rhode Island, New York and Connecticut converge near the eastern end of Long Island Sound, where Napatree Point, Fisher's Island and the borough of Stonington are within a league of each other. Fisher's Island winds east and west eight miles and is in daily communication by steamer with the city of New London, but it is part of the town of Southold on Long Island. After every election a messenger is sent with the returns to the village of that name; and when the weather is too stormy for him to cross from New London to Greenport, he has to go around by way of New York City. This makes a journey of five hundred miles, and is one of the reasons why the island may some day petition to be a separate township. It has fifty registered voters, and the number is steadily increasing. The winter population is estimated at four hundred, including the laborers on the govern-

E VERY island is by nature independent. It may ally itself with the mainland for political reasons or the purposes of trade, but it maintains a separate life and social organization. Wants that would be supplied on the mainland by calling on some neighboring community must here be met at home. Facility of communication is not an unmixed blessing. It encourages dependence and discourages ingenuity. Defoe's hero did not enjoy all the comforts but he cultivated self-reliance. When darkness falls on an island, it is shut off by the sea as was the mediæval castle by its moat. It becomes a world by itself, self-centred and apart.

Of all the islands that skirt the New England coast, there are few pleasanter than Fisher's Island, which

ment fortifications; and the summer population at fifteen hundred.

From the Connecticut shore, Fisher's Island looks like a barren waste, with few trees and many sloping hills. These lie bare and brown in the sunlight—chief among them Chocomount, which rises to the height of one hundred and thirty-six feet. It is visible for many miles north of the coast and can be seen from beyond Montauk at the south. It has for the lover of nature a constant air of dignity and beauty, and there are times

The visitor to Fisher's Island should go to New London and take the steamer *Munnatawket*, Captain Nash, from that city. The boat makes several trips a day in the summer season, but crosses only once in twenty-four hours in the winter, remaining over night at her snug island wharf. She can cover fourteen knots an hour, but usually takes from thirty-five to forty minutes to make the seven miles from dock to dock.

The sail is charming, for New London harbor is one of the most beau-

THE ISLAND FROM THE WATER

when it takes on, in common with its lesser hills, a gorgeous tint of purple, and when it floats in a mirage above the shimmering sea. It is bleak, even at closer range, but there is nothing in the pleasant sweep of surrounding landscape more inspiring. Seen from the sea wall at Stonington as the sun sets, it puts on varied tints, from brightest gold to deepest brown; and as darkness falls, the light on Latimer's reef comes out in range of it and shines like a diamond against its lofty background.

tiful on the coast, and Fisher's Island Sound, whether in turquoise or opal, is ever ready to lure the eye. Up the Thames, as the steamer leaves her wharf, may be seen the high hills of Ledyard and Montville. On the west bank is the city, built on sloping hills, with Fort Trumbull, an antiquated piece of masonry, and the Pequot summer colony, beyond. On the east rises the village of Groton, crowned by its monument, which marks the site of the massacre of 1781. The low mounds of Fort Griswold may still be

THE WINTER SETTLEMENT

seen, silent witnesses to the dreadful carnage that Benedict Arnold inflicted on his native county. Below Groton is Eastern Point, set, like the Pequot settlement, in the midst of lawns and trees.

Emerging from the Thames, the *Munnatawket* crosses the ever changing, ever beautiful sheet of water that separates Fisher's Island from the main shore. The Connecticut villages of Poquonoc, Noank, Mystic and Stonington come one by one into view. Beyond them at the north is Lantern Hill, the highest point in the southeastern part of the state, which rises nearly six hundred feet above the level of the sea and is descried by incoming sailors before Montauk looms into sight. The scene is one of a great variety of color. Poquonoc nestles in its quiet valley, Noank and Mystic flaunt their gay roofs from leafy hills, and Stonington, with its white houses close by the water's edge, shines like a snowy cliff in the distance. At the east are Napatree Point and the great hotels of Watch Hill boldly defined against the ho-

rizon. On clear days even Block Island can be seen beyond them, and Montauk with its white lighthouse at the south. Westward the glance includes the wide waters of Long Island Sound.

Fisher's Island takes on new beauties as we approach it. Where at first there seemed to be only brown hills are all the varied hues of the typical New England upland. Every valley breaks forth in green, with oaks and birches in full leaf, and every barren slope assumes the brilliant colors of its tangled vines and bushes, and, in the autumn, the sunny tint of the golden rod. When the summer guests are gone and the island has settled down to its annual quiet, a journey across the sound and a few days' visit apart from the noise and bustle of the mainland are invigorating. The little steamer reaches her wharf in the late afternoon with half a dozen passengers—housewives who have been shopping in New London, a government engineer or two returning from a consultation with Major Leach—people who do not think it a hardship

WEST HARBOR

to come away from the outside world at nightfall, but are glad to get back to the snug little island. If it were merely a summer resort, it might be desolate in the autumn; but it has a winter as well as a summer life, and its proprietors are doing what they can to attract permanent residents. The district school has fifty scholars, and the "socials" at the Union Chapel bring out a company even in midwinter that fills the house.

One of the first surprises for the stranger as the *Munnatawket* reaches her wharf in West Harbor is a modern electric lighting plant, housed in brick and representing an outlay of twenty thousand dollars. Fisher's Island would not have such a modern institution if it were not for the intelligent enterprise of its principal owners, Messrs. E. M. and W. Ferguson, who purchased the island in 1889. It is reported that the purchase price was not far from a quarter of a million dollars and that they have spent an equal amount in betterments.

From the wharf the road winds across level ground to the Mansion House, a hotel owned by the Messrs. Ferguson and managed by A. T. Hale, formerly of New London. The Munnatawket House, near by, is also the property of the Fergusons and is run by Mr. Hale, but closes its doors at the end of the summer season, while the Mansion House remains open all winter. A third hotel, the Mononotto Inn, is situated nearer the west end of the island, and is the property of Mrs. M. B. Hoppes of Bethlehem, Pennsylvania. This, like the Munnatawket, is a modern hotel and popular with summer guests, but does not keep open during the winter. The vistor is surprised to find an inn of the quality of the Mansion House ready to serve the public at all seasons of the year. Who, he wonders, comes to Fisher's Island in midwinter? Where is the profit in running such a hotel after the summer season has closed? That is one of the secrets of the Messrs. Ferguson. It is an open secret, however. They are bound that the island shall have modern accommodations at all times of the year. They are building for the

MOUNT PROSPECT

future. All the stranger is required to do is to make himself comfortable. The last time the writer visited the island was at evening of a lowering autumn day; but the electric lights in the hotel shone out across the hospitable piazza, and the office was bright and warm, with a wood fire burning in the old-fashioned grate. At dinner there was a pleasant air of cleanliness and homeliness. The windows were hung with snowy muslin curtains, and there was a blossoming geranium in each of the window seats. There are more desolate places than Fisher's Island for a January outing or a midwinter honeymoon.

Down the street from the Mansion House is Post Office Square, dignified with a new stucco building built by the Messrs. Ferguson for the accommodation of their varied business interests and the government mail service. Postmaster Gordon has a "fourth-class office with first-class facilities." On the other side of the building are the Ferguson offices, where the firm transacts its dairy, farm and real estate business. There are three Ferguson farms, occupying the greater part of the island. They produce the usual dairy products, and

send butter to many places, including Pittsfield, Hartford, New London, Stamford and New York. But the Ferguson specialty is fine poultry. Pheasants, Belgian and English hares and ducks are raised, and the eastern part of the island is overrun with rabbits. The Ferguson poultry has taken many prizes at the leading exhibitions of recent years. At the Boston show in 1898 the island won fourteen first prizes, and at the New York show ten. Fifty-dollar specimens of blooded poultry are a regular product. The island produces hay of a fine quality; but as there is no compressor for it, none is exported. In years gone by this was the principal export, and the government might do a profitable business in this line if it would culti-

THE SCHOOLHOUSE

vate its meadows at the west end. It owns more than two hundred acres, the bulk of which was obtained by condemnation proceedings in 1898. The price paid is understood to have been about a thousand dollars an acre, or nearly as much for the whole as the island cost in 1889.

On this property the government engineers are completing large emplacements, which will be an important link in the fortifications designed to protect Long Island Sound. From Long Island to the Connecticut shore an insular chain extends, consisting in order of Plum, Great and Little Gull and Fisher's Islands. "Indian tradition points to no remote time when Plum Island was connected with Long, and there is not a doubt that Fisher's was once part of the encircling reef which made the sound a true Mediterranean." The reef does not end with Fisher's, but continues eastward to Watch Hill Point, between which and Fisher's Island it is well defined. Vessels occasionally are wrecked upon it, and fishermen have found submerged among its rocks the stumps and roots of trees. Taught by the Spanish war, the government is sparing no cost to protect the shores of Long Island and Connecticut from the ravages of a foreign fleet and make fast the "back door" of New York. At Napatree Point, Rhode Island, the work is finished and the mouth of the sound will soon be safe from Montauk to Stonington. On Fisher's Island there are to be several heavy guns, some of them modern rifles with disappearing carriages. At the extreme west end has been placed a fifteen-inch dyna-

mite gun powerful enough to hurl an eight-foot projectile weighing nearly six hundred pounds a mile and a half. It is believed that there will be a large permanent garrison on Fisher's Island, as it is better suited to the maintenance of a strong force than any other of the islands at the mouth of the sound. In the past Fisher's Island Sound has been the rendezvous of the North Atlantic squadron, and blue-jackets from the ships have practised field manœuvres on shore.

The island is chiefly settled at the west end, because this lies nearest to New London. There are fifty or sixty cottages on the high ground overlooking Hay Harbor; but the east end is equally desirable for hotel and cottage sites and lies nearer the mainland. From the east end the view of the ocean is beautiful. If the proposed trolley line running the length of the island should be built, the land between East Point and Chocomount would at once be brought into the market.

There is a pleasant country road that runs along the island, and a good livery stable at the west end, where a stout horse and comfortable carriage can be obtained. The visitor, even in midwinter, should not return to the mainland without driving as far east as Chocomount. The road winds up hill and down dale, across barren moors and through wooded glens. There are sections of it so overgrown with oaks and birches that in summer one hesitates to believe that he is on a wind swept island, especially Fisher's Island, which looks so bare and brown from the Connecticut shore. It skirts the base of Chocomount and at every turn presents a new glimpse of undulating meadow, glistening lake or the encompassing sea. The great gale of 1815, the most terrific in New England history, swept away a forest that covered the island hillsides. Aged persons still living remember it and the havoc it caused on Fisher's Island. A former resident says that when he first went there thirty-five years ago there were thirty or forty acres of land covered with stumps of trees, the wreckage of the great tempest. The same memorable gale stripped Block Island of its trees, devastated much woodland on the main shore and carried the spray miles inland, where it whitened the window panes of the farmhouses.

Fisher's Island's lakes and ponds are one of its most striking features. They are thirty or more in number and ninety acres in extent. Island Lake, the largest, of which a picture is given in this article, contains forty or fifty acres

EPISCOPAL CHURCH

UNION CHAPEL

and is stocked with bass. It is strange, in driving along the road to Chocomount, to find the highway pass between two lakes that are only a few feet apart and yet of differing levels. Some of these bodies of fresh water extend close to the ocean or sound, so that it is hard to tell from a distance whether they are actually fresh water or arms of the sea. It is supposed that they are fed by springs having subterranean connection with the hill country of Connecticut. The government laborers in digging for the emplacements at the west end have found the fresh water bubbling up from the ground with great force, as if from a miniature geyser; and there is a famous spring at the base of Chocomount, which is covered at high tide by the sea.

It is difficult to say when a white man first caught sight of Fisher's Island. Perhaps Thorwald visited it in the year 1003. In 1524 the Florentine voyager Verrazano skirted the southern coast of Long Island from the west and named Block Island "Luisa" after the mother of Francis I of France, in whose service he sailed. It is possible that he and his crew saw the brown hillsides of Fisher's Island on the horizon, if they did not set foot upon the shore. It is thought that the Portuguese Gomez sailed through Long Island Sound a year or two later, in which case he probably caught a glimpse of it. But

NORTH HILL

it is certain that in 1614 Captain Adrian Block discovered the island, for he charted it on the map he presented to the Staats General in 1616. It is said that he named it Visscher's Island in honor of one of his companions— from which the change to the present Anglicized form was easy. The Indians called it Munnatawket, and an early English name for it was Sandy Island. Munnatawket signifies an outlook. The third syllable occurs in the word Montauk, the name of the bold promontory at the eastern end of Long Island.

The younger John Winthrop, son of the governor of Massachusetts and himself at a later date the governor of Connecticut, was in command of the English forces at Saybrook in the year 1635. During his residence there he became familiar with the Pequot country, within the borders of which Fisher's Island is situated. He obtained a grant of the island from Massachusetts, October 7, 1640, though the General Court inserted a proviso in the grant which shows it was uncertain of its jurisdiction. Winthrop thereupon applied for a confirmation of the grant at Hart-

ford, and the Connecticut General Court replied, under date of April 9, 1641: "Vppon Mr. Wyntrops motion to the Courte for Fyshers Iland, It is the mynd of the Courte, that so farre as yt hinders not the publike good of the Country, either for fortifieing for defence, or setting vppe a trade of fisheing or salt & such like, he shall haue liberty to prceed therein." Mr. Winthrop did not immediately occupy his new manor. He returned to England and did not settle upon the island until the spring of 1644, when, it is believed, he began the work of build-

NORTH HUMMOCK LIGHTHOUSE

ing and planting there. In the same year he purchased the land of the Indian proprietors, in this way gaining a triple title. His house, which probably stood near the present site of the brick works at West Harbor, was the first permanent English habitation between the Connecticut River and Narragansett Bay. It antedated the settlement of New London, Stoning-

York. Mr. Winthrop received the grant of a plantation at New London in 1644 from Massachusetts, and the next year he was at that place clearing the land; but when he brought his family from Boston, in October, 1646, making the journey by water and encountering a great storm, he settled them on Fisher's Island, and there they spent their first winter in the

Island Lake

ton, Westerly and all the other towns in the Pequot and Narragansett country. When Mr. Winthrop hewed the logs for his home on this little island estate, the nearest white man's house at the west was on the shore of the Connecticut River, and eastward an unbroken forest reached up to Roger Williams's settlement at Providence Plantations. It is unfortunate that an island so intimately connected with the beginnings of New England history should have been taken away from New England and included in the state of New

Pequot country. The authentic history of the island thus dates back to the first half of the seventeenth century and has its beginnings in the career of the loved and honored Winthrop, whose exceptional accomplishments and admirable personality have caused him to be called the flower of New England Puritanism.

But Fisher's Island was not destined to remain a part of New England. In the year 1664 it was included, together with

E. M. FERGUSON'S COTTAGE

many of the other islands along the southern New England coast, in the King's grant to his brother, the Duke of York, and although Connecticut endeavored to retain it for herself, she was at last compelled to abandon it. The long contention between Connecticut and New York over Long Island and the adjacent islands is picturesque history. As early as 1640 a settlement had been made at Southold, near the eastern end of Long Island, by a company from New Haven, consisting largely of emigrants from Hing-

ham, England. They carried with them to Southold the stern theological ideas of Puritanism, and established there, under the control of the republic of New Haven, a theocratic government. Nobody was allowed to vote unless he was a member of "some or other of the approved churches of New England." This was in accordance with the New Haven law of 1643. Only "God's elect" could legally participate in the administration of public affairs. In 1648 Southold fell away from this strict *régime;* but the New Haven authorities intervened and forced it to promise obedience in the future. In 1662 the new charter obtained for Connecticut by Winthrop merged the New Haven government with that at Hartford, and Southold transferred her allegiance to Connecticut, sending

WALTON FERGUSON'S COTTAGE

Captain Youngs as her deputy to the General Court. Southold included then and still includes Plum, Great and Little Gull and Fisher's Islands. During all the vicissitudes of two centuries and a half, she has retained them within her corporate limits.

Mr. Winthrop received his grant of Fisher's Island from Governor Nicolls of New York, in 1664, in an elaborately worded document, conveying it to him and his assigns "togeth.r w.th all ye Sands Soyles Woodz Meadowes Pastures Marshes Lakes Waters Creeks Fishing Hawking

THE LINDERMAN COTTAGE

Hunting & Fowling and all oth.r Profitts Commodityes Emolum.ts & Hereditam.ts to ye said Island belonging w.th their and every of their appurtenances & of every Parte and Parcell thereof. . . . Ye said Island & premisses now is and forever hereaft.r shall be held deemed reputed taken & be an Intire Enfranchised Towneship Manno.r & Place of itself & shall alwayes from tyme to tyme & at all tymes hereafter have hould and injoye like & Equall privileges & Immunityes w.th any Towne Infranchis'd Place or Mannour w.thin this

Goverm.t . . . only yielding Rendring & Paying yearely & every yeare unto his Royall Highnesse ye Duke of Yorke & his Heires or to such Governo.r or Governours as from tyme to tyme shall be by him Constituted & appointed as an Acknowledgm.t ONE LAMB upon ye first day of May if ye same shall be demanded." Whether this tribute was ever required is not known; but there is on record the attempted gift of a pair of moose deer to Queen Anne. The proprietor of the island wished to honor her Majesty with this unique product of his estate, but one of the deer died, "and the leg of the other being broken in endeavoring to take it, her ladyship was favored only with the horns of the noble stag."

In spite of the stern character of the New Haven government and its successor at Hartford, the people of eastern Long Island preferred them to the autocratic rule of the Duke of York. Under the New England system, at least the church members of the town had the making of laws and the selection of officers; but the Duke's patent gave him the right to frame his own code and choose his own officials. Under Connecticut, Long Island had been as democratic as any portion of New England except Rhode Island, which was ahead of its time. Under New York it became a mere ducal estate governed by the representatives of the Duke, who called the island Yorkshire and termed Southold and the neighboring towns the "East Riding." Connecticut reciprocated the feeling of the people of Southold, Southampton and Easthampton, and on the twelfth of May, 1664, the General Court at Hartford adopted this resolution: "We declare that we claim Long Island as one of the adjoining islands expressed in our charter, except a precedent

against them and sent a counter expedition under Captain Fitz-John Winthrop, son of Governor Winthrop, to bring them to terms. The troops for this enterprise were raised at Stonington and New London. There was a bloodless encounter at Southold, in which a few harmless shots were exchanged, the English being left in possession of the town, while the Dutch, after uttering threats they could not put into execution, sailed

THE MANSION HOUSE

right doth appear approved by his Majesty." New York, on the other hand, claimed not only Long Island, but also all that portion of Connecticut lying west of the Connecticut River. The dispute was carried to the King's Commissioners, who decided that the boundary should run nearly as it does to-day. This gave Southold to New York, and the town remained under the government of that colony until 1673, when the Dutch recaptured Manhattan and made an expedition up the sound. Connecticut determined to move

away. The next year New York came again into the possession of the English and the Duke's agents reasserted their claim upon eastern Long Island. Easthampton, Southampton and Southold all held public meetings and decided to make a stand against Governor Andros. They sent a memorial to Sir Edmund, stating that they had repelled the Dutch with the aid of Connecticut, that they were now under her government, and that they could not secede without her consent. The council at New York immediately issued orders that the three towns should reinstate the officers that had served them before the Dutch invasion, "under penalty of being declared rebels." The town submitted with what grace they could; but again in 1680 the old dispute broke out, this time over Fisher's

THE MONONOTTO INN

Island, which, lying nearer the Connecticut coast than the rest of Southold, was more likely to arouse the interest of the legislators at Hartford. The General Court in May claimed the island by virtue of the royal charter, protesting against the authority of Sir Edmund Andros and declaring "that all such acts are unjust as have or may be exerted by any authority from the sayd S.r Edmund Andross or any other than what hath been or shall be derived from the power given by his Ma.tie vnto this his colony." They forbade obedience to Sir Ed-

mund on the island and ordered notice to be given at New London by the constable at that place. In reply Sir Edmund wrote to Governor Leete: "Honble Sr—Being advised by an order or warrant from yourself and some assistants sent to ffisher's Island, I am much surprised att your Intrenching upon his Maties. Letters Patents to his Royal Highness, as well as the Grant by Governour Nicolls to the Honble John Winthrop, Esq., (late Governor of Connecticut) for sd Island; which Island and Grant it is my duty to assert, as much as this or any other part of the Govermt; And therefore desire that you will, without delay, recall sd. warrant or order, and forbear any the like proceedings for the future, to prevent great Inconveniencys; and remaine your Effectionate neigh-

THE MUNNATAWKET HOTEL

THE POST OFFICE

bour and Humble Servant E. Andros."
The warning was sufficient. New York
has retained possession of Fisher's
Island from that day to this. She has
had to surrender her ancient islands
of Nantucket and Martha's Vineyard,
but she holds fast to this fine little
domain.

As late as 1878 the question of the
boundary between New York and
Connecticut came up for settlement.
Messrs. Allen C. Beach, Augustus
Schoonmaker and Horatio Seymour,
Jr., were appointed commissioners for
New York, and Messrs. Origen S.
Seymour, Lafayette S. Foster and
William T. Miner for Connecticut.
They decided that Mystic Island, sit-
uated at the mouth of the Mystic
River and claimed by New York,
should be Connecticut territory, and
gave it to the town of Stonington;
but adjudged Fisher's Island to be by
long association the rightful
possession of New York. In
their report to the General
Assembly at Hartford, the
Connecticut commissioners
said: "In regard to Fisher's
Island, it ought by reason
of its nearness to our coast
to belong to Connecticut.
It belonged to us, we think,

under a fair construction of the charter of 1662, which by express words
gave us the islands adjacent to the
mainland; but, upon familiar principles
of law, New York has now the title,
having had the actual possession of it
more than a century."

There were at least three houses on
Fisher's Island before the Revolution,
all of which are still standing. They
are the brick house used as an office
by the Fisher's Island Brick Company, a portion of which is said to be
two hundred years old; the Mansion
House, of which the original part is
estimated at from one hundred and
fifty to two hundred years of age; and
the Winthrop house at the east end,
supposed to have been built more
than a century since by Francis
Bayard Winthrop, a descendant of
the first English owner of the island.
The east end house and the Mansion
House are built of brick with outer
facings of wood. Any one interested
in the Winthrop family will find a
number of relics associated with them
in the collection of the Massachusetts
Historical Society at Boston; while

A FAIR CATCH

Mr. Dean Pratt of Saybrook, Connecticut, has in his possession portraits of Francis Bayard Winthrop and his wife, and his brother, John Winthrop. The first two of these are by Trumbull, and the last is by Gilbert Stuart. All three were formerly in the Mansion House.

It is pleasant to think of the island enjoying an uninterrupted history of peaceful rural life through all the years since the first Winthrop carried his family there. We get a glimpse of it more than half a century ago in this account (1843); "The greater portion of the soil is appropriated for grazing, and is capable of sustaining three thousand sheep, three hundred neat cattle and other kinds of stock in proportion." Hay was the most profitable crop, and among other staples produced were Saxony and merino wool, butter and cheese. The beef and mutton were rated of "superior quality and flavor,"and the total number of persons of all ages on the island was forty-five.

At the death of Governor John Winthrop of Connecticut, the island passed from him to his eldest son, Major Fitz-John Winthrop, governor of Sterling Castle, a general in Monk's army and governor of Connecticut from 1698 until his death in 1707. A later owner was his brother,

AN INLAND ROAD

Wait Still Winthrop, chief justice of Massachusetts and a major general of the militia of that province. The island remained in the possession of direct descendants of Governor Winthrop until 1863, when the surviving heirs sold it to Robert R. Fox. Mr. Fox died in 1871, leaving two daughters, Misses Faye and Bessie Fox. During their ownership many small plats of land were sold; but the property was practically intact when, in 1889, it came into the hands of Edmund M. Ferguson of Pittsburg, Pennsylvania,who conveyed an undivided half to his brother, Walton Ferguson of Stamford, Connecticut. Under the firm name of E. M. & W. Ferguson they have largely developed the resources of the island, and are planning generously for its future prosperity.

Fisher's Island has had its marine tragedies—most sorrowful of all the wreck of the *Atlantic* in the year 1846. She left Allyn's Point, on the Thames River, shortly after midnight on the morning of Thanksgiving Day. Soon after her departure, the wind shifted into the northwest and blew with great force. As she rounded Bartlett's Reef lightship off New London, heading westward for New York, an explosion occurred, disabling her and leaving her at the mercy of the gale.

Her anchors were cast overboard, but in spite of them she drifted slowly across Fisher's Island Sound, toward the island rocks. All Thanksgiving Day she struggled with the storm, every hour bearing her stern foremost nearer the sounding breakers. At half past four on the morning of

were drowned, among them six women and a number of children. An eyewitness of the wreck, one of the pilots of the *Mohican*, a sister ship of the *Atlantic*, has recently written: "Never before and never since have I seen and I hope never to look upon such a sight as was the

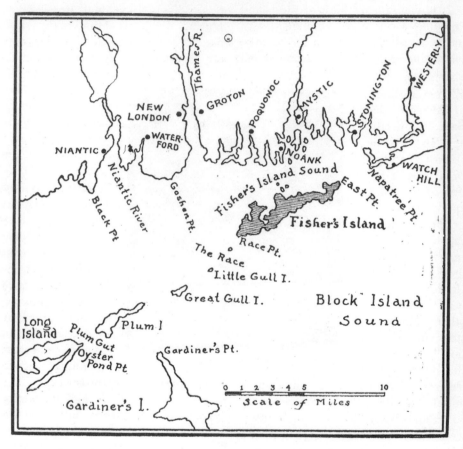

Friday, November 27, a great wave carried her on the rocks, and almost immediately another billow lifted her high upon them. In five minutes she was in pieces, and her seventy or eighty passengers and crew were struggling with the sea. In the darkness and confusion no less than forty

wreck of the *Atlantic*." She seemed to have been ground into kindling wood, with the exception of the portion between the wheel-houses. "The removing of the wreckage," he says, "and the finding of the bodies and parts of the bodies and the broken timbers has always been to me a most painful recollection. Never shall I forget that sorrowful night when the *Mohican* arrived at the depot wharf in Norwich with the remains of those who perished in the wreck, and which were carried into the station to await the recognition of relatives and friends. Nor shall I forget the mournful tolling of the *Atlantic's* bell, which was left so suspended that the rolling of the sea kept it constantly pealing a dirge, as if in memory of the dead." There are many people still living in the near-by Connecticut villages who remember the dreadful knell of that far-off November day.

Race Rock lightship now guards the fierce passageway of waters between the west end of Fisher's Island and Little Gull Island, though no lighthouse would have prevented the Thanksgiving catastrophe of fifty-five years ago. It was built by F. Hopkinson Smith, contractor, artist and author, who tells the story of its construction in "Caleb West." The island is surrounded by lighthouses and lightships. At the north are Bartlett's Reef, New London, North Hummock, Noank, Stonington and Latimer's Reef; at the east, Watch Hill and Block Island; at the south, Montauk; and at the west, Little Gull and Race Rock. At night they flash their various signals over the dark sea, some white, some red, and though they are set to warn the mariner, on pleasant evenings they form a cheerful company. Whatever the weather, they burn warm and bright. They are the "lights along the shore that never grow dim."

The most important single industry on Fisher's Island is that of the Fisher's Island Brick Company.

The president of the company is Philip C. Dunford of New London. The capacity of the yards is sixteen million bricks annually, and the principal markets for this output are the cities of Providence, Pawtucket, Newport, Fall River and New Bedford, where it has gone into some of the finest mills and public buildings. The soil of Fisher's Island is largely clay, and the deep pits of the brick company are an interesting sight. They are on the south side of the island and connected with the kilns on the north shore by a primitive track, along which patient mules draw diminutive clay-laden cars.

The island is as well provided with shops as the ordinary community of equal numbers and has a non-sectarian chapel and an Episcopal church. There are sailboats to be rented, good roads for bicycling, the best of sea bathing in surf and still water, tennis and golf, and hotel accommodations as satisfactory as those of any other New England summer resort. Under the careful oversight of Messrs. Ferguson, everything is being done that can be done to make the island a desirable living place. It is bleak and breezy in winter; but there are those who like its windy January atmosphere. What if the north wind howls and the breaker cries on the reef, if the hearth is warm and the heart glad? With a book for company in the lonelier hours, a friend or two in the long evening, the city papers fresh every day the year round, a morning walk over the salt swept hills, the constant view of ocean, inlet and sound, the sight of the Connecticut shore, village dotted, on the horizon, the various tints of the

A GRAVE BY THE SEA

their birch canoes and gathered in happy idleness on its shore. They fished for perch in its lakes and hunted the smaller game in its thickets. Now it is given over the race that dispossessed the red man; but it is a pleasure ground still. It will never be a "day resort" for its owners are determined to keep the ubiquitous excursionist away. They welcome the permanent cottager, the guest at the hotels and the transient visitor, but they will not tolerate excursion steamers. The seeker for a healthful summer resort who has experienced annoyance from this rival class of pleasure seekers may be sure of finding at Fisher's Island the congenial retirement he craves. Formed by nature to be the resort of those who are looking for health or enjoyment, and furnished by man with many comforts and conveniences, it will in time become one of the best known and most popular of American watering places.

russet island, freedom from care and a tolerable conscience—with all these, life on Fisher's Island in mid-winter is attractive enough. But it is in summer that it stirs itself and blossoms into gayety. The *Munnatawket* brings trunks by the score, and the summer girl, fair creature of the seashore and mountains, is visible everywhere. You meet her on horseback and a-wheel. She drives her pony cart along the leafy roads. She whirls in the gay cotillion and splashes in the foamy ocean.

Fisher's Island was the favorite hunting ground of the Pequot Indians. They crossed the sound in

Ampersand (Adirondacks) (1885)

AMPERSAND.

THERE are many people in the world who profess to love Nature. But if you inquire somewhat closely you shall find that, for the most part, they love her at a distance, and when they have nothing better to engage their affections. I shall never forget the German gentleman whom I met on the top of the Schneekopf, in the Thüringerwald. At first sight of the lovely view he went into a guttural convulsion of ecstasy, "*Ach! wie wunderschön!*"—which lasted just fifty-three seconds; and the rest of the time he was absorbed in the contemplation of sandwiches and beer. It did seem to me that he could have thus employed himself with less trouble at the foot of the mountain, but perhaps also with less appetite. And, after all, his passion for the beautiful may have been sincere; for it is a well-known fact that even the truest love is subject to pains of hunger.

But my own test for the right lover of Nature is a very simple one. He must be one who in making a journey between two points will choose, not the straight line (the mathematical I abhor), nor the smooth line (the sybaritical I contemn), but the crooked line, the line which wanders up hill and down dale, leading him who follows it through sweet and secret places, delaying him with fragrant meadows, babbling streams, cool shadows of trees and rocks, and bringing him at last to his journey's end with a kind of surprise and regret. Those are the brightest flowers which bloom where the crowd never think to look for them. Those are the fairest views which we discover for ourselves. We feel a certain proprietorship in them. It pleases our sense of originality to find that we do not need a hand-board or a guide-book to tell us when to admire. And does not every man owe something to his sense of originality?

In brief, then, I prefer the by-way to the highway. On principle, not in a lax, immoral way, but on the soundest and most reasonable grounds, I love digressions—in books, in sermons, and in journeys; and to tell the truth, I am digressing now. The gentle reader would recall the wandering pen, and pray to be told what Ampersand is.

It is a mountain. It is a lake. It is a stream. The mountain stands in the heart of the Adirondack country, just near enough to the thoroughfare of travel for thousands of people to see it every year, and just far enough away from the beaten track to be unvisited except by a very few of the wise ones who love to digress. Behind the mountain is the lake, which no lazy man has ever seen. Out of the lake flows the stream, winding down a long untrodden forest valley, until at length it joins the Stony Creek waters and empties into the Raquette River. Which of the three Ampersands has the prior claim to the name I can not tell. Philosophically speaking, the mountain ought to be regarded as the father of the family, because it was undoubtedly there before the others existed. And the lake was probably the next on the ground, because the stream is its child. But man is not strictly just in his nomenclature; and I conjecture that the little river, the last-born of the three,

AMPERSAND LAKE.

was the first to be called Ampersand, and then gave its name to its parent and grandparent. It is such a crooked stream, so bent and curved and twisted upon itself, so fond of turning around unexpected corners and sweeping away in great circles from its direct course, that its first explorers christened it after the eccentric supernumerary of the alphabet which appears in the old spelling-books as &.

But in spite of this apparent subordination to the stream in the matter of a name, the mountain clearly asserts its natural superiority. It stands up boldly, and dominates not only its own lake, but at least three others. The Lower Saranac, Round Lake, and Lonesome Pond are all stretched at its foot and acknowledge its lordship. When the cloud is on its brow, they are dark. When the sunlight strikes it, they smile. Wherever you may go over the waters of these lakes you shall see Ampersand looking down at you and saying, quietly, "This is my domain."

Now I never see a mountain which asserts itself in this fashion without desiring to stand on the top of it. If one can reach the summit, one becomes a sharer in the dominion. The difficulties in the way only add to the zest of the victory. Every mountain is, rightly considered, an invitation to climb. And as I was resting for a

month last summer at Bartlett's, Ampersand challenged me daily.

Do you know Bartlett's? It is the homeliest, quaintest, coziest place in the Adirondacks. A score of years or more ago Virgil Bartlett came into the woods, and built his house on the bank of the Saranac River, between the Upper Saranac and Round Lake. It was then the only dwelling within a circle of many miles. The deer and bear were in the majority. At night one could sometimes hear the scream of the panther or the howling of wolves. But now the wilderness has begun to wear the traces of a conventional smile. The desert is blossoming a little—if not as the rose, at least as the gilly-flower. Fields have been cleared, gardens planted; half a dozen log cabins have been scattered along the river; and the old house, having grown slowly and somewhat irregularly for twenty years, has lately come out in a modest coat of paint and a broad-brimmed piazza. But Virgil himself, the creator of the oasis—well known of hunters and fishermen, dreaded of lazy guides and teamsters—"Virge," the irascible, kind-hearted, indefatigable, is here no longer. He will do his friends no more favors, and put his foes to confusion no more. His short, imperious figure will not meet us again at the landing. For he has "gone out of the wilderness," and no man can fill his place. Peace be to thy memory, old friend! There are some who will not forget thy kindnesses in the good days that are past.

The charm of Bartlett's for the angler lies in the stretch of rapid water which flows just in front of the house. The Saranac River, breaking from its first resting-place in the Upper Lake, plunges down through a great bed of rocks, making a succession of short falls and pools and rapids, about a quarter of a mile in length. Here, in the spring and early summer, the

ing over the stones, the same eddy coiling at the edge of the pool. Send your fly in under those hanging branches, where the water swirls around by that old log. Now draw it up toward the foam. There is a sudden gleam of dull gold in the white water. You strike too soon. Your line comes back to you. In a current like this a fish will almost always hook himself. Try it again. This time he strikes the fly fairly, and you have him. It is a good fish, and makes the slender rod bend to the strain. He sulks for a moment as if un-

BARTLETT'S VILLAGE.

speckled trout—brightest and gamiest of all fish that swim—are found in great numbers. As the season advances they move away into the deep water of the lakes. But there are always a few stragglers left, and I have taken them in the rapids at the very end of August. What could be more delightful than to spend an hour or two in the early morning, or about sundown, of each day, in wading this rushing stream, and casting the fly on its clear waters? The wind blows softly down the narrow valley, and the trees nod from the rocks above you. The noise of the falls makes constant music in your ears. The river hurries past you, and yet it is never gone. The same foam-flakes seem to be always gliding downward, the same spray dash-

certain what to do, and then with a rush darts into the swiftest part of the current. You can never stop him there. Let him go. Keep just enough pressure on him to hold the hook firm, and follow his troutship down the stream as if he were a salmon. He slides over a little fall, gleaming through the foam, and swings around in the next pool. Here you can manage him more easily; and after a few minutes' brilliant play, a few mad dashes for the current, and one splendid leap out of water, he comes to the net, and your skillful guide lands him with a quick, steady sweep of the arm. The scales credit him with an even pound of flesh, and a better fish than this you will hardly take here in midsummer.

"On my word, master," says the appreciative Venator, in Walton's *Angler*, "this is a gallant trout; what shall we do with him?" And honest Piscator replies: "Marry! e'en eat him to supper; we'll go to my hostess from whence we came; she told me, as I was going out of door, that my brother Peter (J. R. R.), a good angler and a cheerful companion, had sent word he would lodge there to-night, and bring a friend with him. My hostess has two beds, and I know you and I have the best; we'll rejoice with my brother Peter and his friend, tell tales, or sing ballads, or make a catch, or find some harmless sport to content us, and pass away a little time without offense to God or man."

Ampersand waited patiently while I passed many days in such innocent and healthful pleasures as these, until the right day came for the ascent. Cool, clean, and bright, the crystal morning promised a glorious noon, and the mountain almost seemed to beckon us to come up higher. My photographic camera and a trustworthy lunch were stowed away in the pack-basket. The backboard was adjusted at a comfortable angle in the stern seat of our little boat. The guide held the little craft steady while I stepped into my place; then he pushed out into the stream, and we went swiftly down toward Round Lake.

The motion of these Saranac boats is delightful. They are light and somewhat cranky—frail shells, through the sides of which you can easily put your heel by a careless step—but in the hands of an experienced oarsman they are as safe as a Cunarder, riding the heaviest sea like a duck, and slipping through the water with magical ease. One can travel in them all day long without fatigue, and forty miles is no uncommon journey with a good guide.

Everything depends in the Adirondacks upon your guide. If he is lazy, or selfish, or stupid, you will not enjoy yourself; but if he is the right kind of a guide, he will be at the same time your "philosopher and friend." He will initiate you into the mysteries of wood-craft. He will tell you the secrets of "spring-holes" and "runways." He will cook for you when you are hungry, and find a cold stream for you when you are thirsty. He will tell you endless stories of hunting and fishing when you are in the talking mood, and keep a discreet silence when you are meditative. And when you are sleepy he

will make for you a bed of fragrant balsam boughs on which Insomnia can never find you. Such a guide was mine, rejoicing in the Scriptural name of Hosea, but commonly called, in brevity and friendliness, "Hose."

As we entered Round Lake on this fair morning its surface was as smooth and shining as a mirror. It was too early yet for the tide of travel which sends a score of boats up and down this thoroughfare every day; and from shore to shore the water was unruffled, except by a flock of sheldrakes which had been feeding near Plymouth Rock, and now went skittering off into Weller Bay with great splashing and noise, leaving a long wake of foam behind them. At such a time as this you can see the real color of these Adirondack lakes. It is not blue, as romantic writers so often describe it, nor green, like some of those wonderful Swiss lakes, although of course it reflects the color of the trees along the shore; and when the wind stirs it, it gives back the hue of the sky, blue when it is clear, gray when the clouds are gathering, and sometimes as black as ink under the shadow of storm. But when it is still, the water itself is like that river which one of the poets has described as

"Flowing with a smooth brown current."

And in this broad burnished mirror the mountains and islands were reflected perfectly, and the sun shone back from it not in broken gleams or a wide lane of light, but like a single ball of fire, moving before us as we moved.

But stop! What was that dark speck on the water which I saw away down toward Turtle Point? It was just the color and size of a deer's head. It seemed to move steadily out into the lake. A little ripple, like a wake, appeared behind it. Hose turned to look at it, and then sent the boat darting in that direction with long, swift strokes. It was a moment of pleasant excitement, and we began to conjecture whether the deer was a buck or a doe, and whose hounds had driven it in. But when Hose turned to look again, he slackened his stroke, and said: "I guess we needn't to hurry; he won't get away. It's astonishin' what a lot of fun a man can get in the course of a natural life in chasin' chumps of wood."

We landed on a sand beach at the mouth of a little stream, where a blazed tree marked the beginning of the Amper-

TROUTING.

sand trail. This line, or path, through the forest was first made some fifteen years ago by that ardent sportsman and lover of the Adirondacks Dr. W. W. Ely, of Rochester. Since that time it has been shortened and improved a little by other travellers, and also not a little blocked and confused by the lumbermen and the course of Nature. For when the lumbermen go into the woods they cut roads in every direction, leading nowhither, and the unwary wanderer is thereby led aside from the right way, and entangled in the undergrowth. And as for Nature, she is entirely opposed to the continuance of paths through her forest. She covers them with fallen leaves, and hides them with thick bushes. She drops great trees across them, and blots them out with windfalls. But the blazed line—a succession of broad axe-marks on the trunks of the trees, just high enough to catch

MAKING A PORTAGE.

the eye on a level—can not be so easily obliterated, and this, after all, is the safest guide through the woods.

Our trail led us at first through a natural meadow, overgrown with waist-high grass, and very spongy to the tread. Hornet-haunted also, was this meadow, and therefore no place for idle dalliance or unwary digression, for the bite of the hornet is one of the saddest and most humiliating surprises of this mortal life. Then through a tangle of old wood roads my guide led me safely, and we struck up on the long ridges which slope gently from the lake to the base of the mountain.

Here walking was comparatively easy, for in the hard-wood timber there is little underbrush. The long massive trunks seemed like pillars set to uphold the level roof of green. Great yellow birches, shaggy with age, stretched their knotted arms high above us, sugar-maples stood up straight and proud under their leafy crowns, and innumerable smooth beeches—the most polished and park-like of all the forest trees—offered special opportunities for the carving of lovers' names in a place where few lovers ever come.

As we walked onward the woods were very quiet. It seemed as if all living creatures had deserted them. Indeed, if you have spent much time in our North-

ern forests you must have often wondered at the absence of life, and felt a sense of pity for the apparent loneliness of the solitary squirrel that chatters at you as you pass, or the little bird that hops noiselessly about in the thickets. The middle of the day is an especially silent and deserted time. The deer are asleep in some leafy covert. The partridge has gathered her brood in a quiet nook for their noonday nap. The squirrels are perhaps counting over their store of nuts in a hollow tree, and the wood-thrush spares her sweet voice until the evening. The woods are close—not cool and fragrant as the foolish romances describe them—but warm and still; for the breeze which sweeps across the hill-top and ruffles the surface of the lake does not penetrate into these shady recesses, and therefore all the inhabitants take the noon-tide as their hour of rest. Only the big woodpecker—he of the scarlet head and mighty bill—is indefatigable, and somewhere unseen is "tapping the hollow beech-tree," while a wakeful little bird, invisible though near at hand, pierces the air with his long-drawn "Chick-a-dee-dee-dee-dee-ee!"

After about an hour of this easy walking our trail began to ascend more sharply. We passed over the shoulder of a ridge and around the edge of a fire-slash, and then we had the mountain fairly before us. Not that we could see anything of it, for the woods still shut us in, but the path became very steep, and we knew that it was a straight climb; not up and down and round about did this most uncompromising trail proceed, but right up, in a direct line for the summit. Now this side of Ampersand is steeper than any Gothic roof I have ever seen, and withal very much encumbered with rocks and ledges and fallen trees. There were places where we had to haul ourselves up by roots and branches, and places where we had to go down on our hands and knees to crawl under logs. It was breathless work, but not at all dangerous or difficult. Every step forward was also a step upward; and as we stopped to rest for a moment, we could see already glimpses of the lake below us. But at these I did not much care to look, for I think it is a pity to spoil the surprise of a grand view by taking little snatches of it beforehand. It is better to keep one's face set to the mountain, and then coming out from the dark forest upon the very summit, feel the splendor of the outlook flash upon one like a revelation.

The character of the woods through which we were now passing was entirely different from that on the lower levels. On these steep places the birch and maple will not grow, or at least they occur but sparsely. The higher slopes and sharp ridges of the mountains are always covered with black timber. Spruce and hemlock and balsam strike their roots among the rocks, and find a hidden nourishment. They stand close together; thickets of small trees spring up among the large ones; from year to year the great trunks are falling,

ON THE TRAIL.

one across another, and the undergrowth is thickening around them, until a spruce forest seems to be almost impassable. The constant rain of needles and the crumbling of the fallen trees form a rich, soft forest mould, into which the foot sinks noiselessly. Deep, wonderful beds of moss, many feet in thickness, and softer than feathers, cover the rocks and roots. There are shadows never broken by the sun, and dark, cool springs of icy water hidden away in the crevices. You feel a sense of antiquity here which you can never feel among the maples and beeches. Longfellow was right when he filled his forest primeval with "murmuring pines and hemlocks."

The higher one climbs the darker and gloomier and more rugged the vegetation becomes. The pine-trees soon cease to follow you; the hemlocks disappear, and the balsams can go no farther. Only the hardy spruce keeps on bravely, growing more and more rough and stunted, with branches matted together and pressed down flat by the weight of the winter's snow, until finally, somewhere about the level of thirty-four hundred feet above the sea, even this bold climber gives out, and the weather-beaten rocks of the summit are clad only with the hardiest mosses and Alpine plants.

Thus it is with mountains, as perhaps with men, a mark of superior dignity to be naturally bald. Ampersand, falling short by a thousand feet of the needful height, can not claim this distinction. But what Nature has denied, human labor has supplied. Under the direction of Mr. Verplanck Colvin, of the Adirondack Survey, several acres of trees were cut away from the summit, and when we emerged, after the last sharp scramble, upon the very crest of the mountain, we were not shut in by a dense thicket, but stood upon a bare ridge of granite in the centre of a little clearing.

I shut my eyes for a moment, drew a few long breaths of the glorious breeze, and then looked out upon a wonder and delight beyond description.

A soft, dazzling splendor filled the air. Snowy banks and drifts of cloud were floating slowly over a wide and wondrous land. Vast sweeps of forest, shining waters, mountains near and far, the deepest green and the faintest, palest blue, changing colors and glancing lights, and all so silent, so strange, so far away, that it seemed like the landscape of a dream. One almost feared to speak lest it should vanish.

Right below us the Lower Saranac and Lonesome Pond, Round Lake and the Weller Ponds, were spread out like a map. Every point and island was clearly marked. We could follow the course of the Saranac River in all its curves and windings, and see the white tent of the hay-makers on the wild meadows. Far away to the northeast stretched the level fields of Bloomingdale. But westward from that all was unbroken wilderness, a great sea of woods as far as the eye could reach. And how far it can reach from a height like this! What a revelation it gives to us of the power of sight! That faint blue outline far in the north was Lyon Mountain, nearly thirty miles away as the crow flies. Those silver gleams a little nearer were the waters of St. Regis. The Upper Saranac was displayed in all its length and breadth, and beyond it the innumerable waters of Fish Creek were glistening among the dark woods. The long ranges of the hills about the Jordan bounded the western horizon, and on the southwest Big Tupper Lake was sleeping at the base of Mount Morris. Looking past the peak of Stony Creek Mountain, which rose sharp and distinct in a line with Ampersand, we could trace the path of the Raquette River from the distant waters of Long Lake down through its far-stretched valley, and catch here and there a silvery link of its current.

But when we turned to the south and east, how wonderful and how different was the view! Here was no wide-spread and smiling landscape with gleams of silver scattered through it, and soft blue haze resting upon its fading verge, but a wild land of mountains, stern, rugged, tumultuous, rising one beyond another like the waves of a stormy ocean—Ossa piled above Pelion—McIntyre's sharp peak and the ragged crest of the Gothics, and, above all, Marcy's dome-like head, raised just far enough above the others to assert his royal right as monarch of the Adirondacks.

But grandest of all, as seen from this height, was Mount Seward—a solemn giant of a mountain, standing apart from the others, and looking us full in the face. He was clothed from base to summit in a dark unbroken robe of forest. *Ou-korlah*, the Indians called him—the Great Eye; and he seemed almost to frown upon

HEART OF THE ADIRONDACKS.

us in defiance. At his feet, so straight below us that it seemed almost as if we could cast a stone into its clear brown depths, lay the wildest and most beautiful of all the Adirondack waters—Ampersand Pond.

On its shore, some five-and-twenty years ago, the now almost forgotten Adirondack Club had their shanty—the successor of "the Philosophers' Camp" on Follensbee Pond. Agassiz, of Cambridge, the genial and witty Tom Appleton, of Boston, Charles E. Norton, Emerson, Lowell, Judge Hoar, Judge Gray, John Holmes, and W. J. Stillman, of *The Nation*, were among the company who made their resting-place under the shadow of Mount Seward. They had bought a tract of forest land completely encircling the pond, cut a rough road in to it through the woods, and built a comfortable log cabin, to which they purposed to return from summer to summer. But the civil war broke out, with all its terrible excitement and confusion of hurrying hosts; the club existed but for two years, and the little house in the wilderness was abandoned. Ten years ago, when I spent three weeks at Ampersand, the cabin was in ruins, tenanted only by an interesting family of what the guides quaintly call "quill pigs," and surrounded by an almost impenetrable growth of bushes and

VIEW EAST FROM AMPERSAND.

saplings, among which a brood of partridges were in hiding. The roof had fall-
en to the ground; raspberry-bushes thrust
themselves through the yawning crevices
between the logs; and in front of the sunk-
en door-sill lay a rusty, broken iron stove,
like a dismantled altar on which the fire
had gone out forever. Since that time
two new trails have been cut to the pond,
and it has become more accessible and
more frequented.

After we had feasted our eyes upon the
view as long as we dared, counted the
lakes and streams, and found that we could
see without a glass more than thirty, and
recalled the memories of "good times"
which came to us from almost every point
of the compass, we unpacked the camera,
and proceeded to take some pictures.

If you are a photographer, and have
anything of the amateur's passion for
your art, you will appreciate my pleasure
and my anxiety. Never before, so far as
I knew, had a camera been set up on Ampersand. I had but eight plates with me.
The views were all very distant and all

at a downward angle. The power of the
light at this elevation was to me in my
inexperience an unknown quantity. And
the wind was sweeping vigorously across
the open summit of the mountain. I put
in my smallest stop, and prepared for
short exposures.

My instrument was a Blair tourograph,
which is as compact and useful as anything that is made, but differs from most
other cameras in having the plate-holder
on top of the box. The plates are dropped
into a groove below, and then moved backward or forward into focus, after which
the cap is removed and the exposure made.

I set my instrument for Ampersand
Pond, sighted the picture through the
ground glass, and measured the focus.
Then I waited for a quiet moment, dropped
the plate, moved it carefully forward to
the proper mark, and went around to take
off the cap. I found that I already had
it in my hand, *and the plate had been exposed for about thirty seconds, with a
sliding focus!*

I expostulated with myself. I said:

"You are excited; you are stupid; you are unworthy of the name of photographer. Light-writer! You ought to write with a whitewash-brush!" The reproof was effectual, and from that moment all went well. The plates dropped smoothly, the camera was steady, the exposure was correct. Six good pictures were made, to recall, so far as black and white could do it, the delights of that day.

It has been my good fortune to climb many of the famous peaks of the Adirondacks—Dix, the Dial, Hurricane, the Giant of the Valley, Marcy, and Whiteface—but I do not think the outlook from any of them is so wonderful and so lovely as that from little Ampersand; and I reckon among my most valuable chattels the plates of glass on which the sun has traced for me (who can not draw) the outlines of that loveliest landscape.

The downward journey was swift and pleasant. We halted for an hour or two beside a trickling spring a few rods below the summit to eat our lunch and rest. Then, jumping, running, and sometimes sliding, we made the proverbially easy descent, passed in safety by the dreaded lair of the hornet, and reached Bartlett's as the day was declining to its peaceful close.

Tell me, I pray you, my gentle reader, was not this a day to be grateful for? and are not these pleasures, as Izaak Walton saith, without offense to God or man?

Lake George
(1853)

SOUTHERN APPROACH TO LAKE GEORGE.

LAKE GEORGE.
BY T. ADDISON RICHARDS.

THE rain-drops upon our roof and against our window-pane trip in elfin measure—the harsh voice of old Boreas melts into a zephyrous breathing—glad sunshine illumines the dark clouds—and the gleeful rainbow spreads her magic sceptre of peace over the earth, as we nib our pen this wintry morning to conjure up summer memories of the gentle Horicon. Happy talisman—this remembrance of the Beautiful!

this joyous Abstraction—conquering the pains and fears of the Actual!

"An endless fountain of immortal drink,
Pouring unto us from the heaven's brink."

In a twinkle, dear reader, we leave the deluged city and its dripping causeways far behind us, and drop our fancies down with the glittering sky, the merry mountain-tops, and the laughing island-bowers, deep into the crystal caves of the Queen of Waters: but you, who perchance know not the way so well as we, may need some guidance thither. Geography and topography are not the most alluring studies in the repertory of human lore, yet they have their uses, and claim their meed of deference from the most abstracted gazer from Nature up to Nature's God.

The number, beauty, and variety of the lakes and lakelets is one of the most striking features of American scenery; and the Empire State holds within her boundaries a most Benjamin-like share of these pearls of nature. It is needless for her to boast of Cayuga, Pleasant, Piseco, Schroon, Paradox, Champlain, and numberless other delicious scenes, while with fair Horicon alone she may challenge all the earth. This bright gem—gem of purest water—is befittingly set in a surrounding of kindred beauties, shedding its effulgence upon the most attractive portion of the most picturesque State in the Union. It is as accessible in all directions as steamers, railways, and plank-roads can make it. And what magnificent modes of access! The Canadian, dropping down Lake Champlain, nods to the Adirondacks on one hand, and to the Green Mountains on the other, as he hastens to pay a morning call; while the Southron glides swiftly through the

AMONG THE ISLANDS.

enchanted fastnesses of the Hudson, and peeps into the gay saloons of Saratoga, as he runs up to dinner or tea. And what cordial and hospitable greeting and entertainment they receive—moral and physical! What gracious smiles from the hostess, and what dinners and teas from the stewards of her hotels!

The transit of Lake George is a link in the high road from the States to the Canadas, by which happy accident men of business toils may worship God for a moment through the still, small voice of His handiworks, without abating a jot of their devotion to Mammon. The general scenery-hunter and the fashionable tourist "do" the Lake without trouble, in connection with their devoirs at Saratoga—a good preparation, had Horicon need of such a foil as the intellectual and moral fast of a sojourn at that temple of empty gallantries and unreal life.

The Indian, true to that dominant emotion of his heart—a pure and reverent love of Nature—always fervently worshiped at this shrine, and baptized it humbly—in sympathy with its own character and sentiment—Horicon, or the Silvery Waters; he called it too Canideriout, or the Tail of the Lake, from its relative position to the proximate waters of Champlain. The French Catholics, equally obeying the specialities of their *morale*, christened it, in honor of their religious creed, Lake Sacrament; while the Anglo-Saxon, no less mindful of his highest and holiest love, made it do homage to his egotism, and named it after himself—Lake George! To this hour, well-a-day! the voices of poetry and of religion are drowned in the more clamorous cry of human pride and selfishness.

Who can say what deeds of heroism and horror, of love and hate, the shores and depths of Horicon may have witnessed in the forgotten ages of the past, when the red man alone was lord and master. What unwritten histories, rich and strange, may lie buried in its sealed waters. Certainly, since its story has found chroniclers, numberless events of classic and historic charm have clustered thick around it. The poet and the romancer have embalmed it in the quaint old rhyme and in winsome story. Brave armies lie under its sods, and its ripples now break over the graves of once gay and gallant fleets. Not a few of the most daring and important events of our Colonial wars, and of our Revolutionary struggle, endear these haunts to the national heart. We shall recall these records of the lyre, and these "moving accidents by flood and field," as briefly and comprehensively as we may, as in our traverse of the lake we reach the several points and scenes with whose story they are interwoven.

Let us start, as nine out of ten of you will, from the piazza of one of the giant hotels of Saratoga. We may manage the whole intervening distance of twenty miles, either wholly on an easy plank-road, or in part by the more rapid railway. We say of the latter route, "in part," because not yet has the demon voice of the locomotive profaned the holy stillness of Horicon. By either path, we shall pass over the last and most interesting part of the journey at a decorous and convenient pace.

As we jog on, we may, if we are poetically or archæologically bent—as one is apt to be under such circumstances—recall the woeful story of the ill-fated Jenny M'Crea, and the victory of Gates, and defeat of Burgoyne on Bemis' Heights, both stories of the vicinage. After dinner at Glen's Falls, we may delight us with the angry and tortuous passage of the upper Hudson, over immense barriers of jagged marble; and looking into the past, we may espy the hiding-place of Cooper's fair creations—Alice and Cora Munroe, with their veteran guardians, Uncas and Hawk-Eye. The clamor of human industry at this once quiet spot would now drown the foot-fall of the Mohican better than ever did his stealthy moccasin.

Midway between these famous falls and the lake, we take a peep at Williams' Rock, a venerable boulder on the wayside, remembered with the fate of its god-father, Col. Williams, killed here in the "soul-trying" times. The action which immortalized this ancient druid has given a dreary interest to another spot hard by—a deep-down, dank, and dismal "Bloody Pond," where sleep the poor fellows who were left to pay the scot at this sad merry-making.

From this point we catch our first glimpse of the watch-towers of Horicon; and soon after a joyous gleam of water blesses our vision, growing into a broad, far-spreading sea, studded with mythical isles and edged with gallant hills. Then the little village of Caldwell peeps up to greet us, and hastening to grasp its extended hand, we are soon cosily housed in the parlors of Sherrill's famous house, at the head of the Lake. The unusual course of the Horicon, from south to north, results in a little jumbling of the ups and downs of travel, sending the loiterer down the lake, while he is going up the shore, or road, and *vice versa:* thus leaving the queenly water open to the derogatory imputation of an insane weakness for standing on its head! Sup with the model appetite achieved by your day's travel—puff your Havana lazily as you commune for an hour upon the piazza, with the slumbering waters—sleep serenely, as under such gentle influences you infallibly must—rise betimes, and breakfast befittingly, as you will, upon Sherrill's immaculate trout, and if no very heinous sins press you down (like the leaded ends of the toy pithmen), there is no saying whether you yourself will be found standing upon your head or feet, for it requires but a marvelously short time here to make you a "boy again," and to revive your ancient passion for wild-oats.

It is the custom of many folks to take the steamboat at Caldwell, after breakfast, traverse the entire lake to Ticonderoga, get back again to tea, and consider the thing done: but as these people are only themselves "done," we shall consider their custom more honored in the breach than in the observance. Catch us, forsooth, wasting Lake George on a single day's pleasure! We are not such thriftless prodigals. We are here *chez le* Commodore: we know when we are well off, and we are going to upset our trunks and make ourselves comfortable.

The morning is advancing, and we had well nigh forgotten our bath. To pass a day here without this luxury is to make but a shabby use of the blessings of Providence. What is Stoppani, with his "hot and cold!" or Rabineau, with his "salt!" in comparison with the vast crystal tub in which you here make your daily ablutions! A few steps—your skiff (skiffs abound) is manned; a few pulls, and that dreamy isle whose mazes you threaded last night with the blue wreaths of your cigar, is reached; one plunge, and your youth is renewed—you are in Elysium:

"We have been there, and still would go,
'Tis like a little heaven below!"

Our morning bath accomplished, now let us, like Shakspeare's hero, "sit upon the ground, and tell sad stories of the death of kings." Here, in the cooling shadow of the stately hemlock, so gracefully softened by the lighter humor of the more genial birch—the Socrates and the Alcibiades of the woods. Yonder, to the northward, are gathered, in promiscuous and crowded groups, as if to do honor to your coming, all the mountain-tops of the neighborhood. It is the same glimpse, seen nearer, as that caught occasionally in our approach to the Lake yesternight, and which we have sought to transcribe in our frontispiece. The islands lie chiefly off there in the distance; but so abundant are they, that quite enough still stand around you and dot the

SHELVING ROCK.

SCENE NEAR BOLTON.

water, like exclamation-points, in all directions. With the changing hour—dawn, sunset, and night; with the varying weather; from the calm of drowsy morning to the eve of gathering storm, these islands are found in ever-changing phases. As they sleep for a moment in the deep quiet of a passing cloud-shadow, you sigh for rest in their cooling bowers; anon, the sun breaks over them, and you are still as eager to mingle in their now wild and lawless revelry. You may shake up the Lake like a keleidescope, seeing with every varying change a new picture, by simply varying your relative position to these islands. Now you have a foreground of pebbly beach, or perchance of jagged rock, or of forest *débris*, with the spreading water, and the distance-tinted hills, to fill up the canvas; or, peeping beneath the pendant boughs of the beach and maple, an Arcadian bower discloses vistas of radiant beauty.

Still new volumes open as you thread the shores on either hand. This you may do, for some dozen miles on the western side, upon a comfortable carriage-way. Some four miles onward, you pick up the accompanying picture of "Shelving Rock," a feature which gives saliency to the landscape in all directions. Hereabouts, this particular grouping is seen over and over again, with sundry variations. Behind the Shelving Rock rises Black Mountain, a bold and omnipresent spirit in the scenery of Horicon: to be got rid of only by turning your back upon him—a discourtesy to which there is no temptation.

The charm of many of the islands and localities embraced in the view from Caldwell, is pleasantly heightened by associations of historic incident. Diamond Isle was once (who, now watching its peaceful aspect, would ever think it!) a depôt for military stores and war-clad bands. Long Point, hard by, in 1757 formed with the shore a harbor for the bateaux of Montcalm. Yonder too are still found the ruins of forts, and other adjuncts of the pride, pomp, and circumstance of glorious war. Fort William Henry, the most interesting of these relics, was built by the English during their colonial wars with the French, in 1755. Two years after, it was destroyed by the Gallic general, Montcalm, on the surrender of the English garrison. The circumstances of this capitulation are too tragical to be easily forgotten. As the conquered troops were leaving the fort, under the promise of protection and escort, they were savagely attacked by the Indian allies of the victors, and fifteen hundred were slain or made captives, the French looking calmly and perfidiously on the while, and denying all succor or interference. To complete the horror of the scene, the mangled corses of more than a hundred women strewed the ground.

In this vicinage are the ruins of Fort George; and close by was once a third fortification, named in honor of General Gage. The history of neither recalls to our memory any very active scenes.

Caldwell, though possessing not over two hundred inhabitants, is yet the most considerable village—indeed the only one worthy of the name—until you reach Ticonderoga, at the north end of the Lake. Its position at a terminus, and on the high road of travel, together with its well-ordered summer hotel (the favorite Lake House, at whose table we have thus far in our journey been delighting our souls with the rich products of the angle and of the chase), have made it the place where tourists most do congregate. In every respect it is capital head-quarters. Still there are other resting-places and bivouacs none the less desirable from being more secluded and quiet. Chief among these is Bolton, some three leagues distant by road or water, and Garfield's, still another decade of miles removed. At both of these landings are admirable hotels, with every facility for a satisfactory immolation of Old Tempus. A new inn has been very recently erected opposite Caldwell; and Toole's, some miles beyond, on the eastern shore, is well known to the hunting and fishing visitors.

But of all the haunts on the Lake, Bolton is pre-eminent in its array of natural beauty. In no other vicinage can you put out your hand or your foot, and in one leisurely pull on the water or in one quiet stroll on the shore, possess yourself of so many and so richly contrasted pictures. The genuine lover of nature may linger long at other spots, but here is his abiding place. Bolton is a township which, while having a name to live, is yet dead. It possesses a shadowy conglomeration of huts, which the modesty of the good Bol-tonians themselves dares not dignify with any 'prouder appellation than that of "the huddle." The farm-houses round about are reasonably thick and well to do, certainly; but still Bolton, in the vocabulary of the stranger, is neither more nor less than the "Mohican House," whose esteemed commandant is Captain Gale, a name next to that of "Sherrill" most gratefully inter-woven with the carnal history of Horicon. Yes! the Mohican House is Bolton, and Bolton is the Mohican House; even as Bardolph was his nose, and his nose was Bardolph. Great are both!

Among the genial spirits who were our few fellow guests here during two happy moons, some year or so ago, was one of Italia's most gifted daughters, whose voice has rung in melody through all this wide land, yet never in such sweet and winning harmony, and with such worthy accessories, as under the starry canopy and amidst the enrapt stillness of Horicon. " *Casta diva che in argenti*," floating spirit-like over the glad waters, and gently echoed by listen-ing hill and isle, is not quite the same thing as when sent back from the proscenium of "Astor Place." Our Signorina had "the heavens and earth of every country seen:" had known and loved Katrine and Windermere, Constance, Lo-mond, Geneva and Grassmere, had grown to womanhood on the sunny banks of immortal Como, yet found sweet Horicon more charming than them all. What better evidence of the sweet poetry and power of the lovely theme of our pre-sent memories can we have than the earnest and enduring emotion and sympathy it wins from the most cultivated souls, no less than from the won-der-stricken novice amidst the *chefs-d'œuvres* of nature?

It is no slight task to determine in which di-rection here, to seek the picturesque—whether in the bosom of the Lake, on the variedly indented shores, or on the overlooking mountain tops. Every where is abundant and perfect beauty. Among our poor trophies of the pencil we have preserved a little glimpse looking southward from the edge of the water at Bolton. Our only regret is, as we offer it with its companions, that, with our best seekings, we may still appear to the reader, too much like the pedant in Hierocles, submitting a brick as a sample of the beauty of his house.

The average width of Lake George is between two and three miles. At the Mohican House, this average is exceeded; indeed, at one other point only, is it any where broader than here. All the leading features of the locality are hap-pily commanded here. The islands within range of the eye are many and of surpassing beauty—and among them is that odd little nautical eccen-tricity, called Ship Island, from the mimicry in its verdure of the proportions and lines of the ship. The landing is near the mouth of the northwest bay—a special expanse of five miles, stolen from the main waters by the grand mount-ain promontory aptly called the Tongue. It is

SHIP ISLAND AND BLACK MOUNTAIN.

THE NARROWS.

the extension into the Lake of this ridge of hills which forms the Narrows, entered immediately after passing Bolton. Contracted as the channel is at this point, it seems yet narrower from the greater elevation of the mountains among which are the most magnificent peaks of the neighborhood. Here is the home of Shelving Rock, with its hemisphere of palisades, and its famous dens of rattlesnakes; here too, monarch of hills, the Black Mountain, with his rugged crown of rock, holds his court. Tongue Mountain is the favored haunt of the Nimrods in their search for the luscious venison. Speaking of the chase reminds us that we owe a line to the sister sport of the angle. It is in the vicinage of Bolton that both these delights may be best attained, and particularly is it the field, *par excellence*, for piscatory achievements. Were it not that so very little credence is placed in the avoirdupois of fishermen, we would allude modestly to the weight of certain astonishing creatures of the trout and bass kind, which we have ourselves persuaded to the hook.

Charming as are the scenes from the surface of the Lake, they are surpassed by the glimpses continually occurring in the passage of the road on the western shore (the precipitousness of the mountains on the other side admits of no land passage), and commanded by the summits of the hills. Leaving Bolton, the road which has thus far followed the margin or the vicinity of the water, steals off, and sullenly winds its rugged and laborious way across the mountains, offering nothing of interest until it again descends to the Lake near Garfield's—a tedious traverse of a score of miles or more. The interval is much more rapidly and pleasantly made on the steamer. From Sabbath-Day Point and Garfield's, the road again jogs on merrily in the neighborhood of the water. Descending the mountains at the northern end of this central portion of the Lake road, you catch a noble and welcome panorama of the upper part of the Horicon. But returning to Bolton—we were about speaking of the delightful scenes from the shore thereat. Within a short walk northward, an exceedingly characteristic view is found looking across the mouth of Northwest bay to the Narrows. From all the eminences or from the shore, the landscape is here of admirable simplicity, breadth, and grandeur. It is seen most justly as the morning sun peeps over Black Mountain and its attendant peaks. Looking southward from various points yet further on, fine views of the head of the Lake are obtained—among them our sketch of the master feature of the southern extremity—the French mountain—terminating a pleasant stretch of lawn, hill, and islanded water.

It is while the eye is filled with such scenes as these modest hill-tops offer, more perhaps than when embowered in the solitudes of the island shades, or than when wandering by the rippling shore, that the soul is most conscious of the subtle nature of the charms which make us cling to and desire ever to dwell near Horicon. This secret and omnipotent essence is the rare presence of the quiet and grace of the beautiful—heightened, but not overcome, by the laughing caprices of the picturesque, and the solemn dignity of the grand in nature. The beautiful alone, wanting that contrast and variety which keeps curiosity alert and interested, soon wearies and cloys—the sublime calling forth feelings of astonishment, and sometimes even of terror, stretches the fibres so much beyond their natural tone as to create pain, so that the effect, however great, can not be very enduring. When these several qualities are united, as they are in the luxuriant, change-ful, and wide-spreading landscape of Lake George, a pleasant and lasting sensation of delight is the result—a healthy tone of pleasurable excitement, in which are avoided the extremes both of the languor of beauty and the painful tension of emo-tion produced by the sublime

The attractions of Horicon will be yet more perfect when time shall effect the additional infu-sion of the picturesque, which will follow the enterprise, opulence, and taste of increasing pop-ulation Though now exhibiting all the elements of perfect beauty, she yet bides her time for com-plete development. She is now, to her sister waters of the Old World, as the untaught forest maiden is to the peerless queen of the boudoir and saloon The refining and spiritualizing hand of art will soon enliven her quieter features, and

soften her rougher characteristics Ruined bat-tlements and legendary shrines may never deck her bluffs and promontories in the mystic veil of romance, but happy cottages and smiling homes of health and content will climb her rude accliv-ities, and merry summer villas will peep glee-fully out of the clustering shrubbery of her lovely isles, bringing to the heart more grateful thoughts and hopes than would the vaunted accessories of older spots, inasmuch as they will whisper of a yet higher civilization and of a nobler life.

So admirably attuned are all the elements of beauty in the scenery of Lake George, that on our first acquaintance with the region we could scarcely imagine it ever to appear under a differ-ent aspect than the sunny phase in which we then saw it. So perfect did nature appear, both in the general sentiment and in the most minute detail, that we could think of her doing

> "Nothing but that, more still, still so, and own
>   No other function—"

As we gazed around upon the chattering waters and upon the rejoicing hills, we wondered whether storm and cloud ever darkened their radiant face —whether the wrath of the mad and unchained elements ever managed to break the spell of calm repose But we learned in due time that, as the mildest eye will sometimes glance in wrath, and the rosiest lip will curl in scorn, so the black scowl of the tempest would gather upon the brows of the peaceful hills, and hide the smile of the gentle floods of Horicon—only, though, soon to pass away, and leave hill and water more verdant and sparkling than before. When the air is thus cleared by storm or shower, the surrounding hills glitter in almost painful distinctness, each stem and stone from the base to the crown of the mountains seeming to come within the grasp of your hand. Once—deceived by this false sem-

FRENCH MOUNTAIN.

SABBATH-DAY POINT

blance—we were persuaded to undertake the passage of the Lake and the ascent of the Black Mountain. "It is so easy and simple a matter," said our adventurous friends, "and may be managed so readily and so rapidly" Alas! poor deluded wretches! Well was it that our fancy came with the rising of the sun, and that no delay followed in the execution, for night fairly overtook us before we regained our domicile, under a firm conviction of the verity of the old proverb touching the deceitfulness of appearances. As a memento of this excursion, we brought back a rattle-snake, which we demolished on the way; and the skin of which one of our party, following the sumptuary habits of the people, afterward wore as a hat-band. Turning from the position whence we have been gazing upon the French Mountain, we may detect, upon the extreme left, the petite area of Fourteen Mile Island, lying at the base of Shelving Rock, and near the entrance to the Narrows. This is a famous temporary home of the Nimrods who chase the deer over the crags of the Tongue Mountain, opposite. The domestic appliances of this rude resting-place are as nomadic as the roughest hunter could desire

On the Pinacle, a lofty peak west of the hotel, a more extended panorama of the Lake is obtained. We often climbed to the summit of the hills on the road westward from Bolton; once we found ourselves there at the very peep of day, when the stern and rugged phiz of Black Mountain was bathed in the purple light of the rising sun; the few fleeting clouds visible in the heavens were

tinged with gold, doubly gorgeous in contrast with the gray hue of the unillumined hills beneath, the blue waters, and the yet sleeping islands. Still a few moments, and "heaven's wide arch was glorious with the sun's returning march." Floods of living light swept over the extended landscape—the hundred islets rubbed their sleepy eyes, and joyously awoke again; while the waters threw off the drapery of their couch in the shape of long lines of vapor, which the jocund king of day—merrily performing the rôle of chamber-maid—busied himself in rolling carefully up on the hill-side, and hiding away until they should be again required. It was one of those magical scenes of which the poet and painter more often dream than realize.

Thus far our panorama gazings have (from the intervening of the Tongue) shown us only the southern end of Horicon. At the 2200 feet elevation of the Black Mountain, the eye sweeps the entire extent of the Lake—of Champlain, lying at its eastern base—and of all the region round, to the peaks of the Adirondacks, and the green hills of Vermont. But very few tourists, few of the Nimrods even, brave the toils of an ascent to the crown of this stately pile. The way is wearisomely steep and beset with dangers. Watching with due precaution for the rattlesnake, an indigenous product of all this region, you may overlook the approach of the bear, or unexpectedly encounter the catamount—not to mention the host of less distinguished animals, "native here, and to the manner born."

When you are ready, or necessitated rather,

to say adieu to Bolton (for continual parting is the sad alloy of the traveler's rare privilege of varied greeting), the little steamer will pick you up all in the morning betimes, and whisk you through the Narrows to your next bivouac, at Sabbath-Day Point.

The passage of the Narrows, either in storm or sunshine, at noon-tide or night, is not the least agreeable item in your Lake experience. The waters here reach a depth of four hundred feet, and so surprisingly translucent are they, that you may watch the gambols of the finny peoples many fathoms below the surface. In most parts of the Lake you may count the pebbles at the bottom as your skiff glides along.

We shall be set ashore at Sabbath-Day Point in a batteau, for want of a steamboat landing. Such a convenience was once found here. Once Sabbath-Day Point was a point every body longed to know. A commodious and fashionable summer hotel stood here, and a miraculous old landlord did the honors in his own remarkable way. Hotel, landlord, and visitors have all vanished. Nature, though, yet remains—young, lovely, and *riant* as ever. The pleasant strip of meadow pokes its merry nose into the Lake with the saucy impudence of other days, and scans with wonted satisfaction the glorious sweep of the waters, as they vanish southward in the defile of the Narrows; or northward, reflect on their broad expanse the Titan phiz of good Saint Anthony, and the rocky flanks of Roger's Slide.

In 1756, a handful of colonists here successfully repelled a stormy onslaught of the Indians and French. Here too, in 1758, General Abercrombie and his gallant army lunched, *en route* from Fort George, at the head of the Lake, to attack the French at Ticonderoga. The sky was gemmed with stars, and the disc of the moon fell unbroken upon the motionless waters, as this glorious array of a thousand boats, bearing sixteen thousand men, pursued their stealthy march. As the brilliant cavalcade debarked, the bright uniforms sparkled in the beams of the rising sun, and the morning being the Sabbath, the little cape was happily called Sabbath-Day Point. Here again, in the memorable 1776, the patriot militia dealt some successful back-handers to the Tories and their Indian allies.

From Sabbath-Day Point we may re-embark on the steamer, or continue our journey by land, as the road now touches the Lake again. Three miles onward we make the little village of Hague, if village it can be styled. The visitor will remember the locality as Garfield's—one of the oldest and most esteemed summer camps. Judge Garfield would seem to have an intimate acquaintance with every deer on the hill-side, and with every trout in the waters, so habitually are these gentry found at his luxurious table. An excellent landing facilitates the approach to Garfield's, and the steamboat touches daily, up and down.

The shore route hence to Ticonderoga is through a pleasant country, well worth exploration. We will pursue our journey now by water. Just beyond, the Lake is again reduced to Procrustean limits, as it brushes between the opposing walls of Roger's Rock and Anthony's Nose. The reader is doubtless familiar with the ruse by which Major Rogers, flying from the Indians in 1758, persuaded them that he had achieved the marvelous feat of sliding down this grand declivity; thus cleverly reversing the

ROGER'S SLIDE AND ANTHONY'S NOSE.

RUINS OF TICONDEROGA.

theory of the sublime Western poet—seeking to—

    —— "Prove that one Indian savage
    Is worth two white men, on an av'rage!"

North of Roger's Rock the character of the Lake changes; the wild mountain shores yield to a fringe of verdant lawn and shady copse, and the water grows momently more shallow. This last variation was a god-send to the first English captives, detained by the French and Indians in the olden time, upon Prisoner's Island, hereabouts. At a quiet moment they took French leave, and waded ashore!

Directly west of Prisoner's Island is Howe's Landing, the point of debarkation of the mighty flotilla which we met at Sabbath-Day Point: and here, too, good reader, is *our* landing, and the end of our voyage of Horicon.

You will now collect your traps, and stepping with us, into one of the carriages which await—take a pleasant jog of four miles down the merry outlet of Lake George, and through the two villages of Ticonderoga, or "Tye," as they are familiarly called, to the brave old fort which the sturdy Ethan Allen so audaciously seized, "in the name of the Great Jehovah and the Continental Congress." In this little four-mile gallop of Horicon to Lake Champlain, the water makes a descent of two hundred and thirty feet, forming in the journey two series of very considerable cascades, called the Upper and the Lower Falls; both made industrially available by the denizens of the villages just mentioned. This ride, with its opening vistas of the valleys and hills of Vermont; its foaming cataracts; its charming revelations of the grand waters of Champlain; and, above all, its termination amidst the remains of the famed old Fort, is a welcome sequel to the day's delights.

Nothing could be more charmingly picturesque than the position and surroundings of the hotel at this memorable spot: the fairly-like air of the verandahed and latticed little house, its dainty walls gleaming in the drops of sunshine which steal from beneath the "sloping eaves" of the verdant grove which encircles it, and the rich velvety lawn sloping so gently to the very edge of the water.

Within immediate reach of this quiet and secluded retreat, stands the ancient Fort, looking proudly down, even in the feebleness and decrepitude of age, upon the scenes which once looked to its strength for protection and defense.

Ticonderoga, though geographically belonging to Lake Champlain, is essentially, in all its historical associations, and in all its natural beauties, part and parcel of Horicon; and nowhere may we more appropriately end our day's rambles than within its quiet shades.

Let us linger yet a moment, while the moonlight holds, amidst these eloquent mementoes of the past. Once these aged and tottering piles braved the defiance thundered from the frowning brow of yonder mountain. Here many of that glad and gorgeous array which we have twice met, found a gory resting-place. Here the feeble arm of a young nation first grew strong to humble the pride of tyrant power.

Feeble and mouldering walls, too weak to bear even the tender embrace of the clinging ivy! You were once the envied and the vaunted glory of the three great powers of the earth. France, Britain, and America successively confessed your strength. You are no more a contested prize, and never again may you be. Quiet is within your walls, and Peace dwells among the nations.

Niagara
(1853)

NIAGARA.*

NIAGARA should be first approached from above, and from the Canada shore. Let the tourist who, with his face Niagara-ward, stands at Buffalo some bright summer morning, resist the voice from within that whispers in his ear—"Take the cars · in an hour you will be there!" Let him choose rather the little steamer that plies down and across the lake to Chippewa There let him forget the Americanism which holds it undignified to walk when one can ride, and pass on foot over the three miles which separate him from Niagara.

For awhile the way lies through level green fields along a railway which looks venerable enough to be the grandfather of all railways. But as you reach a point where the river makes a sharp bight inshore, descend the bank to the water's edge. You are now a little below the first ledge of rocks that break the smooth current, forming the entrance to the Rapids, which stretch before you in white lines far away to the American shore. The prospect is soon shut out by a low crescent-shaped island, at the distance of a stone's throw. The intervening water is as smooth and placid as that of the quiet brook in which long ago you were wont to bathe, and comes rippling up to your feet with a low whisper which almost overpowers the deep murmur that overloads the air, but which you know to be the voice of the great cataract, hitherto unseen.

You round the green point of the island, and the Rapids are full before you. You have gradually descended until you are below the level of their summit, and as you look backward their white foaming crests are drawn sharply against the horizon. Down they sweep, rapid, multitudinous, apparently illimitable, seeming to pour from the blue sky.

You have never seen Niagara, but you have all along had fancies as to what it should be. You have read that the river is the outlet of the Great Lakes, the reservoirs of almost half the fresh water upon the globe; so you have tried to picture to yourself an Atlantic plunging down a precipice of unknown depth. But you know also that the stream has been measured, the precipice gauged, the quantity of water esti-

mated, and the whole stands recorded in some quite finite number of yards, feet, and gallons. But now, as you look upon this mad rush of waters whirling down the slope, you feel that your most imperial fancies fall far short of the great reality. You had placed the sublime wholly in extent, forgetting entirely the more potent elements of motion and velocity. The ocean stretching beyond reach of vision, or swooping upon the sternest lee-shore, is a feebler emblem of power than is the inevitable and despairing rush with which these tortured waters plunge down. The Rapids are a fit portal for Niagara.

How slowly you now pace along, though the sun has passed mid-heaven, and the shadows of the trees are lengthening eastward toward the river. At length your eye fixes upon some special white crest of foam, and follows it down until it melts away into a smooth green surface rounding gently over, and disappearing in an abyss the depth of which you can not see. This green slope sweeps round in a magnificent curve to the right; beyond this is a purple-gray precipice, and still further on a white cataract flashing back the sunbeams. From the centre of the curve, a pillar of spray floats calmly up, with the crown of a rainbow just rising above the verge of the abyss

You have unconsciously paused within a hundred paces of the brink of the cataract. Pass that space, and you will see all. Yet you hesitate and linger. We always, I think, pause before any great experience which is the highest of its kind we can ever know. We tremble to clutch a pleasure, beyond which there can be no other, when it is fairly within our grasp. We dally with our own feelings in order to prolong the thrill which precedes the supreme moment, which once known can never be experienced again. Did not the youth at Sais pause long with his hand upon the vail that shrouded the mysterious statue? Did you not hesitate within the vestibule of St. Peter's, and almost refuse to look upward into the vast dome that overarches the stately aisles? Were you not prompted to close your ear as the marvelous Swede opened those lips from which were to pour forth notes whose like you should never again hear upon earth? Who has not hesitated long before he would give utterance to that unbounded love which vailed eye and flushed cheek had long ago assured him would meet with a like unbounded and generous return?

THE FALLS FROM ABOVE, ON THE CANADA SHORE.

"See Naples and die," says the Italian proverb. You knew that with the view of Niagara one great chapter of your experience would be closed up. So you seat yourself in the cool shadow, light a cigar, and watch its blue smoke curling up between you and the white rainbow-tipped spray rising from before the great cataract. You pore lazily over the columns of a last week's journal which you have brought with you, and have forgotten to throw away. Yet ever and anon you lift your eye toward that innumerable rush of waters, and sweep around the circumference of that majestic curve, and feel that you are growing into Niagara. And now, at the distance of months, or years it may be, as you close your eyes and in imagination look again upon that scene, you do not wonder that we have chosen it for our opening illustration; or that the Swedish Singer should twice have commissioned the artist to paint it for her.

You spring up with a sudden impulse, and hurry over the space which separated you from Table Rock, and the Fall is full before you. You had been told by some who had approached Niagara from below, that their first feeling was one of disappointment at its apparent want of elevation. But you feel nothing of the kind. Had honest old Father Hennepin stood by your side, and told you that the height of the Fall was six hundred feet, you would have believed him.

Your mood has now changed; you no longer pause to note details; you have taken the plunge, and are eager to advance; you wish to master Niagara at once. So you hurry along the brink of the gorge, across which gleam the woods of Goat Island and the white descent of the American Fall.

A small lad, with a large head and faded yellow hair, sidles up to you, and says something about "Ing'n Work," or "Cur'osities," or "Cam'ra 'bscura," or "Guide." You give some sharp, quick answer; the small boy collapses and vanishes. You shake your head negatively at the cab-man who, catching your eye, asks, "Car-ge, S'r!" A man shambles frantically from a shanty upon the edge of the cliff, and thrusts toward you a yellow handbill, announcing that the biggest giant, the smallest dwarf, the leanest man, or the fattest woman in the world can be seen within for a trifling consideration. You look negation; whereupon the shambling individual adds persuasively that you can enter and "not pay nothink if you aren't satisfied." Still reading denial in your eye, he whispers hysterically that "if the gen-'lm'n 'd please to give the hunfort'nit hobjec hany think, it 'd be a hact of ra'al char'ty." You remain obdurate. Are you growing hard-hearted? It would seem so; for you hardly notice the good-natured smile with which the ebony gentleman, seated at a small table under the shade of a friendly tree, suggests, "May be, then, Massa 'll take some when he comes back," in reply to your gruff rejection of his small refreshments You are not even moved to sympathy by the weather-beaten canvas that marks the spot whence the unfortunate Martha Rugg fell from the bank "while picking a flower ."—in fact, it does not strike you just then that she was particularly unfortunate.

A hollow-cheeked man accosts you. His hair seems to be in a perpetual drip, and he exudes a faint odor of wet oil-skin, which you somehow imagine must be inseparable from him. He speaks in a low, mysterious tone, as though he were a hierophant proffering to you the exposition of some sacred mystery He wishes to conduct you "behind the Fall." He has evidently a theory of life He supposes the "chief end of man" to be to go behind the sheet of water.—Not now You are satisfied to stand in the outer court, and have no present desire to penetrate within the vail.

"But all this is not describing Niagara ; it is merely hinting at one's own impressions upon his first visit."

Well, then, for the Falls themselves, by way of running commentary upon our artist's clever sketches

From the bank just below the Clifton House there is a fine panoramic view of both Falls. Their general outline bears a close resemblance to the shape of the human ear ; the Horseshoe Fall constituting the upper lobe, while Goat Island and the American Fall represent the remaining portion. The river, whose general course has been east and west, makes a sharp turn to the right just at the point where the Fall now is. Its breadth is here contracted from. three-fourths of a mile to less than one-fourth. The Horseshoe Fall only occupies the head of the chasm, while the American Cataract falls over its side ; so that this Fall and a part of the Horseshoe lie directly parallel with the Canada shore, and its whole extent can be taken in at a single glance. It is this oneness of aspect which renders the prospect from this side so much the more impressive for a first view of Niagara. It gives a strong, sharp outline which may afterward be filled up at leisure.

The most complete view of the Horseshoe Fall is that from the bottom of the cliff, at a point near the ferry landing. If, however, the water is unusually high, the quiet pool which the artist has depicted in the foreground, becomes a fierce and angry rush of waters, foaming above and around the jagged rocks. If the water is very low, the bed of this pool is entirely dry. Two years ago the scene presented the aspect here represented during the whole summer Last year there were but few days when the whole spot was not overflowed. The current nearest the Canada shore runs up-stream, as though seeking an outlet in the direction from which it came. The middle distance is

THE HORSESHOE FALL, FROM NEAR THE FERRY, CANADA SHORE.

THE TOWER, FROM NEAR THE FERRY, CANADA SHORE.

caught through a clump of trees which stand a little above the ferry landing. The limitation of view heightens the effect, when contrasted with the unlimited prospect of the Fall presented from almost every other point on the Canada side.

It is no very difficult task for a stout pedestrian to make his way along under the edge of the precipice from the Ferry up to the foot of the Fall. The path winds among huge fragments of rock which have tumbled from above, and is slippery with the falling spray. You stop to rest upon a huge rock, where a couple of rough-coated men are fishing. They tell you that it is named "Bass Rock," and you recognize the propriety of the appellation, as you observe the finny spoil that has repaid their labor. The water rushes foaming and eddying around the fragments of rock, sometimes rising in great swells to the spot on which you stand. Fragments of timber, their ends rounded and worn like pebbles on a wave-beaten shore, are scattered around; some groaning and tossing in the water, others stranded high and dry upon the rocks, where they have been flung by some swell higher than usual. You are so near the foot of the Fall that the descending sheet of

marked by a line of white foam, beyond which the current runs down-stream. The centre of the Horseshoe Fall is directly in front, defined on the right by the verge of Table Rock, and on the left by the upper extremity of Goat Island. Just below the tower which seems to rise from the midst of the waters on the American side, an immense mass of rock is dimly visible, which became detached from the precipice in February, 1852.

A very charming glimpse of that portion of the Fall directly in front of the tower may be

THE HORSESHOE FALL, FROM BASS ROCK.

water occupies the entire field of vision; the immense rock which interposes between Bass Rock and the descending water has as yet received no distinctive name.

The path now begins to ascend the sloping bank, winding around huge boulders, and among gay shrubs which the perpetual spray nourishes in luxuriant greenness, wherever there is a resting-place for a patch of soil. At last you reach the dilapidated staircase which descends the perpendicular face of the cliff, and clambering around its base upon a rotten and slimy plank, you find yourself below the overhanging mass of Table Rock. You are close at the edge of the falling water, which descends in a mass apparently as solid as though carved from marble. You now begin to comprehend the height of the Fall. It makes you dizzy to look up to the upper edge of the rushing column. You stand just midway between the top and the bottom. Above you hangs the imminent mass of Table Rock; below, far down by the wet and jagged rocks, is the seething whirlpool, where the water writhes and eddies as though frenzied with its fearful leap. Round and round it goes in solemn gyrations, bearing with it whatever floating object may have been plunged into its vortex.

A year ago, this very month of August, a young woman walked in the cool gray morning down to the brink of the cliff, and flung herself into the whirlpool below. So resolute was the leap, that she shot clear of the jagged rocks at the base, and plunged sheer into the water beyond. When the visitors came sauntering down to the Fall, her body was seen whirling round and round in the mad eddies, now submerged for an instant, and then leaping up, as though imploring aid.

A day or two thereafter, I was one of a group to whom a rough-looking man was describing the scene. He told how he and two others had descended amid the blinding spray close to the foot of the Fall. A rope was then fastened to his body, which was held fast from above by the others, while he groped his misty way down to the very edge of the water, where he waited till they whirled the corpse close inshore. He then darted a spear with a spring barb into the body, but the force of the current tore out the hold, and it drifted away. Again it came within reach, and again the hold of the spear was too weak to overcome the force of the current. A third time, the body approached, and the spear was darted. This time it caught among the strong muscles of the thigh, and held, so that the body was drawn to shore.

The narrator was a rough man, roughly clad, and told his story roughly; but there was in his voice a low thrill of horror as he told how he was obliged to cut the spear-head out of the flesh with his knife, before the weapon could be extracted: "It was too bad," said he; "but it couldn't be helped." And it was with unconscious pathos that he told how they stripped off their own rough garments, and tenderly covered the poor maimed and mutilated body before they bore it up the bank. It was a commentary, wrought out into practice, upon Hood's immortal "Bridge of Sighs."

From behind the curtain of water, you now see a troop of figures slowly emerging in single file, clinging to the side of the cliff. They look like overtasked firemen or half-drowned mermen. As they draw near, you recognize in the foremost the hollow-voiced guide who, a few hours before, offered to be your Virgil, to conduct you into the Inferno before you. He smiles a ghastly recognition, for he knows that sooner or later the spell will be upon you, and you will essay the gloomy way. Among the uncouth figures is one whose light elastic step can not be disguised by the dripping oil-skin. A few hours later, as you pace the piazza of the "Clifton House," looking now at the cataract shining in the calm moonlight, and now through the open windows into the illuminated parlors, your eye catches the same light step and lithe but vigorous form.

With the exception of the Fall itself, the Canada side presents little of interest. The brink of the gorge is bare and naked, the trees which once clothed it having been cut away. The regular "drive" seems to be up to the Burning Spring, and thence back by way of Drummondville and Lundy's Lane.

At the Burning Spring you register your name, pay your fee, and are introduced into a small apartment in the floor of which is a spring in constant ebullition from the escape of an inflammable gas. The flaxen-pated children of the show-woman place a receiver over the spring, and set fire to the gas, as it comes out of the jet; they then remove the receiver, and light the gas as it rises to the surface of the water; and that is all. You take your departure, looking vastly edified; while the driver thrusts his tongue into his cheek, as though he were mentally quoting a certain proverb touching "a fool and his money."

In the gray little tumble-down village of Drummondville, the driver shows you a petty shop kept by Sandy McLeod, notorious for his connection with the burning of the "Caroline;" a fellow upon the safety of whose worthless neck once apparently depended the question of war or peace between America and England. "Eh, but that Sandy's a great rogue," said a hard-featured Scotchman with whom I fell into conversation; "but it's no that easy to catch him."

The battle-ground at Lundy's Lane is marked by two rival observatories. The old campaigner who does the honors at the "original" has, they say, two versions of the action, which he produces as he supposes may suit the nationality of his auditors. The story goes, however, that at the "celebration," a year ago, General Scott was regaled by him with the English version, and then learned for the first time how thoroughly he was beaten upon that well-contested field.

THE AMERICAN AND HORSESHOE FALLS, FROM PROSPECT POINT.

In the early morning you commit yourself to the little boat in which you are to be ferried over to the American shore. Your half-felt misgivings are dissipated as you see the dexterous manner with which the brawny boatman handles his oars, and takes advantage of the "up-eddy" and "down-eddy;" and in a few minutes you are landed close at the foot of the American Fall.

Half-way up the ferry stairs is an opening which gives access to a path along the foot of the perpendicular precipice to the verge of the falling water. From this point, in the early morning, may be gained one of the most picturesque v' vs of Niagara. Your position gives you the full perception of the height of the Fall, which forms a standard by which you measure that of the Horseshoe Fall which stretches away in the distant perspective.

I was standing, one glorious Autumn morning, looking now up to where the crown of the Fall, illuminated by the early sun, shone like opal, now downward where the gray mist curled up in the deep shadow, or across the chasm which seemed bridged over by the rainbow, whose feet were planted by the American shore, while its summit, which not long before had topped the height of the Canadian precipice, flinging a glory over the bare rocks and scanty shrubbery, crept slowly down, as the sun climbed its steep way up the eastern sky. I was suddenly roused from a reverie by a sharp voice:

" It's a-bilin' and a-sizzling down there fust-rate !"

Looking down into the seething caldron below, I could not but assent ; though mentally excepting to the phrase in which the opinion was expressed.

" But, I say, Mister," continued my interlocutor, " is the water really bilin' hot down there, so that you can't hold your hand into it ?"

Upon inquiry, I found that my new friend had fallen into the hands of one of those ingenuous youths who are on the watch to earn a few shillings by officiating as guides. He had amused his patron by a number of fables, of which this may pass as a fair specimen.

Completing the ascent of the ferry stairway, you reach Prospect Point, at its head, from whence the same general view is gained, from a more elevated point. It is hard to say whether the view from above or below is the finer The latter brings more into notice the height of the falling column of water, thus gaining an additional element of grandeur, while the latter embraces a view of the wooded islands above the Fall, adding greatly to the picturesque effect. The precise point from which the artist has taken this sketch is not now attainable. It was a projecting shelf of rock, a few feet below the precipice, which has been cut away to make room for the terribly unpicturesque, but most convenient stairway.

This was apparently the point from which honest Father Hennepin, who has left us the earliest written account of Niagara, gazed upon that " prodigious Cadence of Waters, which falls down after a surprising and astonishing Manner, insomuch that the Universe can not afford its parallel."—" The Waters," goes on the quaint narrative, "which fall from this horrible Precipice, do foam and boyle after the most hideous Manner imaginable, making an outrageous Noise more terrible than that of Thunder." The good Jesuit would seem to have been deeply moved by this " dismal Roaring ;" for in the curious picture which he gives of the Falls, he represents the spectators holding their hands to their ears to shut out the din ; and he hints that the Indians were forced to abandon the neighborhood of the Falls lest they should become deafened by the uproar.

The good Father must have heard the " horrid Noise of the Falls," as he elsewhere calls it, with the imagination rather than with the ear. You hardly notice it, as you loiter along the brink, except when some sudden atmospheric change varies its deep and solemn monotone. The sound is like the continuous and pervading murmur of the wind through a forest of sombre pines. You are not forced to raise your voice in conversing with the friend by whose side you loiter along the brink of the Fall, toward the bridge which gives you access to the wooded islands that beckon you on.

Nothing can exceed the picturesque beauty of the small wooded islands which stud the Rapids upon the American side. Two of rare beauty, known as " Ship" and " Brig" Islands, stem the current a little above the bridge which connects Goat Island with the shore. It needs but little effort of the imagination to fancy them vessels under full press of sail, endeavoring to sheer out of the current that hurries them inevitably down. The former of these Islands is accessible by a bridge which connects it with Bath Island, and is one of the loveliest spots imaginable. The old cedars, whose gnarled and contorted trunks overhang the waters, dipping their branches into the current, seem to cling with desperate clutch to the rocks, as though fearful of losing their hold and being swept away.

From the bridge leading to Goat Island the Rapids present that same appearance of plunging from the sky which renders their view from the Canadian shore so impressive. So thought

THE AMERICAN RAPIDS, FROM THE BRIDGE.

THE AMERICAN FALLS, FROM HOG'S BACK.

a young man whom I saw one calm moonlight evening leaning on the railing, and contemplating the rush of waters.

"They are beautiful, wonderful—but not quite what I expected," said he, as we fell into conversation. "I had supposed that the Falls were higher"

He had hurried from the hotel, ignorant which way to go, and supposed that he was now looking at the Great Cataract.

Goat Island—so let it still be called in spite of the foppery which has of late attempted to change its name to Iris Island—presents an aspect almost as wild as it did before it had been rendered accessible to human foot. Were it not for the path which girdles its entire circumference, and the rustic seats disposed here and there, one might fancy that he was the first who had ever sauntered through its grand and stately woods. The beauty and variety of the trees on this island are wonderful. There is the maple, greeting the early spring sunshine with its fire-tipped buds; spreading out in summer its broad dome of dark green leaves in masses so thick that beneath them you have no fear of the passing shower; and in autumn wearing its gorgeous crimson robe like an Oriental monarch. The beech shows its dappled trunk and bright green foliage at every point, giving perpetual life and vivacity to the scene. The silvery trunks of the white birch gleam among the underwood. An occasional aspen, with its ever-quivering leaves, which almost shed a sense of breezy coolness in the stilliest, sultriest day, contrasts finely with the dark evergreens by which it is relieved. Almost all of our northern Fauna have their representatives here. Even upon the little Ship Island, which can be crossed in any direction in a dozen strides, and which appears to a hasty view but a mass of twisted and gnarled cedars, there are at least seven distinct species of trees. Those trees, however, which immediately overhang the Falls have an aspect peculiar to themselves. They are bent, broken, twisted, and contorted in every direction. They seem to be starting back in horror from the abyss before them, and to wind their long finger-like roots around the rocks, in order to maintain their hold.

One of these, an aged birch, growing upon the ridge known as the "Hog's Back," affords a resting place from which to gain one of the finest views of the American Falls. Right in front is the small Central Fall, and the footbridge which leads to Luna Island, with its trees dwarfed and stunted by the weight of frozen spray which loads them in the winter. Beyond is the serrated line of the American Fall;

while the distance is filled up with the receding lines of the banks of the river below.

A few paces—past groups of blithe tourists, past companies of sombre Indian girls in blue blankets and high-crowned hats, with their gay wares spread out at their feet—brings you to the Biddle staircase, down which you wind to the foot of the precipice.

The path to the left leads along the foot of the overhanging cliff, up to the verge of the Horse-shoe Fall, only a portion of whose circumference is visible from any point on the American shore. You are here close upon the fragments of rock that fell from just in front of the tower, in February, 1852, the latest of those changes which are slowly and almost imperceptibly altering the form and position of the Falls. This fall of rock was seen by the artist who has given us so faithful a picture of its effects. He was just recovering from an illness, and while sitting in his room at the Clifton House, on the opposite Canadian shore, he was startled by a crash, almost like that of an earthquake. Tottering to the window, he beheld the immense curtain of rock in front of the tower precipitated from its ancient hold, and lying in huge masses upon the ice below; while a few streams of water trickled down the brown cliff, where but a moment before nothing had been seen but a surface of dazzling ice. The water at this extremity of the Fall descends in light feathery forms, contrasting finely with the solid masses in which it seems to plunge down the centre of the sweeping curve. The tower is perched upon the very brink of the

HORSE-SHOE FALL, FROM BELOW THE TOWER.

ENTRANCE TO CAVE OF THE WINDS

precipice, so close that the next fall of rock must carry it along with it.

The path to the right·from the foot of the staircase, leads to the entrance to the Cave of the Winds, which lies behind the Central Fall. It is hard to imagine how this cavern missed being called the "Cave of Æolus" by those classicists who have exhausted ancient mythology for appellations for our American scenery. But it has escaped this infliction; and the "Cave of the Winds" it is, and will be. From the little house close by the entrance, where the requisite changes of dress are made, you look down into an abyss of cold gray mist, driven ever and anon like showers of hail into your face, as you grope your way down the rocky slope. Haste not, pause not. Here is the platform, half-seen, half-

felt amid the blinding spray. Shade of Father Hennepin, this is truly a "dismal roaring" of wind and water. We are across—and stand secure on the smooth shaly bottom of the cave. Look up : what a magnificent arch is formed by the solid rock on the one side, and the descending mass of water on the other. Which is the solider and firmer you hardly know. Yet look again—for it is sunset—and see what we shall see nowhere else on earth, three rainbows one within another, not half-formed and incomplete, as is the scheme of our daily life ; but filling up the complete circle, perfect and absolute.

Upon an isolated rock at the very brink of the cataract stands a round tower. It is approached by a long, narrow bridge, resting now upon ledges of solid rock, and now upon loose boul-

THE TOWER, FROM THE HEAD OF THE BRIDGE.

ders. From the balcony upon its summit, you can lean far over the edge of the precipice, and there catch the freshness of the cloud of spray that rises evermore from the unseen foot of the great Fall. Or you can climb down the low rock upon which the tower stands, and gather shells and pebbles from within arm's length of the verge of the descent, so gentle, to all appearance, is the current. But be not over-bold. These waters, apparently so gentle, sweep down with a force beyond your power to stem. Not many months ago, a man fell from the bridge into their smooth flow, and was in the twinkling of an eye swept to the brink of the descent. Here he lodged against one of those rocks that lie apparently tottering upon the brow, looking over the fearful descent, with as little power to retrace his course, as he would have had to re-ascend the perpendicular Fall. A rope was floated down to him, which he had just strength to fasten around his body, and he was drawn up from his perilous position.

It is usual to speak of the Horseshoe Fall as Canadian ; and our rather slow neighbors across the river have been wont to plume themselves upon the possession of the more magnificent part of Niagara ; while Young America has been heard to mutter between his teeth something about "annexation," on the ground that the lesser nation has no fair claim to the possession of the major part of the crowning wonder of the Continent. But the portion of Niagara belonging to Canada is hardly worth contending for. The boundary line between the two countries is

the deepest water, which runs far over toward the Canadian shore. The line passes through the lonely little isle in the centre of the river, which has never been trodden by human foot. Right through the very centre of the Horseshoe Fall, where the water is greenest, cutting the densest pillar of spray — through the inmost convolution of the whirlpool — through the calmest part of the quiet reach of water above the Suspension Bridge — through the maddest rush of the rapids below — goes the boundary line — leaving to Canada nothing of Niagara except Table Rock, which yearly threatens to fall, and the half of the great Fall : while to America it gives, together with full one half of the Horseshoe Fall, the varying beauties of the lesser Cataracts, and the whole wealth of the lovely islands which gem the Rapids.

The general form of the Fall is slowly changing from age to age. When good Father Hennepin saw them, a century and three-quarters ago, they presented little of that curved and indented outline which now forms their most striking peculiarity. The Fall on the western side extended in nearly a straight line from the head of Goat Island to Table Rock, which terminated in a bluff that turned a portion of the water from its direct course, forming another cataract which fell to the east. A century later, this projecting rock had disappeared, but the spot which it had occupied was distinctly traceable. From the character of the strata through which the water has slowly worn its way back from the shores of Lake Ontario, we learn what must have been the appearance of the Fall at any period of its history. Thus, it can never have overcome the descent of three hundred and fifty feet at Lewiston at a single leap, but must have formed at least three cataracts separated by intervening rapids. When the Falls occupied the position of the Whirlpool, three miles below their present site, the descent was evidently greater than at any period before or since. But there never can have been a period when their beauty equaled that which they present at the present age. The immense breadth of the sheet of falling water, its graceful sweep of curves, and the picturesque islands that stud the brink, belong solely to our present Niagara. The Falls recede at present, we are told, at the rate of something less than a foot in a year. Geology is able to predict that when a recession of a mile has taken place—some five or six thousand years hence—the height of the Fall will be reduced by a score of feet. Another five thousand years will subtract two score more of feet. Ten thousand years more, when the Fall shall have worn its way four miles farther back, all that constitutes Niagara will have disappeared, and the whole descent will be accomplished by a series of rapids like those near the Whirlpool.

It is strange how little of direct human interest is connected with Niagara. One would have supposed that it would have been a sacred spot with the Indians; but, with the exception of a few graves on the upper extremity of Goat Island, no special memorial of the aborigines exists here. In truth, the actual North American Indian was a terribly unpicturesque and un-

heroic animal. The Falls have been known to the white race for too short a time to gather around them legendary associations. One or two points are associated with the memory of a young Englishman who, something like a score of years ago, set up as the "Hermit of the Falls." A picturesque little break in the Rapids between Goat Island and one of the rocky islets known as the "Three Sisters," has been named from him the "Hermit's Cascade." It is a lovely spot by the side of which one may lie under the overarching trees, and while away the noontide hour, lulled into dreamy slumber by the deep voice of the Cataract. This "Hermit" seems hardly worthy of being made the hero of the Falls. Little is told of him except that he was fond of music and of pacing by night along the margin of the river; that he was alike indisposed for human society and for clean linen. It is said, indeed, that he was accustomed to record his musings in Latin, but as no fragments of these were discovered after

THE HERMIT'S CASCADE.

THE SUSPENSION BRIDGE, FROM THE MAID OF THE MIST

his death, we may set the story down as apocryphal. A deeper tragic interest is attached to a tale, now some three years old, which will be told you as you stand by the margin of the Lesser Fall. A party of visitors stood here, in gay discourse. Among them were a young man, his affianced bride, and a laughing child. The young man caught the child in his arms, saying gayly, " Now I shall throw you over." She glided from his hold in affright, half real, half feigned, and plunged into the stream ; he sprang after, but the current was stronger than his strength, and swept them both down the smooth slope, and over the Fall Their bodies, mangled and bruised, were recovered from the rocks below.

The pedestrian can hardly find a pleasanter summer day's ramble, than that along the river to Lewiston, descending on the American side, and returning by the opposite bank For a mile below the Falls, where the channel is narrowest, the current is so smooth, that one might fancy he was gazing down into some quiet tarn embosomed in the mountains, were it

BANK BELOW THE WHIRLPOOL.

not that you catch the white margin of the lower Rapids just where the Suspension Bridge stretches its slender line from the summits of the opposing cliffs.   In this quiet reach of water plies the little steamer, the "Maid of the Mist."   After passing the ugly, bustling little village growing up around the American extremity of the bridge, a path leads through quiet fields and woods along the very verge of the precipice.   Here and there some tree growing upon the brink forms a safe balustrade over which you lean, and look down upon the green water dashing furiously through its confined channel far below.

The Whirlpool, three miles below the Falls, is an adjunct worthy of Niagara.   The stream makes a sharp bend just where the channel is narrowest and the descent of the Rapids the steepest.   At the angle the current has scooped out an immense basin, around whose whole circumference the water circles before it can find an outlet.   All floating bodies that pass down the river are drawn into the Whirlpool, where they are borne round and round for days, and weeks sometimes, it is said, before they make their escape.   A practicable path winds down the bank to the water's edge

The character of the banks gradually changes as we descend toward the outlet of the river. The hard limestone overlying the softer rock, and forming the perpendicular portion of the cliff, becomes thinner ; the sloping *talus* at the

foot grows higher, and the rocks are clothed with a luxuriant forest growth.

A half mile below the Whirlpool is a deep cleft in the precipitous bank, which is connected with a wild Indian legend ascribing terrible convulsions of nature, and even the approach of the fatal white men, to an unauthorized violation of the privacy of a great demon who once abode here   This was the scene of a terrible tragedy in the old Franch wars   A convoy of British soldiers fell into an ambush of Indians at this point, and were all, with the exception of two, slain outright or driven over the edge of the chasm.   The little rivulet which flows over the brink, ran red with the blood of the slaughtered, and thus gained the name, which it still bears, of the "Bloody Run."

Close by the Devil's Hole the railroad now in course of construction from Lewiston to the Falls, gains the level of the top of the bank. From this point downward, it is excavated in the face of the cliff, forming a steep grade to its bottom   An almost continuous line of *shanties* occupied by the laborers engaged in the excavation extends along the very verge of the preci-

THE WHIRLPOOL, FROM THE CANADA SIDE.

pice. It was curious, as I passed along in the early April days, to see children whom we should scarcely trust out of the nurse's arms, sprawling upon the very verge of the cliff. The laborers are apparently all Irish, and it is noteworthy to see how much more intelligent is the aspect of the younger than of the older children. I thought I could distinguish by their mere physical appearance those who were born under the freer and happier auspices which surround them here.

At the foot of the cliff the Suspension Bridge stretches like a slender thread across the stream, its supporting towers resting on a ledge above the level of the roadway. No line of guards watches the quiet frontiers of two great nations. The sole police is a small boy at the gate, and the only passport demanded is a shilling for toll. You climb the smooth slope to the summit, where the shattered monument to the noble Brock is the only memorial of the day when the thrice-won victory was at last wrenched from the hands of the Americans.

THE AMERICAN FALL BY MOONLIGHT.

A flock of sheep are cropping the tender herbage; a couple of lambs have found a shady resting-place in the crumbling archway of the monument. To the right the white village of Lewiston presents an aspect of bustling activity; while to the left, on the opposite Canadian shore, Queenstown rests gray and sombre. At your feet, just below the dilapidated memorial of war, the bridge—symbol of union—binds the two shores: may it never be a pathway for the march of hostile armies!

There are two or three things in the way of excursion which must sooner or later be performed. Some bright afternoon, when the west is all a-glow, as you sit upon Table Rock, watching the clouds of spray momently torn from the face of the descending column, the guide with the hollow voice, whose mission is to conduct visitors behind the great sheet, presents himself. You commit yourself to his guidance, and don-

ning the suit of yellow oil-skin follow him down the spiral staircase, along the base of the precipice up to the verge of the cataract. You shudder, and hesitate to enter the blinding spray along that winding path which seems in the dimness like a slender line drawn upon the face of the rock. The guide whispers a word of encouragement, deftly insinuating how boldly "the lady" trod its slippery length. You take courage and advance. You can scarcely breathe, much less see—but you feel that the torrent is plunging from the immeasurable height above into the unfathomable depth below. Somehow, how you hardly know, you have passed through the thick curtain of blinding spray, and are peering eagerly into the gray depth beyond. You are on Termination Rock, and farther than' this mortal foot may never penetrate within the vail. Whichever way you turn, it is all cold gray mist, shrouding the overhanging rock and the over-arching water above, and the profound depths below :—all mist, cold gray mist above, below, around, except when you turn your eyes back along the path by which you entered, where you behold a strip of golden sky between the grim rock and the edge of the descending flood. Drenched and dripping, spent and exhausted, as a shipwrecked sailor flung by the surf upon some inhospitable shore, you follow your guide back along the misty path, and emerge gladly enough into the clear outer air, into the free sunshine, and beneath the bright sky. You have been within the vail. As you doff the heavy oil-skin integuments, a printed paper is put into your hand, certifying that you "have been under the great sheet of water, the distance of two hundred and forty feet from the commencement of the Falls to the termination of Table Rock," verified by the signature of the proprietor of "Table Rock House." Your guide looks on you complacently, as though he would assure you that the great end of life was now attained, and you might take up your "*Nunc dimittis.*"

Or you take your place upon the deck of the "Maid of the Mist," hard by the Suspension Bridge, and are steamed up to the foot of the cataract. The little steamer answers but poorly to her romantic name. She swings wearily from her moorings, and goes panting and tugging up the current. Yet she manages to hold her course, unless the wind blows too strong down-stream, and slowly wins her way close up

to the huge rocks upon which the waters of the American Fall are broken and shattered, into the thickest of the spray. A sharp gust of wind tears a sudden rent through the spray, dashing it in arrowy sleet against your upturned face ; but through the rent you catch a glimpse of the green crest of the Horseshoe Fall, sinking grandly into the ocean of vapor below.

Or better still, on some calm moonlight night, you invoke the aid of "Charley Jones" or his brother "'Ras," the ferrymen, and glide up along the foot of the American Fall, keeping just outside the dark line of shadow. There is nothing on earth so weird and ghostlike as the spectacle before you. The column of spray rises from the blankness below, like the spectre of some gigantic tree, and spreads solemnly up into the clear air above.

The mere summer tourist sees, however, but half of Niagara. In the winter the great rocks at the foot of the Fall are piled with an accumulation of frozen spray to the depth of half a hundred feet. By creeping cautiously up the slippery ascent, you may stand face to face with the cataract, half-way up its height. Every shrub on the margin is loaded with glittering ice. The thick-branched evergreens are bowed beneath its weight, and bend to the ground like enormous plumes. The face of the cold gray rock is cased in glittering ice, and ribbed with pillars and pilasters, which flash back the reflection of all gems, in the slant rays of the sun.

WINTER VIEW AT NIAGARA.

These are but words, and words can only faintly suggest some of the more salient features of Niagara. Even the painter's pencil is inadequate to express that in which lies its deepest charm—everlasting motion and perpetual change, conjoined with an all-pervading sense of unity. The artist from whose labors we have so largely borrowed, has made the study of the Great Cataract a labor of love. He has summered and wintered by it. He has painted it by night and by day; by sunlight and by moonlight; under a summer sun, and amid the rigors of a Canadian winter, when the gray rocks wore an icy robe, and the spray congealed into icicles upon his stiffened garments. The sketches from which we have selected, have grown up under his hands for a half score of years; and we can not doubt that many to whom Niagara wears the face of a familiar friend, will find themselves transported to it in imagination, as they look upon the results of his labors; and many who may never behold the Falls, will gain some just though inadequate conception of their magnificence and beauty.

J. W. ORR N.Y.

THE ARTIST AT NIAGARA.

An Excursion to Watkins Glen (1871)

AN EXCURSION TO WATKINS GLEN.

By PORTE CRAYON.

GLEN MOUNTAIN HOUSE.

THE wise Solomon snubs a class of people who are eternally babbling about the superiority of "the former days," and lamenting the decease of the good old times; but if any one has reason to complain, it is surely the modern traveler, who may be permitted to look back with envy and regret to those by-gone ages when the means of locomotion were so limited, and popular credulity so unlimited.

When the tourist, on taking up his staff and scrip, or settling himself in his dug-out for an excursion, was stimulated by the reasonable hope of seeing something new under the sun; in the days when Jason went in search of the golden fleece; when sage Ulysses spent so many adventurous years paddling about in that shallow puddle, the Mediterranean; when the pious Æneas made that famous subterranean journey to explore a country which the pious folks of the present day are not supposed to visit; when traveled Herodotus told his entertaining stories; and when, instead of one great overshadowing publishing concern, every prince and hero entertained a "Harper" of his own to publish his life and actions, not in cloth and gilt bound volumes, to be sneered at and discredited by unfriendly and hireling critics, but issued *viva voce* at high festivals and jolly suppers, to audiences filled with meat and drink and amiable credulity.

Those were, indeed, the days for travelers, bards, historians, and all other professors of the imaginative arts. But since the insatiable Anglo-Saxon has done our world so thoroughly, where shall we direct our restless steps with the rational hope of discovering a novelty, or what chance for indulgence in the poetic luxury of aberration, when any free-school brat may question your facts or criticise your geography?

Indeed, for the romance of travel, we may as well concede that the surface of our present establishment is about used up, and until the coming man discovers a practicable entrance to the interior, or perfects aerial navigation sufficiently to enable us to visit our neighboring Lunatics, the tourist may as well lay aside pen and pencil, take half a dozen magazines and newspapers, light his pipe, and imitate the clever M. Gonzalez with his "Voyages en Pantoufles."

In accordance with the foregoing reflections we had sat down in our slippers, lighted our pipe, and cut the leaves of our fresh magazine, when the mail brought us an invitation to visit the region of the minor lakes in Western New York.

At the reading the air was balmy with the buds and blossoms of early May; the bluebirds warbled lovingly as they worked at their cottage-building in the eaves; and boon Nature seemed to have put on all her blandishments to induce acceptance.

Then we were promised a select company in a special car. Among the excursionists there would be editors, artists, clergymen, scholars, poets, and philosophers, such as travel to gather ideas rather than dimes; men who live and labor to develop the true, the beautiful, the elevated, rather than to heap up the mere means of living; whose labors are so often futile and whose lives failures for lack of those very means, which old Gradgrind accumulates so easily, and don't know how to spend.

We were to meet in Baltimore, at the dépôt of the Northern Central Railroad, on Monday, the 9th of May. The hour of starting 12.40 by bell and whistle.

Accepted.

ENTRANCE TO WATKINS GLEN.

All aboard! Fizzle—squeak—ding-dong—
rumble-rumble, and away we go, out of the
hurry-skurry, smoke, and suffocation of the dépôt into the open air and sunlight. Puffing
and rolling onward through the long, wearisome vistas of brick and mortar streets, until
at length, the dusty corporation limits passed,
our noses scent the incense-laden breath of the
country. The free, buxom, artless country, all
buds and blossoms and blushes, like a May
queen—her bashful charms enhanced by a thin
veil of violet haze, whose transparency but stimulates the ardent glances of her accepted lover,
the sun.

Reclining on spring-cushioned, cut velvet
seats, realizing the luxury, if not the poetry, of
motion, our excursionists revel in the perfumed
atmosphere and tender-tinted landscapes, diluted a little and the garishness toned down by
dense clouds of tobacco smoke, and express
their æsthetic emotions in stenographic phrase-
ology.

"Fine day."

"Very."

"Nice weather."

"Hottish."

Puff; puff.

"Cigar?"

"Thank you, no—prefer a pipe."

Puff; puff.

"What baskets are those?"

"Grub."

"And the bottles?"

"Ale and Bourbon."

"Ah! how invigorating and appetizing!"

"What? pure country air and water? Try
this ale—with a toast:

> 'A country duck,
> But a city cook.'

Here's another to the same purpose:

> 'A country lass
> In a city dress.'"

But, like the light skirmishing which preludes
the general engagement, this presently closed
in more earnest conversation; for our company
was composed of men of travel, elegant culture,
and varied abilities—many-sided men, as the
Germans call them, who are readily jostled into
social congruity, whose characteristic angulari-
ties are easily adjusted, like hexagonal figures;
whose differences and dogmatisms were domi-
neered and harmonized by a mysterious sympathy, like that which unites the votaries of a
common religion. Fellow-worshipers at the
shrine of the beautiful, this sweet May day
was dedicated to their divinity. The universal
majesty, before whom all conceits, prejudices,
and opinions bend the knee; in whose homage
all ages, languages, and civilizations unite; at
the gates of whose temple all the ascending
paths of human progress must finally meet; in
whose service all sincere and honorable workers, whether in politics, society, science, art, or
religion, are brethren.

Most people go through the world with eyes

and hearts both blind to its greatest beauties
and highest enjoyments; or if they look at all,
it is, through a gimlet-hole, at such objects only
as may be connected with their own narrow occupations and interests. Thus, while our untiring Yankee has pretty thoroughly reconnoi-
tered the agricultural, mineral, manufacturing,
commercial, and gullible capacities of our broad
inheritance, called (why mince matters?) "the
Western Continent," its nobler resources and
attractions are so commonly ignored that the
tourist, with artistic and poetic eyes, in passing
through regions which have been pastured,
plowed, catacombed with mines, gridironed with
railroads, and smoked by factory chimneys for
years, stumbles continually upon delightful surprises, natural picture-galleries of exquisite
beauty and surpassing grandeur, of which the
world has never heard, and which are scarcely
known, much less appreciated, by the busy
muck-rakes in their immediate vicinity.

Thus, in sweeping across Central Pennsylvania, we saw a region teeming with intelligent
industry and material wealth, covered with well-
cultivated farms, and dotted with thriving villages and stately cities. We had heard of
these things, boastfully reiterated, and were
not disappointed. But we had in addition—
what we had never heard talked of—a succession of the most beautiful scenic pictures that
ever regaled the eye of an artist or warmed the
fancy of a poet. We do not remember to have
seen any where a panorama superior to that
exhibited by the broad Susquehanna, with its
green islands, limpid waters, and blue mountain embankments. As we glided smoothly and
rapidly along the well-conducted thoroughfare,
it was enjoyable as an opium dream to watch
how each vanishing picture was replaced by another equally charming ere one had time to regret its passage.

It was, indeed, quite equal to standing on a
corner in Charles Street, on a pleasant afternoon, with a full stream of Baltimore beauties
flowing along the sidewalks.

Having left York, Harrisburg, and Sunbury
behind, evening overtook us as we approached
Williamsport, one hundred and seventy-eight
miles distant from our starting-point.

There is a limit to all emotions, even to our
purest and most healthful enjoyments, and we
experienced a certain sense of relief when Mother Night kindly drew her curtain over the pictures.

We had seen quite enough for one day, and
having switched off in front of the Herdic
House, we land and say good-by until to-morrow morning.

This elegant railroad hotel and summer resort is the nucleus of a handsomely improved
suburb of Williamsport—a town of fifteen or
twenty thousand inhabitants, living and thriving on saw-mills and the lumber trade.

In size and appointments the Herdic com-
pares with our first-class city hotels, with the
advantage, however, of being located in the

VIEW FROM GLEN ALPHA.

Rising from the valley by the inclined planes we cross a summit level which shows us a more open and cultivated country, with a wider horizon, and divers fresh-looking villages, with an inordinate proportion of church steeples.

At length we find ourselves in the State of New York, and, during a brief stoppage, catch a glimpse of Elmira, a beautiful town with whole streets of handsome villas and ornate cottages embowered in trees and blooming shrubbery.

Anon we enter the Slashes, at the head of Seneca Lake, and after running for several miles through water up to the hubs of the car-wheels, emerge at Watkins.

This pretty village stands high and dry at the head of lake navigation, overlooking the submerged meadows through which we had traveled, and commanding a charming view of the lake and the grand amphitheatre of hills which encircle its head waters.

The look-out in every direction was pleasant, and the air hazy with the perfume of flowers and blooming orchards. Seneca, like a blue mirror framed in gently sloping hills, is "beautiful exceedingly;" but we had by this time become familiarized with pretty things, and enjoyed it mildly. Dinner was served, and after that we sallied forth to see the village wonder—the Glen.

Our route led us directly up the main street of the town, with pretty cottages and ornamented grounds on either side. The surrounding country appeared so smooth-featured that we wondered, as we walked, where those savage scenes, vaguely described to us, could be located.

About half a mile from our hotel we reached a bridge spanning a limpid stream. Looking to the right, a quarter of a mile distant, we perceive this stream issues from a cavernous opening at the base of a perpendicular cliff some three hundred feet in height above the road.

As we approach nearer we see a steep rustic

midst of an extensive and umbrageous park, where its guests may sit in the shade and indulge in rural conceits, uninterrupted by the harsh screaming of the locomotives; for here all movements of trains are arranged by silent signals—which may be noted, by-the-way, as an advance toward a higher civilization in railway management.

After a night's repose and a solid breakfast we took the road again, leaving the Susquehanna and running up the fertile and picturesque valley of the Lycoming.

As we ascend, the hills grow wilder and more abrupt, the valley more limited, and the scenery, although still charming, loses much of its breadth and grandeur. On this portion of the route there are numerous summer resorts, which offer mineral waters, pure air, and trout-fishing to the wearied cit who would escape for a season from the heat and business of the town.

At Hinnequa, the most ambitious of these hotels, the attractions consist of a sulphur spring and a bear—the water weakly mineralized, and the bear rather small and uninteresting.

stairway raised against the face of the rock, crossing the fissure by a narrow bridge, and connecting with other steps which are hidden beneath the shadows of overhanging trees.

Still nearer, the impressiveness of the scene is reinforced by a deep-toned, subterraneous roaring, and glimpses of a column of water leaping from a height of thirty feet into a black caldron beneath the bridge.

Now we see the sharp-cut, narrow rift extending from the summit to the base of the cliff—closed in above the bridge by masses of evergreen foliage; below, all bare and black, like the mouth of a cavern.

It was not necessary for our guide to name it. This is the entrance to the Glen, and with one accord we all stood still to take in the full measure of its impressiveness.

"This," said the poet, "is a suggestive gateway to a region of wonders."

"And this," said the artist, "is worthy of a sketch." And, having selected his point of view, he went to work with crayon and sketchbook, while the rest of the company entered the Glen and disappeared from our sight.

Attracted by the novelty, some boys who had been angling for minnows left their sport, and gathered around to stare. Presently the artist made an impatient gesture, and quoted the Ancient Mariner—

"Water, water every where,
And not a drop to drink."

"My boy,"said he, addressing one of the juvenile gapers, "wouldn't you like to have a hand in getting up this picture?"

The boy seemed a little mystified, but expressed his willingness to be useful in any way that he could.

"Then run to that house and get me a cup of water." The errand was promptly accomplished, and rewarded by thanks and a small item of fractional currency.

"Thankee yourself," replied the boy, with effusion. "I say, mister, I'm jist going down here to fish a little; and if you want any thing more, jist call me, for I likes to run errands for people that gives me money."

Our sketcher was not thirsty, as we had supposed, but only in need of water to liquefy his India ink, to deepen the shadows of his picture. It was speedily completed, and pronounced a success. The artist observed, with some complacency, that the rudest drawing conveyed ideas more graphically and geographically than the most elaborate word-painting; "and yet," he continued, looking up and around, "how feeble all our arts appear in the majestic presence of nature!"

Then we go forward together; mount the stairway, light with expectancy; crossing the bridge, not without a tremor as we glance downward into the black, tumultuous abyss. Ascending a few more steps we turn a corner, and are in the Glen. A dramatic surprise—startling, savage, hideous! But we are not yet hopelessly engulfed—swallowed by these horrible jaws; for, looking outward, we may still catch a glimpse of the bright, luxurious world we are leaving. There we may see the stream, glad of its escape from the torturing tumult of its dark prison, dancing in the golden sunlight, hastening through blooming orchards and green meadows down to the lake, rejoicing like a wandering child that has found its mother; over all the blue mountains and bright sky— the most smiling and loving of nature's pictures, set in a narrow frame of black, slimy, frightful crags.

But it becomes us not to linger here, to gaze upon this melting beauty. Kiss your hand to her like a knightly lover, say farewell, and summon up your spirit for the rugged work before us. It is like the sudden plunge from peace into war. We anticipate with fear and trembling. We recoil with horror from the verge. We take the frantic leap; and, now now that our blood is up, we feel that the red glare ceases to offend, but even stimulates the eye more gratefully than the gentle blue. War has its horrible charms, its grand emotions, its glories, which at times render the memory of peace insipid. So, now we have fairly entered the Glen, and adjusted our faculties to the subject, we will find therein wonders, sublimities, grim beauties, and tumultuous excitements fully to compensate us for the tame, easy-going world we have left outside.

Encouraged by the success of his external picture, our artist made his *entrée* with an air of assurance; but ere he had reached Glen Alpha his countenance fell, and his look of complacency departed.

"This," he exclaimed, "is stunning! Rembrantesque! Gustave Dorésque!—confounded chaos! There's no place to sit down, no point of view, no perspective—unless one lies on his back and looks upward, or leans over a handrail face downward. To get a picture here the horizontal line must be perpendicular, with the vanishing point in the clouds or the bowels of the earth."

Advancing, however, a short distance into Glen Alpha, the prospect began to improve, for there were four cascades in perspective, and a glimpse of blue sky through the narrow rift above.

Choosing a convenient seat just beneath a projecting ledge, secure from annoyance of the dripping water or a chance fragment of rock scaling from above, the artist again began his labors. As the work progressed, and by the skillful management of light and shade the flat surface of the paper began to exhibit the cavernous depths and distances of the actual scene before us, the workman resumed his strain of cheerful enthusiasm:

"What a glorious picture this would make if skillfully rendered in color, by such a hand, for example, as that of Church or Bierstadt! And yet," he continued, "there appears to be little or no color in it—all light and shadow, sharply defined, with very little middle tint or gradation.

GLEN ALPHA.

"One might suppose, too, that these grim, silent, hard-featured rocks were steady sitters, and the laughing, dancing cascades, all froth and motion, were hard to catch; but it is just the reverse.

"The leaping waters perform their gymnastic evolutions, foaming, fretting, flashing, dimpling, by certain rules, so rapidly and continuously repeated that the eye soon catches the method, and the likeness is easily fixed; but what with the changing shadows from the clouds, or the sunlight creeping over their foreheads, the rocks are continually showing new profiles and changing their aspect, so as frequently to lose all resemblance to themselves from hour to hour."

But here comes something to enliven our solitude—a comely matron, followed by two little girls carrying baskets. They mount the dizzy ladders, and hasten along the slippery, shelving

THE CATHEDRAL.

paths with an incurious assurance which indicates that they are not strangers here. Now they turn aside, and scrambling up the banks, begin to fill their baskets with choice specimens of mosses, ferns, and wild flowers. These are some tasteful dwellers in the village below, who gather material in this wild conservatory to replenish their vases, borders, and hanging baskets at home.

When they were gone there followed up from the gorge below a confusion of articulate sounds—loud talking mingled with shouts and merry laughter. Then came a troop of young people—gentlemen and ladies, doubtless, but it sounds pleasanter to call them boys and girls. From their eager gestures and wondering exclama-

tions it is easy to see they are strangers, doing the Glen for the first time. We will, moreover, risk our reputation on the assertion that the last couple are lovers—else why do they linger so far behind their fellows, instead of emulating their adventurous activity? Why, instead of screaming, screeching, and exclaiming in tones that drown the laughter of the water-falls, do they glide along the narrow paths so quietly, looking on the surrounding sublimities with cold glances of dutiful admiration, and lightening with enthusiasm only when their faces are turned inward toward each other? Why clings she so timorously to his arm, claiming protection where there is no danger? Why does he watch and guide each step of hers with knightly tenderness, when she could take better care of her draggled skirts walking alone?

How those gay colors and animated figures warm up and humanize these heartless rocks and water-falls! I wish they would stop for ten minutes; my pencil yearns for just such a group to enliven the foreground of this damp and dismal sepulchre. They did not tarry, however, and the moment after voices were heard as if descending from the clouds: "Come up here, Josey! Hurry, hurry! What a lovely view!"

Aroused from their trance by these calls the rear-guard hastened forward, and the visitors disappeared amidst the intricacies of the ravine like a gleam of sunlight suddenly quenched, leaving the Glen enshrouded in deeper shadows than before.

"I wish they had tarried a while longer," said the artist, as he resumed his work; "I wish they had waited; for, with all nature's grandeurs and sublimities, the world would be dreary without them."

Under the influence of these reflections the sketch was hastily finished, and we, too, resumed our explorations.

Perched like an eagle's nest upon the brow of the cliff which overhangs the abyss from which we emerged, we first beheld an edifice, the work of human hands, whose architectural features are singularly adapted to the wild and rugged nature around it.

Ascending a long flight of steps, steep but secure, we reached the broad veranda of the Mountain House, and, with agreeable surprise at the sudden transition, find ourselves high up out of the cavernous Glen, in the genial sunlight, and surrounded by a gay and excited company of visitors, all agog with what they have seen and what they still expect to see.

The change was as dramatic as an entre-act in "Der Freischütz" or "Robert le Diable," when the curtain falls on the terrors of the Wolf's Glen or the Haunted Cloister, and one steps out to stretch his legs in the saloon, in the society of ice-creams, lemonades, simpering smiles, and every-day affectations.

We had all these refreshments at the Mountain House, and, what was more, we enjoyed them with a zest.

Our companions were all there waiting, and we found them discussing the Glen over some empty glasses and a table slopped with ale.

ABOVE THE CATHEDRAL.

"Hillo, Porte, what have you made of it? Show us your sketches."

"First, let our poet laureate recite his verses composed on the occasion."

"Verses!" exclaimed the poet. "I give it up. The place reminds me of the Mammoth Cave with the lid lifted off; but as for verses—although rhymes come pat and plentiful, I could make no reason out of it all. I sat upon a wet rock down there, and for half an hour puzzled myself by stringing together all the wondering, thundering, roaring, pouring, flashing, splashing, crashing, dashing, roaming, foaming, rumbling, tumbling, jagged, cragged, onerous, sonorous adjectives that I could think of, until I got such a buzzing in my ears that I was fain to come up here and calm my excited imagination with a glass of beer."

"And, pray, can you tell us the name of this?" said the artist, exhibiting a wild flower of singular beauty. "I plucked it as I came along."

"That," replied the professor, "is—ah—that is—that is—" snapping his fingers three times, and tapping his forehead impatiently—"that is—my memory is vexatiously bad."

"I'm glad you've forgotten it," said the laureate, "for I am sure it is some jaw-breaking Latin or Greek derivative that might wither so sweet a blossom in the baptism."

The professor retorted, with some asperity, "Its name belongs to a technical vocabulary with which every scholar, and especially a rhymer, should be acquainted, as it might help you out of many a metrical hobble, and, perhaps, save the sense of your verses on a pinch."

"Save me from such assistance!" exclaimed the poet. "They would be like a handful of gravel in my rhyming mill."

Here the discussion was terminated by the departure of the gay party we had seen below.

"And is there more of it?" asked one with eagerness.

THE CASCADE.

"More of it! They say that we have seen nothing compared to what is to come."

"Why, it is frightful to think of, Joe," whispered the pretty girl whom we had remarked in Glen Alpha.

"Don't be scared, Kate, but just stick close to me, and I'll insure you safe through worse places than this Glen."

And Kate clasped his arm as if she had made up her mind to stick through thick and thin.

"There go our future electors," observed our conservative friend. "What is the world coming to? When women get into public life all the romance of chivalry must perish and be forgotten."

"Nonsense!" cried the poet. "Did you see him make an umbrella of his hat when they passed under that dripping rock? Talk to me of the decadence of chivalry, when any cock-sparrow of a merchant's clerk is ready to sacrifice a new hat to protect his sweetheart's false curls! I tell you the sentiment is ineradicable, perennial—"

"Sempervirens is the botanical term," suggested the professor.

Our friend perceived that the poet had just emptied his third glass, so he ignored the interruption, and addressed his discourse pointedly in another direction.

"When woman insists on giving up the sacred seclusion of domestic life, abandoning the dignified and elevated position in society which high civilization has accorded to her, and descends into the filthy arena of politics—"

"Then," interrupted the poet, "she will bring her broom with her, and sweep the dirt out of it, and make it a fit place for gentlemen and good citizens, as she has swept and purified every other arena to which she has been admitted."

As the subject was supposed to be one of general interest the company soon became involved in a general and simultaneous debate, the conclusion of which it was difficult to foresee, as all talked and none listened.

At this stage the champion of the dames withdrew from the lists, and occupied himself in scribbling over the blank page of a letter with a lead-pencil. In an incredibly short time he rose to his feet with the paper in his hand, and stopping the talk with an authoritative ahem, he said:

"Gentlemen, this is really not worth talking about, and so please listen to my views, in verse:

"ON WOMAN'S RIGHTS.

"'Ce qui ne vaut pas le peine d'être dit—on le chante.'

"Thunder and earthquakes! what a scare;
Sultan and Pope for war prepare,
    A new rebellion's brewing.
In all the newspapers we note
Our women have resolved to vote:
    'Twill be mankind's undoing.

"'Twill quite upset that ancient board
Of registration, which ignored
    Her rights, by nature given—
From mundane politics debarred,
Dismissed her to be registered
    With marriages—in heaven.

"'Oh, woman, in our hours of ease
Uncertain, coy, and hard to please'—
    Thus sings the Scottish poet.
Will she be more uncertain when
In politics, more false and mean
Than we have found her fellow-men?
    If so, we'd like to know it.

"She'll practice law; God help the judge;
The printed code may pass for 'fudge,'
    Scarce worth his Honor's reading.
When law and logic fail she'll weep,
In fluent tears her kerchief steep;
    Then who'll reverse her pleading?

THE WELL.

"The thought's enough to strike one dumb,
  You're sick—the lady doctor's come
    Your fevered pulse to finger.
  At once your heart begins to drum—
  'Tis in the pericardium;
    This case is like to linger.'

"Our churches next will be perplexed;
  In pulpit she'll expound her text—
    She's half 'divine' already.
  'Mulier'—we quote forgotten law—
  'Taceat in ecclesia'
  (Woman in church must hold her jaw)—
    What language to a lady!

"A-soldiering with right good-will,
  She'll gayly march to camp and drill,
    With musket, fife, and drumming.
  The lines she'll dress with nicest skill,
  And e'en when sallying forth to kill,
    Still dress to look becoming.

"When empty drums sound loud alarms
  She'll march, arrayed in all her charms,
    To meet the opposing gender.
  Still lovelier 'mid impending storms,
  She only need 'present' her arms—
    'Don't shoot, girls—we'll surrender.'

"Victorious in election races,
  Our halls of state at length she graces,
    Regardless of expenses.
  Then policy, in all high places,
  Will be to cheapen foreign laces
    And multiply the census.

"Well, let her have it as she will,
  She'll be the sculptor's model still,
    Queen of the poet's rhymes.
  The painter still his pallet mix
  To match the warm life in her cheeks,
    As in the good old times.

"Yes, let it come, for evermore
  'Twill be as it has been before,
    Since apples grew in Eden:
  Should she invite we all must bite;
  Refusal would not be polite,
    Nor sanctioned by good-breeding.

"Then courage, boys, fair play for all,
  Though girls should vote the sky won't fall,
    So love we one another.
  The candidates we nominate
  Be blue-eyed Mary, blushing Kate;
  And if they'll but reciprocate
    We'll rule the world together."

This effusion was received with loud applause and a rattling of glasses. The company rose and resumed their walk; and the debate was abandoned, not without some murmuring. The professor hinted that there was more wit in the French motto than in the verses; while the conservative was shocked at the levity manifested in the consideration of so awful a subject.

The path for some distance now winds along a hill-side sunlit and spangled with wild flowers. Far below, under the shadows of pines, cedars, and hemlocks, half hidden by the dark foliage, the persistent stream toils through the contorted windings of Glen Obscura. Down there it appears as if Nature had been trying experiments to ascertain what might be done with water and rocks without actually stultifying her own laws or overleaping the narrow limit between facts and impossibilities; and queer work she has made of it.

En route the professor lectured on the botany of the Glen, declaring that, except in an artificial conservatory, he had never seen so great a variety in one locality. Many of the plants

LOTT D. DAVIS, AGED 57.

found here are exotic in this region outside; and the growth embraces a climatic range from Labrador to the Carolinas.

But as we crossed a narrow foot-bridge all eyes were lifted upward, while the handfuls of innocent fresh-gathered flowers were cast carelessly into the rushing current of forgetfulness. We stood at the entrance of the Cathedral; and from the consideration of microcosmic infinity our minds were suddenly turned to a scene of infinite grandeur.

This is, by common consent, the most striking view in the Glen; and it is certainly very impressive and emotional, with its towering cliffs, its broad flag-stone flooring, its transparent, glassy pools, reflecting the blue heavens and the overhanging sunlit trees; its flashing water-fall, like a high altar, adorning its upper extremity; its shelving strata, supported by rows of gigantic caryatides, weird mimicry of the sculptor's art.

But why waste words? The artist has already pointed his crayons, selected his point of view, and assumed the task of description.

He says the view is grand, open, charming; but not near so astounding and impressive nor so picturesque as some others. But this is not the age for new dogmas, even in matters of taste; and we magnanimously invite each visitor to see for himself, and enjoy his own opinions.

This picture finished, we move on, crossing

had tipped him to hold his tongue. A nice, respectable Mr. Furness had got hold of! And Flower would take care that all Horsingham knew his story. But presently he had broken out in a still more insulting and ruffianly strain. Well, he wished Miss Anne joy, then, of the letters she had written to "Lacer," that was all! She might be sure they would be made public enough if it suited "Lacer's" book to do so, unless Mr. Furness would buy him off. And finally Flower took his departure, after treating my mother to this scene, with a volley of coarse sneers and low abuse, which he uttered aloud on his way through the kitchen and across the garden, for the benefit of the two women-servants and any others who might be at hand to hear.

"What did he mean, Anne, by letters you had written to Gervase Lacer?" asked my mother. "The man was not quite sober, but I do not believe he was so intoxicated as not to know what he was saying. You never wrote to Mr. Lacer, did you?"

"I wrote to him twice. Once at your bidding to ask him to dine or drink tea here—a mere commonplace note of three lines. The other time I wrote to him was after I had learned from him that my father was concerned in having a race-horse trained secretly. I was disturbed by the thought night and day. I kept turning it over this way and that way in my mind. At length I wrote a little letter to Mr. Lacer, asking him if there were *no* means to prevent—to prevent all the trouble that did happen, after all. It was not very wise, perhaps, so to write. But I was so restless and unhappy I could have caught at the merest straw. The letter was one which—*now*—all the world might read."

"Of course, darling! But I was doubtful of the fact of your having written at all. And how did Flower ascertain it?"

"Perhaps he posted the letter; I don't remember. Nor is it worth a second thought. Dearest mother, don't let such a wretch's low malignity disturb you. But you had a second trouble, you said. What was it?"

"The second trouble, Anne, is a more serious one. And—I'm afraid it will hurt you a good deal. Your father went to Horsingham. He was obliged to do so. There he heard that Matthew Kitchen had put an execution into the Arkwrights' house. That was a blow to him, for I think it opened his eyes to the hard, grasping character of the man. Father has always said that Matthew was more reasonable and forbearing than people gave him credit for. Then there came worse. He saw Mrs. Arkwright somewhere—in a shop or in the street—and she began to rail upon him, laying her misfortunes at *his* door. Poor father!"

"She is violent, mother. But consider—five little children! And then her husband, whom she so idolizes—"

"Oh, Anne, I can't forgive her! It was too unjust. Your father attacked publicly in that way! Charged with the ruin of her family! It was too monstrous. And the worst is that father has so taken it to heart! He won't hear me blame the woman. 'No,' he says; 'she was right, perhaps. I bring trouble and misery on every one. My name is a by-word where it had been honored for generations!' And so he goes on. It was cruel. I can't forgive her. And are we not making sacrifices to do right? Shall not we, too, be forced to go away from our pleasant home, and give up all we have in the world?"

I felt that that was no time to plead or make excuses for Mrs. Arkwright. I thought that the letter I had brought with me would be the best means of soothing my mother, and turning her thoughts away from the thorny present to green pastures where we might hope, at least, for peace.

I took it from my pocket, and held it up before her eyes, telling her at the same time how I had come by it, and that grandfather had directed she should open it in his absence. Mother's face paled and flushed, and paled again, as she devoured the square, red-sealed envelope with her eyes.

"Oh, Anne!" she said, and clasped her hands tightly together. "Oh, Anne! if it should be—if it is—"

"Surely it is a bearer of good tidings, dear mother. The matter was nearly settled before. Ought not father to be present when we open it? Where is he? Let me call him."

"He is wandering about the shrubbery. But stay, Anne! Don't go, my child! If it should not be good news, after all! Let us spare him the chance of disappointment. Give it to me."

Her hands shook so much that she tore the cover across in trying to open the letter. And she breathed quickly, and kept her lips parted, like a person parching with thirst.

There were two letters—one from Colonel Fisher to my grandfather, the other from the new proprietor of the Scotch estate to Colonel Fisher himself.

Mother looked at the latter first. It was very brief—a few lines, as I could perceive without distinguishing the words, very neat and straight, and headed by a big gilt monogram. Mother kept her eyes fixed upon it for a much longer time than it could have taken to master its contents. She seemed to be reading it over and over again. At length, as she did not look up, I said, in a low voice,

"Well, mother?"

But the chill of her silence had struck to my heart. I knew—I knew! She glanced at me for a moment, and heaving a deep, long sigh, shook her head slightly. Then she looked down again at the letter lying open on her lap.

I took it up and read it. But to this hour I can not recollect a word of it, although I gathered the sense of it instantly. It seemed to me as if the paper were covered by one word—No! no! no! no!—in characters that quivered before my quivering eyes.

The Romance of the Hudson (1876)

THE ROMANCE OF THE HUDSON.
[Third Paper.]

WASHINGTON'S HEAD-QUARTERS BELOW NEWBURGH.

WHAT a magnificent theatre of romantic events bursts suddenly upon the vision as the steamboat sweeps around the lofty promontory of Anthony's Nose on a fine summer afternoon! The aerial perspective is charming, and a picture of marvelous beauty and grandeur is presented to the eye of the voyager. We are in the heart of the Highlands, and seem to be traveling upon a narrow lake with rugged shores, broken by islands and pierced by promontories. Through a narrow vista in the great hills, where the head of the Storm King is more than a thousand feet above the tide, may be seen in the far distance, sixty miles away, the pale blue line of the Katsbergs. In the immediate foreground is Anthony's Nose, rising full 1300 feet, its base pierced for the passage of the Hudson River Railway only a few feet above the water. From its northern verge stretches a wet meadow toward the foot of the Sugar Loaf, whose purple cone shoots up sharply in the northern sky. It is the first conspicuous object that attracts the eye when the enchanting scene opens. It is the highest part of a range of lofty hills on the eastern side of the Hudson, upon which the Americans planted batteries and lighted beacon fires in the time of the old war for independence.

On the western shore, opposite the Sugar Loaf, rises Mount Independence, crowned with dark evergreens, that cluster around the gray ruins of Fort Putnam. Below it you

WEST POINT.

may see the high promontory of West Point, with glimpses of the buildings of the Military Academy. On the brow of a rocky precipice nearer is Cozzens's summer hotel, and below it you may see the white foam of a mountain stream, as it falls in a gentle cascade into the river over a smooth rocky bed, after a turbulent passage among the bowlders above. This the prosy Dutch skippers called Buttermilk Falls.

Fort Putnam, now in ruins, was built under the direction of the accomplished Polish patriot, Kosciusko. The latter was only a little more than twenty years of age when he came to America, the disappointed lover of a Lithuanian maiden. Recommended by Franklin, he asked Washington for employment. "What can you do?" asked the chief. "Try me," was the laconic answer. He entered Washington's military family, and soon became colonel of engineers. We shall meet his works on the Upper Hudson in those strong military lines on Bemis's Heights which Burgoyne could not break through. He was beloved by all. In testimony of the respect which their fathers cherished for the gallant Polander, the cadets at West Point, fifty years after Fort Putnam was constructed, erected a beautiful white marble monument to his memory within the ruins of Fort Clinton, on the extremity of the promontory of West Point.

Fort Putnam was the most important of all the numerous military works in the Highland region. It commanded all others, the plain below, and the river for miles up and down. Could the voyager ascend to its crumbling walls, one of the grandest scenes in nature would be opened to his view. Almost every rood of the wild and beautiful domain has been consecrated by historic deeds. With the eye of retrospection, he might see the *Half-Moon* running "up into the Riuer twentie leagues, passing by high Mountaines," as the chronicler tells us, where the hopes of her commander were extinguished by the freshening of the water; he might see the dusky tribes fighting for the mastery upon the mountains and in the ravines before the advent of the white man; flotillas of vessels bearing armies for northern campaigns during the French and Indian wars, sweeping around the magnificent curves of the river, while the voices of men and the resounding drum awoke the echoes of the hills; he might see the camp fires of Continental soldiers engaged here and there in building fortifications, or spanning the river with a great chain, or watching the mountain passes, and the growth, upon a plain at his feet, of a grand military school from which have gone out soldiers and engineers to conquer armies and rugged nature, and astonish the nations by their prowess and skill; he might see the commerce of an empire expanding, in the space of a few decades of years, from trade with a few Indian trappers, to the mighty bulk which now floats hourly upon the waters, or is hurried with the speed of a gale along the railway from field to mart. Glancing his eye, as he awakes from his reverie, to the mouth of a broad hollow, scooped from the hills, he would see the smoke of furnaces and forges at Cold Spring, where the great Parrott guns of our army and navy have been wrought for many years. Such are the heads of some of the chapters in the romance of the Hudson unfolded among these everlasting hills.

At the verge of the Buttermilk Falls is a modest house, with its back against the overhanging precipice. There, more than twenty years ago, the writer found an old waterman, who ferried him across the river. He was eighty years of age, and well remembered sitting upon Washington's knee and admiring his silver buckles and big gilt buttons. He remembered, too, a romantic scene on the plain above that dazzled his eyes and made a lasting impression upon his memory. It was at a *fête*, given by Washington, in obedience to the command of Congress, in honor of the birth of an heir to the throne of the French monarch, who had been the active ally of the Americans in their struggle for independence. It took place on the last day of May, 1782. A beautiful arbor was made, more than two hundred feet in length and eighty in width, constructed of evergreen trees, which formed a colonnade of more than a hundred pillars. It was roofed with boughs and tent cloths. Branches curiously woven formed a sort of pediment, on which were displayed emblematic devices, the *fleur-de-lis* being prominent. Every column was encircled by muskets with bayonets; and the interior was decorated with festoons and garlands of evergreens, with devices significant of the alliance. Prominent among these also was the *fleur-de-lis*. Appropriate mottoes were scattered about the edifice.

At five o'clock in the afternoon more than five hundred ladies and gentlemen partook of a grand banquet in the arbor. These represented the *élite* of civil and military society in America. Early in the afternoon General Washington and his wife and suit, Governor George Clinton and his wife, Generals Knox and Hand with their wives, Egbert Benson, the Attorney-General of New York, Mrs. Margaret Livingston, of the Lower Manor, and Janet, the widow of General Montgomery, and a large number of ladies and gentlemen from the States of New York and New Jersey, had arrived in their barges. They were conducted through the grand arbor, situated on the gently rising ground in the rear of Fort Clinton, on which the West Point Hotel now stands. It was on the upper verge of the plain, with the magnificent

THE FÊTE OF MAY 31, 1782.

river and mountain scenery at the north in full view.

The Continental army was paraded on each side of the river. At the signal of three cannon discharges the regimental officers left their commands and repaired to the quarters of General M'Dougal. When the banquet was on the table, General Washington, with his wife and suit, left those quarters, followed by the invited guests, and went to the arbor, where a martial band played sweet airs during the repast, suggestive of peace and reconciliation. After the banquet of meat came a banquet of wine, when thirteen toasts were drunk, each followed by thirteen discharges of cannon, accompanied by music. Then the regimental officers returned to their commands, and as night came on the arbor displayed the splendors of a grand illumination by scores of candle-lights. At that moment cannon and musketry throughout the whole army gave a *feu de joie* which, like peals of thunder, awoke a thousand echoes among the grand old hills. This was followed by a consentaneous shout of the whole army—a wild huzza, with the benediction, " Long live the Dauphin!"

A ball in the arbor followed these noisy demonstrations without, in which the commander-in-chief heartily joined. "He attended the ball in the evening," wrote an eye-witness, "and with dignified and graceful air, having Mrs. Knox for his partner, carried down a dance of twenty couples in the arbor on the green grass." That partner was the wife of General Knox, the Boston bookseller—the "beautiful Lucy," as she was familiarly spoken of, the belle of the camp, and then about thirty years of age. The festivities ended toward midnight with a brilliant display of fire-works.

As the steamboat sweeps around the short curve in the river here, after leaving the government landing, you behold a white marble monument erected to the memory of more than a hundred United States soldiers who were massacred by the

Indians in Florida many years ago. Near it may be seen a sheltered nook in the rocks at the brow of the cliff, which is known as "Kosciusko's Garden." There the eminent Polander constructed a pretty fountain; and there, it is said, he retired for reading and repose. His monument may be seen a little further on; and across the river at the turn, on Constitution Island, the crumbling walls of a part of old Fort Constitution may be seen. It is the relic of a work that guarded the immense iron chain which the Americans stretched across the river there, buoyed up by logs, after the obstructions at Fort Montgomery had been broken.

As the steamboat goes out at the upper gate of the Highlands, a picture of rare beauty opens upon the vision of the voyager. The great hills disappear on the right and left. The broad expanse of Newburgh Bay is before him, harmonizing in its aspect of repose with the rolling, cultivated country of Dutchess and Orange counties on each side of the river. Looking eastward, the eye wanders to the theatre of many of the exploits in the life of "Harvey Birch" (Enoch Crosby), the hero of Cooper's *Spy*. You may almost see the spire of the old Dutch church at Fishkill, wherein he was a manacled and willing prisoner, after a mock trial before the Committee of Safety. Around that old church cluster many historical romances of the valley of the Middle Hudson, of deepest interest. Near its ancient walls the fugitive Legislature of the State of New York met, after flying before British bayonets from the neutral ground in Westchester. There was the place of deposit for a large amount of stores for the northern army; there the New York Committee of Safety held their meetings; and by that old church passed the captive army of Burgoyne, British and Hessians, on their way to Virginia.

Nestled in a quiet spot on the western shore, a little below the city of Newburgh,

KOSCIUSKO'S FOUNTAIN.

part of the time, and the cultivated wives of several of the officers; and until a comparatively few years ago the remains of the borders around the beds of a little garden which Mrs. Washington cultivated for amusement might have been seen in front of the mansion.

That building, now the property of the State of New York, is preserved in the form it bore when Washington left it. There is the famous room, with seven doors and one window, which the owner used for a parlor, and the commander-in-chief for a dining hall. In that apartment, at different times, a large portion of the chief officers of the Continental army, American and foreign, and many distinguished civilians, were entertained at Washington's table.

is New Windsor, famous as the head-quarters of Washington for many months during the Revolution, and as the residence of a charming little maiden named Anna Brewster, a lineal descendant of Elder Brewster, of the *Mayflower*. Her height in womanhood was three feet, her form was perfect, her face beamed with intelligence and sweetness, and her mind was pure and active. She was loved and admired by every one; and she lived a charming maiden until she was seventy-five years of age. She possessed such dignity and self-respect that she declined an invitation from Mrs. Washington to visit her at head-quarters, because she improperly thought it was curiosity rather than respect that prompted the kind act.

As the steamboat approaches the wharf at Newburgh, the voyager beholds on the southern verge of the city a low broad-roofed house, built of stone, with a flag-staff near, and the grounds around garnished with cannon. That is the famous "Head-quarters of Washington" during one of the most interesting periods of the war and at its close. Then the camp was graced by the presence of Mrs. Washington a greater

More than fifty years after the war a counterfeit of that room was produced in the French capital. A short time before Lafayette's death he was invited, with the American minister and several of his countrymen, to a banquet given by the old Count de Marbois, who was the secretary to the first French legation in this country during the Revolution. At the hour for the repast, the company were shown into a room which strangely contrasted in appearance with the splendors of the mansion they were in. It was a low boarded room, with large projecting beams overhead; a huge fire-place, with a broad-throated chimney; a single small uncurtained window, and numerous small doors, the whole having the appearance of a Dutch or Belgian kitchen. Upon a long rough table was spread a frugal repast, with wine in decanters and bottles and glasses and silver goblets, such as indicated the habits of other times. "Do you know where we now are?" Marbois asked the marquis and the American guests. They paused for a moment, when Lafayette exclaimed: "Ah! the seven doors and one window, and the silver camp goblets, such as the marshals of France used in my youth. We are at Washington's head-quarters on the Hudson, fifty years ago!" So the story was told by Colonel Fish, father of our Secretary of State, who was one of the company. Close by the "Head-quarters" is a modest monument of brown freestone, beneath which rest the remains of Uzal Knapp, the last survivor of Washington's Life-Guard.

On the eastern side of the river, about two miles above Fishkill Landing, stands a mansion of similar form, a mile back from the shore, which has been for more than a century the country-seat of the Verplanck family. It was the head-quarters of the Baron de Steuben while the army lay back of Newburgh. There, a little while before that army was disbanded, the officers formed the notable association known as the *Society of the Cincinnati*, which still exists. It was suggested by General Knox, and approved by Washington. Its object was to perpetuate and cherish the mutual friendship of the officers of the Continental army, and to provide a fund for the aid of the indigent among them. Membership was made hereditary in the masculine line; that failing, it might be perpetuated in worthy collateral branches. State societies were formed for convenience, which were subordinate in a degree to the general society. Washington was the first president of that general society—an office now filled by Secretary Fish. This is the only institution in this country which bears the primogeniture feature of English society.

Not far above Newburgh is a low rocky peninsula known as the Dans - Kamer—Dance Chamber. On that spot, for a century after the discovery of the Hudson, the Indians held their *kinte-kayes*—fearful orgies, in which they danced and yelled around great fires on the eve of an expedition for war or the chase. They appeared more like fiends than human creatures, and the Dutch skippers called the place the Devil's Dance Chamber. There it was, according to the veracious Knickerbocker, that Peter Stuyvesant's crew were "most horribly frightened by roystering devils."

Poughkeepsie, which bears the corrupted form of an Indian word signifying "safe harbor," has historical associations of great interest. Here were dock-yards, at which vessels for the Continental navy were built, and where they were burned on the stocks to prevent their falling into the hands of the marauders. In the old court-house in that village the Legislature of the State of New York held its sessions after Kingston was burned in the autumn of 1777; and here was held the State Convention which ratified the national Constitution. The house in which Governor Clinton resided, and where several of Washington's letters were written, yet stands on Upper Main Street.

At Krom Elbow, a few miles above Poughkeepsie, is the head of the Long Reach, which extends to the Dans-Kamer. Near there, on the western shore, is a smooth rock, with an inscription chiseled by the ancient inhabitants of the valley—a hieroglyphic record of some event in their history. As the steamboat sweeps around the short curve of the "crooked elbow"—as the name means—the river widens into the appearance of a lake, with the lofty Katsbergs in full view. On the left there is a low light-house in the shallows, and beyond it is the village of Rondout, now a part of old Kingston or Esopus, on the Esopus Creek, two miles from the river.

That region was a theatre of stirring historical events from its first settlement by Europeans, two hundred years ago, to the close of the old war for independence. The Indians and the white intruders there contended for the mastery many years, until the pale-faces conquered, as usual, after seasons of bloodshed, terror, and distress. At Kingston the Convention sat which framed the first Constitution of the State of New York. There the new commonwealth was organized in the summer of 1777, and there the first Legislature was in session when Forts Clinton and Montgomery fell. When news of that event and the coming of a squadron under Sir James Wallace (piloted by a Dutchess County Tory), with almost four thousand soldiers under General Vaughan, reached Kingston, the members of the Legislature fled. They supposed that the then capital of the State would feel most cruelly the strong arm of the enemy. And so it did. The British frigates anchored above Kingston Point, and large detachments of soldiers landed and marched upon the doomed town of almost four thousand inhabitants. They laid nearly every house in ashes, driving the affrighted people back upon the Wallkill settlements, where they were exposed to the dangers of attacks from savage war parties in the interior, under Brant.

From Kingston the British went up the river as far as Livingston's manor, on the eastern shore. They spread desolation by the torch at intermediate places, and burned the manor-house. Their object was to assist Burgoyne, then struggling with the Americans at Saratoga, either by drawing away a part of Gates's army for the defense of the country below, or by actually joining the crippled British force above. The news of the surrender of Burgoyne, which reached them at the manor, quenched their hopes, and they fled to New York with all possible speed.

From a point a little north of Tivoli, on the river or on the land, may be obtained the most comprehensive views of the Katsbergs, lying bold and lofty against the west-

RIP VAN WINKLE.

ern sky. The Indians called the range *On-ti-o-ra*—Mountains of the Sky—and the Dutch, less poetic, named them Katsbergs—Cats' Mountains—because of the abundance of wild-cats found there. They are commonly called Catskill Mountains.

High up on the Katsbergs are the two famous summer resorts, the "Mountain House" and the "Overlook House," from both of which magnificent views of the country may be seen.

In a hollow near which the road passes up to the old Mountain House is the scene of Rip Van Winkle's encounter with the

Dutch ghosts and the bewitching flagon. The story of Rip is one of the most charming of Irving's legends. He tells us that he was a good-for-nothing idler about the village tavern that stood in the evening shadows of these mountains, and was properly a hen-pecked husband. Rip feared nothing so much as Dame Van Winkle's tongue, which was sharp and lively when the good woman was irate. He was much away with his dog and gun hunting in the mountains. On one of these occasions he heard the rumbling of the ghostly nine-pins among the hills, which often sounded in the ears of dwellers near; and he soon came upon a queer-looking company, who were solemnly and silently engaged in that game. They were doubtless the ghosts of Hendrick Hudson and his crew in carnal form. He was introduced to them by a man who was bearing a keg of liquor on his shoulder. That liquor was poured into a flagon, out of which the ever-thirsty Rip drank freely, fell asleep, and did not awake until twenty years had passed away.

When Rip awoke, his first thought was of his wife's tongue. "Oh, that flagon! that wicked flagon!" he exclaimed. "What shall I say to Dame Van Winkle?" Alas! all had changed. His rusty gun-barrel, without a stock, lay by his side; his dog was gone; his beard was white and flowing, and his clothes were rags. What could it mean? As he wandered back to the village, he saw nothing that was familiar to him—men, politics, the tavern, all were changed. Every thing was a mystery to him, and he was a mystery to every body. At length some recognitions occurred, and the first real happiness that beamed in Rip's dim eyes was when he was assured that death had silenced Dame Van Winkle's tongue. His story of the mysterious nine-pin players was finally believed; and "even to this day," said the romancer, "the Dutch inhabitants never hear a thunder-storm of a summer afternoon about the Katskill but they say, Hendrick Hudson and his crew are at their game of nine-pins."

The story of the birth and growth of the city of Hudson is a notable romance. It was founded in 1780 by thirty families, chiefly Quakers from New England. At the end of three years from the time the farm on which the city stands was purchased, one hundred and fifty dwelling-houses, and wharves, storehouses, workshops, and out-buildings, were seen there, and a population of fifteen hundred souls, who possessed a city charter. The history of cities has no parallel to this.

Between Hudson and Albany the river is dotted with islands, the most notable of which is one off the mouth of Norman's Kill, the Indian *Ta-wa-sen-tha*, or "place of many dead," that comes into the Hudson from the west a little below Albany. It was named by the Dutch Castle Island, from the circumstance that a stockade fort was built upon it as a protection to Dutch traders with the Indians. This was the first fort built by the Hollanders on the Hudson River, and there a large trade in furs and peltries was carried on with the Indians.

On the eastern shore, about four miles below Castle Island, is the village of Schodac, the name of which is derived from the Indian word *is-cho-da*, a "meadow," or "fire-plain." There in ancient times was the seat of the council fire of the Mohegans, and there, it is believed, Uncas, the eminent sachem and chief in Connecticut, sometimes presided over the great assembly. It is a beautiful region of country, and, like all the chosen seats of Indian society, attests their wisdom and taste in selection. From this point to Albany, where the ascending voyage of the *Half-Moon* was ended, the passage is soon made; and when the steamboat from New York reaches the wharf at the political capital of the State, it has traversed the length of the Lower and Middle Hudson

region. Henceforth the traveler must be content with various and less luxurious vehicles of conveyance over the beautiful region of the Upper Hudson, from Albany to its head waters in the Northern Wilderness.

On the northern verge of the city of Albany is one of the finest of the old mansions of the State. It is the Van Rensselaer manor-house. On the southern verge of the city there is another of the finer dwellings. It was the town residence of General Philip Schuyler. Both were erected at about the same time—a little past the middle of the last century. The Van Rensselaer mansion is associated with the settlement of the colony of New Netherland; the Schuyler mansion is associated with the heroic age of that colony as the State of New York, and with the fortunes of the Six Nations of Indians.

The Dutch West India Company, trading along the Hudson River with the savages, built a small military work on the site of Albany, and named it Fort Orange. Wishing to colonize the country, they offered certain privileges and exemptions to any person who should lead or send a colony to New Netherland, and within four years afterward should have there at least fifty permanent residents over fifteen years of age, one-fourth of whom should be located there within the first year. Killian Van Rensselaer, a pearl merchant of Amsterdam and one of the directors of the company, undertook a settlement on these terms. With three other persons he bought of the Indians over seven hundred thousand acres of land on and around the site of Albany, and planted a colony near Fort Orange. He received the title of *patroon*, or patron, and was invested with its privileges. A reed-covered mansion was built near the site of the later manor-house, in which for more than a hundred years the patroons or their agents entertained the best society of the Province, and received delegations from the dusky monarchs of the forest. So great were the delegated powers and privileges of the patroon that he defied the local authorities, and there was a grand quarrel between his agent and Governor Stuyvesant. When the English took possession of the Province, these privileges ceased, but the patroon enjoyed his title and rights under the law of primogeniture until 1840. The last patroon was General Stephen Van Rensselaer, a son-in-law of General Schuyler.

The Schuyler family were conspicuous as friends of the Indians from the earliest period of their residence in this country, and through several generations they were popular with the red men. They held peculiar relations with the Iroquois confederacy under government appointment, controlling in a great degree the political action of the Six Nations until Sir William Johnson obtained

RESCUE OF SCHUYLER'S CHILD.

his ascendency over them. For many years General Schuyler was at the head of the Indian commissions for the transaction of government business with them, and his house was a place of frequent resort of the chiefs and sachems of the confederacy. During the Revolution his personal influence, wisdom, skill, and watchfulness enabled him to hold a large portion of these savages in a position of neutrality, and so secured the State from any disastrous invasions, and the cause from ruin.

The spacious Schuyler mansion is at the head of Schuyler Street. It was seldom without guests when the family were there. The most distinguished citizens of America and travelers from abroad found a generous welcome there during the forty years that Schuyler and his wife dispensed princely hospitality under its roof.

The Schuyler mansion was the theatre of a romance in the summer of 1781. General Schuyler was not then in active military service, but, at his house at Albany or at Saratoga, he was the vigilant eye of the Northern Department. His person as a pris-

oner was coveted as a capital prize by his Tory neighbors. Walter Meyer, a Tory colleague of the famous Joe Beltys, was employed to execute a scheme for the seizure and abduction of the general. With a party of his associates, Canadians and Indians, he prowled in the woods near Albany for many days, and ascertained the exact situation of affairs at Schuyler's house from a Dutchman whom he had seized at his work. He learned that a guard of six men were there for the protection of Schuyler's person, three of them alternately on duty continually. The Dutchman was compelled to take an oath of secrecy. He did so with a mental reservation, and as soon as he was released, he hastened to Schuyler and warned him of his peril.

As the twilight of a sultry day in August was yielding to the night, Schuyler and his family were sitting in the great hall of the mansion; the servants were about the premises; three of the guard were asleep in the basement, and the other three were lying on the grass in front of the mansion. A servant announced that a person at the back gate wished to speak with the general. His errand was understood. The doors and windows of the mansion were immediately closed and barred, the family were gathered in an upper room, and the general ran to his bedroom for his arms. Looking out of a window, he saw the house surrounded by armed men. To alarm the town, half a mile distant, he fired a pistol from his window. At the same moment the intruders burst open the front-door. At that instant Mrs. Schuyler perceived that in the confusion she had left her infant in a cradle in the hall below. She was about to rush down the stairs after it, when the general interposed and prevented her. Her third daughter, Margaret (who was afterward the wife of the last patroon), instantly flew down the great stairway, snatched the sleeping babe from the cradle, and bore it up to its mother. One of the Indians hurled a sharp tomahawk at her. Its keen blade just grazed the infant's head, and was buried in the railing of the stair. Meyer, supposing her to be a servant, called to her, as she flew up the stairs, "Where's your master?" With quick thought she exclaimed, as she reached the verge of the upper hall, "Gone to alarm the town!" Her father heard her, and with as quick thought threw up a window and called out, as to a multitude, "Come on, my brave fellows! Surround the house, and secure the villains!" The alarmed marauders, who were plundering the general's dining-room of the plate, fled in haste, carrying away some of the booty. That infant was the late Mrs. Catherine Van Rensselaer Cochran, General Schuyler's youngest child, who died at Oswego in the summer of 1857.

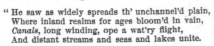
ALBANY IN THE OLDEN TIME.

In that mansion General Schuyler, the father of the canal system of the State of New York, worked out his plans, and revealed to his guests his knowledge and his hopes concerning the feasibility of inland lock navigation. Joel Barlow, who visited him, prophesied as follows, in his "Vision of Columbus," published thirty years before the work on the great Erie Canal was begun:

" He saw as widely spreads th' unchannel'd plain,
   Where inland realms for ages bloom'd in vain,
   Canals, long winding, ope a wat'ry flight,
   And distant streams and seas and lakes unite.

" From fair Albania toward the setting sun,
   Back through the midland lengthening channels run;
   Meet the fair lakes, their beauteous towns that lave,
   And Hudson join'd to broad Ohio's wave."

That prophecy was fulfilled when canal-boats from Lake Erie came to Albany, and formed a part of the grand nuptial procession already mentioned in honor of the wedding of the lakes with the Hudson and the sea. That procession was ended at Sandy Hook, where Governor Clinton poured a keg of the water of Lake Erie into the Atlantic—a ceremony more significant of the true greatness of a state than that of the Doge of Venice who cast his ring into the waters, and so symbolically wedded the Adriatic. That canal, which enters the Hudson at Albany, may now bear to the bosom of the river 4,000,000 tons of the products of the West annually; when enlarged to the width of seventy feet, it may bear 24,000,000 tons.

We might linger long in recounting the romances of this old Dutch-founded city. We might tell strange stories of the primitive society, where, on the benches at the front-doors, were seen nearly the whole population in the evening, the old men smoking, the old women knitting, and the young people chatting loudly upon current topics or softly on love-making. We might tell of military events at Fort Frederick, that stood in the middle of State Street, on the hill, where General Charles Lee (then a captain) whipped one of Abercrombie's aids for insulting a citizen's daughter; or of the troubles of Sexton Brower, of the old Dutch church that stood in the middle of State Street, near the river. Poor old bell-ringer! It was his duty to pull its rope every evening at eight o'clock, to ring out the "suppaan bell"—the curfew bell of the Dutch—when it was the duty of all good citizens to eat their *suppaan*, or hasty-pudding, and go to bed. The old bell-ringer was faithful and superstitious. The "horrid boys" of those days teased him dreadfully. While he was ringing the bell, by the light of a dim lantern, they would steal into the church, unfasten a side door, and remain hidden until his departure. When the old man was quietly seated at home, taking his last smoke before going to bed, they would ring the bell furiously. The old sexton would hasten down to the church, and the boys would slip out of the side door, leaving him puzzled and half frightened with the idea that invisible hands were pulling at his rope—those

> " people—ah, the people—
> They that dwell up in the steeple,
>   All alone;
> And who, tolling, tolling, tolling,
>   In that muffled monotone,
> Feel a glory in so rolling
>   On the human heart a stone:
> They are neither man nor woman,
> They are neither brute nor human—
>   They are ghouls."

We might tell of the adventures of that queer old bachelor, Balthazar Lydius, tall, bullet-headed, and so ugly in features and manners that the boys would shun him in the streets as they would an ogre of a fairy tale. He was a Lothario in his young manhood. Jilted at Greenbush, he became a misanthrope. He loved his pipe and applejack better than human kind. He lived in a fine house, with mahogany partitions, the beams carved into pictures of vines and fruit, and a dresser that glittered with pewter plates so long as his mother lived, whom he loved tenderly. When she died, his locks were thin and white. He had no one to sew on his buttons, and so, to show his contempt for womenkind, he bought a squaw for a pint of gin, and lived with her as his wife the remainder of his life.

Not far up the street from Balthazar's dwelling was the grand "Van der Heyden Palace," where sumptuous hospitality was dispensed. The owner figures in Irving's charming story of Dolph Heyliger in *Bracebridge Hall*, and the iron vane from his double-fronted mansion now swings over the pinnacle of the cottage at Sunnyside.

But we must here bring to a close our record of romance. The valley of the Hudson above Albany is associated with stirring events in our Revolutionary history. These, however, would not have full justice done them within the limit which we have assigned to ourselves in these pages.

THE PURSUIT OF A HERITAGE.

"MY beloved nephew," said the Honorable Mr. Brewster, one morning recently, to a large party of guests assembled upon a memorable occasion, "has developed a talent in his profession as rare as it is commendable, a patience and originality in research, an independence and reticence in action, which evince the highest capability for the pursuit of our noble calling. I have always entertained for him the warmest aspirations, and I now predict for him a brilliant future!"

Then followed a burst of applause and acclamation, in the midst of which the honorable gentleman wiped his gold-ribbed spectacles and sat down. There may have been tears upon those pebbles; probably the eminent barrister meant every word that he said. When he got upon his legs in response to the toast in his nephew's honor, and cast that beaming, refulgent look to his side of the table, he considered him probably at that moment not only the light of his existence, but a planet of no ordinary magnitude to a benighted world.

Nevertheless, candor compels me to state that only a short period previous he had called him a disreputable young scoundrel, an idle, unprincipled dog, a disgrace to his name, and a blight to his profession.

And he had not had recourse to these strong expressions to relieve a momentary outburst of wrath, but Tom was assailed with them upon all the occasions in which he was unfortunate or stupid enough to allow himself to be left alone with his uncle. Mr. Brewster had too much respect for himself and the tie between them to descend to this abuse in the presence of others; he then maintained a cold and severe silence, eying Tom with the malignity of a basilisk, and asking him if he'd have a bit of mutton in the same tone he desired of a hardened culprit the reason why he should not be hanged.

The fact was, the uncle and nephew didn't get on together. The qualities that had descended in a direct line from the remote branches of a respectable genealogical tree were altogether wanting in Tom's composition. The mantle of dignity, eloquence, research, etc., had not fallen gracefully upon his shoulders, but was rather given to lopping aside, and not long since had been nearly trampled under his feet.

It was not Tom's fault that the womenfolks had been out late at a festivity the night before, had come down to the morning meal in a rather chaotic state, had sipped their chocolate, dallied with their steak, and gone back comfortably to bed. Mr. Brewster insisted that his household should arise at a certain hour, and assemble together at breakfast. His feminines, who had inherit-

Adirondack Days
(1881)

EDMONDS'S POND.

ADIRONDACK DAYS.

"Under the greenwood tree,
  Who loves to lie with me,
  And tune his merry note
Unto the sweet bird's throat;....
  Who doth ambition shun,
  And loves to live i' the sun,
  Seeking the food he eats,
  And pleased with what he gets;
Come hither, come hither, come hither;
    Here shall he see
    No enemy,
But winter and rough weather."
                    —*As You Like It.*

THERE is a saying of quaint Izaak
Walton's which has often given me
much inward pleasure, not only because
it is true, but because it flatters that secret vanity which makes every man like
to believe himself the possessor of some

quality or taste which does not belong to
mankind in common. "Angling," says
honest Piscator, "is somewhat like poetry—men are to be born so. I mean with
inclinations to it, though both may be
heightened by discourse and practice; but
he that hopes to be a good angler must
not only bring an inquiring, searching,
and observing wit, but he must bring a
large measure of hope and patience, and
a love and propensity to the art itself;
but having once got and practiced it, then
doubt not but angling will prove to be so
pleasant that it will prove to be, like virtue, a reward to itself."

Well said, thou genial father of our
gentle craft! And is not the same thing
true of all that wild, free life in the woods
and mountains of which angling often

457

forms so large a part? It is good and pleasant only for those who have some natural bent and fitness for it, and to them its delights are always new and always increasing. This has often come to my mind in the Adirondacks, when I have seen how many of the people who travel through that beautiful mountain land are unhappy and discontented, or find their chief pleasures in the comforts and amusements of the large hotels which have sprung up through the region. But there are others who love the rough hills and spreading forests for their own sake, and turn with unfailing gladness from the cares of the world and the noisy whirl of cities to a fresh and vigorous life in close contact with nature. It restores the jaded mind and body. It is like coming out from a crowded room into the clear cool air of night. Every breath is a delight.

This is what we four friends felt when we met again, after some years of separation, in the little Adirondack village of Elizabethtown. Never had the "Pleasant Valley" looked more lovely; never had the outline of the western mountains seemed more grand than as we sauntered up the road together on that fair August evening, and watched the sunset glow fading away, and the first star trembling into sight above the sharp peak of Hurricane. It filled us with honest joy to find ourselves once more in the old haunts, and look forward to a month of wandering in the woods.

The morning of the next day was bright and glad. Our wagon stood waiting before the porch of the Windsor; the miscellaneous *impedimenta* were stowed away under the seats; the mouse-colored horses were leaning patiently against the pole, after the manner of their tribe; and nothing remained to be done save to say good-by, and start away for our distant camping ground. A merry shout, a blowing of horns, and ringing of bells, and waving of handkerchiefs, a spasmodic burst of speed from the Gothic steeds, and we were out of sight around the corner of the road.

Our course lay due west, toward the opening of the Keene Pass, the road following up the bed of a rushing mountain stream once full of trout, and still repaying the patient angler with a few fish and many picturesque pools and cascades. As we mounted through the narrowing val-

ley, each mile gave a wider outlook behind us over the slopes of Lake Champlain and the far-away ridges of the Green Mountains. Every bridge that we crossed, and every thicket we passed, the little red school-house with its grove of pine-trees, and the dismantled saw-mill—all were associated with some pleasant memory or jolly story, and the talk and laughter flowed merrily as we rattled on our way.

Within the pass all was still and desolate. On either side rose high cliffs, stripped by fire and scarred by frost, with skeleton trees still standing here and there, the new growth of pale green poplar and birch but thinly veiling the rugged slopes. The narrow strip of arable land between the mountains was silent and deserted. The two or three adventurous farmers who had tried to wring a living from the niggard soil had at last given up the attempt, and their houses stood gray and lonely in the bright sunshine. The stillness of mid-day rested over the place. There were no inhabitants and no travellers. The current of our merriment had ceased, and the only sound that stirred the air was the scream of a blue jay in some distant thicket, or the tinkle of a far-away cow-bell. How many times we had come and gone along this high and lonely road, tramping with staff and knapsack, swinging along with a jolly party on a buckboard, or returning from camp with merry companions! And where were they all now? and could those good old times ever come again?

"Perhaps not," said the Governor. "But there is one sense in which we can never lose them; and no matter what changes take place in us, there is always sunshine for us, and beautiful things make us glad. What is it that Wordsworth says?

> 'My heart leaps up when I behold
>   A rainbow in the sky;
> So was it when my life began,
> So is it now I am a man,
> So be it when I shall grow old,
>   Or let me die.'

Surely as long as we can see a landscape like this, it will fill us with delight."

And indeed it was a lovely scene that now opened before us from the brow of the hill. A thousand feet below lay the Keene Valley, with its soft green meadows and feathery elms. Beyond it we saw range upon range of dark fir-clad mount-

MIST RISING OFF MOUNT WHITEFACE.

ains, and beyond all rose the long pyramidal slope of Whiteface.

Down we plunged into the valley by a steep sandy descent, through the sleepy little village of Keene, with its dreary tavern and loafer-haunted post-office, and then up again on the other side by a stony hill covered with acres of blackberries. At the top of this the road passed into a dark and beautiful forest, and then, after a few miles, emerged at the foot of the lower Edmonds's Pond. These ponds are twin sheets of water, which completely fill a long and narrow defile in the mountains. I will not compare them to great pearls fallen into a crevice of malachite, nor to mirrors in which the mountains, like Narcissus, study their own beauty, for I must confess that such comparisons always seem to me trivial and unworthy. No jewels or works of art ever equalled the strange, wild loveliness of these little lakes.

The road wound along a narrow ledge beside the water. It was rough, and none too safe. The driver showed us the place where the traditional peddler's wagon had pitched off into the water a few years ago.

"How many of that peddler were there?" asked Gad, "and how many times did he fall off? For I have been shown at least a dozen spots where the peddler fell off, and my mind is a little confused."

Now this remark was neither kind nor sensible; for the driver only meant to give us a gentle thrill of sensation with his favorite story, and could not be expected to know how often we had heard it before; and, indeed, for that matter, if our imaginations had only been vivid enough, we ought to have been glad to have as many spots as possible connected with the thrilling tale, for then we should have had just so many more sensations. For my part, I never could sympathize with those people who cavil at slight discrepancies like this; it is really a great advantage to have two or more birth-places of Franklin, for it just doubles our opportunity of reverent emotion; and I can not see why every city in the United States should not have a Washington's Head-quarters, simply as a means of moral education.

But the real reason why Gad spoke so hastily and with such acerbity was to be found in the fact that he was hungry, as we all were, and therefore irritable. We had travelled a long way since breakfast, the blackberries had been but trifles light as air to appetites like ours, and we were inwardly rejoiced when we arrived at Miller's Silver Cascade House.

Shudder not at the name, unsentimental reader! I know it is ominous, suggestive of artificial water-falls and romantic but famine-stricken summer boarders. It is a name which fills the wise traveller, bent on a good dinner, with dark forebodings. But here they are unfounded and needless. For we who remember the days when Mrs. Miller used to keep the little tavern down in the valley know that she has lost none of her ancient skill in cooking, and can give us a dinner worthy of the Dutchman's in Jamaica Bay, or old Rockwell's by Lake Lucerne. Dishes of fried trout as dainty to the eye as to the taste, huge snowy potatoes, broiled chickens, and scrambled eggs as light and golden as—as Beaconsfield's novels: these all were set before us by a little maid with a fleet step and large soft eyes, like a gentle, shy daughter of the forest.

From the ponds the road wound onward through a still heavier forest, broken only by a few new and fertile clearings, and then emerged on the high rolling plain of North Elba. Here at last the great mountains came in view, a majestic range of dark and solemn forms outlined against the sky—the weird fantastic ridges of the Gothics, Marcy's granite dome, the scarred and sullen face of Colden, the giant mass of McIntyre, and, most wonderful of all, the Indian Pass opening like a huge gateway into a boundless world of light. What power and delight dwell in this vision! These green fields, sloping to the long valley of unbroken forest, rest and rejoice the eye. The silent hills beyond lift themselves to heaven in the glory of enduring strength, changeless

amid the fleeting forms and fashions of earth, calming and uplifting our restless hearts, speaking to us of the truth which abides forever. And above all this marvellous pass into the luminous distance, this sole and splendid portal in the rocky wall, flooded with illimitable radiance, seems like the gateway into another life, the entrance of the Infinite. These are the words which Nature speaks to us: *repose*, untroubled by the storms of human passion, unshaken by the ebbings and flowings of the tide of life; *strength*, enduring, inexhaustible, based upon a changeless and inviolate will; *infinity*, opening with glorious vistas ever beyond that which is seen, and touching the earth with gleams of far-off splendor. Shall we not say rather that these are the words and messages of Him whose dwelling is deeper than the bases of the hills, and high above their sun-clad peaks, and far beyond the farthest light? Not vain and visionary are the hours in which we seem thus to hear His voice, and catch glimpses of His glory beneath

"The outward shores of sky and earth."

They are the moments of true strength and insight amid the dreams and delusions of life. Not the vision, but the awakening, in which a Divine voice calls us to ourselves, and a sight of the everlasting realities flashes through the forms of things into our souls.

The afternoon sun was slowly declin-

INDIAN PASS.

"I AIN'T GOT NO FISH-HOOKS."

ing in the western sky as we rode through the fields of North Elba, past the dilapidated gray houses where the early abolitionists had once endeavored to plant a colony of negroes (a strange and futile fancy), and the barren little farm where John Brown's body lies mouldering beneath a bowlder of native granite. Here and there we saw a better farm-house, which looked as if the owner had succeeded in making the cold and stony earth yield him a more generous tribute. Occasional groups of children stared at us with quiet and indifferent faces. Once we passed a wagon full of young people from the hotels of Lake Placid, singing the refrain of some merry college song. And then the road crossed Chub River, and entered the woods beyond.

At moonrise we reached Cameron's, a new hotel which has sprung up on the site of an old white farm-house. Here Peter and Howard disembarked with knapsacks and fishing-rods, for they had obtained permission of the Governor (whose word was law by consent of the little company) to stay over a day and fish Ray Brook, while he and Gad went on to Harrietstown, four miles beyond, to buy provisions and make ready for camp.

The next day was bright and warm, and the two fishermen vainly whipped the stream through the natural meadows where it flows. They came back to the house discouraged. "Patience," said Peter; "every day has an evening; for the present, this hammock is comfortable." So, as the sun went down behind the tall tamaracks, the brothers stood on opposite sides of a certain dark still pool, and knotted on their best casts of flies. Softly the lines went curling out over the quiet water. A rise! that was a good trout. Another! now you have him. How he fights, rushing down the pool, and lashing the water into foam! But the supple rod holds well, and soon he is landed on the grassy bank. Then another rises, and as he swings away, tautening the line, there is a flash of yellow in the water beside him, and two fish are hooked at once. And so it goes on—exciting work, for the fish are quick and strong, and it needs a steady hand to cast and strike and land in this half-darkness. But presently the moon steals up behind the trees, and looks down upon us over their dark tops. And now we can see more clearly. Still the fish are rising and fighting hard. Still the flies go darting out through the air, and drop softly on the surface of the gleaming water, until at last our wrists are tired and our desires contented, and we climb up the little hill to Cameron's with two fine strings of trout, running from half a pound upward. Cameron gears up his colts to a springy buckboard, and in half an hour the party is reunited at Harrietstown.

Gad and the Governor had spent a busy day. The great trunk, with our tents and blankets and tin dishes and all the paraphernalia of camp, which had been left in the care of Reub, our faithful guide, must be looked over, defects repaired, wants supplied, and provisions laid in for a three weeks' trip. I think the Governor rather enjoyed the hours in Tip Spalding's store. Like many men whose lives are spent in professional or literary work, he has a practical trait, and delights in dealing with such concrete realities as pork and flour and sugar and "canned things."

A group of brown-faced little boys stood by, and watched the purchases with an interest which was but ill concealed under the guise of carelessness. When it was all finished, one of the smallest urchins came up to the Governor, with an easy and indifferent air, and said, in a casual sort of way, "Mister, be you fond o' fishin'?"

"Why yes," said the Governor, "of course I am."

"Wa'al," said the youngster, "I know a hole where there's lots o' trout—big ones too; none o' yer little sardines; reg'lar *gee-whollopers;* and, mister, if ye want a *guide,* guess I ken take ye thar 'most any day."

"But," said the Governor, "why don't you catch the fish yourself, if they are such big ones?"

The bright brown eyes dropped to the floor, and the "guide" curled up one of his brown toes, and began to trace figures with it on the boards, in genteel embarrassment. But nothing could equal the suggestiveness of the tone with which he answered, "'Coz I can't, mister; I ain't got no fish-hooks."

This was irresistible, and the Governor must stand treat all around—for each boy a fish-hook and a candy bull's-eye, and for the clever little "guide" a double share.

Harrietstown is on the Saranac River. A mile away, at the foot of the Lower Saranac Lake, is Martin's Hotel, well known to sportsmen. The scene from the piazza on the morning of our departure was bright and busy. A cool breeze blew down from the distant islands, and the broad sheet of water sparkled and danced between its dark green shores. People were coming and going, laughing and talking, hurrying about to get ready for various expeditions; guides were loading their boats beside the little dock; hounds were tugging at their chains, and whimpering impatiently for their masters. A stage-load of passengers "going out" drove away for Au Sable station. Little groups of boats, heavily laden for camp, or lightly laden for some fishing excursion, pushed out from the narrow landing-place, and slipped away up the lake. At last, after much tribulation, packing and repacking, our own three boats were ready, and we were off, with long steady strokes, for Big Tupper Lake.

Our three guides were good men whom

A CARRY—THE START.

we had long known, and engaged for this trip some months beforehand. Reub and Raut are brothers—small men, but tough as pine knots, with muscles like whip-cord, and tremendous endurance. They are fine oarsmen, and while Raut is perhaps a little ahead as a hunter, Reub is one of the best cooks in the woods. They can swing an axe mightily, and know how to make a comfortable camp. Above all, they are kind and faithful and steady. Steve is a well-known guide of the older generation, a tall, thin man, with a red beard and keen eyes, a quick and sure shot, a most taking fisherman, and no man in the region can beat him at starting deer. He has a laugh like thunder, and an endless fund of stories.

There are guides and guides. It is folly to praise or trust them all alike indiscriminately. Some of them are poor sticks—stupid, surly, conceited, lazy. But most of them are good men. Drinking, I am glad to say, is becoming more and more uncommon. And some of them are noble specimens of manhood—honest, skillful, devoted, and pleasant companions, respecting themselves as well as their employers, to whom they are often united by very warm attachments on both sides. Everything depends on getting such men to go with you into the woods.

Meanwhile our tiny fleet went creeping up the lake, past rocky points and islands, through narrows, and across curving bays. Forest fires have destroyed much of the beauty of the shores. But the Saranac River, up which, after seven miles, we turned, has still the charm of a wild stream. The brown current flows steadily and swiftly between its banks. The quiet bays and "slews" are filled with many-colored aquatic plants; the broad dark leaves and coarse yellow flowers of the splatterdock mingle with the lighter and more delicate leaves and shining white blossoms of the pond-lily; tall, jointed water grasses like miniature thickets of bamboo; patches of moose-weed, with lance-shaped leaves, and flowers of the brightest blue; and scarlet Indian sage flaming beneath the sombre shadow of the woods. After the wearisome olive green and old gold of modern art decoration, these living hues seemed to us a new and joyful revelation of what true color is—a thing of light and gladness.

Half way up the stream we had to take out the boats, and carry them over the Middle Falls.

"Do you remember our fishing here last May?" said the Governor to Howard. "How different everything looked then —the pale green of the early foliage, the faint smell of the trailing arbutus, and the great trout leaping all along the full, rushing stream!"

"Yes," said Howard. "And particularly well do I remember how *you* looked when you made that long cast, and then stepped on the end of a loose plank, and subsided into the water. It was much deeper then than it is now, and colder too. Don't you think so?"

"Never mind that," said the Governor. "We had good enough sport to make up for a dozen duckings."

An hour more up the river and across the beautiful but tempestuous Round Lake brought us to Bartlett's, on the Upper Saranac Carry, where we were warmly welcomed by Mrs. Bartlett, most excellent of forest landladies. The long low house was crowded with guests, but we preferred to recall it as it is in the spring, the chosen resort of a few ardent fishermen, who come in when the leaves are few and the trout are plenty. Many are the huge "lakers" brought down from the Upper Saranac and laid out on the fresh grass at the door; many the brace of river trout caught at sunset from the bridge in front of the house; many the happy evenings passed around the fire in the snug little parlor. O good father Walton, and gentle Cotton, would that your pens might worthily record these pleasures!

A wet and windy pull of three miles brought us across the Upper Saranac. The little boats were tossed like cockle-shells by the white-capped waves. But the craft were stanch and the oarsmen skillful, and we had not shipped more than a pint or two of water when we reached the Sweeny Carry. This is a well-worn road, three miles long, leading across the divide between the waters of the Saranac, flowing eastward into Champlain, and the waters of the Raquette, flowing westward into the St. Lawrence. Our boats were placed on the wagon racks to be hauled over, and we set out on foot, following the road through a noble hardwood forest. Tall, straight sugar-maples lifted their leafy crowns high above us; smooth beeches, with round gray trunks, stood like massive pillars; and great yellow birches, with shaggy curling bark and gnarled limbs, rose like monarchs above the lesser trees.

As we came down the last hill, and through the clearing to the bank of the Raquette, Howard was silent. Five years had passed since he had seen that river, and he had only heard from the others of the melancholy change which had befallen it. But the reality was far worse than the description. He stood silent for a moment on the muddy bank, and then there came a flood of untranslatable German.

"*Donnerwetter noch einmal!* What a hole!"

It was indeed a hideous change. The most beautiful of wild rivers, a swift, dark current, flowing for miles between high

A CARRY—THE END.

A DIFFICULT PASSAGE.

banks and through broad natural meadows fringed with water-maples, with bold, clear sweeps and shining reaches, bordered with lilies and overhung with trees, had been transformed into a dreary, sluggish stream, the water foul and slimy, the banks covered with mud, the dead trees standing on either side like two long lines of skeletons, leaning already to their fall across the stream. And all this destruction simply because some lumber merchants wanted a dam at Piercefield Falls to enable them to get out their logs more easily!

"Do you call this the progress of civilization," said Howard, as we rowed sullenly down the stream between the spectral rows of tree trunks, "to destroy one of God's fairest works in order that a few men may have more money to decorate their houses with poor pictures and hideous furniture? I call it barbarism, vandalism—worse than breaking statues and pulling down cathedrals."

That night we spent at Mart Moody's, at the foot of Big Tupper Lake, and the next morning pushed our way against a heavy wind to the head of the lake, where the Bog River comes tumbling in over a wall of rock. This was once a famous place for trout, but the glory of it has departed since the snaky and all-devouring pickerel found their way down from Long Lake into these waters. But while these fresh-water sharks can easily go down a water-fall, they have not yet learned to go up one; and as we carried around the falls, and launched our boats in the dark winding stream above, we rejoiced in the thought that we were again in trout waters.

It was hard work going up the stream, for the water was low and the rocks far too numerous. Reub's emphatic, "By jolly!" and Steve's grunt of discontent, were heard as we occasionally left a streak of paint on a hidden bowlder, or bumped heavily and had to back off. The carries around the rapids and then across into Round Pond were longer than we could have wished, and we were all thoroughly tired when we reached, just after dark, the house on Little Tupper Lake kept by Pliny Robbins, an old guide of ours.

This was the end of our journey, and we slept the sleep of the just.

The next morning we set out to choose a camp ground. Little Tupper is a beautiful sheet of water, about six miles long, with deep branching bays on both sides. There is not a clearing on it; it is all unspoiled by fires, and the great pines still fringing the shores bear witness that the forest here is still virgin. We selected our ground near the head of the lake, at the entrance of a little bay so sheltered from the wind that it made a perfect harbor for the boats. A circle, perhaps fifty yards across, had been cleared away in the forest. On the upper edge of this, on a slight rise of ground, we pitched the tents. Below, and nearer the boat-landing, were the guides' shanty, the kitchen, and the pantry, made of bark. On a level with the tents, and continuing their line in a sort of crescent toward the lake, was the dining-table, with a sloping roof of bark, open on all sides, and commanding a fine outlook through the trees into the lake. A winding path led back from the boat-landing a few yards into the forest to a never-failing spring of ice-cold water; and a hard-wood ridge, rising directly behind the camp, supplied us with the best of fire-wood. Back of the tent, under a great yellow birch, the Governor swung his hammock, and we built a rustic table and a seat looking out over the water.

To accomplish all this was no slight task, nor was it done in a single day. The making of a camp, like the furnishing of a house, to be done rightly, must be done slowly. And, indeed, it can hardly be said to be done at all. It is always, as the Germans would say, *im Werden*.

The first night, however, saw the tents pitched and the beds comfortably laid, with odorous balsam boughs, and covered with blankets. Three of the weary campers had unpacked their knapsacks and settled themselves to sleep. But the fourth place was vacant. A figure, scantily arrayed, stood outside in the dim light of the fire, wrestling mightily with a huge round canvas bag.

"Come to bed, Gad," said a sleepy voice from the tent.

"Can't find my night-cap. That's the worst of these bags. You never can find anything in them. And I packed everything on top too, so that I could get it when I wanted it. Where the— Oh, here it is."

Then at last he crept in between the blankets, and silence came upon the camp.

How shall I describe the pleasures of our life in the forest? It is impossible to put them into words, or to make one who has never experienced the like understand what they are. There is a sense of freedom and freshness in every hour; the

IN CAMP.

wretched cares and complications of our artificial existence, the strifes and rivalries and hypocrisies of society, are far away and forgotten; we possess ourselves in quietness; a round of simple, natural toils fills up each day; and we have such mirth as Izaak Walton loved — "mirth that does not make friends ashamed to look

GUIDE LETTING LOOSE THE DOGS.

upon one another next morning, nor men that can not well bear it to repent the money they spend when they be warmed with drink." Above all, there is a constant influence of delight encircling us in the ever-changing beauty of sky and forest, mountain and lake, stream and meadow.

It is the morning of a hunting day. The guides are up and stirring before it is fairly light, and the sun has not risen above the tree-tops when Raut's bald head appears between the tent flaps, and he reminds us of our solemn promise to make an early start. The air is eager and nipping, and we hurry to get dressed, putting on an extra coat, and sitting down with a little shiver to a breakfast of steaming coffee and venison steak and potatoes. Steve is already starting into the woods with the hounds. He fastens their chains to his belt, and sets off with a long swinging stride, following no path, but making for a certain ridge far back in the forest, where he hopes to find a stag or two not yet awakened from their morning nap. It will be a hard tramp, through swamps and thickets, jungles of underbrush and tangles of fallen wood, with the dogs pulling and tugging at his belt, and nosing the ground impatiently for scent. After an hour or two, if he finds a fresh track, he will let one of them loose, and then go on to start a second, and, if he can, a third. The dogs are noble creatures, two of them thorough hounds with long hanging ears, and the other a rough Scotch dog, with

the keenness and pertinacity that belong to his race. They will follow the track with untiring vigor, crawling through the densest slash of burned and fallen timber, rushing along the more open hard-wood ridges, threading the tangled alder thickets, dashing through marshes, swimming narrow streams, until at last the deer crosses some runway where a hunter stands, or takes some larger water, and is captured or escapes. Then, if there be no one there to take the dog in, he turns and follows his track back until he comes to the camp, and creeps in, wet and hungry and tired, to lie down by the fire, and wait for his master to feed him.

In the mean time we have finished our

preparations, and are pushing out in our boats to take possession of the watch grounds. The light mist of the morning is curling up in fantastic shapes from the water, and the air is yet unwarmed by the sun, as we turn away each to his appointed station—one on a little pond some three miles up a winding stream, another on an island at the head of the lake, another down at Red Island, and Peter alone, for he is a ready oarsman, has charge of the island in front of the camp. It is tiresome work watching alone, for your eyes must be strained to catch the first sight of the deer as he enters the water, or moves, visible only as a black spot, across the surface. Fancy often plays you tricks, so that a floating piece of wood, or a loon swimming across some distant bay, seems to be a deer's head, and you set out in pursuit, and almost break your back, until you discover your mistake.

But if you have a good guide with you, you may leave the larger part of the watching to his sharp eyes, and finding a shady place, amuse yourself with a book, or watch the ants crawling through the grass forest, or lie and dream, letting your thoughts wander lazily along the curving shores and among the drifting clouds.

Presently there comes a faint sound, very different from those constant noises of the woods and waters to which you have been listening. Reub straightens himself on the projecting limb of the dead pine where he is sitting. Hark! A faint mellow note of a hound's voice coming over the trees. It is Jack. He is running. Now the chase is coming toward us. You can hear the sharp ringing bark distinctly. How eagerly he runs! There is a moment of silence. He is puzzled, or is struggling with some difficulty. Now the cry rings out again in quick, clear notes. The wind sweeps it away, and then brings it back with new power. It grows fainter and fainter. He is passing around some hill or ridge in the forest. He is turning away. No, here he comes again, clearer and louder than ever. He is making for the lake. But what is this? The music ceases. Then it begins more slowly. The deer has made a turn, and is swinging away for Stony Pond. Jack follows him, and his voice grows fainter, and then is lost as he passes back into the forest. We are disappointed.

We look down the lake again. Suddenly Peter's boat puts out from the island where he is watching. He is pulling for

A SWIM FOR LIFE

IN THE FOREST.

dear life He must see something. We will go down. Reub's sinewy arms make the oars bend, and the boat flies through the water. Do you see that dark spot moving out from the shore? It is a deer, a buck, a noble head. Peter is still a little in advance of us. But the deer swims fast. Will he get away? Peter pulls bravely, and at last his boat shoots between the stag and the point for which he was making. The great head, with its branching horns, turns out into the lake. Steady now, for the boat is dancing, and the stag is almost springing from the water. We must not spoil the antlers. A ball just below the ear. The rifle-crack rings sharp, and the buck is ours.

This is certainly the easiest way to kill a deer—so easy, in fact, that it hardly de-serves the name of sport, and is only to be justified on the ground that it is the only way to get venison in that season of the year which intervenes between jack-hunting and still-hunting. But even hounding may try the skill of the marks-man if he has a narrow piece of water to watch, and has to make a long shot as the deer is going out or skirting along the shore. And if this watch ground be a runway in the woods or on some narrow stream, then the hunter must have a quick and sure aim. It is a strange ex-perience to spend a day for the first time on one of these forest runways. The first sensation is one of pleasure in the wild beauty of the woods. Then the si-lence begins to oppress you. Through all the maze of mighty tree trunks no creature seems to be moving. There are no birds in the high branches, which are but feebly stirred by the wind, and through which only the thinnest rays of sunlight fall into the sombre green atmosphere below. Even the mimic forests of undergrowth and moss with which the ground is covered seem barren of all life. It is such a wood as Mage Merlin slumbered in when lissome Vivien slid from his embrace, and vanished with swift steps down the glade. But after a while your ear becomes attuned to the surroundings, and you begin to hear a gentle sound, like the dropping of ceaseless rain. It is the pattering of minute spiculæ falling from spruce and pine and hemlock, and mingling with the decaying roots and underbrush to form the dark rich forest mould on which every step falls so softly. Lying closer to the ground, you become aware of a busy insect life hurrying to and fro. Then there is a rustle of leaves, a patter of quick, light feet, and a red squirrel runs along a fallen trunk, peers at you curiously, and half in fear, half in

ON THE WATCH GROUND.

audacity, gives his sharp, shrill bark. A little bird which you can not see pierces the air with a slender, long-drawn note. A woodpecker beats his sounding tattoo on a hollow tree, and growing bolder, comes nearer and nearer, until perhaps he ventures to try the very trunk against which you are leaning. The influence of the place is soothing. You are very still, possibly a little drowsy. There is a louder rustling in the brush; you turn your head; a deer is looking at you with great startled eyes; you reach for your rifle, but at the first motion he is gone like a flash, bounding lightly over the great logs, and your random shot only awakes the echoes. You have lost your chance, and must come home empty-handed.

At our camp we usually had dinner at four o'clock; and never banquet was more delightful than these hearty feasts of venison and trout, eaten in the fresh air, with the living picture of the lake ever changing before our eyes. The fare was by no means that of anchorites. For besides the juicy saddles and tender steaks with which good fortune kept our larder supplied, we enjoyed the fruits of the Governor's forethought and Reub's skill in soups and sauces, and crisp baked beans, and flapjacks browner and more tempting than those which the fisherman in Shakspeare's play promised the shipwrecked Pericles. But two difficulties troubled us. One was subjective—the inability to eat enough. And this Gad solved by a simple rule. "Never," said he, with a mouth full of flapjack and maple syrup— "never eat too much at any one time, and then you will be able to eat a great deal all the time." Solon never said a wiser thing.

The other trouble was objective. The good things on the table attracted a swarm of yellow-jackets, who insisted on sharing our meals with us. In justice to them, I must say that they did not sting unless provoked; but at first their presence was embarrassing. Once they were so numerous and persistent that Gad and Peter and Howard were driven away to eat their dinner at the tent, leaving the Governor in solitary dignity at the table. "Foolish boys!" said he; "these are harmless creatures if you do not molest them. They do but seek their natural sustenance. Treat them— Whew !" The Governor's hand had rested too heavily

on one of the harmless creatures, and he joined the party by the tent with a very much lower opinion of the innocence of yellow-jackets. But a judicious use of hot water and sugar traps, and a ceaseless war of extermination which Steve waged at all times and with all weapons, soon reduced the troublesome visitors to control.

After dinner, Howard, the indefatigable angler, usually rowed away to cast the fly for trout in one of the dark winding streams at the head of the lake. He loved much to be alone at this hour, and the fishing was little more than an excuse. Peter was fond of exploring the neighboring bays, sometimes returning from his expeditions with a duck, and once bringing home with pride a great northern diver, the hardest of all birds to shoot. The Governor retired to his hammock with a cigar and his inevitable volume of Milton. Gad sat on the shore, placidly smoking a huge pipe, and trying to sketch the sunset effects.

The sun descended to his rest amid soft and glowing clouds, lingering, as it seemed, to caress the forest and the lake with an ineffable tenderness of light. When he was gone, hues of yellow and rose and orange spread over the sky, and were reflected with infinite gradations of paler color in the smooth water. Then came deeper tones of saffron and of red, fading slowly through purple into silvery gray. Low on the horizon dwelt

"That green light that lingers in the west";

the first star faintly twinkled on the edge of the night, and the pine-covered shores were clad with dark shadows.

When it was dark, we had our supper of oatmeal porridge and chocolate, and gathered around the camp fire. This, after all, is the centre of camp life. The great pile of burning logs sends out a cheerful heat and a steady glow. The straight tree trunks, gleaming in the light, surround us in a solemn circle. Beyond that is utter darkness, except on one side, where we can see a pallid gleam of the lake. A column of smoke, mingled with darting, twisting sparks, goes up to the stars. Now we recount the experiences of the day, and make plans for the morrow, and tell innumerable stories. Steve relates his marvellous history of the blueberry deer. Raut tells of that memorable night when Gad went out "jacking" with him, and jumped right over the bow of the boat to catch a deer that he had wounded; whereat Raut laughed so consumedly that he almost fell overboard. At this a hoot-owl, sitting unseen above our heads, startles us with a derisive Hu-hu-hu-whoo-oo-oo! And this reminds Gad of the time when he ran into a nest of them, when night-hunting, and was frightened almost out of his skin. Thus one story suggests another, and the fragrant smoke wreaths curl away into the night, until the white disk of the moon shines like an oriel-window through the branches of the trees, and climbing higher, sheds a flood of light into the camp.

We made many excursions from our camp: to Rock Pond, a wild and lovely sheet of water; to Charley Pond; to Smith's Lake, beautiful despite its name; and often in the evening we manned a boat with double sculls, and ran down to Robbins's cozy hostelry to get our letters and hear the news. It is strange how fast news travels in the wilderness; and by news I do not mean the stock quotations and the foreign telegrams, but the report of what is happening from day to day in the woods. If a bear was killed on the Raquette, or if some one shot a huge buck at Big Wolf, or if some scoundrel poisoned a lot of dogs on the Saranac, or if they had a fortunate day's hunt at Smith's Lake, or if some one caught a monstrous trout at Big Clear, we were sure to hear of it within forty-eight hours.

Indeed, we rather regretted this facility of transmission, for the report of the excellent sport on Little Tupper brought more people there than we cared to see. But there was room enough for all, and, as it happened, game enough. And our position at the head of the lake was thoroughly secluded.

During the last week of our stay the air was filled with smoke from distant forest fires. The effect was strange and beautiful. A gray luminous haze came floating down, filled with the faint odor of burning pine. The high mountain far beyond the foot of the lake grew first purple, then misty and indistinct. The nearer hills were covered with a mysterious veil. The long ridges became more dim and distant. Every vista was prolonged, and the islands seemed to recede and float mirage-like in the air. At sunset the sun was a glowing ball of fire, deepening as it sank into rosy mist, which spread and darkened into purple, and at last into the gloom of night.

Under this veil of smoke we could dimly see that the autumn colors were beginning to glow on the hills; and when, on the morning of our last day, the west wind, blowing fresh, made the air as clear as crystal, every hard-wood ridge was glorious with gold and scarlet leafage. Thus our woodland home never seemed so fair as when we turned our faces away from it, and went out again into the busy world.

SWAN LAKE.

The Adirondack Forests (1885)

THE ADIRONDACK FORESTS.

THE preservation of the Adirondack forests involves an economic question of great public interest to the people of New York. These forests, or their remnants, cover the high and broken Adirondack plateau ; — a region of heavy rain-fall, low mean annual temperature, and poor and barren soil. This region, which embraces all the country from the shores of Lake Champlain to the valley of the Black river on the west, and from the Mohawk, north to the St. Lawrence plain, is a great natural reservoir, from which flow the principal streams of the State.

The Adirondack forests have three distinct and valid claims for care and consideration at the hands of the public. The first of these, and the most important, is this : Forests retard evaporation from the surface of the ground, and thus store up and hold the moisture discharged from clouds, and furnish rivers a constant and regular supply of water. It is important, therefore, that high and broken ground, where the precipitation of moisture is always greater than at the sea-level, and where great rivers take their rise, should be permanently covered with forests. The chief argument for the preservation of the Adirondack forests must rest upon the fact that they are necessary to the existence of many important streams which head among them, and which will be seriously injured, and perhaps ruined by the denudation of their water-sheds. The Adirondack rivers already feel the effects of forest destruction in increasing freshets and diminished summer water-supply. Many of the small streams disappear entirely every year ; and it is evident that if the devastation which has already turned large areas about the borders of the forest into dangerous deserts is allowed to extend to the slopes of the higher mountains, serious consequences must ensue from the ruin of great rivers of widespread and far-reaching influence.

These forests should be preserved for their influence upon the flow of the rivers of the State, if for no other reason ; and this in itself is a matter of such great and vital importance that it is hardly necessary to mention any others. There are, however, two excellent additional economic reasons why all of that portion of northern New York which is occupied by the Adirondacks plateau should be kept as a great forest. It is adapted by nature to produce forests and nothing else. It is unfit for agriculture, and all attempts to make of it a farming or grazing country have resulted in disastrous failure. The cold and barren soil refuses to produce more than one or two scanty crops ; and starvation soon drives the settler to seek fresh fields of operation. It is a forest region, and nothing else, and as a forest region, so long as the forests are protected from fire, — their worst enemy, — it is of immense value to the community.

These forests make the whole region pleasant and attractive, and draw to it every year thousands of visitors or travelers who spend there, in the aggregate, large sums of money, and give employment to whole communities, who are supported in caring for the tourists who visit this region for rest and recreation, or to enjoy the forests and what the forest can give them.

If these forests, however, are allowed to perish, and the devastation of the borders extends over the whole region, the Adirondacks will cease to be a great summer resort ; the public will lose the benefit of a health and pleasure resting-place hardly surpassed in the United States in beauty, accessibility, and extent ; a great and permanent industry capable of vast future development will be irrevocably ruined, and the persons who conduct it will be forced to find other occupations.

The third claim of the Adirondack forests for preservation is, also, in a purely economic sense, well founded.

The lumber-product of this region is considerable; it depends, of course, upon the continuance of the forests. If they are allowed to burn up, and the soil which supports them is destroyed, there will be no more lumber manufactured in northern New York, the general lumber supply of the country will be reduced, and a considerable population who are now supported by preparing for market the products of the Adirondack forests will be deprived of their means of existence.

There are, therefore, three reasons, looking at this matter from a purely business point of view, why these forests should be preserved. They protect rivers necessary for the commercial prosperity of the State; they attract visitors, who bring money into the State, and so give employment to a large population, and they produce lumber needed by the community, and which, in the production, gives employment to many men.

It is easy to show why the Adirondack forests should be preserved. It is a much more difficult matter to inaugurate and put into execution any system for accomplishing this result. The greatest difficulty which stands in the way of forest preservation in this particular region is found in the apathy and ignorance of its inhabitants in regard to the value of the forests to themselves as a community. They have gone on for years seeing the forests burn up before their eyes, without protest and without effort to stop the devastations until it has become a matter of course for them to look upon forest destruction as inevitable. They do not realize that these forests are all they possess in the world; that the prosperity of the entire community is dependent upon them; and that, as a community, they must perish with the forests. The lumbermen cannot believe that these forests can be made perpetually productive under a system of selection in cutting, and that unless such a system is introduced their entire productive capacity will be destroyed. The owners of the hotels, the guides, boatmen, and teamsters, the army of men who look after the summer tourists, do not realize that it is the forests, and the forests only, which make the Adirondacks pleasant, and that when the forests are all burned up there will be no more travelers to take care of, and that their occupation will be gone. If the people who own the forests, and those who live upon them, could be made to understand their dependence upon them it would not be difficult to build up, upon local public sentiment, an effective system of forest management and protection. The first efforts of those persons who desire the preservation of these forests will be wisely devoted to increasing the knowledge and arousing the interest of the inhabitants of northern New York in their forests. They, next to the population living on the shores of the Hudson river, are most interested in their preservation. Knowledge of this sort comes slowly to a community; too often it comes too late. Fortunately, in this case, the State of New York is already in possession of a considerable part of these forests. It is easier for a State than it is for an individual to inaugurate and execute a system of control intended to develop and perpetuate the forest; and if such a system can be adopted for the care of these State lands, it will at least remove them from immediate danger, and gradually, it is to be hoped, bring about the introduction of better methods of forest management upon the neighboring lands of individuals.

New York already owns great forests extending over and protecting the watersheds of rivers of the greatest commercial importance. It is, therefore, in an exceptional position for testing the possibility of State forest management. The experiment can be made without any great outlay of money and without inflicting injury upon invested rights of any sort. If forest protection in the Adirondack region can be made successful, the material prosperity of the State will be increased, and the result will be felt from one end of the continent to the other.

The Adirondack forest is the arena where the future of the forests of the country will be decided. If they cannot be preserved it is useless to hope that scientific forest management can be adopted, during this generation, at least, in any part of the United States. The question is one of national import, and the action of the present Legislature of New York in this matter will be watched with deep interest by all persons who have the future prosperity of the country at heart.

C. S. Sargent.

Brookline, Massachusetts, February, 1885.

I have been a practical horticulturist for over twenty years, and know by experience that disastrous droughts occur with increasing frequency as the country is denuded of trees. To a lover and student of nature it is scarcely possible to understand how even a pot-house politician can be so short-sighted and utterly reckless in regard to the future of the country as to be indifferent to the wasting of our forests. Certainly those who have the interests of the State at heart should not neglect the plain and imperative duty of preserving large tracts of woodland as reservoirs of moisture. I truly believe that destructive forest fires will prove more disastrous in the end than conflagrations in cities; for, after all, cities depend on the country. I believe that the simple law of self-preservation should lead the State to make ample provision to cope with this consuming element, and that stolid, ignorant men, whose one principle of action is, "After me the flood," should be met with stern, definite law in their disposition, like the locusts of Egypt, to destroy every green thing. The time will come when we shall learn that not only must mountain forests be preserved, but good arable land given up to groves, in order to secure the rain-fall essential to our crops.

E. P. Roe.

Cornwall-on-the-Hudson, New York, Feb. 10, 1885.

You have my hearty sympathy in your efforts to stay the hand of the destroyer in the Adirondack forests. We are perhaps the most wantonly destructive people under the sun. We sweep away vast forests without a moment's thought of the deleterious effect upon our rivers and water-courses.

I read in Herodotus that the ancient Persians held rivers in such veneration that they would not even wash their hands in them or spit in them for fear of currupting them. We not only empty all our mountains of filth in them, but we throttle them, cut them off in their sources, by stripping the land of its forest covering. The land in the Adirondack wilderness is comparatively worthless for agricultural purposes, and the destruction of its forests would be an irreparable injury to the State, as well as a blot upon the face of the earth.

John Burroughs.

West Park, New York, Feb. 9, 1885.

This matter is one not of local, but of national importance. In my judgment, the State of New York could better afford, as a mere matter of physical prosperity, to let its great city be burned flat to the ground, from the Battery to the Harlem, than to let the Adirondack hills be stripped of their covering. If New York city were totally destroyed by fire to-day, its imperial mastery of American commerce would cause it to be rebuilt, fairer and larger than ever, within the space of ten years, as, indeed, Chicago has been after its great wreck. But no man can estimate the extent or the duration of the calamities that would spring from the destruction of these forests by the greed of lumber speculators

Francis A. Walker.

Massachusetts Institute of Technology, Boston, Jan. 31, 1885.

The preservation of forests is one of those duties which only the very thoughtful and provident are likely to urge. The thoughtless, who form the bulk of the community, are always ready to kill the goose that lays the golden eggs. The idea of present gain absorbs them. Their intense selfishness cries, "After me, the deluge;" and the few who call for a helpful consideration of the future are seldom heard. What is the advantage of health and comfort for posterity to the man who can sell his wood on his acres for a thousand dollars? All the blessings of life to innumerable families kick the beam on his balance when that thousand-dollar bill is placed on the other scale. Legislation in this direction of Providence is therefore always slow, and they who seek it have a very severe task. They are the few fanatics who believe in the golden rule and also in common-sense. They are, nevertheless, the few fanatics who salt this world from corruption and perdition.

Any observing and well-informed man must see that the Adirondack region is a magnificent reservoir of health, for the valleys of the Mohawk and Hudson, supply water both for the rivers and for the rain-fall. It is, moreover, a sanitarium for refugees from city heats and business cares, readily accessible from some of the largest centers of busy life. If the forests of the Adirondacks be removed, all this priceless advantage is gone. Agriculture, commerce, and the public health will all suffer over an area of fifty thousand square miles and a population of four millions. The work of stripping the mountains has begun and has advanced. Now is the moment to save this source of health and wealth. Laws restraining the vandalism should at once be passed by the New York Legislature. Most effective penalties should be attached to their breach. The higher power should interfere and make private gains subordinate to the public welfare. Only in this way can the prospective stoppage of mills, drying up of rivers, parching of the soil, failure of crops, contraction of commerce, spread of malaria, and increase of the death-rate be avoided. Will the Legislature of New York be wise — or otherwise?

Howard Crosby.

New York, Feb. 5, 1885.

———

I am glad that you mean to draw attention to the necessity of protecting the Adirondack forests. All forests covering the regions where the great rivers of the country take their rise ought to be carefully preserved. Most of our large streams have their sources in one or more States or Territories, and traverse several others on their way to the sea. These latter have a deep interest in preserving the sources unimpaired, but they have not the power, since the region is out of their jurisdiction. The central government may, therefore, reasonably be called upon to interpose for their relief. In New York the case is different. Not only the sources of the Hudson, but its entire course, lie within her territory, so that her future is in her own hands. If she wishes to secure an even and moderate flow of waters in that important stream she will carefully watch over the forests where it springs; if she wishes to see it capricious, fitful, and dangerous, now swelling with freshets and now dwindling into a scanty current, a peril in the spring floods, and robbed of half its value in the summer droughts, she will abandon the Adirondacks to be laid bare by fire and the axe. Considered as a measure of practical utility, the preservation of the forests that shelter the sources of the Hudson calls imperatively for legislative attention. Considered as a matter of feeling and taste, none but the dullest materialism can be indifferent to it.

Francis Parkman.

Boston, Feb. 5, 1885.

Kings and noblemen are accustomed to have sanitariums and retreats, and why should not the people? Especially why not if a great water-way of commerce will thereby be made more serviceable? If the great State of New York can and will do for its citizens and those of the neighboring States what the General Government is doing for the whole country, but more especially for the West, it will be an honor to the State and a benefit for all time.

Mark Hopkins.

Williams College,
Williamstown, Massachusetts, Feb. 9, 1885.

———

I beg leave to say that I am too much occupied with public business to express at any length the views I entertain in regard to the preservation of the Adirondack forests. The discussion of the subject, however, which has taken place in the public journals, and in the official reports which have been printed from time to time, leave no doubt in my mind that the State of New York ought to take prompt and efficient steps to prevent the further destruction of the trees, and to guard its property in such wise as will make it of value to the State not only as a sanitarium and a pleasure-ground, but as the source of its water supply for the Erie canal. I am in full sympathy with the efforts which have been made to this end, and regret that I have not been able to take an active part in the movement for the preservation of a domain so fortunately situated for the recreation of our citizens.

Abram S. Hewitt.

House of Representatives, U.S.,
Washington, D.C., Feb. 5, 1885.

———

Under certain circumstances, it is the plain duty of the government of a State to make efficient arrangements for the preservation and regulation of forests. The grounds of this duty are the same with those on which rest the duties of preparing to repel invasion, suppress insurrection, restrict crime, limit epidemics, or otherwise guard citizens from evils with which it is impracticable for them to contend privately by voluntary association or without scientific guidance.

The time has come when this duty should be accepted by the State of New York with respect to the Adirondack forests. The means now proposed for the purpose have been well considered, and are moderate and economical.

The profit to the State that will *incidentally* result from preserving and enlarging the value of the region as a resort for recreation and health will be of constantly increasing importance.

The adoption of the measure will be a step in civilization for which the time is ripe.

Frederick Law Olmsted.

BROOKLINE, MASSACHUSETTS, Jan. 31, 1885.

I am in hearty accord with the measures on foot for the preservation of the forests of the Adirondack.

While I have never visited them as yet, I have many friends accustomed to do so, and have heard their glowing accounts of the healthfulness and pleasures of that vast region.

I have not the time, however, to furnish you more in detail my views on the subject, as requested in your letter.

E. G. Lapham.

UNITED STATES SENATE,
WASHINGTON, D.C., Feb. 9, 1885.

The Adirondack forests are invaluable, in my judgment, not merely because they supply lumber, but because they furnish sanitary elements indispensable to New York State. Outside of the question of using the forests for a grand respite for wearied people from the cities, my observation in foreign countries, notably along the Mediterranean, and most especially in Spain, Judea, and Asia Minor, leads me to believe that the denuding of the land of timber is a sure way to invite barbarism, unthriftiness, and every element that belongs to a laggard people. Every fiber that grows in our forests, therefore, particularly in New York, is indispensable to health, to navigation, to comfort, and delectation.

S. S. Cox.

HOUSE OF REPRESENTATIVES,
WASHINGTON, D.C., Feb. 5, 1885.

I have some very clear and strong convictions on the subject of forestry laws : —

1. We are destroying our timber at a frightful rate, mortgaging our future, and foreclosing the mortgage, and living on our children, by our extravagance and unwisdom. By our absurd tariff on foreign lumber we are actually giving a premium to men to cut down what we ought to be trying to save. The first thing for us to do is to admit lumber free of duty. Now we can take Canadian lumber and put our own price upon it; if we wait until we have exhausted our own forests, we must buy it at the seller's price.

2. It is impossible for the government, either State or National, to purchase the timber lands, and so secure their preservation. It may be wise for New York to buy enough for the great park in the Adirondacks, though I confess myself in doubt about such a policy. At all events, this will not be a cure for the present evil. We must abandon totally, as we have already abandoned in part, the notion that a man may do what he will with his own ; we must recognize the truth that the rights of society are the supreme rights, and that, as we may and do prohibit the shooting of game in certain seasons, in order that we may preserve game, so we may prohibit the cutting of timber, except under restrictions and limitations as to size and proportion, etc. In order that we may protect our forests I would have every State appoint a forestry commission, with power to make, or at all events to devise and submit to the legislature, rules for the regulation of timber-cutting and the preservation of forests, equally applicable to private and public lands ; and I would have a "forest warden" or "wardens" appointed, as we now have game constables, to enforce these regulations and prohibitions.

3. There should be some comity and conjoint action between the States, or else action by the National Government ; and this would require, I suppose, a constitutional amendment. At present, the reckless destruction of the forests in the Alleghanies in Pennsylvania threatens the whole valley of the Ohio with alternate flood and drought, and only by some conjoint action can this evil, inflicted on one State by the selfishness or folly of another, be prevented, or even checked.

I am very glad you are taking this matter up, and I wish it were possible for me to render you more efficient service.

Lyman Abbott.

NEW YORK CITY, Feb. 7, 1885.

I am glad of the opportunity to express my hope that the Adirondacks will never be interfered with by the worshippers of real estate and manufactories. To cut down those forests would not make a single poor man less poor ; but it would seriously and permanently impoverish a large portion of the inhabitants of this country ; and the wealth of which it would deprive them is wealth of a kind more valuable than can be expressed in terms of dollars and cents. The mere knowledge that such a place as the Adirondacks had ceased to exist would be a cause of genuine sorrow even to those who had never personally enjoyed the pleasure and refreshment of being there. The spirit which would destroy these splendid regions is a squalid and unhandsome spirit, which, should it be indulged, will reflect lasting discredit upon our country. Europe might well ask whether America be not large enough, morally as well as physically, to forbear to perpetrate so short-sighted and stupid an outrage as this. No true American will give his support to such a scheme ; and I cannot but think that it would meet with a veto practically unanimous could means of giving expression to the popular opinion be devised. I myself have never visited the Adirondack region, and may, perhaps, never find an opportunity to do so ; and it is not on my own account that I speak, but in behalf of the commonwealth, the common health, and of the posterity for whose sake we exist.

Julian Hawthorne.

Sag Harbor, New York, Feb. 1, 1885.

———

There exist the strongest economic reasons why the great forests of the Adirondack region should be preserved : they are the magnets of clouds, the regulators of storms, a reservoir of rains, and a rush of streams ; they should be protected as a perpetual source of lumber supply, as well as a guard against extensive climatic changes, terrible freshets and terrible droughts, which are known to be the disastrous results of the destruction of forests in some other parts of the world. But they have higher than mere material uses ; and we should urge the preservation of that vast natural park, with all its wildness and beauty, for the sake of health and sanity, for symbol and inspiration, for rest and refreshment to the souls of weary men.

J. T. Trowbridge.

Arlington, Massachusetts, Feb. 10, 1885.

I am not at all certain that a legislative body in this country is insensible to an appeal to sentiment, although it is generally supposed to be. Probably it would often like an excuse for yielding to sentimental considerations ; and in the case of the Adirondacks it has an excuse of the best sort.

Any legislator who has ever taken his vacation in the northern woods — if he was not on a lumber errand — would no doubt vote to keep that fascinating and agriculturally worthless domain for his and the people's pleasure. He would say that the pleasure and the health to be got out of it were advantages outweighing any practical one to which the destruction of these forests as a pleasure-ground could lead ; but when the so-called practical people accuse him of being influenced by sentiment, he is very glad to be able to show them by figures and calculations that the destruction of the Adirondack woods would be a pecuniary calamity. In short, that it is not a mere matter of trout-fishing and deer-stalking and weak-lung nursing, but that these great forests are necessary to the physical prosperity of New York.

The Adirondack forest is the great sponge which gathers and holds moisture, regulates climate, and prevents sudden and violent changes ; but it is very fortunate for all this part of the country that there is a vast region of swamps and mountains, practically useless for settlement (in comparison with other lands). And we are just apprehending the many parts it plays in the economy of nature.

As a frequenter of the Adirondacks, for a good many years, I feel very strongly the devastation that has been wrought there by the recklessness of men, and the necessity of protection by State authority. The lumbermen, by damming the outlets of the lakes and flooding standing timber, have made a considerable portion of the Saranac country ghastly. But hunters and fishers and pleasure-seekers need looking after as well as the lumbermen. Many of the destructive fires are set going by the carelessness of hunting and camping parties ; and some of the most lovely lakes in the world (lakes that for beauty of shore and contour of the surrounding hills, that is for artistic qualities, have no equal in Switzerland or England) have been almost ruined in appearance by camping-parties, who have peeled the spruces for shanty covers, and slashed among the woods for fuel. This work of devastation will go on.